Exploring the Cybersecurity Landscape Through Cyber Forensics

Mohd Shahid Husain
College of Applied Sciences, University of Technology and Applied Sciences, Oman

IGI Global
Scientific Publishing
Publishing Tomorrow's Research Today

Vice President of Editorial	Melissa Wagner
Managing Editor of Acquisitions	Mikaela Felty
Managing Editor of Book Development	Jocelynn Hessler
Production Manager	Mike Brehm
Cover Design	Phillip Shickler

Published in the United States of America by
IGI Global Scientific Publishing
701 East Chocolate Avenue
Hershey, PA, 17033, USA
Tel: 717-533-8845
Fax: 717-533-8661
Website: https://www.igi-global.com E-mail: cust@igi-global.com

Library of Congress Cataloging-in-Publication Data

Names: Husain, Mohd Shahid, 1981- editor.
Title: Exploring the cybersecurity landscape through cyber forensics / edited by Mohd Shahid Husain.
Description: Hershey, PA : IGI Global Scientific Publishing, [2025] | Includes bibliographical references and index. | Summary: "This book delves into the intricacies of cyber forensics, offering insights and methodologies essential for uncovering and interpreting digital evidence in today's technologically advanced landscape"-- Provided by publisher.
Identifiers: LCCN 2024059915 (print) | LCCN 2024059916 (ebook) | ISBN 9798369329603 (hardcover) | ISBN 9798369349502 (paperback) | ISBN 9798369329610 (ebook)
Subjects: LCSH: Computer crimes--Investigation. | Computer security.
Classification: LCC HV8079.C65 E97 2024 (print) | LCC HV8079.C65 (ebook) | DDC 363.25/968--dc23/eng/20250218
LC record available at https://lccn.loc.gov/2024059915
LC ebook record available at https://lccn.loc.gov/2024059916

British Cataloguing in Publication Data
A Cataloguing in Publication record for this book is available from the British Library.

Table of Contents

Preface

Cyber forensics is a crucial field within forensic science focused on the recovery, analysis, and presentation of digital evidence. As digital technology becomes integral to virtually all aspects of modern life, the ability to investigate and resolve cyber-related incidents through systematic and scientifically grounded methods has never been more essential.

Cyber forensics is indispensable for investigating and addressing cyber incidents with scientific rigor and legal integrity. By adhering to core principles, employing systematic methodologies, and leveraging specialized tools, cyber forensic professionals play a key role in uncovering digital evidence and resolving cyber-related challenges. Despite ongoing challenges, the field remains vital for maintaining security and integrity in our increasingly digital world.

EMERGING NEED

In an era where digital technology touches every aspect of our lives, the necessity for advanced cyber forensic methods has never been more pressing. The proliferation of digital devices and the internet has brought about profound changes in the way we communicate, conduct business, and manage personal information. However, with these advancements come significant challenges in securing and analyzing digital evidence to address and resolve cyber-related incidents.

"Exploring the Cybersecurity Landscape Through Cyber Forensics" is designed to serve as a comprehensive guide for professionals, researchers, and students in the field of digital forensics. This book delves into the intricacies of cyber forensics, offering insights and methodologies essential for uncovering and interpreting digital evidence in today's technologically advanced landscape.

Purpose

This comprehensive book covers a cutting-edge exploration of the latest trends and challenges in the field of cyber forensics, ensuring that readers gain a thorough understanding of the subject and are equipped with the state-of-the-art knowledge needed to navigate the evolving landscape of digital investigations.

In this volume, we explore the fundamental principles of cyber forensics, the tools and techniques used for evidence collection, and the challenges posed by emerging technologies. Each chapter is meticulously crafted to provide a thorough understanding of both theoretical concepts and practical applications.

As you journey through this book, it is our hope that you will gain not only a deeper understanding of cyber forensics but also a heightened awareness of its critical role in safeguarding our digital world. The challenges we face in the digital age are substantial, but with robust forensic methodologies and a proactive approach, we can navigate these complexities and secure our digital future.

Audience

This book " Exploring the Cybersecurity Landscape Through Cyber Forensics " is designed for a diverse audience, including:

- **Forensic Professionals:** Practitioners in the field of digital forensics will find this book an essential resource for understanding the latest techniques and tools. It offers practical guidance and advanced methodologies that can be applied directly to forensic investigations, enhancing their ability to handle complex digital evidence.
- **Cybersecurity Experts:** Professionals focused on cybersecurity will benefit from the book's in-depth exploration of forensic methodologies and incident response strategies. Understanding cyber forensics is crucial for developing comprehensive security measures and effectively addressing cyber threats.
- **Law Enforcement and Legal Practitioners:** Law enforcement agencies and legal professionals involved in cybercrime investigations will gain insights into the forensic processes that underpin the collection, preservation, and presentation of digital evidence. This book provides a solid foundation for integrating forensic findings into legal contexts and ensuring the admissibility of evidence in court.
- **Academic Researchers and Students:** Scholars and students in the fields of computer science, cybersecurity, and forensic science will find this book a valuable educational resource. It covers fundamental concepts as well as

advanced topics, making it suitable for both introductory study and advanced research.

- **Industry Professionals and Decision Makers:** Executives and decision-makers responsible for managing IT and security strategies will benefit from understanding the role of cyber forensics in mitigating risks and responding to incidents. The book provides a strategic perspective on integrating forensic capabilities into organizational security frameworks.

Emphasis

This book aims to equip its readers with the knowledge and tools required to navigate the complexities of modern cyber investigations. From the basics of data recovery to the complexities of cloud computing, virtual reality and deepfakes, this book delves into the cutting-edge topics and advanced methodologies shaping modern digital investigations.

What You Will Learn

By going through the material presented in this book, you will learn:

- Forensic Methodologies in the Digital Age including ML & DL techniques for cyber forensics
- Concept and methodologies in Blockchain Forensics and Incident Response in the Cloud
- Current Trends in Cyber Forensics like Social Media Forensics, AI-Powered Behavioral Analysis in Digital Investigations.
- Forensic Analysis of AI-Generated Content, Forensic Challenges in Augmented Reality (AR) and Virtual Reality (VR) and Deepfake Detection and Analysis
- Concepts of Biometric Data Forensics
- Legal and Ethical Challenges in cyber forensics
- Future trends and directions in cyber forensics

BOOK ORGANIZATION

The book is divided into three sections. ***Section A*** (Chapters 1–5) of the book provides conceptual background, starting with Forensic Methodologies in the Digital Age including ML & DL techniques for cyber forensics, Concept and methodologies in Blockchain Forensics and Incident Response in the Cloud. This is followed by

Section B (Chapters 6–11) which discusses Current Trends in Cyber Forensics like Social Media Forensics, AI-Powered Behavioral Analysis in Digital Investigations, Forensic Analysis of AI-Generated Content, Forensic Challenges in Augmented Reality (AR) and Virtual Reality (VR) and Deepfake Detection and Analysis, and Biometric Data Forensics. The final part of the book, ***Section C*** (Chapters 12–14) deals with legal and ethical aspects of cyber forensics, including privacy concerns and compliance issues, best practices for law enforcement agencies conducting digital investigations and ethical considerations and challenges associated with the use of artificial intelligence in cyber forensic investigations.

Below is the summary of the book chapters:

Chapter 1. Forensic Methodologies in the Digital Age: The rapid advancement of technology has transformed forensic methodologies, demanding new approaches to evidence collection, preservation, and analysis. This chapter explores the evolution of forensic practices in response to digital innovations. Readers will gain insights into state-of-the-art techniques that address the unique challenges of contemporary digital environments, ensuring that forensic methodologies remain effective and relevant in an era characterized by exponential data growth and technological complexity.

Chapter 2. Machine Learning in Digital Forensics: Digital forensics is an essential field within cybersecurity and law enforcement, focused on recovering, preserving, and analyzing electronic data to uncover evidence of criminal activities. With the exponential growth of digital devices and the increasing complexity of cybercrimes, digital forensics has become more challenging. Machine Learning (ML), a subset of artificial intelligence (AI), is emerging as a transformative tool in this domain, offering advanced techniques for data analysis, pattern recognition, and anomaly detection. This chapter provides a comprehensive analysis of the role of machine learning in digital forensics, including its principles, applications, challenges, and future directions.

Chapter 3. Deep Learning Techniques in Digital Forensics: Deep learning techniques have the potential to significantly enhance digital forensics, offering powerful tools for analyzing complex and voluminous data. By automating and improving various forensic processes, deep learning can address challenges that traditional methods struggle to overcome. However, successful implementation requires careful consideration of data privacy, model interpretability, and resource requirements. As deep learning continues to evolve, its integration into digital forensics will likely yield even more innovative and effective solutions, paving the way for advancements in the fight against cybercrime. This chapter explores how deep learning techniques are applied to digital forensics, examining their impact, methodologies, and potential future developments.

Chapter 4. Blockchain Forensics: As blockchain technology becomes more widespread, it introduces new dimensions to forensic investigations. Blockchain forensics involves analyzing blockchain transactions and smart contracts to uncover illicit activities and trace financial flows. The chapter offers in-depth coverage of blockchain forensics, including the tools and techniques used to investigate cryptocurrency-related crimes and the unique challenges posed by decentralized and anonymized systems.

Chapter 5. Incident Response in the Cloud: With the proliferation of cloud computing, incident response strategies must adapt to the complexities of cloud environments. This chapter examines best practices for handling incidents in the cloud, including data recovery, evidence collection, and coordination with cloud service providers. Readers will learn about the nuances of cloud-based forensics and how to address the unique challenges of investigating incidents across distributed and multi-tenant systems.

Chapter 6. Social Media Forensics: Social media platforms are rich sources of digital evidence but also present unique challenges for forensic investigations. This chapter explores methodologies for extracting, analyzing, and interpreting data from social media platforms, including techniques for handling user-generated content, metadata, and interactions. Social media forensics is crucial for understanding the context of cyber incidents and uncovering critical evidence in both criminal and civil cases.

Chapter 7. AI-Powered Behavioral Analysis in Digital Investigations: Artificial Intelligence (AI) plays a transformative role in behavioral analysis within digital investigations. This chapter highlights how AI-powered tools can analyze user behavior, detect deviations, and predict potential threats based on historical data and real-time analysis. By leveraging AI, investigators can enhance their ability to anticipate and respond to cyber threats with greater precision and speed.

Chapter 8. Forensic Analysis of AI-Generated Content: This chapter provides a comprehensive overview of the forensic analysis of AI-generated content, highlighting key techniques, case studies, and implications. The field continues to evolve, and staying informed about advancements in AI and forensic methodologies will be crucial for addressing future challenges and ensuring the authenticity of digital content.

Chapter 9. Forensic Challenges in Augmented Reality (AR) and Virtual Reality (VR): Augmented Reality (AR) and Virtual Reality (VR) are transforming forensic analysis by enhancing visualization and interaction with digital evidence. This chapter provides discussion on how AR can overlay forensic data onto real-world environments, aiding investigators in contextualizing and understanding crime scenes. Readers will gain insights into how VR offers immersive simulations, allowing forensic experts to reconstruct and explore crime scenes in a controlled virtual environment. These technologies facilitate detailed analysis and training, improve evidence presentation, and enable more effective communication of complex findings to stakeholders.

Chapter 10. Deepfake Detection and Analysis: The rise of deepfake technology poses significant challenges for digital forensics, as manipulated media can undermine the authenticity of evidence and complicate investigations. This chapter addresses techniques for detecting and analyzing deepfakes, including forensic methods for verifying media integrity and combating misinformation. Readers will gain insights into the latest advancements in deepfake detection and the implications for forensic practice.

Chapter 11. Biometric Data Forensics: This chapter provides a detailed examination of biometric data forensics, covering its definition, types of biometric data, analysis techniques, applications, challenges, and future directions. Each section is designed to offer a comprehensive understanding of the field and its implications in forensic science.

Chapter 12. Data Privacy and Legal Considerations in Cyber Forensics: This chapter provides a thorough examination of legal frameworks, privacy concerns, and ethical considerations that impact forensic investigations. It covers topics such as data protection laws, consent, and the admissibility of digital evidence, ensuring that forensic practices adhere to legal and ethical standards while maintaining investigative integrity.

Chapter 13. Digital Forensics in Law Enforcement: Best Practices: Digital forensics is a crucial field in contemporary law enforcement, bridging the gap between technology and criminal investigations. As our world becomes increasingly digitized, the role of digital forensics in law enforcement has expanded from a niche area to a core component of criminal investigations. This chapter explores the multifaceted domain of digital forensics, covering its principles, methodologies, challenges, and the evolving landscape shaped by technological advancements. The readers will get insight to a comprehensive overview of digital forensics in law enforcement, exploring its fundamentals, processes, challenges, and future directions.

Chapter 14. AI Ethics in Cyber Forensics: As AI technologies become increasingly integrated into forensic investigations, a host of ethical considerations arise. These considerations revolve around privacy, bias, transparency, accountability, and the potential misuse of technology. This discussion will explore these ethical issues in detail, examining the implications for individuals, organizations, and the legal system. The chapter outlines the key ethical considerations in AI-driven cyber forensics, providing a comprehensive overview of the challenges and potential solutions.

Acknowledgment

This work was a great experience for me in the domain of cyber forensics. There are lots of people who helped me directly and indirectly to make this book a reality. I would like to acknowledge the contribution of each individual who helped me in the conception and completion of this book.

I want to take this opportunity to offer my sincere gratitude to them. A very special thanks to IGI global publication team, particularly Mikaela Felty (Managing Editor of Acquisitions), Cassandra Martin (Assistant Acquisitions Editor), Melissa Wagner (Vice President of Editorial) and Nina Eddinger (Assistant Book Development Editor) without their continuous encouragement and support this book would not have been possible.

I also thank esteemed technical experts Dr. T J Siddiqui (Prof. University of Allahabad), Dr. Rashid Ali (Prof. AMU Aligarh), Adil Kaleem (Cloud Delivery Technical Architect at NCS Group, Australia), Dr. Mohammad Suaib (Asst. Prof, Integral University), Dr. M Z Khan (Asst. Prof, University of Bisha) and Dr. M Akbar (Asst. Prof, Integral University) for their efforts in time constrained impartial and critical review, proof reading and providing constructive feedbacks. I also appreciate my friends and colleagues for providing help wherever and whenever necessary.

This acknowledgement will not be complete until I pay my gratitude and regards to my parents and family members for their unflinching and encouragement to me in all my pursuits. It's the confidence of my family members in me that has made me the person that I am today. I dedicate this book to them.

Finally, I wish to thank the organizations and individuals who granted me permission to use the research material and information necessary for the completion of this book.

Last but not the least I am heartily thankful to almighty God for showering His blessings forever during my entire life.

Mohd Shahid Husain

Section 1
Emerging Techniques in Cyber Forensics

Chapter 1
Forensic Methodologies in the Digital Age

ABSTRACT

The advent of sophisticated Information and Communication Technologies and exponential growth in the usage of internet has enabled the cybercriminals to exploit the vulnerabilities of digital systems and networks, to perform crimes like hacking, phishing, identity theft, ransom ware, cyber espionage, cyber terrorism and cyber warfare. These Cybercrimes can cause significant financial losses, reputational damage, operational disruption, legal liability and national security risks. Today almost all criminal activity has a digital forensics footprint, and digital forensics experts can provide critical assistance to case investigations by identifying, acquiring, and analyzing electronic evidence. Digital evidence ranges from emails, images of child sexual exploitation, messages, to the location of a mobile phone. Digital forensics plays an important role in identifying, mitigating, and eradicating cyber threats and is also useful in the aftermath of an attack, to provide information required by auditors, legal teams, or law enforcement.

1. INTRODUCTION

The advent of sophisticated Information and Communication Technologies and exponential growth in the usage of internet has enabled the cybercriminals to exploit the vulnerabilities of digital systems and networks, to perform crimes like hacking, phishing, identity theft, ransom ware, cyber espionage, cyber terrorism and cyber warfare. These Cybercrimes can cause significant financial losses, reputational damage, operational disruption, legal liability and national security risks. Today almost all criminal activity has a digital forensics footprint, and digital forensics experts can provide critical assistance to case investigations by identifying, acquiring, and analyzing electronic evidence. Digital evidence ranges from emails, images of child

DOI: 10.4018/979-8-3693-2960-3.ch001

sexual exploitation, messages, to the location of a mobile phone. Digital forensics plays an important role in identifying, mitigating, and eradicating cyber threats and is also useful in the aftermath of an attack, to provide information required by auditors, legal teams, or law enforcement. For analysis purposes, various computerized systems can be used to acquire digital evidence like computers, portable or mobile devices, remote storage devices, wearable devices, internet of things (IoT) devices. Digital forensics includes many other subdomains as mentioned in Figure 1.

Figure 1. Cyber forensics: An interdisciplinary science

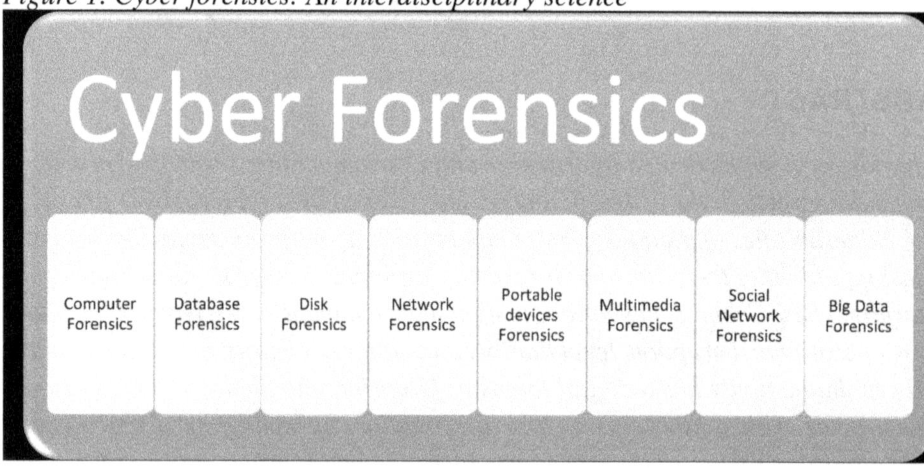

This chapter explores the evolution of cyber forensic over the years and various forensic methodologies employed in the digital age, examining their challenges, and the crucial role they play in modern law enforcement. With a focus on real-world case studies, enriched by current facts and figures, this exploration aims to illuminate the multifaceted landscape of digital forensics.

2. EVOLUTION OF CYBER FORENSICS

Cyber forensics, also known as digital forensics or computer forensics, has evolved significantly since its inception. Initially focused on computer-based crimes, it has expanded to encompass a broad spectrum of digital devices, including smartphones, tablets, and IoT devices (Husain & Khan, 2019). The evolution is driven by the surge in cybercrimes and the increasing complexity of digital systems.

2.1. Historical Perspective

The need for digital forensics began when the first computer crime occurred in 1971 when Bob Thomas wrote the virus named "The Creeper." This virus was just a general nuisance but not harmful. However, it did indicate the growing need for computer crime experts. However, during the early days, the forensics team were mostly representatives of federal law enforcement agencies with a computer background. By the 1990s, the term "computer crime" had become common in the world of investigation. In 1984, the FBI launched the first official program called Magnet Media program (later known as CART program) headed by Michael Anderson, the father of digital forensics. In the early 21st century, the federal government began to put together policies on digital forensics.

- ***Some of the milestones in the evolution of the cyber forensics are:***

  1966: The first computer crime was reported and federally prosecuted in the USA, where a bank consultant stole money from the bank by modifying the program so that the overdraft access will not be reported.

  1976: A book titled "Crime by Computer" by Donn Parker was published providing the description of how computer can be used for committing crimes and the use of digital information to investigate and prosecute such crimes.

  1978: To enact law against unauthorized modification and deletion of computer data, 'Florida Computer Crimes Act' was introduced.

  1986, Cliff Stoll, a Unix System Administrator at Lawrence Berkeley National Laboratory, created the first honeypot trap.

  1987, The first commercial antivirus was launched.

  1990: Internet becomes more accessible for the public and opens a new avenue for criminals.

  1993: The First International Conference on 'Computer Evidence' hosted by FBI was attended by participants from 26 countries.

  1995: Establishment of the International Organization on Computer Evidence (IOCE).

  2000: Development of new techniques to acquire digital evidence from a variety of devices as the use of mobile devices like cellphones, USB sticks, and memory cards has increased.

  2004: A Convention on Cybercrime treaty was signed by 43 nations to settle the laws and methodologies for countering cybercrimes.

  2005: ISO 17025 - The standard regarding the general requirements for the competence of testing and calibration laboratories for cyber forensics was published by International Organization for Standardization (ISO).

2006: U.S. implemented a mandatory regime for 'electronic discovery' in its Rules for Civil Procedure.
2007: With the emergence of technologies like cloud computing, big data, and virtualization has influenced digital forensics and demanded more sophisticated techniques to deal with the huge volume of decentralized data.
2012: Details of more than 400,000 credit cards were published by hacker OXOMAR.
2013: Around 3 billion users' accounts and personal information were compromised by hackers attacking yahoo server.
2019: New Zealand's stock market had to temporarily shut down due to multiple DDOS attacks.
2022: more than 270,228 malware variants that have never been seen before were identified by Cyber security experts, Sonicware.
2023: Almost 81% of organizations were affected (at least once) by ransomware in 2023.

Current Landscape: The increasing use of refined encryptions, the Internet of Things (IoT), sensor networks, block chain, wearable devices, and other emerging technologies has presented new challenges as well as opportunities for digital investigators.

A significant increase has been observed in cyber-attacks using generative AI tools.

- o A malicious Internet of Things (IoT) malware, Mirai, was detected 103,092 times worldwide in 2022.
- o According to a report by Sky High Security, in 2023, 78% of financial services organizations have experienced a security breach.
- o According to Forbes, in Feb 2024, 94% of hospitals experienced a disruption from cyber-attacks.

2.2. Domain Evolution in Cyber Forensics

The evolution of cyber forensics starts with the analysis of digital data stored in a computing device, a computer. There are two types of investigation which are dealt in ***Computer forensics***:

- o Crimes where computers are used as a tool to perform illegal/criminal activities.
- o Crimes where computers are the target like viruses, hacking, and information theft.

Database forensics is considered as a subfield of computer forensics, where investigative techniques are used to analyze who gets access to database content and metadata to gather evidence for any criminal activity.

Memory forensics started as a subcategory of computer forensics where investigation is done to analyze the volatile memory (Random Access Memory) to get the (approx.) real-time image of the system like running processes, encryption keys, or open connection ports and identifying malicious software or changes in the system. However, now memory forensics is in itself a whole discipline because memory is part of almost all the smart devices in use, not only the component of a typical computer machine.

Image forensics or file forensics deals with using methods to extract the content of the image and creating a verified bit for bit copy of an entire disk to generate digital evidence in legal matters.

Network forensics focuses on connected devices in the digital world by investigating network traffic data and log files to examine network traffic patterns and collecting evidence for unauthorized access or malicious activities. Server forensics, SDN (Software Defined Networks) forensics and internet forensics are subdomain of network forensics focusing on specific objectives.

Figure 2. Cyber forensics domain evolution

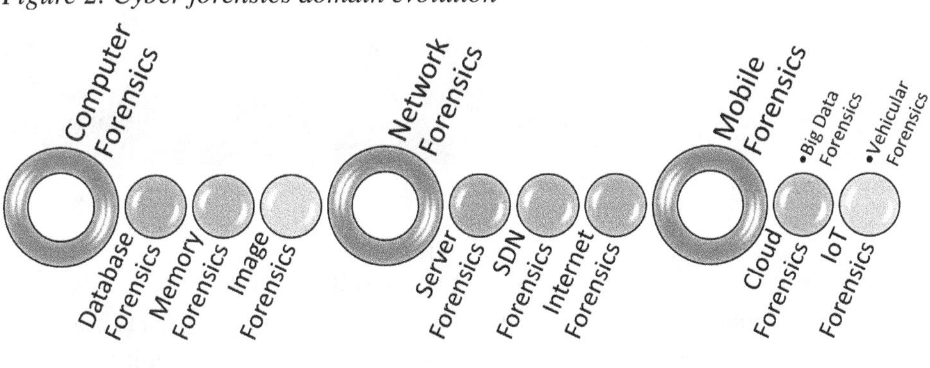

Mobile forensics is similar to computer forensics but emerged due to the need for customized approaches for portable computing devices.

New forensic disciplines like cloud forensics, big data forensics, IoT forensics, and vehicular forensics are also emerging because new case scenarios and sophisticated devices keep emerging, such as autonomous cars, drones, wearable devices etc.

3. STATISTICAL OVERVIEW AND TRENDS

Threats in cyberspace are not just escalating in frequency but are also becoming more sophisticated, challenging traditional security paradigms. In this rapidly evolving digital landscape, understanding the upcoming trends is a matter of foresight and a necessity for preparedness. Figure 3 shows the cybercrime index i.e., ranking of countries based on cybercrime threat level.

Figure 3. Cybercrime index

CYBERCRIME INDEX

Ranking countries by cybercrime threat level

Ranking	Country	WCI score	Ranking	Country	WCI score
1	Russia	58.39	11	Iran	4.78
2	Ukraine	36.44	12	Belarus	3.87
3	China	27.86	13	Ghana	3.58
4	United States	25.01	14	South Africa	2.58
5	Nigeria	21.28	15	Moldova	2.57
6	Romania	14.83	16	Israel	2.51
7	North Korea	10.61	17	Poland	2.22
8	United Kingdom	9.01	18	Germany	2.17
9	Brazil	8.93	19	Netherlands	1.92
10	India	6.13	20	Latvia	1.68

(Bruce, Lusthaus, Kashyap, Phair, & Varese, 2024)

Figure 4 shows the impact of cyber-attacks on different industries in 2023. The statistics show that more than 50% of total attacks have been on manufacturing, finance, and energy sectors to weaken the economy and cause instability.

Figure 4. Cyberattacks across industries

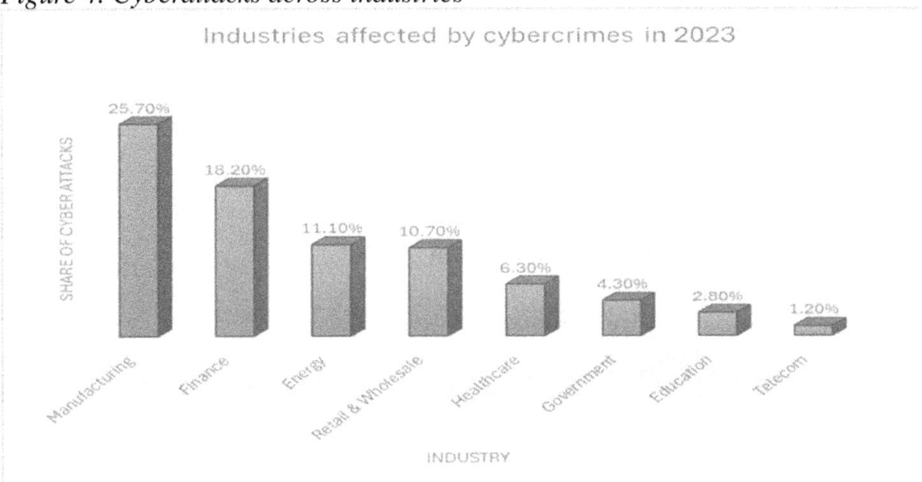

(Petrosyan, Share of cyberattacks in global industries worldwide 2023, 2024)

Figure 5 shows the ranking of cyberthreats by cyber security professionals worldwide on a scale of 1-5.

Figure 5. Ranking of cyber threats

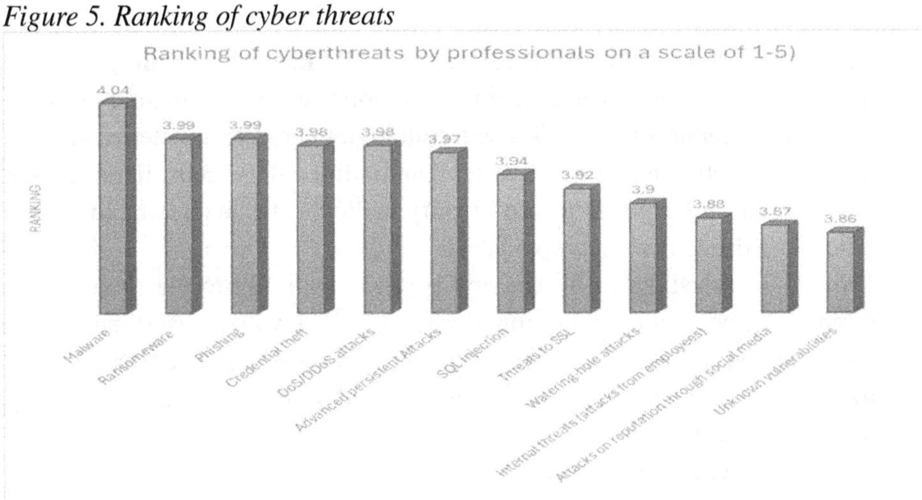

(Petrosyan, Leading IT security threats according to cyber security professionals 2022, 2023)

Figure 6 shows the complaints of cyberthreats received worldwide by IC3 (Internet Crime Complaint Center) and the losses it incurs during the period from 2018-2022.

Figure 6. Cybercrime complaints and losses

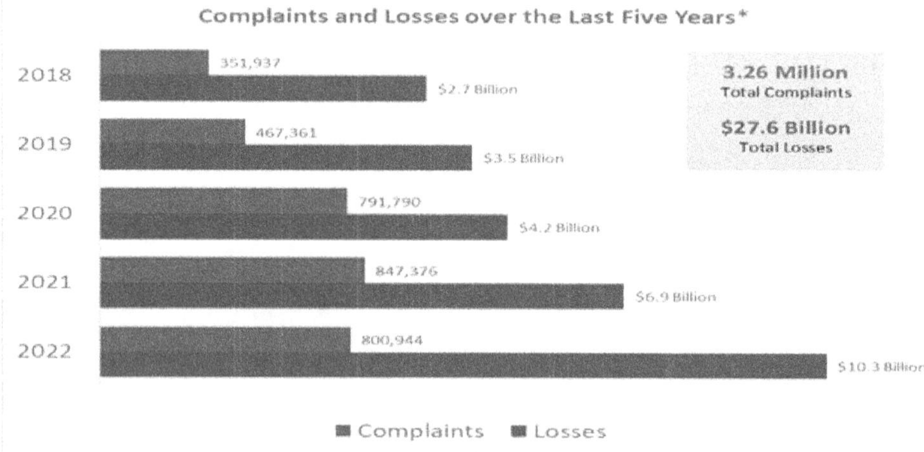

(Langan, 2022)

3.1. Current Trends

The current trends in cyber forensics are:

- **Increased Use of Artificial Intelligence and Machine Learning:** AI and machine learning are revolutionizing cyber forensics by automating the analysis of vast amounts of data. These technologies can detect patterns, anomalies, and potential threats much faster than traditional methods. For example, machine learning algorithms can identify malicious behaviors or extract significant evidence from encrypted data.
- **Cloud Forensics:** As more data and applications move to the cloud, cloud forensics is becoming increasingly critical. This involves investigating and analyzing data stored in cloud environments. Challenges include dealing with multi-tenant architectures and ensuring data integrity across geographically dispersed servers.
- **Mobile Device Forensics:** With the proliferation of smartphones and tablets, mobile device forensics has become a crucial aspect of investigations. The focus is on extracting and analyzing data from mobile devices, including text messages, call logs, app data, and GPS information. Challenges include the diversity of mobile operating systems and encryption.
- **IoT Forensics:** The Internet of Things (IoT) introduces a vast number of connected devices that can be sources of forensic evidence. Investigating

data from IoT devices such as smart home systems, wearables, and industrial control systems involves new techniques and tools to handle the variety and volume of data.

- **Ransomware Investigations:** Ransomware attacks are on the rise, and investigating these incidents has become a significant trend. Cyber forensics professionals are developing new methods to analyze ransomware strains, recover encrypted data, and track the criminal networks behind these attacks.
- **Blockchain and Cryptocurrency Forensics:** With the growing use of cryptocurrencies and blockchain technology, forensics in these areas are gaining prominence. Investigators are developing techniques to trace cryptocurrency transactions, analyze blockchain data, and uncover fraudulent activities or illicit transactions.
- **Data Privacy and Legal Compliance:** Data privacy laws, such as GDPR and CCPA, are influencing cyber forensics practices. Forensic experts need to ensure that their investigations comply with these regulations, balancing the need for evidence collection with the protection of personal data.
- **Advanced Persistent Threats (APT) Detection:** APTs are sophisticated, prolonged attacks designed to remain undetected. Cyber forensics is evolving to address these threats by improving detection techniques, analyzing indicators of compromise, and understanding the tactics, techniques, and procedures (TTPs) of attackers.
- **Memory Forensics:** Memory forensics involves analyzing a computer's volatile memory (RAM) to uncover evidence. This method is becoming more important as it can reveal details that are not stored on disk and provide insights into active processes and recent activities.
- **Integration with Threat Intelligence:** Integrating cyber forensics with threat intelligence is becoming a trend. By combining forensic data with real-time threat intelligence, investigators can enhance their understanding of cyber threats, correlate evidence with known attack patterns, and improve their overall investigative strategies.
- **Rise of Quantum Computing:** Quantum computing has the potential to revolutionize many fields, including cryptography, which is foundational to cybersecurity. Classical encryption algorithms, such as RSA and ECC (Elliptic Curve Cryptography), could be rendered vulnerable by quantum algorithms like Shor's algorithm, which can factor large numbers exponentially faster than classical methods. This threat necessitates the development of quantum-resistant cryptographic methods. Quantum computing could also influence forensic techniques by introducing new methods for analyzing and processing data. Research is ongoing into how quantum algorithms might enhance data analysis capabilities, potentially leading to breakthroughs in how digital

evidence is managed and interpreted. Forensic tools and methodologies will need to adapt to accommodate quantum computing advances. This includes updating algorithms for hashing and data integrity verification to ensure they remain secure against quantum attacks.

- **Public-Private Partnerships in Cybersecurity Education:** Public-private partnerships can create platforms for collaboration among different stakeholders in the cybersecurity community. Forums, conferences, and professional networks facilitated by these partnerships can encourage knowledge sharing and collaboration, driving the field forward. Such partnerships can play a role in raising awareness about cybersecurity issues and promoting best practices. Through joint campaigns, workshops, and seminars, they can educate both the public and private sectors on the importance of cybersecurity and the role of forensics in protecting digital assets. Public-private partnerships can also focus on workforce development programs, such as internships, apprenticeships, and job placement services. These programs can help bridge the transition from education to employment, ensuring that graduates have practical experience and are well-prepared for the demands of the cybersecurity workforce.

These trends reflect the ongoing evolution of cyber forensics as it adapts to new technologies, threats, and regulatory landscapes. The field continues to advance, leveraging innovative tools and methodologies to address complex digital crime challenges. Figure 7 shows the current trends in cyber forensics.

Figure 7. Trends in cyber forensics

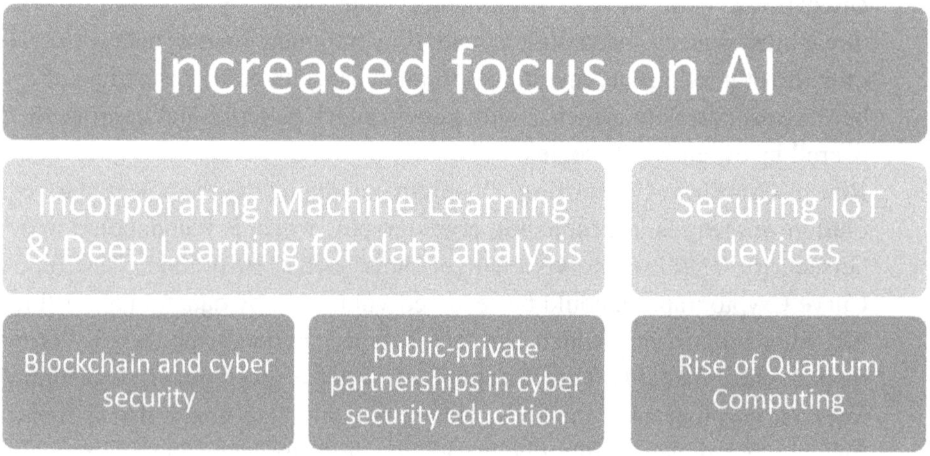

4. THE CYBER FORENSICS PROCESS

Though investigations vary, cyber forensics follows a rigorous scientific process to present findings of fact to prove or disprove a hypothesis in a court of law. Zatyko, the former director of the Defense Computer Forensics Laboratory, mentioned the scientific cyber forensics process containing eight steps which can be grouped into three phases as shown in below Figure 8.

Figure 8. Cyber forensics scientific process

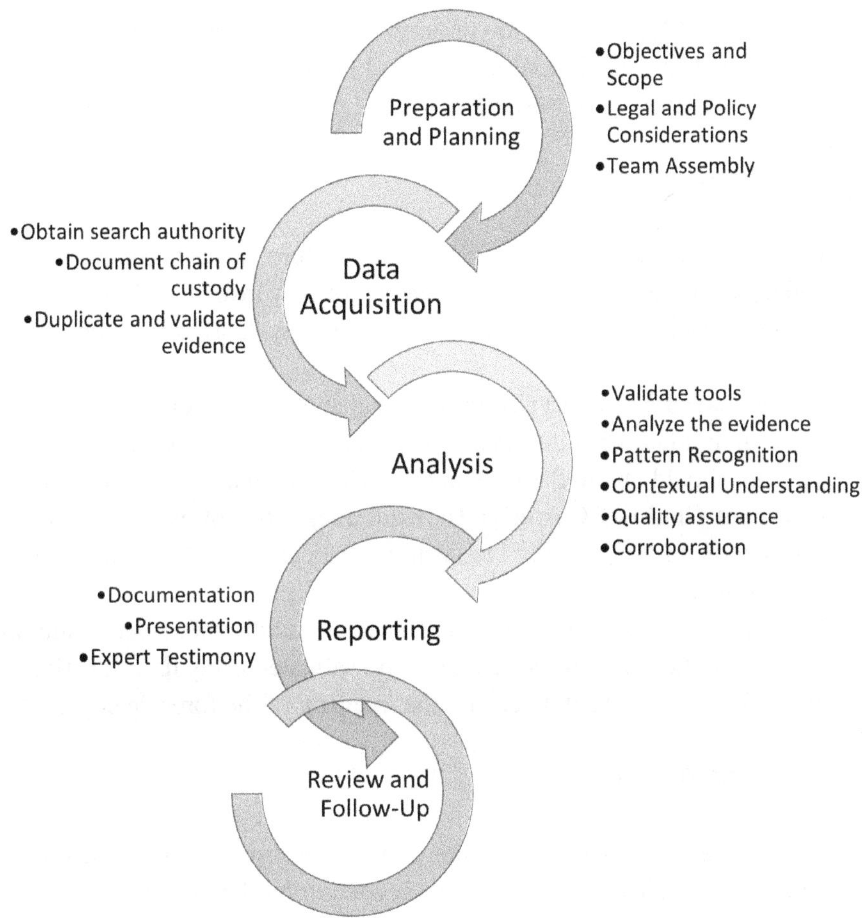

4.1. Preparation and Planning

- **Objectives and Scope:** Before initiating an investigation, it's essential to define the objectives and scope. This includes understanding the nature of the incident or crime, determining what data might be relevant, and identifying the resources and tools needed.
- **Legal and Policy Considerations:** Ensure that the investigation complies with relevant laws and organizational policies. This includes obtaining necessary permissions, understanding legal constraints, and adhering to privacy regulations.
- **Team Assembly:** Form a team of experts with the required skills, including forensic analysts, legal professionals, and IT specialists. Clearly define roles and responsibilities to ensure an organized approach.

4.2. Data Acquisition

In this phase digital evidence is collected to capture suspect media or network traffic and logs, post breach. The acquisition of data may involve making a copy of a hard disk, downloading data from a mobile, or recovering data from a remote system.

- **Obtain Search Authority:** To follow local and country jurisdiction laws and respect individual's/institution's privacy, before seizing materials the forensics team should obtain the legal authority to search and seize the data.
- **Document Chain of Custody:** To avoid allegations of evidence tampering or misconduct in the court of law, a chronological documentation of evidence handling is required.
- **Duplicate and Validate Evidence:** The acquired digital evidence should be carefully duplicated as forensic image and validated using hash functions like MD5, SHA1 or SHA256 to ensure the integrity of the forensic copy.

4.3. Evidence Analysis

The forensic experts analyze and interpret the forensic copies of the collected evidence using specialized tools to expose deleted or hidden material.

- **Validate Tools:** To ensure reliability and correctness of the data analysis the tools used by the experts in the forensic process should be validated.
- **Analyze the Evidence:** The forensic investigative team employs various analytical tools and techniques to examine the evidence. The data collected from different sources like hard disk, emails, browsing history, and portable

devices has been analyzed to identify people, places, items and events and determine how they are related to a particular incident.

- **Pattern Recognition:** Identify patterns, trends, and relationships within the data. This may involve correlating findings with known attack signatures, understanding the tactics used by attackers, and identifying the sequence of events.
- **Contextual Understanding:** Interpret the findings in the context of the incident. This involves understanding the motives, methods, and impacts of cyber activity and how it relates to the broader case or incident.
- **Quality Assurance:** To ensure the quality of the forensic procedure applied, the forensic analysis applied should be repeatable and any independent third party should be able to reproduce the same results by repeating the same procedure.
- **Corroboration:** Cross-check findings with other sources of evidence to verify their accuracy and relevance. This helps in building a comprehensive picture of the incident.

4.4. Reporting

After analyzing the evidence, the forensic team prepares a report of findings to present it in the court of law.

- **Documentation:** The forensic team must document all the findings, and the analytical procedure used in the task. They should document all the information they have uncovered with details like data ownership, login/logoff times, emails, chats, logs etc.
- **Presentation:** The document prepared by the forensic team provides facts and scientific basis so that the court may use the unbiased evidence and gain a better understanding of events. In some cases, the forensic analyst gives expert testimony in the court of law by presenting his/her findings and conclusions to confirm or disprove alibis and provided statements.
- **Expert Testimony:** In legal cases, forensic experts may be required to provide testimony in court. This involves explaining the forensic process, findings, and the significance of the evidence in a manner that is comprehensible to judges and juries.

4.5. Review and Follow-Up

- **Post-Incident Review:** Conduct a review of the forensic process to identify lessons learned and areas for improvement. This helps in refining procedures and preparing for future investigations.
- **Redress:** Based on the findings, recommend, and implement corrective actions to address vulnerabilities and prevent recurrence of similar incidents. This may involve updating security measures, revising policies, and providing training.
- **Compliance and Updates:** Ensure that all forensic practices and tools are up-to-date and comply with current legal and technological standards. Regularly review and update forensic procedures to adapt to evolving threats and advancements in technology.

The cyber forensics process is intricate and demands meticulous attention to detail to ensure that evidence is properly managed and analyzed. By following a structured approach, forensic professionals can effectively uncover the truth behind cyber incidents and support legal and organizational outcomes.

5. DIGITAL FORENSIC METHODOLOGIES

It is important for the forensics experts to consider the following areas of analyses to prepare an effective report and conclusion which can be presented in the court of law to prove /disprove an alibi.

5.1. Multimedia Forensics

- **Image Analysis:** Acquired images are analyzed for identification of faces and objects hidden in the image.
  - o Examine Exchangeable Image File Format (EXIF) metadata for information such as camera make, model, and settings used. This can reveal inconsistencies or alterations.
  - o Analyze file headers for signs of tampering or inconsistencies with known file formats.
  - o Perform Error Level Analysis (ELA) i.e. Detect modifications by analyzing changes in image error levels. ELA can highlight areas where an image has been edited.
  - o Examine pixel patterns and colors for signs of tampering, such as cloning or splicing.

- Use photogrammetry techniques to measure and analyze physical dimensions and relationships within an image, helping to verify its authenticity.
- Detect and analyze digital watermarks embedded in images to verify their authenticity and trace their origin.

- **Audio analysis:** The audio forensic experts examine the audio recordings to assess their legitimacy. Other common aspects of audio forensics are checking for integrity, transcribing dialogue, enhancing speech clarity, comparing voices, and reconstructing event timelines.
    - Examine the frequency spectrum of audio recordings to identify anomalies or signs of manipulation.
    - Compare voice recordings to known samples to verify the identity of speakers or detect audio splicing.
    - Use noise reduction techniques to enhance the clarity of audio evidence and detect subtle alterations.
    - Analyze compression artifacts to identify inconsistencies or manipulations in the audio file.
    - Determine the authenticity of an audio recording by analyzing its source and comparing it to known standards or references.
    - Assess timing and synchronization issues in audio to detect potential tampering or manipulation.
- **Video analysis:** The forensic team scientifically inspect and evaluate the videos recovered from multiple sources to identify suspects or potential sources of evidence.
    - Analyze video frames for consistency in temporal elements, such as frame rate and motion patterns. Detect irregularities that might indicate tampering or frame insertion.
    - Examine scene changes, lighting, and shadows to detect inconsistencies or alterations in video content.
    - Analyze video compression artifacts to identify signs of editing or recompression. Detect inconsistencies in compression patterns that could indicate tampering.
    - Use forensic coding techniques to detect and decode hidden data or metadata embedded in video files.
    - Generate and compare hash values of video files to verify their integrity and detect any alterations.
    - Analyze and detect digital watermarks or embedded signatures to verify the authenticity of video content.

5.2. Text Forensics

The experts analyze the textual data recovered from different sources like emails, chats and logs to discover keywords, patterns, and sentiments in large volumes of text data.

- **Stylometry:** Analyze various aspects of writing style, such as word choice, sentence structure, punctuation, and grammar, to identify patterns that may indicate authorship.

Extract stylistic features from the text and compare them with known samples from potential authors to determine similarities or differences.

- **Forensic Linguistics:** Examine linguistic features, including syntactic structures, lexical choices, and discourse patterns, to support authorship attribution or detect linguistic anomalies.

Compare the language used in the text with known samples from individuals to assess authorship or detect potential forgeries.

- **Metadata Examination:** Review metadata associated with digital documents to uncover information about creation, modification, and access history. This can help identify alterations or confirm the document's origin. Use cryptographic hash functions to verify the integrity of digital documents and detect any unauthorized modifications.
- **Text Alteration Detection:** Compare different versions of a document to identify changes, deletions, or insertions. This can reveal unauthorized modifications or track the evolution of the text.
- **Linguistic Anomaly Detection:** Identify linguistic anomalies or inconsistencies that may indicate tampering. Look for unusual patterns in language use, such as abrupt changes in style or tone.

5.3. Behavioral Analysis

To understand the behavior of suspects, data such as activity logs of users, browsing history and network traffic are analyzed to identify unusual or suspicious patterns.

- **Behavioral Profiling:** Examine patterns in user activities, such as login times, access patterns, and resource usage, to identify anomalies or deviations from normal behavior. This can help in detecting insider threats or compromised accounts.

Use profiling techniques to create behavioral profiles of users or entities based on their historical behavior. Compare these profiles to current activities to identify suspicious behavior.

- **Anomaly Detection:** Establish a baseline of normal behavior for users or systems by analyzing historical data. This baseline helps in identifying deviations that may indicate malicious activity or operational issues.

Apply statistical methods and algorithms to detect outliers or anomalies in behavior. Techniques such as clustering and regression analysis can help in identifying unusual patterns.

- **User and Entity Behavior Analytics (UEBA):** Collect and integrate data from various sources, including network traffic, system logs, and application usage, to gain a holistic view of user and entity behaviors.

Develop models of normal behavior based on historical data. These models help in understanding typical patterns and identifying deviations. Use machine learning algorithms to continuously learn and adapt behavioral models based on new data. This helps in improving the accuracy of anomaly detection over time.

- **Risk Scoring:** Assign risk scores to behaviors based on their deviation from normal patterns and their potential impact. Higher risk scores indicate more suspicious or potentially harmful activities.

Generate alerts based on risk scores and predefined thresholds. Implement automated or manual responses to address detected anomalies or threats.

- **Behavioral Indicators for insider threat detection:** Identify behavioral indicators of potential insider threats, such as unusual access to sensitive data, excessive data transfers, or anomalous login times. Monitor for signs of social engineering, such as unusual requests for sensitive information or changes in communication patterns.
- **Contextual Analysis:** Analyze contextual factors, such as the user's role, recent changes in job responsibilities, or organizational changes, to better understand the context of suspicious behaviors. Assess potential motivations

behind suspicious behaviors, such as financial gain, personal grievances, or coercion, to better evaluate the risk.

- **Transaction Analysis:** Analyze patterns in financial transactions, such as payment amounts, frequencies, and locations, to identify anomalies indicative of fraudulent activities. Look for behavioral red flags, such as rapid changes in transaction patterns or frequent requests for unusual transactions.

Cross-reference behavioral data with other data sources, such as credit reports, social media profiles, and communication logs, to identify inconsistencies or evidence of fraud.

Use link analysis techniques to map relationships and interactions between entities to uncover hidden connections and potential fraud rings.

- **Proactive Cyber Threat Monitoring:** Continuously monitor behavioral indicators of cyber threats, such as unusual network traffic, unexpected system changes, or unfamiliar process executions. Integrate threat intelligence feeds to enhance behavioral analysis with information about known threats, attack patterns, and adversary tactics.
- **Behavioral Forensics:** Analyze the behavior of users and systems during security incidents to understand the nature and scope of the attack. This includes examining login patterns, file access, and communication logs.

Use behavioral analysis to attribute attacks to specific actors or groups based on their behavior, tactics, and techniques.

6. CHALLENGES IN CYBER FORENSICS

With the evolving landscape of technology and exponentially growing ICT (Information and communication technology) users, cyber forensic experts are facing several challenges. The increasing complexity and diversity of digital devices, systems, and networks, coupled with the sheer volume of data generated have created new challenges for cyber forensic investigators. These challenges include technical, legal, and ethical issues that require careful consideration and innovative solutions.

- **Growing Size of Storage Devices:** With the growing size of data storage devices, experts don't get sufficient time to create a forensic image or to process the data.
- **Data Volume and Complexity:** The continuously increasing volume of data and the speed of data generation amount to exponential growth in digital ev-

idence that needs to be analyzed. The variety of data generated (structured/unstructured, audio, video, sensor data etc.) is also posing a challenge to experts to use more sophisticated tools and techniques.

- **Prevalence of Embedded Flash Storage:** With the rapid increase of HW interfaces with embedded flash storages, it is not easy to remove or image storage devices for forensic analysis.
- **File Formats:** Rapid enhancement of Operating Systems and increase in different file formats has increased the requirements, complexity and cost of cyber forensic tools.
- **Data Heterogeneity:** With the advancement of technologies like IoT devices, cloud environment, social media applications, sensor networks etc., the data generated in different formats and structures, making it challenging for forensic experts to collect, analyze, and correlate the data to reconstruct the events.
- **Prevalent Encryption:** The excessive use of sophisticated encryption techniques hampers the processing and interpretation of data.
- **Cloud Environment:** Pervasive Cloud environment for remote storage and data processing has intricated the identification and acquisition of digital evidence.
- **Data Privacy and Security:** The digital forensic investigators face challenges of maintaining privacy and securing sensitive personal data such as health, financial and location data, while acquiring digital evidence for forensic analysis.
- **Anti-Forensic Techniques:** Cyber criminals are using Anti-forensic techniques such as encryption, steganography, DoS attacks, covert channeling, storage space data hiding, and residual data wiping to hide evidence or to distract the investigation process. The use of anti-forensic techniques makes it challenging to locate and obtain digital evidence.
- **Lack of Standards and Best Practices:** The lack of standardized procedures, and universally accepted guidelines & best practices for conducting digital forensic investigations lead to inconsistencies and errors in the investigation process and can make it difficult to share and compare results between investigators.
- **Rapidly Changing Technology:** The rapid pace of technological change poses a significant challenge to forensic experts. Forensic experts need to be aware of the technological advancements so that new techniques can be developed and tested to discover reliable information of forensic value.
- **Resource Challenges:** Technological advancement has created a lot of avenues for criminals to do cybercrimes and dodge investigations. Digital forensics is an emergent field, and there are still significant limitations to

the resources needed as new technology poses new threats. To counter this threat there is a need of sophisticated tools and technologies as well as skilled professionals.

- **Legal Challenges:** Cyber forensic investigations often involve legal and regulatory issues, such as data ownership, data retention, and privacy laws. Law & Privacy Limits the scope of forensic investigations. Forensic experts need to be aware of these issues and comply with the relevant laws and regulations.

7. CASE STUDY EXAMPLES

- **Equifax Data Breach - Unraveling a Corporate Cyber Catastrophe:** The Equifax data breach of 2017 serves as a poignant case study showcasing the application of forensic methodologies in a large-scale cyber incident. The data breach has exposed the personal information of 147 million people. The company has agreed to a global settlement up to $425 million with the Federal Trade Commission, the Consumer Financial Protection Bureau, and 50 U.S. states and territories. The case study provides a detailed analysis of how investigators navigated through the aftermath, emphasizing the crucial role of digital forensics in attributing responsibility and mitigating further damage (FTC, 2024).
- **Maze Ransomware - Decrypting the Cryptocurrency Trail:** The Maze ransomware case exemplifies the evolving sophistication of cyber threats. This case study explores how forensic experts followed the cryptocurrency trail left by the attackers, showcasing the intricate interplay between forensic methodologies and emerging trends in cybercrime (Research, 2020).
- **Silk Road - Unraveling the Dark Web:** The Silk Road case serves as a paradigmatic example of digital forensic methodologies in action. This study provides a detailed analysis of how investigators navigated the complexities of the Dark Web to bring down one of the most notorious online marketplaces for illegal goods and services (Case, 2018).
- **SolarWinds Cyberattack - A State-Sponsored Operation:** The SolarWinds cyberattack, discovered in 2020, exemplifies the sophistication of modern cyber threats. This case study explores how forensic experts pieced together the puzzle of a state-sponsored cyber-espionage operation, emphasizing the importance of forensic methodologies in attributing cybercrimes (Siolu, 2021).
- **The Target Data Breach:** Hackers gained access to Target's network through credentials stolen from a third-party vendor, compromising the personal and payment information of over 40 million customers. Target says the data

breach was caused by malicious software on the POS card-swiping devices in the checkout aisles of its stores (Gopal, 2022).

Investigators used network forensics, log analysis, and malware analysis to trace the breach's origin and identify the attackers. The breach led to significant financial and reputational damage for Target. The case emphasized the importance of securing third-party vendor access and led to enhanced focus on supply chain security.

- **The Sony Pictures Hack:** North Korean hackers infiltrated Sony Pictures, stealing and releasing sensitive data, including unreleased films, employee information, and internal communications. Using a destructive malware called "Wiper," the attackers erased data from the company's servers and deployed ransomware. The breach exposed confidential internal emails, unreleased movies, and sensitive employee data, causing an estimated damage of $15 million in the immediate aftermath (Framework Security, 2024).

Forensics involved malware analysis, digital trail investigation, and reverse engineering of the malware used in the attack. Investigators also analyzed data exfiltration methods.

The hack resulted in extensive media coverage, significant financial losses, and discussions about state-sponsored cyberattacks. The case highlighted the need for robust data protection and incident response plans.

- **The Capital One Data Breach (2019):** On July 19, 2019, Capital one, a credit card company determined that an outside individual gained unauthorized access and obtained certain types of personal information about Capital One credit card customers and individuals who had applied for our credit card products (CapitalOne, 2022).

The forensics investigations used cloud forensics, access control analysis, and vulnerability assessments to trace the breach and identify the attacker. A former employee of Amazon Web Services exploited a vulnerability in Capital One's configuration, accessing sensitive data of over 100 million individuals.

The breach led to significant legal and regulatory consequences for Capital One. The case highlighted the importance of securing cloud configurations and monitoring cloud environments.

- **Uber Data Breach:** In 2022, an 18 year old hacker gained access to the Uber's VPN and discovered Microsoft Powershell scripts containing the login credentials of an admin user in Thycotic - the company's Privileged Access

Management (PAM) solution. This breach provided him full admin access to all of Uber's sensitive services, including DA, DUO, Onelogin, Amazon Web Services (AWS), and GSuite. The hacker also allegedly accessed Uber's bug bounty reports which usually contain details of security vulnerabilities yet to be remediated (Uber Team, 2022).

In 2026, Uber experienced a breach in which two attackers stole personal data of 57 million riders and drivers. Uber paid the attackers to keep the breach secret (Dara Khosrowshahi, 2016).

Forensic analysis focused on how the breach occurred, the methods used to exfiltrate data, and Uber's response to the breach. The breach resulted in legal actions and fines against Uber for failing to disclose the breach. The case underscored the importance of transparency and timely breach reporting.

- **The Ashley Madison Hack:** In 2015, hackers breached Ashley Madison, a dating site for people seeking extramarital affairs, leaking sensitive user data, including personal information and payment details of 37 million users (Lynsey Eidell, 2024).

Forensic efforts included analyzing the leaked data, understanding the breach vector, and investigating the data release methods. The breach had significant reputational and legal consequences. It highlighted the risks associated with storing sensitive user data and the importance of robust security measures.

- **The Marriott International Data Breach:** In 2018, Marriott International discovered a data breach affecting up to 500 million guests, with attackers accessing personal and payment information from its Starwood reservation system. However, the breach took place in 2014 when Starwood network was compromised before the acquisition by Marriott International. (Hollander, 2023).

Investigations involved network forensics, analysis of the compromised reservation system, and tracing the data access methods used by the attackers. The breach led to significant regulatory scrutiny and fines. It emphasized the importance of comprehensive data protection strategies and thorough investigations into breaches.

These case studies provide valuable insights into the complexities of cyber forensics and underscore the importance of continuous improvement in cybersecurity practices.

7.1. Key Lessons from these Cases

- **Proactive Security Measures:** Regular vulnerability assessments, patch management, and robust access controls are essential for preventing breaches.
- **Incident Response Planning:** Having a well-defined incident response plan helps organizations respond swiftly and effectively to cyber incidents.
- **Data Protection:** Ensuring the protection of sensitive data through encryption, secure storage, and minimal data retention practices is crucial.
- **Transparency and Reporting:** Timely and transparent reporting of breaches is important for regulatory compliance and maintaining stakeholder trust.
- **Advanced Threat Detection:** Leveraging advanced threat detection and behavioral analytics helps in identifying and mitigating sophisticated attacks.
- **Supply Chain Security:** Securing third-party vendors and software supply chains is critical to prevent supply chain attacks and related breaches.
- **Legal and Regulatory Compliance:** Adhering to legal and regulatory requirements helps in mitigating legal risks and financial penalties.

8. FUTURE HORIZONS: INNOVATIONS IN DIGITAL FORENSICS

The field of digital forensics is rapidly evolving, driven by advancements in technology and the increasing sophistication of cyber threats. Integration of sophisticated AI and machine learning techniques holds significant potential for enhancing investigative precision and efficacy, particularly in addressing the escalating prevalence of cybercrime (Haroon, Misra, Husain, Tripathi, & Khan, 2023) (Khan, et al., 2023) (Siddiqui, Yadav, & Husain, 2018).

- **AI-Based Incident Response:** Expert systems using artificial intelligence can be used to expedite forensic investigations and reduce the time and resources needed by crime investigators. With proper training and implementation, these systems can be effective in detecting unauthorized system access, Log Analysis, User Behavior Analytics (UBA), Anomaly Detection, Multi-Factor Authentication (MFA), Vulnerability Scanning, and Honeypots. Effective implementation of these systems can predict any crime and independently solve new and future crimes.
- **Data Mining Methods:** Data mining techniques such as decision trees, rule-based classifiers, Naïve Bayes classifiers, and ANN (Artificial Neural Networks) have been proved to be quicker and more accurate method for evaluating large volumes of data than traditional forensic analysis through lab experiments, which can be challenging and expensive. Future research

evaluating data mining approaches should not only concentrate on accuracy but also consider other crucial factors such as dependability and utility.

- **Advanced Data Recovery Techniques:** Innovations in data recovery techniques are improving the ability to retrieve information from damaged or corrupted storage media. This includes the development of new methods for dealing with encrypted or partially overwritten data. Enhanced recovery tools and techniques for physical damage, logical errors, and encryption challenges.
- **Automated Evidence Collection:** Automation in evidence collection is streamlining the forensic process. This includes automated scripts and tools that can gather and preserve evidence with minimal human intervention. Deployment of forensic bots, automated evidence documentation, and integration with other forensic systems for streamlined workflows.
- **Malware Classification Using Feature Engineering:** Feature-extraction tools and techniques such as Scikit Learn are very helpful in extracting features from high volume of data. Feature sets extracted from memory analysis of live malware infections can be used to effectively classify malware families to identify the specific areas affected or compromised by malware and guide digital forensics analysts as to where to concentrate their examinations.
- **Cloud Forensics:** With the growing use of cloud services, digital forensics is adapting to address challenges related to data stored in the cloud. Cloud forensics involves the collection, preservation, and analysis of data from cloud environments. Techniques are evolving to handle multi-tenant environments, manage data fragmentation, and ensure compliance with legal standards across different jurisdictions.
- **Big Data Digital Forensic Investigation:** In the fight against cybercrime, Big data driven framework for conducting digital forensic investigations utilizing all aspects of data collection, processing, analysis, and presentation proved to be an effective and cost-effective solution.
- **Blockchain Forensics:** Blockchain technology, used in cryptocurrencies and other applications, presents unique forensic challenges. Innovations are focusing on tracing transactions on decentralized networks and understanding the flow of assets.

Tools are being developed to analyze blockchain data, track cryptocurrency transactions, and identify patterns associated with illicit activities.

- **IoT Forensics:** The proliferation of Internet of Things (IoT) devices introduces new challenges in digital forensics. These devices often collect and transmit data, which can be crucial in investigations. Forensic methodologies are being refined to handle the diverse data formats and communication protocols of IoT devices, as well as to address issues related to device security and privacy.

- **Real-Time Forensics:** Real-time digital forensics involves analyzing data as it is being generated or transmitted. This innovation is crucial for responding to active cyber threats and breaches. Tools and methodologies for live system analysis, real-time data collection, and immediate incident response.
- **Enhanced Mobile Forensics:** As mobile devices become more advanced, so do the techniques for extracting and analyzing data from them. Innovations include dealing with new operating systems, encryption, and app data. Advanced tools for bypassing security features, recovering data from encrypted backups, and analyzing data from diverse mobile applications.
- **Legal and Ethical Frameworks:** As digital forensics evolves, there is a growing need for updated legal and ethical frameworks to guide investigations. This includes considerations for data privacy, cross-border data issues, and the admissibility of digital evidence in court. Development of international standards for digital evidence handling, protocols for maintaining data integrity, and guidelines for ethical conduct in forensic investigations.

These trends reflect the dynamic nature of digital forensics and highlight the need for ongoing research and adaptation to keep pace with technological advancements and emerging threats.

9. SUMMARY

The digital age has transformed the landscape of forensic methodologies, presenting both opportunities and challenges. The science of digital forensics has a seemingly limitless future and as technology advances, the field will continue to expand as new types of digital data are created by new devices logging people's activity. Although digital forensics began outside the mainstream of forensic science, it is now fully absorbed and recognized as a branch of forensic science.

REFERENCES

Bruce, M., Lusthaus, J., Kashyap, R., Phair, N., & Varese, F. (2024). Mapping the global geography of cybercrime with the World Cybercrime Index. *PLoS One*, 19(4), e0297312. DOI: 10.1371/journal.pone.0297312 PMID: 38598553

CapitalOne. (2022). *Information on the Capital One cyber incident*. Retrieved from Capital One: https://www.capitalone.com/digital/facts2019/

Case, S. (2018). *Silk Road: The Dark Web's Most Infamous Marketplace*. Oxford University Press.

Dara Khosrowshahi, C. (2016). *2016 Data Security Incident*. Retrieved from Uber Newsroom: https://www.uber.com/newsroom/2016-data-incident/

Framework Security. (2024). *The Sony Pictures Breach: A Deep Dive into a Landmark Cyber Attack*. Retrieved from Framework Security: https://www.frameworksec.com/post/the-sony-pictures-breach-a-deep-dive-into-a-landmark-cyber-attack

FTC. (2024). *Equifax Data Breach*. Federal Trade Commission.

Gopal, R. V. (2022). *Complete Case Study — Target Data Breach*. Retrieved from Medium: https://medium.com/thedeephub/complete-case-study-target-data-breach-2-ba4bb365a82e

Haroon, M., Misra, D. K., Husain, M., Tripathi, M. M., & Khan, A. (2023). Security Issues in the Internet of Things for the Development of Smart Cities. In Husain, M. S., Faisal, M., Sadia, H., Ahmad, T., & Shukla, S. (Eds.), *Advances in Cyberology and the Advent of the Next-Gen Information Revolution* (pp. 123–137). IGI. DOI: 10.4018/978-1-6684-8133-2.ch007

Hollander, J. (2023). *Marriott Data Breach FAQ: What Really Happened?* Retrieved from hoteltechreport.com: https://hoteltechreport.com/news/marriott-data-breach

Husain, M. S., & Khan, M. Z. (2019). *Critical Concepts, Standards, and Techniques in Cyber Forensics*. IGI Global.

Khan, W., Ishrat, M., Haleem, M., Khan, A. N., Hasan, M. K., & A, F. N. (2023). An Extensive Study and Review on Dark Web Threats and Detection Techniques. In M. S. Husain, M. Faisal, H. Sadia, T. Ahmad, & S. Shukla (Eds.), *Advances in Cyberology and the Advent of the Next-Gen Information Revolution* (pp. 202-219). IGI.

Langan, T. (2022). *INTERNET CRIME REPORT*. FEDERAL BUREAU OF INVESTIGATION.

Lynsey Eidell. (2024). *What Happened to Ashley Madison? The True Story of the Dating Site's Infamous 2015 Hack — and How It Bounced Back.* Retrieved from People.com: https://people.com/ashley-madison-dating-website-2015-hack-true-story-8644849

Petrosyan, A. (2023). *Leading IT security threats according to cyber security professionals 2022*. Statista.

Petrosyan, A. (2024). *Share of cyberattacks in global industries worldwide 2023.* Statista 2024.

Research, C. P. (2020). *The Maze Continues: Exploit Trends in 2020.* Check Point Software Technologies Ltd.

Siddiqui, M. Z., Yadav, S., & Husain, M. S. (2018). Application of artificial intelligence in fighting against cyber crimes: A review. *Int. J. Adv. Res. Comput. Sci.*, 9(2), 118–122.

Siolu, N. (2021). *SolarWinds State-Sponsored Supply Chain Attack vs. Standard Supply Chain Attacks.* Aiden.

Uber Team. (2022). *Security update*. Retrieved from Uber newsroom: https://www.uber.com/newsroom/security-update

ADDITIONAL READING

Abdel-Basset, M., Hawash, H., Chakrabortty, R. K., & Ryan, M. J. (2021). Semi-supervised spatiotemporal deep learning for intrusions detection in IoT networks. *IEEE Internet of Things Journal*, 8(15), 12251–12265. DOI: 10.1109/JIOT.2021.3060878

Afaq, S. A., Husain, M. S., Bello, A., & Sadia, H. (2023). A critical analysis of cyber threats and their global impact. In *Computational Intelligent Security in Wireless Communications* (pp. 201–220). CRC Press.

Akbar, M., Suaib, M., Husain, M. S., & Shukla, S. (2020). A Compendium of Cloud Forensics. In Critical Concepts, Standards, and Techniques in Cyber Forensics (pp. 215-227). IGI Global. DOI: 10.4018/978-1-7998-1558-7.ch012

Akbar, M., Suaib, M., & Hussain, M. (2023). The Rise of Deepfake Technology: Issues, Challenges, and Countermeasures. In Advances in Cyberology and the Advent of the Next-Gen Information Revolution (pp. 178-201). IGI Global.

Daradkeh, M. (2023). The Link Between Privacy and Disclosure Behavior in Social Networks. In Advances in Cyberology and the Advent of the Next-Gen Information Revolution (pp. 38-61). IGI Global. DOI: 10.4018/978-1-6684-8133-2.ch003

Golomingi, R., Dobay, A., Franckenberg, S., Ebert, L., & Sieberth, T. (2023). Augmented reality in forensics and forensic medicine – Current status and future prospects. *Science & Justice*, 63(4), 451–455. DOI: 10.1016/j.scijus.2023.04.009 PMID: 37453776

Halima, N. B., Alluhaidan, A. S., Khan, M. Z., Husain, M. S., & Khan, M. A. (2023). A service-categorized security scheme with physical unclonable functions for internet of vehicles. *Journal of Big Data*, 10(1), 178. DOI: 10.1186/s40537-023-00865-7

Khan, W., Ishrat, M., Haleem, M., Khan, A. N., Hasan, M. K., & A, F. N. (2023). An Extensive Study and Review on Dark Web Threats and Detection Techniques. In M. S. Husain, M. Faisal, H. Sadia, T. Ahmad, & S. Shukla (Eds.), Advances in Cyberology and the Advent of the Next-Gen Information Revolution (pp. 202-219). IGI.

Mei, Y., Han, W., Li, S., Lin, K., Tian, Z., & Li, S. (2024). A Novel Network Forensic Framework for Advanced Persistent Threat Attack Attribution Through Deep Learning. *IEEE Transactions on Intelligent Transportation Systems*, 25(9), 12131–12140. DOI: 10.1109/TITS.2024.3360260

Voigt, P., & Bussche, A. v. (2017). *The EU General Data Protection Regulation (GDPR). A Practical Guide* (1st ed.). Springer International Publishing. DOI: 10.1007/978-3-319-57959-7

KEY TERMS AND DEFINITIONS

Anomaly: Anomaly refers to an occurrence or data point that deviates significantly from the expected or usual pattern. In various fields, anomalies are considered deviations from the norm that may indicate underlying issues, irregularities, or important insights.

Big Data: Big Data refers to large, complex datasets that are too vast and intricate to be processed, managed, and analyzed using traditional data processing tools and techniques. The concept encompasses the enormous volume, velocity, and variety of data generated from various sources, which can provide valuable insights when properly harnessed.

Blockchain: Blockchain is a decentralized, distributed ledger technology that securely records and verifies transactions across a network of computers. It ensures the integrity and transparency of data by maintaining a continuously growing list of records, called blocks, which are linked and secured using cryptographic principles. Each block contains a collection of transactions and is connected to the previous block, forming a chain.

Cyber Espionage: cyber espionage refers to the use of cyber techniques to secretly collect sensitive or confidential information from individuals, organizations, or governments. Unlike traditional espionage, which often involves physical surveillance and human intelligence, cyber espionage leverages digital tools and methods to gain unauthorized access to data and systems. The motives behind cyber espionage can range from political or economic gain to strategic advantage.

Cyber Forensics: Cyber forensics, also known as digital forensics, is a branch of forensic science focused on the recovery, analysis, and presentation of digital evidence from electronic devices and networks. Its primary objective is to investigate and uncover evidence related to cybercrimes or security incidents in a manner that is legally admissible in court. Cyber forensics involves various techniques and methodologies to identify, preserve, and analyze digital information, ensuring that the evidence is handled and processed in a way that maintains its integrity and chain of custody.

Cyber Terrorism: cyber terrorism refers to the use of cyber tools and techniques to carry out attacks that aim to cause significant disruption, harm, or fear, typically with political or ideological motives. Unlike traditional terrorism, which often involves physical violence and acts of terror, cyber terrorism utilizes digital methods to target computer systems, networks, or data.

Cyber Warfare: cyber warfare refers to the use of digital attacks and strategies by nation-states or other organized groups to conduct warfare through cyberspace. Unlike conventional warfare, which involves physical battles and military engagements, cyber warfare utilizes cyber tools and techniques to achieve strategic objectives, disrupt or damage critical infrastructure, steal information, or influence political and military outcomes.

Hacking: hacking refers to the practice of gaining unauthorized access to computer systems, networks, or data, often with the intention of exploiting, modifying, or manipulating information for various purposes. Hacking can be conducted for ethical reasons, such as security testing, or for malicious purposes, such as stealing data or disrupting operations. The term "hacking" encompasses a range of activities and motivations, and it is crucial to distinguish between different types and intents of hacking.

Identity Theft: identity theft is a crime in which an individual's personal information, such as Social Security numbers, credit card details, bank account information, or other identifying data, is stolen and used without their permission. The stolen information is typically used for fraudulent purposes, such as financial gain or accessing services under the victim's name. Identity theft can have serious consequences for individuals, including financial loss, reputational damage, and emotional distress.

IoT: Internet of Things (IoT) refers to the network of interconnected physical devices that communicate with each other and with centralized systems via the internet. These devices, often embedded with sensors, software, and other technologies, collect and exchange data, enabling automation, monitoring, and control over various applications and environments.

Linguistics: Linguistics is the scientific study of language and its structure. It encompasses the analysis of language form, language meaning, and language in context. Linguistics explores how languages are constructed, how they function, and how they are used by people in various social and cultural settings.

Malware: Malware, short for "malicious software," refers to any software intentionally designed to cause harm to, exploit, or otherwise negatively affect computers, networks, or devices. Malware encompasses a wide range of harmful programs and code, each with specific functions and methods of attack. Its purpose is typically to compromise the integrity, confidentiality, or availability of data and systems.

Phishing: phishing is a type of cyber-attack that aims to deceive individuals into providing sensitive information, such as usernames, passwords, credit card numbers, or other personal data. The attacker uses fraudulent communication, typically via email, text message, or social media, to impersonate a trustworthy entity or organization. The goal is to trick the victim into disclosing sensitive information or performing actions that can compromise their security.

Quantum Computing: Quantum Computing is an advanced computational paradigm that leverages the principles of quantum mechanics to perform complex calculations at speeds far exceeding those of classical computers. Unlike classical computers, which use bits as the basic unit of information, quantum computers use quantum bits or qubits.

Ransomware: ransomware is a type of malicious software (malware) that encrypts a victim's data, rendering it inaccessible, and demands a ransom payment from the victim to restore access. Ransomware attacks can target individuals, businesses, and organizations, and they often cause significant disruption and financial damage.

Chapter 2
Machine Learning in Digital Forensics

ABSTRACT

In the intricate landscape of digital forensics, the integration of machine learning has ushered in a transformative era. Digital forensics is a discipline concerned with the recovery, analysis, and presentation of digital evidence in a manner that is legally admissible. The field is increasingly important due to the growing dependence on digital technologies and the proliferation of cybercrimes. With the exponential growth of digital devices and the increasing complexity of cybercrimes, digital forensics has become more challenging. Machine learning (ML), a subset of artificial intelligence (AI), has emerged as a pivotal technology in context of cyber forensics, offering sophisticated methods for analyzing large volumes of data, detecting anomalies, and automating complex tasks (Suaib, Akbar, & Husain, 2020).

1. INTRODUCTION

In the intricate landscape of digital forensics, the integration of machine learning has ushered in a transformative era. Digital forensics is a discipline concerned with the recovery, analysis, and presentation of digital evidence in a manner that is legally admissible. The field is increasingly important due to the growing dependence on digital technologies and the proliferation of cybercrimes. With the exponential growth of digital devices and the increasing complexity of cybercrimes, digital forensics has become more challenging. Machine learning (ML), a subset of artificial intelligence (AI), has emerged as a pivotal technology in context of cyber forensics, offering

DOI: 10.4018/979-8-3693-2960-3.ch002

sophisticated methods for analyzing large volumes of data, detecting anomalies, and automating complex tasks (Suaib, Akbar, & Husain, 2020).

This chapter provides a comprehensive insight into the application of machine learning in cyber forensics. It explores foundational concepts, key applications, challenges, and future directions. The objective is to offer an in-depth understanding of how ML can be leveraged to enhance forensic investigations and address the evolving challenges in the digital landscape.

2. EMERGENCE AND IMPORTANCE OF MACHINE LEARNING

The emergence of machine learning as a powerful analytical tool for diverse applications forms the foundation for its integration into digital forensics. Machine learning is a branch of artificial intelligence (AI) that enables systems to learn from data and improve their performance over time without explicit programming.

2.1. Foundations of Machine Learning

Machine Learning (ML) is a subfield of artificial intelligence (AI) focused on developing algorithms and statistical models that enable computers to learn from and make predictions or decisions based on data. Unlike traditional programming, where explicit instructions are given to perform a task, machine learning systems use data to learn patterns and improve their performance over time without being explicitly programmed for specific tasks. The core of ML lies in its ability to recognize patterns and make decisions based on data inputs. Key concepts in ML includes:

2.1.1. Machine Learning Techniques

Machine Learning approaches are generally categorized into supervised learning, unsupervised learning, and reinforcement learning as shown in Figure 1.

Figure 1. Machine learning categorization

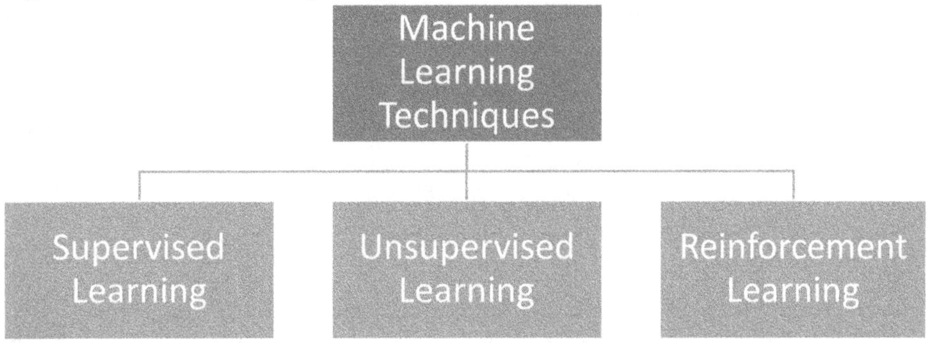

- **Supervised Learning:** This approach involves training algorithms on labeled data, where each training example is paired with an outcome. The goal is to learn mapping from inputs to outputs that can then be used to predict outcomes for new data. Supervised learning techniques include regression analysis (e.g., linear regression) and classification (e.g., decision trees, and neural networks).
- **Unsupervised Learning:** Unsupervised learning deals with unlabeled data. The algorithm seeks to identify patterns or groupings within the data. Grouping similar types of digital evidence (i.e. Clustering) and reducing the number of features while preserving important information (i.e. dimensionality reduction) are typical examples of tasks performed using unsupervised machine learning approaches. Common unsupervised machine learning techniques include clustering (e.g., k-means), association mining (e.g., Apriori) and dimensionality reduction (e.g., principal component analysis).
- **Reinforcement Learning:** This machine learning technique involves training an agent to make a sequence of decisions by rewarding it for correct actions and penalizing it for incorrect ones. It is less commonly used in digital forensics but has potential applications in automated decision-making systems.

2.1.2. Algorithms and Models

At the core of ML are algorithms that process data to build models. These models can then make predictions or decisions based on new data.

- **Algorithms:** A set of rules or procedures that a machine learning model uses to learn from data and make predictions. Common algorithms include linear regression, decision trees, support vector machines, and neural networks.
- **Models:** Mathematical or computational representations created by algorithms based on training data. A model is used to make predictions or decisions based on new, unseen data.

Several ML algorithms are commonly used in digital forensics:

- **Decision Trees (DT):** Decision Trees are a supervised learning method used for classification and regression that involves splitting the data into subsets based on feature values. These algorithms use a tree-like model of decisions and their possible consequences. They are intuitive and useful for classification tasks. In forensics investigations it is used for analyzing structured data to extract meaningful insights and identifying patterns indicative of unauthorized access or attacks.
- **Support Vector Machines (SVM):** Support Vector Machines are supervised learning algorithms used for classification and regression tasks. SVMs are quite effective for classification tasks, particularly in high-dimensional spaces. They work by finding the optimal hyperplane that separates classes in the feature space. SVM are mainly incorporated in cyber forensics for malware detection and spam filtering based on features extracted from the file.

However, Performance of SVM can be sensitive to the choice of kernel function and parameters. Another issue with SVM is that it requires substantial computational resources for large datasets.

- **Artificial Neural Networks (ANN):** These algorithms are inspired by the human brain and are capable of learning complex patterns through layers of interconnected nodes. Deep learning, a subset of neural networks, is particularly powerful for tasks such as image and speech recognition.
- **Random Forests (RF):** Random Forest is an ensemble learning method that constructs multiple decision trees during training and outputs the mode of the classes (classification) or mean prediction (regression) of the individual trees to improve classification accuracy and robustness. Random Forest Assists in identifying the most relevant features in forensic data and helps in categorizing large datasets of digital evidence.
- **Naïve Bayes:** Naive Bayes is a probabilistic classifier based on Bayes' theorem with strong independence assumptions between features. It is a useful approach for classification like identifying spam mails or categorizing docu-

ments. Naïve Bayes is quite Efficient with high-dimensional data and requires a relatively small amount of training.

- **Clustering Algorithms:** Techniques like k-means and hierarchical clustering group data points into clusters based on their feature similarities. These are useful for anomaly detection and data organization based on hidden features.
- **K-Nearest Neighbors:** K-Nearest Neighbors is a simple, instance-based learning algorithm used for classification and regression. It classifies a data point based on the majority class among its k nearest neighbors. K-Nearest Neighbor approach is useful for recognizing patterns in user behavior or file usage and identifies unusual patterns or behaviors in network traffic or file activities.
- **Logistic Regression (LR):** Logistic Regression is a statistical method for binary classification that models the probability of a certain class or event. In digital forensics it is useful for distinguishing between two classes, such as legitimate vs. malicious files and identifying fraudulent activities by analyzing patterns in transaction data.
- **Principal Component Analysis (PCA):** Principal Component Analysis (PCA) is a statistical technique used to simplify and reduce the dimensionality of data while preserving as much variance as possible. It transforms the data into a new coordinate system where the axes (principal components) are ordered by the amount of variance they capture from the original data. PCA is widely used in data analysis, machine learning, and pattern recognition for exploratory data analysis, feature reduction, and visualization.
- **Singular Value Decomposition (SVD):** Singular Value Decomposition (SVD) is a fundamental matrix factorization technique in linear algebra and numerical analysis. It is used to decompose a matrix into three other matrices, revealing important properties of the original matrix. SVD is widely used in various fields, including data science, machine learning, and signal processing, due to its ability to simplify complex problems and analyze large datasets.
- **Generative Adversarial Networks (GANs):** GANs are a class of deep learning models that consist of two networks, a generator and a discriminator, which are trained adversarially. GANs are used to generate synthetic data for training other models and are especially useful in scenarios with limited real data.
- **Apriori:** The Apriori algorithm is a classical data mining technique used for association rule learning. While it is primarily associated with market basket analysis, its principles and methods are also applicable to cyber forensics, particularly in the context of pattern recognition and anomaly detection.

Table 1. Summary of common ML techniques used for digital forensics

ML Algorithm/Model	Pros	Cons	Applications
Decision Trees	• Easy to interpret and visualize. • Can handle both numerical and categorical data.	• Prone to overfitting, especially with complex datasets. • Pruning techniques are needed to improve generalization.	• Intrusion Detection • Data Analysis
Support Vector Machines (SVM)	• Effective in high-dimensional spaces. • Robust against overfitting.	• Performance sensitive to the choice of kernel function and parameters. • requires substantial computational resources for large datasets.	• Malware Detection • Spam Filtering
Deep Neural Networks	• Capable of handling very complex patterns and large amounts of data. • Suitable for a variety of forensic tasks, including natural language processing and image recognition.	• Requires large amounts of labeled data. • Requires substantial computational resources. • Models can be difficult to interpret.	• Image and Video Analysis • Feature Extraction
Random Forests	• Handles large datasets • Reduces the risk of overfitting compared to single decision trees.	• Model interpretability can be challenging due to the complexity of the ensemble.	• Digital evidence Classification • Helpful in identifying the most relevant features in forensic data.
Naïve Bayes	• Efficient with high-dimensional data. • Requires a relatively small amount of training data.	• Assume independence between features, which may not always be true. • May not capture complex relationships between features.	• Email Classification • Document Classification
Clustering Algorithms	• Useful for exploratory data analysis. • handle large datasets to discover hidden patterns.	• The choice of the number of clusters (for K-Means) or parameters (for DBSCAN) can impact results. • Require domain expertise to interpret clusters meaningfully.	• summarizing large volumes of forensic data. • Anomaly Detection
K-Nearest Neighbors	• Simple to implement • Easy to understand. • Flexible to different types of data.	• Computationally expensive for large datasets. • Performance heavily depends on the choice of k and the distance metric.	• Anomaly Detection • Pattern Recognition

continued on following page

Table 1. Continued

ML Algorithm/Model	Pros	Cons	Applications
Logistic Regression	• Provides probabilities and confidence levels for predictions. • Simple and effective for binary classification tasks.	• Assumes a linear relationship between features and the log-odds of the outcome. • May not perform well with complex, non-linear data.	• Fraud Detection in transaction data. • Binary Classification Tasks such as legitimate vs. malicious files.
PCA	• aids in understanding complex datasets by reducing dimensionality while preserving as much information as possible	• computationally intensive for very large datasets	• Dimensionality Reduction • Data Visualization • Noise Reduction • Feature Extraction. • Pattern Recognition
SVD	• Suitable for applications requiring precise computations due to numerical stability.	• computational complexity can be intensive for large matrices	• Dimensionality Reduction • Data Compression • Noise Reduction
Generative Adversarial Networks (GANs)	• Capable of generating high-quality synthetic data. • Useful for tasks that require realistic data simulations.	• Training GANs can be complex and resource intensive. • Requires careful tuning of hyperparameters and network architectures.	• Data Augmentation • Image Generation
Apriori	• Helpful in identifying frequent patterns and associations in large datasets. • Scalable i.e. can be applied to datasets of varying size including large datasets.	• Computationally intensive and slow for very large datasets.	• Detection of Suspicious Patterns • Incident Analysis • Behavioral Profiling • Forensic Data Analysis • Threat Intelligence

2.1.3. Data Preparation and Feature Engineering

Effective machine learning requires careful data preparation and feature engineering:

- **Data Collection:** Gathering relevant data is crucial. In digital forensics, this might include system logs, network traffic, or file metadata.
- **Data Cleaning:** Ensuring the data is accurate and free of inconsistencies is essential for model performance.
- **Feature Selection:** Identifying the most relevant features or attributes of the data helps improve model accuracy and efficiency.

- **Normalization:** Scaling features to a standard range can improve the performance of many ML algorithms.

2.1.4. Training and Testing

ML models are trained on historical data (tagged/labelled data in case of supervised learning and unlabeled data in case of unsupervised learning), known as training data. They are then tested on unseen data to evaluate their performance and generalizability.

- **Training Data:** The dataset used to teach the machine learning model. This data includes both the input features and the corresponding output labels or values. Training is done to tune up the parameters used and optimize the model.
- **Testing Data:** A separate dataset used to evaluate the performance of the machine learning model after it has been trained. This data helps assess how well the model generalizes to new, unseen examples. Testing is done to measure the model's accuracy and effectiveness.

2.2. Emergence of ML in Digital Forensics

Machine learning, as a concept, started gaining traction in the 1950s with the work of pioneers like Alan Turing and Arthur Samuel. Turing's work on artificial intelligence (AI) and Samuel's development of the first learning algorithms laid the groundwork for the future of ML. However, it wasn't until the 1980s and 1990s, with the advent of more powerful computers and the refinement of algorithms, that machine learning began to emerge as a practical tool for various applications, including forensics.

- **Early Machine Learning Research (1990s–2000s)**

Early research in ML for digital forensics focused on techniques such as clustering algorithms, decision trees, and support vector machines (SVMs). These techniques were used to analyze and classify data, offering new ways to identify patterns and relationships within digital evidence.

- **The Emergence of Advanced Machine Learning Techniques (2000s–2010s)**

The 2000s marked a significant shift with the introduction of more advanced machine learning techniques and algorithms. The development of ensemble methods, such as random forests and gradient boosting machines, enhanced the accuracy and robustness of predictive models. This era also saw the rise of neural networks and deep learning, which provided powerful tools for complex data analysis tasks.

A landmark moment was the application of natural language processing (NLP) to digital forensics. NLP techniques allowed forensic experts to analyze textual data from emails, chat logs, and documents, enabling more effective information extraction and categorization.

- **Integration of Machine Learning in Commercial Tools (2010s–Present)**

As machine learning techniques matured, they began to be integrated into commercial digital forensic tools. Modern forensic software suites, such as Cellebrite's UFED and Magnet AXIOM, now incorporate ML algorithms for tasks like data classification, anomaly detection, and predictive analysis. These tools have significantly enhanced the efficiency and effectiveness of digital investigations.

One notable advancement is the use of ML for automated data triage. With the increasing volume of digital evidence, manual analysis became impractical. ML algorithms now assist forensic experts in prioritizing and categorizing data, allowing them to focus on the most relevant evidence and streamline the investigative process.

2.3. Milestones in Adoption of ML in Digital Forensics

- **Development of Predictive Analysis (2010s)**

The adoption of predictive analysis in digital forensics represents a major milestone. By applying machine learning algorithms to historical crime data, forensic experts can predict potential criminal activity and identify patterns that may indicate future crimes. This capability has been particularly useful in investigating organized crime and identifying connections between seemingly unrelated incidents.

Predictive analysis has also improved the efficiency of data recovery. ML algorithms can prioritize data extraction based on the likelihood of relevance, reducing the time required to sift through large volumes of digital evidence.

- **Advances in Facial and Voice Recognition (2010s–Present)**

Facial and voice recognition technologies have seen substantial advancements due to machine learning. Deep learning algorithms, particularly convolutional neural networks (CNNs), have greatly improved the accuracy of facial recognition systems. These systems are now capable of identifying individuals in images and videos with high precision, even in challenging conditions such as low lighting or partial obstructions.

Voice recognition has also benefited from ML techniques, with improvements in speaker identification and transcription accuracy. These advancements have enhanced the ability of forensic experts to analyze audio recordings and match them to known individuals.

- **Development of Automated Data Analysis Platforms (2010s–Present)**

Automated data analysis platforms have become a crucial component of modern digital forensics. These platforms leverage ML algorithms to perform tasks such as data filtering, pattern recognition, and anomaly detection. Forensic investigators can now process vast amounts of data quickly and accurately, significantly accelerating the investigation process.

One example is the use of ML for email and communication analysis. Algorithms can automatically categorize and flag suspicious messages, identify key contacts, and uncover hidden relationships within communication data. This has been particularly valuable in investigations involving large-scale data breaches or cybercrimes.

- **Ethical and Legal Considerations (2010s–Present)**

As machine learning became more integrated into digital forensics, ethical and legal considerations have gained prominence. The use of ML in forensic investigations raises questions about privacy, data security, and the potential for algorithmic bias. Ensuring that ML algorithms are transparent, accountable, and free from discriminatory biases is essential to maintaining the integrity of digital forensic practices.

The development of ethical guidelines and best practices for the use of ML in forensics has become an important milestone. Organizations such as the International Association for Computer Investigative Specialists (IACIS) and the National Institute of Standards and Technology (NIST) have published guidelines to address these concerns and promote responsible use of ML technologies.

3. APPLICATIONS OF MACHINE LEARNING IN DIGITAL FORENSICS

Machine learning has numerous applications in digital forensics, each addressing specific challenges in analyzing and interpreting digital evidence (Qadir & Noor, 2021) (Khan, Shoaib, Husain, Nisa, & Quasim, 2024) (Halima, Alluhaidan, M Z

Khan, Husain, & Khan, 2023) (Shukla, et al., 2024) (Khan, Husain, & Shoaib, Introduction to email, web, and message forensics., 2020). ML applications help forensic experts in enhancing both the efficiency and accuracy of investigations. Key applications of ML in forensics are shown in Figure 2.

Figure 2. Machine learning applications in digital forensics

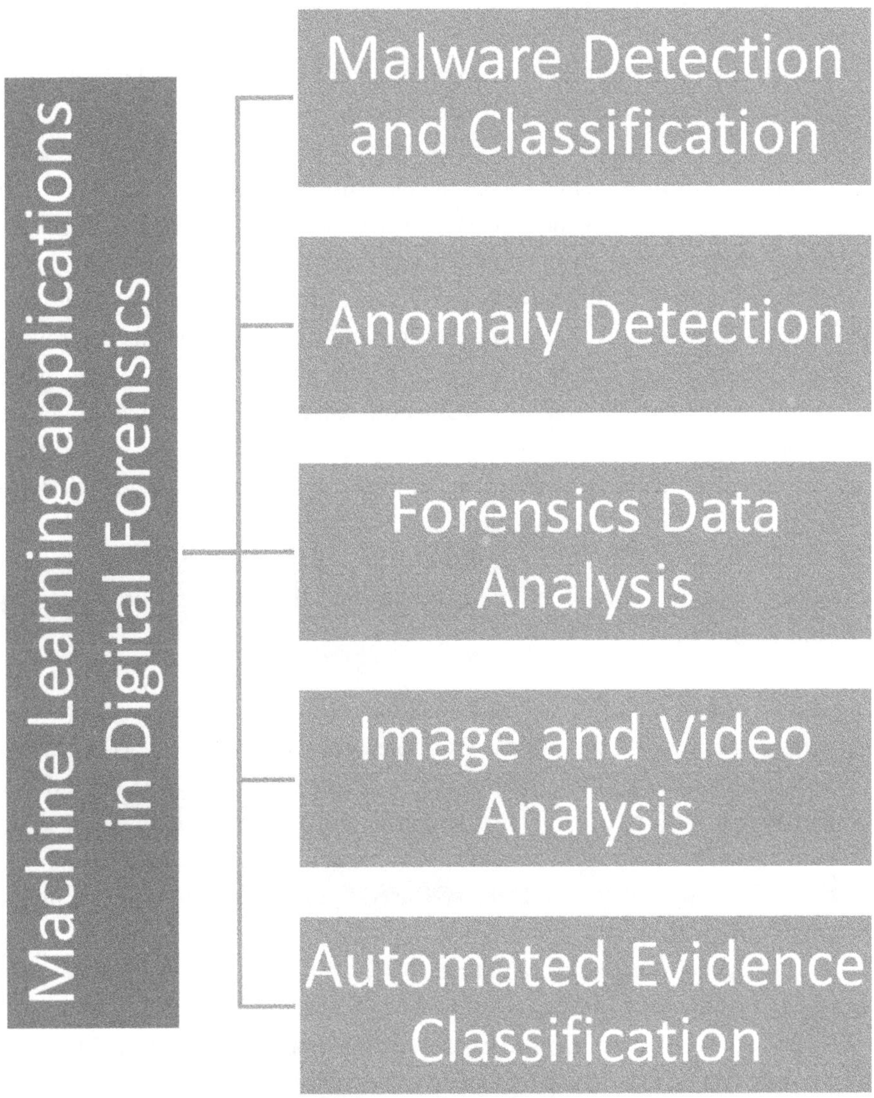

3.1. Malware Detection and Classification

Machine learning algorithms can analyze patterns in code to identify and classify malware. Supervised learning techniques, such as neural networks and support vector machines, are used to recognize malicious software based on known examples. Machine learning offers advanced capabilities for detecting and classifying both known and unknown malware.

- **Static Analysis:** Machine learning models analyze the static features of files, such as byte sequences or API calls, to detect malware. For instance, deep learning models can learn to identify patterns associated with malicious code.
- **Dynamic Analysis:** This approach involves analyzing the behavior of files during execution. ML models can track and classify behaviors such as file system modifications or network activity. Techniques like behavioral analysis using recurrent neural networks (RNNs) are employed to detect anomalies.
- **Hybrid Approaches:** Combining static and dynamic analysis improves the accuracy and robustness of malware detection systems. Machine learning models can integrate features from both approaches to enhance detection capabilities.

Various machine learning algorithms used for malware detection are:

Machine learning offers a powerful alternative by enabling systems to learn from data and improve over time. There are several ML algorithms used in malware detection, including:

- o **Classification techniques:** used to categorize files as either benign or malicious based on their features. Examples are Decision Trees (DT), Support Vector Machines (SVM), Random Forests (RF), Neural Networks (NN).
- o **Clustering Algorithms:** These are used to group similar malware samples together, which can help in identifying new malware strains. Examples include K-means Clustering, Density-Based Spatial Clustering of Applications with Noise (DBSCAN).

Challenges in Malware detection:

While machine learning helps in improving the system performance in detecting malware, there are challenges which need to be addressed:

- o **Evolving Threat Landscape:** The hackers keep updating their approach in creating malware, making it challenging for static models to keep up.

- o **Data Quality and Quantity:** High-quality, labeled data is essential for training robust models. Obtaining such data can be difficult.
- o **Feature Overfitting:** Overfitting occurs when a model learns noise instead of the actual pattern, leading to poor generalization.

Future Directions in malware detection using ML:

Ongoing research and development in machine learning and system automation are improving the effectiveness and efficiency of the traditional Machine learning techniques.

- o **Deep Learning:** Advanced neural networks like convolutional neural networks (CNNs) and recurrent neural networks (RNNs) are being explored for their ability to handle complex patterns and sequences.
- o **Adversarial Machine Learning:** Researchers are developing methods to make ML models more resistant to adversarial attacks, where attackers manipulate input data to deceive the model.
- o **Explainability:** Improving the interpretability of ML models to understand why certain decisions are made, which is crucial for forensic investigations.

In conclusion, machine learning algorithms significantly enhance malware detection in cyber forensics by providing more adaptive and scalable solutions compared to traditional methods. In a forensic investigation, ML algorithms can be integrated into a larger toolkit that includes data collection, analysis, and reporting tools. Automated malware detection helps forensic analysts quickly identify threats and focus on detailed investigations.

3.2. Anomaly Detection

Anomaly detection algorithms are used to identify unusual patterns or activities within large datasets, such as network traffic or system logs. In cyber forensics, anomalies may indicate various forms of cyber threats, such as intrusions, insider threats, or malware activity. Unlike traditional methods, which rely on predefined signatures or rules, anomaly detection aims to identify novel or previously unseen threats by analyzing deviations from expected behavior. Unsupervised learning methods, including clustering and isolation forests, help detect deviations from normal behavior that may indicate security breaches or suspicious activities.

- **Network Traffic Analysis:** Machine learning models analyze network traffic to identify unusual patterns, such as sudden spikes in data transfer or unexpected connections. Techniques like clustering and outlier detection are used to flag anomalies.

- **System Log Analysis:** Anomaly detection in system logs helps identify unusual activities, such as unauthorized access attempts or abnormal system behavior. ML algorithms can classify log entries and detect deviations from normal patterns.
- **User Behavior Analysis:** Machine learning models can analyze user behavior to detect anomalies, such as unusual login times or atypical file access patterns. This can help identify potential insider threats or compromised accounts.

Machine Learning Approaches for Anomaly Detection

Several ML algorithms and techniques are employed for anomaly detection, each with its strengths and limitations:

- **Statistical Methods:** These involve modeling the normal behavior of a system and identifying deviations from this model. For example, *Z-Score* which identify the anomaly using standard deviation of a data point from the mean value and *Gaussian Mixture Models (GMM)* where the models represent data as a mixture of several Gaussian distributions and detects anomalies based on the probability density of data points.
- **Distance-Based Methods:** These techniques rely on the distance between data points to identify anomalies. For example, *k-Nearest Neighbors (k-NN)* where data points that are far from their neighbors are considered anomalies.
- **Complex Machine Learning Models:** More complex ML models can also be used for anomaly detection like *Autoencoders* which uses neural networks that learn to compress and reconstruct input data and identify anomalies by using high reconstruction errors. *Recurrent Neural Networks (RNNs)* are particularly useful for identifying anomalies in sequence data, such as network traffic over time by detecting deviations in traffic patterns.

Challenges in anomalies detection

The challenges in anomaly detection using machine learning in cyber forensics investigations are:

- **Data Imbalance:** Anomalies are often rare compared to normal data, leading to class imbalance. This can affect model performance and requires techniques to handle imbalanced datasets.

- o **Dynamic Nature of Attacks:** Cyber threats evolve rapidly, and models trained on historical data may not always detect new types of anomalies. Continuous updating and retraining of models are necessary.
- o **False Positives and Negatives:** High false positive rates can lead to alert fatigue, where genuine threats may be ignored. Balancing detection sensitivity and specificity is critical.

Future Directions:

- o **Explainable AI:** Developing models that provide clear explanations for why certain anomalies were detected, aiding forensic investigations by providing insights into the nature of the anomalies.
- o **Real-Time Detection:** Advancements in processing power and algorithms are enabling real-time anomaly detection, which is crucial for timely responses to security incidents.
- o **Hybrid Approaches:** Combining multiple anomaly detection methods to leverage their strengths and mitigate their weaknesses.

Anomaly detection using machine learning provides a sophisticated approach to identifying potential security threats in cyber forensics. By leveraging various ML algorithms and techniques, organizations can enhance their ability to detect and respond to novel and evolving threats.

3.3. Forensics Data Analysis

Forensic data analysis involves examining and interpreting large volumes of digital data to uncover relevant evidence. Machine learning algorithms can assist in analyzing and interpreting complex datasets. For instance, natural language processing (NLP) techniques are used to extract relevant information from unstructured text data, such as emails or documents, helping investigators identify key evidence (Iqbal & Alharbi, 2020).

- **Natural Language Processing (NLP):** NLP techniques are used to extract meaningful information from unstructured text data. For example, named entity recognition can identify individuals, organizations, or locations mentioned in emails or documents.
- **Data Correlation:** Machine learning can correlate data from different sources to uncover relationships and patterns. For instance, correlating log data with network traffic can help identify coordinated attacks or malicious activities.

- **Sentiment Analysis:** Analyzing the sentiment of textual data, such as social media posts or communication records, can provide insights into the motivations or intentions behind certain actions.

Machine Learning Approaches in Forensic Data Analysis

Machine learning enhances forensic data analysis through several key approaches:

- o **Data Classification:** ML algorithms classify data into predefined categories. Forensic data analysis uses classification to perform tasks like Classifying files as malicious or benign based on their characteristics, Classifying user activities as normal or suspicious or detecting Phishing emails by analyzing content and metadata and classifying as legitimate or spam. Common classification algorithms include Support Vector Machines (SVM), Random Forests, and Neural Networks.
- o **Anomaly Detection:** Identifies deviations from expected behavior, which can signal potential security incidents. For example, Behavioral Analysis to detect abnormal user behaviors or system activities, and Intrusion Detection. Anomaly detection methods include Autoencoders, RNNs, Isolation Forest etc.
- o **Clustering:** Clustering algorithms groups similar data points together, which helps in identifying patterns and relationships. In cyber forensics clustering is used for different tasks like Network Traffic Analysis by grouping similar traffic patterns to identify and analyze attack vectors, and File Grouping to clusters similar files or malware samples for further analysis. Popular clustering algorithms are K-Means Clustering and DBSCAN.
- o **Natural Language Processing (NLP):** Analyzes text data for forensic purposes, such as: Sentiment Analysis i.e. analyzing the sentiment of communication to detect suspicious behavior, Topic Modeling which is used to identify topics or themes in communication to understand the context of an incident. NLP techniques used for forensics purposes include *Bag of Words* to represents text as a collection of words, ignoring grammar and word order and *Word Embeddings* which represents words in continuous vector space, capturing semantic meanings.
- o **Predictive Analytics:** Predicts potential future incidents or outcomes based on historical data. Risk Assessment is used to predict the likelihood of a future attack based on past incidents. Common algorithms for prediction include Regression Analysis and Time Series Analysis.
- o **Feature Engineering and Selection:** Effective forensic data analysis relies on extracting relevant features from raw data. Feature Extraction involves deriving meaningful attributes from raw data, such as file metadata, network

traffic patterns, or system logs and Feature Selection is used to identify the most relevant features that contribute to accurate model performance, reducing dimensionality and improving efficiency. Techniques for feature selection include *Principal Component Analysis (PCA)* which reduces the number of features while retaining most of the variance and *Recursive Feature Elimination (RFE)* which iteratively removes less important features to improve model performance.

Challenges in data analysis:

- **Data Quality:** Incomplete, corrupted, or biased data can impact the accuracy of ML models.
- **Scalability:** Handling large volumes of data efficiently is crucial for real-time analysis.
- **Interpretability:** Understanding and explaining ML model decisions is essential for forensic investigations and legal proceedings.
- **Privacy and Security:** Ensuring that data handling and analysis comply with privacy regulations and security best practices.

In conclusion, machine learning algorithms significantly advance forensic data analysis by automating processes, identifying complex patterns, and improving efficiency. As technology evolves, integrating ML into forensic investigations will continue to enhance the ability to detect, analyze, and respond to cyber threats effectively.

3.4. Image and Video Analysis

Multimedia evidence plays a significant role in digital forensics. Machine learning models can enhance the analysis and interpretation of images and videos. These models assist in identifying individuals, verifying the authenticity of media, and reconstructing events.

- **Facial Recognition:** ML algorithms can identify and match faces in images or videos, assisting in verifying identities and tracking individuals. Techniques such as convolutional neural networks (CNNs) are used for facial recognition tasks.
- **Object Detection:** Object detection models can identify and classify objects within images or videos. This is useful for identifying evidence, such as weapons or stolen items, in multimedia evidence.
- **Video Forensics:** Machine learning can be used to enhance video quality, detect tampering, or extract relevant frames for analysis. Techniques such as

deep learning-based video enhancement are employed to improve the quality of video evidence.

- **Frame Manipulation:** Detects alterations in individual video frames. Machine learning models analyze temporal and spatial inconsistencies across frames.
- **Spatio-Temporal Anomalies:** Identifies anomalies in motion or object behavior that could indicate tampering. Recurrent neural networks (RNNs) and temporal convolutional networks (TCNs) are often used for this purpose.

- **Image Forgery Detection:**
  - **Copy-Move Forgery:** Detects when a part of an image is copied and pasted within the same image. Machine learning algorithms, particularly those based on convolutional neural networks (CNNs), are used to identify inconsistencies in texture or patterns.
  - **Splicing:** Involves stitching together multiple images. ML models can identify boundaries and discontinuities that are not visible to the naked eye.
  - **Image Retouching:** Detects subtle alterations, such as smoothing or object removal. Techniques often involve deep learning models that analyze pixel-level changes.

    Challenges in multimedia forensics:

  - **Data Quality and Quantity:** High-quality labeled datasets are crucial for training effective models. Generating and annotating these datasets can be time-consuming and expensive. Also, models trained on specific datasets may not generalize well to new types of manipulations or novel attack methods.
  - **Evasion and Counter-Forensics:** Attackers may use techniques to deliberately avoid detection by forensic models. Sophisticated manipulations, especially those using advanced generative models, can be challenging to detect.
  - **Ethical Considerations:** Ensuring that forensic analysis is used responsibly and respects individuals' privacy. There is potential for misuse of forensic techniques, such as for false accusations or surveillance.

Machine learning has significantly advanced the field of image and video forensics, but ongoing research and development are needed to keep pace with evolving manipulation techniques and ensure the technology remains effective and ethical.

3.5. Automated Evidence Classification

Automated evidence classification streamlines the process of organizing and indexing digital evidence. Machine learning can automate the classification and tagging of digital evidence, speeding up the process of organizing and indexing large volumes of data. This automation reduces manual effort and helps forensic analysts focus on more critical tasks.

- **File Classification:** ML models can categorize files based on their content and metadata, facilitating the organization of evidence and improving searchability. Techniques like text classification and clustering are used for file classification.
- **Tagging and Indexing:** Automated tagging and indexing of evidence help forensic analysts quickly locate and retrieve relevant information. Machine learning models can assign tags based on file content, context, or metadata.

  Machine Learning Approaches in Automated Evidence Collection

  - **Data Identification and Retrieval:** ML algorithms can automate the identification and retrieval of relevant data based on specific criteria from various sources, such as: File Systems, Network Traffic, and Logs. Techniques used for data identification and retrieval are Pattern Recognition and Intelligent search algorithms, enhanced by ML.
  - **Data Categorization and Classification:** Once data is retrieved, it needs to be categorized and classified to facilitate further analysis. Supervised and unsupervised techniques like SVMs, Random Forests, Neural Networks, and clustering algorithms are used to classify the data such as users' activities, logs, emails, files as malicious or legitimate.
  - **Metadata Extraction and Analysis:** Extracting and analyzing metadata such as File Metadata which includes information such as creation dates, modification times, and file origins and Network Metadata including details about network connections, protocols, and packet sizes provides context and additional information about files and activities. ML models can extract relevant features from metadata to assist in identifying patterns or anomalies. NLP techniques can be used for analyzing textual metadata, such as comments or descriptions.
  - **Automated Evidence Correlation:** Correlating evidence from different sources helps in building a comprehensive picture of the incident. Tasks like *Cross-Referencing* which allows automati-

cally linking related pieces of evidence from files, logs, and network traffic, and *Timeline Creation* by constructing timelines of events based on correlated evidence to understand the sequence of activities are very vital in forensics Investigation. Techniques used for evidence correlation are machine learning based Graph Algorithms which help in visualizing and analyzing relationships between different pieces of evidence. Machine learning algorithms are also useful in Link Analysis to identify connections and relationships between entities in the evidence.

Machine learning significantly enhances automated evidence collection in cyber forensics by improving efficiency, accuracy, and consistency. By automating the retrieval, classification, and analysis of digital evidence, ML helps forensic investigators to focus on critical aspects of their work and respond more effectively to cyber incidents.

Recent work in forensics investigation using Machine Learning:

Machine learning plays a vital role in cyber forensics. Cyber forensics investigators use machine learning algorithms to analyze vast amounts of data to perform various forensics tasks like pattern recognition, feature classification, behavioral analysis, discovering relation between digital evidence and suspects etc. (Balushi, Shaker, & Kumar, 2023). Table 2 summarizes the prominent work done in digital forensics using machine learning algorithms.

continued on following page

Table 2. Continued

Table 2. Summary of prominent work in digital forensics investigation using ML

Forensic Purpose	Reference	Work objective	ML approach
Malware forensics	(Tuncer, Ertam, & Dogan, 2021)	Anti-malware framework for forensics analysis	SVD, PCA
	(Ali, Shiaeles, Clarke, & Kontogeorgis, 2019)	Determine malware location in Windows Registry	LR, DT
Network forensics	(Sudha & Rupa, 2019)	Features classification	K-Means
	(Usman, et al., 2021)	Classify attack behavioral	DT, SVM and Naïve Bayes
	(Kachavimath, Nazare, & Akki, 2020)	DDoS attack	KNN, Naïve Bayes
	(Yudhana, Riadi, & Ridho, 2018)		NN, Naïve Bayes
Video forensics	(Barra, Bisogni, Nappi, Freire-Obreg´on, & Castrill´on-Santana, 2019)	Gender classification	RF, KNN, SVM
	(Ferreira, Antunes, & Correia, 2021)	Detect manipulated videos and photos	SVM
	(Durall, Keuper, Pfreundt, & Keuper, 2019)		
Image forensics	(Barni, Nowroozi, & Tondi, 2018)	Contrast enhancement and identify JPEG-Compressed image	SVM
	(Roy, Dixit, Naskar, & Chakraborty, 2020)	Determine image source	PCA, RF
	(Islam, et al., 2018)	Copy-move and splice attacks	SVM
	(Ahmed, Gulliver, & alZahir, 1-12)	Image falsification	SVD
Mobile forensics	(Li, Xi, Wu, Jiang, & Rao, 2018)	Mobile forensics	Apriori, K-Means
Email forensics	(Hina, et al., 2021)	Email classification	LR, SVM, RF, DT
File system/ memory forensics	(Ruriawan, Anggono, Siahaan, & Purwanto, 2019)	Identify and recover digital evidence	K-Means

4. CHALLENGES AND CONSIDERATIONS

While machine learning offers significant benefits for digital forensics, several challenges and considerations as shown in figure below, must be addressed to effectively integrate machine learning techniques in forensics.

Figure 3. Key challenges in using machine learning for digital forensics

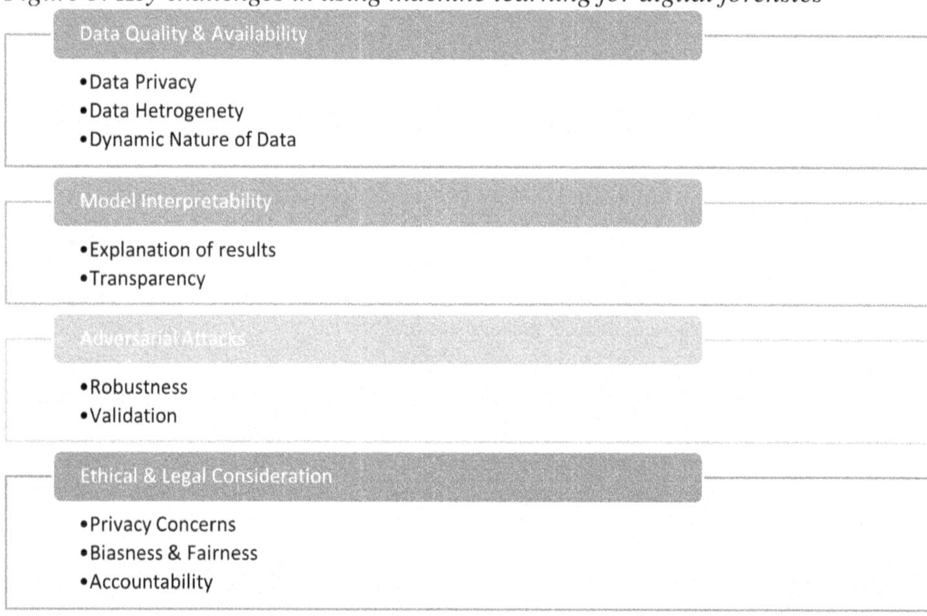

4.1. Data Quality and Availability

The effectiveness of machine learning models depends on the quality and availability of data. Machine learning models require high-quality, representative datasets for training. In digital forensics, obtaining such datasets can be challenging due to privacy concerns, data heterogeneity, and the dynamic nature of digital evidence. Ensuring that the data used for training is comprehensive and unbiased is crucial for effective model performance. In digital forensics, obtaining such datasets can be challenging due to:

- **Data Privacy:** Obtaining and using digital evidence must comply with privacy laws and regulations. Ensuring that data is handled responsibly and ethically is essential for maintaining trust and legal compliance.
- **Data Heterogeneity:** Digital evidence comes in various formats and from diverse sources, making it challenging to create uniform training datasets. Addressing data heterogeneity involves developing methods to handle different data types and formats.
- **Dynamic Nature of Data:** The rapid evolution of digital technologies and cyber threats requires continuous updates to datasets and models. Machine learning systems must adapt to new types of data and emerging threats.
- **Scalability:** Handling large volumes of data efficiently is crucial for real-time analysis.

4.2. Model Interpretability

Many machine learning models, particularly deep learning approaches, operate as "black boxes," providing limited insight into their decision-making processes. In forensic contexts, it is important to understand and interpret model outputs to ensure that evidence is presented accurately and can be scrutinized by courts. In this context the key challenges are:

- **Explanation of Results:** Forensic analysts and legal professionals need to understand and explain how ML models arrive at their conclusions. Lack of interpretability can undermine the credibility of ML-based findings in legal proceedings.
- **Transparency:** Ensuring transparency in ML processes, including model development, validation, and deployment, is crucial for maintaining the integrity of forensic analyses.

4.3. Adversarial Attacks

Machine learning systems can be vulnerable to adversarial attacks, where malicious actors manipulate inputs to deceive the model. In digital forensics, adversarial attacks could undermine the integrity of evidence analysis and detection systems. Implementing robust security measures and validating models against such threats are essential.

- **Robustness:** Developing robust ML models that can withstand adversarial attacks is essential for maintaining the reliability of forensic analyses.

Techniques such as adversarial training and defensive algorithms are employed to enhance model robustness.

- **Validation:** Regular validation and testing of models against potential adversarial scenarios can help identify and mitigate vulnerabilities. This includes evaluating models with synthetic adversarial examples and conducting stress tests.

4.4. Ethical and Legal Considerations

The use of machine learning in digital forensics raises several ethical and legal issues, such as privacy concerns and the potential for algorithmic bias. Forensic professionals must navigate these issues carefully, ensuring that ML applications comply with legal standards and ethical guidelines.

- **Privacy Concerns:** Handling sensitive data requires adherence to privacy laws and regulations. Ensuring that ML applications do not infringe on individuals' privacy rights is crucial for ethical practices.
- **Biasness and Fairness:** ML models can inadvertently introduce biases based on the training data. Addressing biases and ensuring fairness in model predictions is essential for equitable and accurate forensic analyses.
- **Accountability:** Determining accountability for decisions made by ML models and ensuring that human oversight is maintained are important considerations. This involves defining the roles and responsibilities of forensic analysts and ensuring that ML-based decisions are subject to human interpretation and validation.

5. EXAMPLE CASE STUDIES

Machine learning (ML) has revolutionized digital forensics by automating complex tasks, enhancing detection capabilities, and improving the analysis of large datasets. Below are few case study examples demonstrating the application of ML in digital forensics:

- **Automated Malware Detection**

VirusTotal: VirusTotal, a popular online service, uses machine learning models to analyze files and URLs for malware detection. It aggregates data from various antivirus engines and uses ML algorithms to improve the accuracy of malware classification. They have incorporated Random Forest for feature-based classification and Deep Learning models for behavioral analysis.

The integration of ML models improved detection rates and reduced false positives, enabling faster identification of malicious files and enhancing overall security.

CrowdStrike Falcon: CrowdStrike Falcon is a cybersecurity platform that uses machine learning to detect and classify malware. The system aims to address the challenge of identifying new and sophisticated malware variants that traditional signature-based approaches might miss. Deep neural networks (DNNs) employed to analyze and classify executable files based on their behavior and characteristics have achieved high accuracy in detecting both known and unknown malware, significantly improving the ability to prevent attacks.

CrowdStrike Falcon's ML-based malware classification has led to more effective endpoint protection, minimizing the risk of successful attacks and improving incident response times.

- **Network Intrusion Detection by Cuckoo Sandbox**

Cuckoo Sandbox is an open-source automated malware analysis system that employs machine learning to detect network-based intrusions and anomalies. The system uses Support Vector Machines (SVM) for classification of network traffic and K-Means Clustering approach for anomaly detection in network patterns.

By leveraging ML, Cuckoo Sandbox significantly enhanced its ability to identify suspicious network behavior and isolate potential threats in real-time.

- **Phishing Email Detection by Google's Gmail Spam Filter**

Google's Gmail uses machine learning algorithms to filter out phishing and spam emails from users' inboxes. To classify emails based on content and metadata it uses Naïve Bayes classifiers and Deep Learning models for contextual analysis and pattern recognition.

The ML-based spam filter drastically reduced the number of phishing emails reaching users and improved overall email security.

- **Digital Image Forensics by Adobe Photoshop Content Authenticity Initiative**

Adobe's Content Authenticity Initiative uses machine learning to verify the authenticity of digital images and detect tampering. For detecting image manipulations and inconsistencies the Adobe's system uses Convolutional Neural Networks

(CNNs) and to create realistic synthetic images for training Generative Adversarial Networks (GANs).

The initiative improved the ability to verify the integrity of digital images, addressing issues of image tampering and misinformation.

- **Social Media Analysis by Hunchly**

Hunchly is a digital investigation tool that utilizes machine learning to track and analyze social media data related to criminal investigations. It implements Natural Language Processing (NLP) techniques to analyze and categorize social media posts. To group related posts and identify patterns it uses Clustering Algorithms.

Hunchly enhanced the capability of investigators to find relevant social media content, track suspects, and uncover crucial evidence.

- **Fraud Detection in Financial Transactions by Visa's Neural Network System**

Visa employs machine learning to detect and prevent fraudulent transactions in real-time. To analyze transaction patterns and user behavior it employs different Deep Neural Network (DNN) models. The system implements Anomaly Detection Algorithms to identify unusual transaction patterns.

The system reduced the rate of fraudulent transactions and improved the accuracy of fraud detection, protecting consumers and financial institutions.

- **Forensic Data Recovery by X1 Search**

X1 Search uses machine learning to enhance forensic data recovery and analysis by indexing and searching through large volumes of data. The system utilizes various Text Classification techniques to categorize and prioritize recovered data and different Similarity Detection Algorithms to find related documents and evidence.

The tool streamlined the process of recovering and analyzing forensic data, making investigations more efficient.

- **Behavioral Profiling by Darktrace**

Darktrace utilizes machine learning to create behavioral profiles and detect anomalies in network traffic. In the first phase, the system uses Machine Learning-based Behavioral Analysis to establish normal behavior patterns. At the second level it uses Anomaly Detection techniques to identify deviations from established norms. The system detected unusual patterns and behaviors indicative of potential security incidents, such as unauthorized access or data exfiltration. By learning normal network behavior, the system minimized false alarms and improved the accuracy of threat detection.

Darktrace improved the ability to detect insider threats and advanced persistent threats (APTs) by providing real-time alerts on unusual behavior.

- **Forensic Audio Analysis by Voice Biometric Systems**

Voice biometric systems use machine learning to analyze and verify speaker identities from audio recordings. Feature Extraction Algorithms are implemented to analyze vocal characteristics and then Deep Learning models are used for speaker recognition and voice matching. The ML based system enhances the accuracy of speaker identification and voice authentication, assisting in criminal investigations and legal proceedings.

VoiceBiometrics' use of deep learning for voice analysis has advanced the field of forensic audio analysis, providing reliable tools for verifying speaker identities and supporting legal investigations.

- **Digital Evidence Correlation using FTK Imager and EnCase**

FTK Imager and EnCase are forensic tools that incorporate machine learning to correlate and analyze disparate pieces of digital evidence. They use the concept of Entity Recognition to identify and link related pieces of evidence. To correlate data across different sources Pattern Recognition Algorithms are used.

Improved the efficiency of forensic investigations by enabling investigators to link and analyze evidence more effectively, leading to quicker case resolutions.

- **Digital Evidence Extraction from Encrypted Devices**

Passware Kit Forensic is a digital forensic tool used to extract and analyze evidence from encrypted devices. The tool incorporates machine learning to enhance the decryption and analysis of encrypted files and disk images. ML algorithms are used to optimize brute-force attacks on encrypted files, increasing the efficiency of the decryption process. Various Pattern Recognition methods are used to identify patterns in encryption keys or passwords based on historical data and known attack vectors.

ML-enhanced techniques help in reducing the time required to crack encryption and access valuable data and improving the accuracy in identifying encryption keys and passwords, leading to successful extraction of encrypted evidence. Passware Kit

Forensic's use of machine learning has significantly advanced the capability to access and analyze encrypted data, aiding in criminal investigations and legal proceedings.

- **Forensic Analysis of Social Media Data**

Geofeedia, a social media monitoring tool, uses machine learning to analyze and extract relevant information from social media platforms. The tool helps forensic investigators gather evidence from posts, images, and interactions. Implemented ML algorithms identify and categorize images based on their content, such as locations, objects, or people. The system uses NLP techniques for text data analysis to determine the sentiment of social media posts and interactions. The tool automated the process of collecting and categorizing social media content, saving time and effort for investigators and provides valuable context and insights by analyzing sentiment and identifying key entities related to the investigation.

Geofeedia's application of machine learning has facilitated more effective social media investigations, enabling forensic experts to uncover crucial evidence and connections.

6. FUTURE DIRECTIONS

The integration of machine learning into digital forensics is an evolving field, with several promising directions for future research and development:

6.1. Enhanced Algorithms

Developing more sophisticated ML algorithms that can handle complex and diverse data types will improve the accuracy and efficiency of forensic investigations. Advances in generative models, transfer learning, and explainable AI hold promise for addressing current limitations.

- **Deep Learning:** Advances in deep learning, including novel neural network architectures and training methods, offer potential for improving accuracy and performance in tasks such as image recognition and natural language processing.
- **Transfer Learning:** Transfer learning allows models trained on one task to be adapted for related tasks, enabling faster and more efficient development of forensic models with limited data.

6.2. Cross-Domain Applications

Machine learning techniques developed for other domains, such as finance or healthcare, could be adapted and applied to digital forensics. Leveraging cross-domain knowledge and technologies could lead to innovative solutions for forensic challenges.

- **Integration with Other Technologies:** Combining ML with other technologies, such as blockchain for data integrity, AR to provide immersive investigative tools or edge computing for real-time analysis, can enhance forensic capabilities.
- **Cross-Domain Knowledge Transfer:** Applying ML methods developed for fields like finance or healthcare to digital forensics can lead to new insights and approaches.

6.3. Enhanced Predictive Analytics

Future ML algorithms may offer even more accurate predictive capabilities, helping forensic experts anticipate and prevent criminal activities with greater precision. Advances in deep learning and AI could lead to more sophisticated models for analyzing complex data patterns and trends.

6.4. Collaboration and Standards

Establishing standards and best practices for the application of machine learning in digital forensics will be crucial for ensuring consistency and reliability. Collaboration among researchers, practitioners, and policymakers will help shape the development and implementation of these standards.

- **Industry Collaboration:** Collaboration between researchers, practitioners, and policymakers can help develop standardized methodologies and frameworks for ML in digital forensics.
- **Best Practices:** Developing and sharing best practices for model development, validation, and deployment can ensure consistency and reliability across forensic investigations.

6.5. Improved Data Privacy and Security

Future advancements will likely focus on addressing privacy and security concerns associated with ML in digital forensics. Developing algorithms that ensure data confidentiality and mitigate risks of misuse will be crucial for maintaining public trust and protecting individual rights.

6.6. Ethical and Legal Frameworks

As machine learning technologies continue to advance, developing comprehensive ethical and legal frameworks will be essential. These frameworks should address issues related to privacy, transparency, and accountability to ensure the responsible use of ML in digital forensics.

- **Developing Frameworks:** Creating comprehensive ethical and legal frameworks for ML applications in digital forensics can guide the responsible use of technology and protect individuals' rights.
- **Transparency and Accountability:** Ensuring transparency in ML processes and maintaining accountability for decisions made by ML models are crucial for upholding the integrity of forensic analyses.

7. SUMMARY

Machine learning represents a powerful tool for analyzing complex data and automating decision-making processes across various domains. Its ability to uncover patterns, make predictions, and continuously improve through experience makes it a cornerstone of modern AI and data science. Machine learning has the potential to revolutionize digital forensics by enhancing the analysis, detection, and classification of digital evidence. While the integration of ML presents numerous opportunities, it also introduces challenges that must be carefully managed. By addressing these challenges and advancing research in the field, digital forensics can leverage machine learning to improve investigative processes and contribute to the pursuit of justice. As the field evolves, ongoing collaboration, innovation, and adherence to ethical standards will be key to harnessing the full potential of machine learning in digital forensics.

REFERENCES

Ahmed, B., Gulliver, T. A., & alZahir, S. (2020). (1-12). Blind copy-move forgery detection using svd and ks test. *SN Applied Sciences.*

Ali, M., Shiaeles, S., Clarke, N., & Kontogeorgis, D. (2019). A proactive malicious software identification approach for digital forensic examiners. *Journal of Information Security and Applications*, 47, 139–155. DOI: 10.1016/j.jisa.2019.04.013

Balushi, Y. A., Shaker, H., & Kumar, B. (2023). The Use of Machine Learning in Digital Forensics: Review Paper. *International Conference on Innovation in Information Technology and Business* (pp. 96-113). Springer Nature. DOI: 10.2991/978-94-6463-110-4_9

Barni, M., Nowroozi, E., & Tondi, B. (2018). Detection of adaptive histogram equalization robust against jpeg compression. *International Workshop on Biometrics and Forensics (IWBF)* (pp. 1-8). IEEE. DOI: 10.1109/IWBF.2018.8401564

Barra, P., Bisogni, C., Nappi, M., Freire-Obreg'on, D., & Castrill'on-Santana, M. (2019). Gait analysis for gender classification in forensics. *International Conference on Dependability in Sensor, Cloud, and Big Data Systems and Applications* (pp. 180-190). Springer. DOI: 10.1007/978-981-15-1304-6_15

Durall, R., Keuper, M., Pfreundt, F.-J., & Keuper, J. (2019). Unmasking deepfakes with simple features. *arXiv preprint arXiv:1911.*

Ferreira, S., Antunes, M., & Correia, M. E. (2021). Exposing manipulated photos and videos in digital forensics analysis. *Journal of Imaging*, 7(7), 102. DOI: 10.3390/jimaging7070102 PMID: 39080890

Halima, N. B., Alluhaidan, A. S., Khan, M. Z., Husain, M. S., & Khan, M. A. (2023). A service-categorized security scheme with physical unclonable functions for internet of vehicles. *Journal of Big Data*, 10(1), 178. DOI: 10.1186/s40537-023-00865-7

Hina, M., Ali, M., Javed, A. R., Srivastava, G., Gadekallu, T. R., & Jalil, Z. (2021). *Email classification and forensics analysis using machine learning. IEEE Smart-World, Ubiquitous Intelligence & Computing, Advanced & Trusted Computing, Scalable Computing & Communications, Internet of People and Smart City Innovation (Smart-World/SCALCOM/UIC/ATC/IOP/SCI).* IEEE.

Iqbal, S., & Alharbi, S. A. (2020). Advancing automation in digital forensic investigations using machine learning forensics. *Digital Forensic Science, 3.*

Islam, M. M., Karmakar, G., Kamruzzaman, J., Murshed, M., Kahandawa, G., & Parvin, N. (2018). *Detecting splicing and copymove attacks in color images. Digital Image Computing: Techniques and Applications (DICTA)*. IEEE.

Kachavimath, A. V., Nazare, S. V., & Akki, S. S. (2020). Distributed denial of service attack detection using na¨ıve bayes and k-nearest neighbor for network forensics. *2020 2nd International conference on innovative mechanisms for industry applications (ICIMIA)* (pp. 711-717). IEEE.

Khan, M. Z., Husain, M. S., & Shoaib, M. (2020). Introduction to email, web, and message forensics. In *Critical concepts, standards, and techniques in cyber forensics* (pp. 174–186). IGI Global. DOI: 10.4018/978-1-7998-1558-7.ch010

Khan, M. Z., Shoaib, M., Husain, M. S., Nisa, K., & Quasim, M. T. (2024). Enhanced mechanism to prioritize the cloud data privacy factors using AHP and TOPSIS: a hybrid approach. *Journal of Cloud Computing, 13(1), 42., 13*(1).

Li, H., Xi, B., Wu, S., Jiang, J., & Rao, Y. (2018). The application of association analysis in mobile phone forensics system. *International Conference on Intelligence Science* (pp. 126-133). Springer. DOI: 10.1007/978-3-030-01313-4_13

Qadir, S., & Noor, B. (2021). Applications of machine learning in digital forensics. *International Conference on Digital Futures and Transformative Technologies (ICoDT2)*. DOI: 10.1109/ICoDT252288.2021.9441543

Roy, A., Dixit, R., Naskar, R., & Chakraborty, R. S. (2020). *Digital Image Forensics: Theory and Implementation*. SpringerLink. DOI: 10.1007/978-981-10-7644-2

Ruriawan, M. F., Anggono, B., Siahaan, I. A., & Purwanto, Y. (2019). Development of digital evidence collector and file classification system with k-means algorithm. *Asia Pacific Conference on Wireless and Mobile (APWiMob)* (pp. 64-68). IEEE. DOI: 10.1109/APWiMob48441.2019.8964232

Shukla, S., Hussain, S., Irshad, R. R., Alattab, A. A., Thakur, S., Breslin, J. G., Hassan, M. F., Abimannan, S., Husain, S., & Jameel, M. S. (2024). Network analysis in a peer-to-peer energy trading model using blockchain and machine learning. *Computer Standards & Interfaces*, 88, 88. DOI: 10.1016/j.csi.2023.103799

Suaib, M., Akbar, M., & Husain, M. S. (2020). Digital forensics and data mining. In *Critical concepts, standards, and techniques in cyber forensics* (pp. 240–247). IGI Global. DOI: 10.4018/978-1-7998-1558-7.ch014

Sudha, T. S., & Rupa, C. (2019). *Analysis and evaluation of integrated cyber crime offences. Innovations in Power and Advanced Computing Technologies (i-PACT)*. IEEE.

Tuncer, T., Ertam, F., & Dogan, S. (2021). Automated malware identification. *Multimedia Tools and Applications*, 80(7), 10881–10900. DOI: 10.1007/s11042-020-10317-6

Usman, N., Usman, S., Khan, F., Jan, M. A., Sajid, A., Alazab, M., & Watters, P. (2021). Intelligent dynamic malware detection using machine learning in ip reputation for forensics data analytics. *Future Generation Computer Systems*, 118, 124–141. DOI: 10.1016/j.future.2021.01.004

Yudhana, A., Riadi, I., & Ridho, F. (2018). Ddos classification using neural network and na¨ıve bayes methods for network forensics. *International Journal of Advanced Computer Science and Applications*, 9(11). Advance online publication. DOI: 10.14569/IJACSA.2018.091125

KEY TERMS AND DEFINITIONS

Cross-Validation: A technique used to assess the performance of a machine learning model by dividing the data into multiple subsets, training the model on some subsets, and validating it on the remaining ones. Cross validation is used to ensure that the model's performance is robust and not dependent on a particular subset of data.

Evaluation Metrics: Evaluation metrics are the measures used to quantify how well the model performs and guide improvements. Common metrics include accuracy, precision, recall, F1 score, and mean squared error.

Features: The individual measurable properties or characteristics of the data used as input to the model.

Hyperparameters: Parameters set before the training process begins that control the learning process, such as the learning rate, number of layers in a neural network, or the depth of a decision tree. Hyperparameters are used to tune the model and improve its performance.

Labels: The output or target values that the model is trained to predict. Labels are used in supervised learning to guide the training process.

Overfitting: When a model learns the training data too well, including noise and outliers, leading to poor performance on new data. The model is too complex and captures details that do not generalize.

Underfitting: When a model is too simple to capture the underlying patterns in the data, leading to poor performance on both training and testing data.

Chapter 3
Deep Learning Techniques in Digital Forensics

ABSTRACT

As cybercrime becomes more intricate and sophisticated, the field of digital forensics faces challenges that traditional techniques struggle to address. Deep learning, a subset of machine learning has revolutionized various fields by enabling computers to learn from vast amounts of data and perform complex tasks with remarkable accuracy. Deep learning characterized by its use of neural networks with multiple layers, has shown great promise in enhancing the accuracy, efficiency, and scope of forensic investigations. This chapter explores the transformative role of deep learning in digital forensics, highlighting its applications, advantages, challenges, and potential future prospects.

1. INTRODUCTION

Digital forensics has evolved rapidly in recent years, forcing increasingly sophisticated methods to tackle the growing complexity and volume of digital evidence. Traditionally reliant on manual methods and heuristic techniques, digital forensics is increasingly benefiting from advances in artificial intelligence (AI), particularly deep learning.

As cybercrime becomes more intricate and sophisticated, the field of digital forensics faces challenges which traditional techniques struggle to address. Deep learning, a subset of machine learning has revolutionized various fields by enabling computers to learn from vast amounts of data and perform complex tasks with remarkable accuracy. Deep learning characterized by its use of neural networks with

DOI: 10.4018/979-8-3693-2960-3.ch003

multiple layers, has shown great promise in enhancing the accuracy, efficiency, and scope of forensic investigations. This chapter explores the transformative role of deep learning in digital forensics, highlighting its applications, advantages, challenges, and potential future prospects.

2. FUNDAMENTALS OF DEEP LEARNING

Deep learning involves neural networks with multiple layers, known as deep neural networks (DNNs), which are designed to automatically learn and extract hierarchical features from data. These networks are capable of learning from vast amounts of data through a process of feature extraction and pattern recognition, making them highly effective for tasks involving complex and unstructured data. Unlike traditional machine learning techniques that rely heavily on manual feature extraction, deep learning models learn features directly from raw data through their multiple layers (Husain M. S., 2023).

2.1. Components of Deep learning model

At the heart of deep learning are artificial neural networks (ANNs), inspired by the human brain's structure and functioning. The basic components of deep learning include:

- **Neural Networks:** Networks of interconnected nodes (neurons) organized into layers, including an input layer, multiple hidden layers, and an output layer.
- **Neurons:** The fundamental units of a neural network, akin to biological neurons, that process input and transmit signals to other neurons.
- **Layers:** Neural networks are organized into layers: an input layer that receives the data, one or more hidden layers that process the data, and an output layer that produces the final result.
- **Weights and Biases:** Parameters that the network adjusts during training to minimize error and improve predictions.
- **Activation Functions:** Activation functions applied to the output of each neuron to introduce non-linearity, enabling the network to learn complex patterns. Common activation functions include:
    - **Sigmoid:** Maps values to a range between 0 and 1. Useful for binary classification.

- ReLU (Rectified Linear Unit): Outputs the input directly if it is positive; otherwise, it outputs zero. It's efficient and helps with vanishing gradient issues.
   - **Tanh:** Maps values to a range between -1 and 1. It's a scaled version of the sigmoid function.
- **Learning:** A training algorithm that adjusts the weights of the connections based on the error of the network's predictions, improving its performance over time. The learning rate controls how much the weights are updated during training. A too-high learning rate can cause the model to converge too quickly to a suboptimal solution, while a too-low rate can result in a slow convergence.
- **Optimization Algorithms:** Techniques like gradient descent that minimize the loss function by adjusting network parameters.

2.2. Training Deep Learning Models

Training a deep learning model involves optimizing its parameters to minimize a loss function that quantifies the difference between the predicted and actual values. Key steps in training include:

- **Forward Propagation:** The process where input data passes through the network, layer by layer, each layer applying weights, biases, and activation functions to produce the output.
- **Loss Calculation:** The loss function measures the error of the model's predictions compared to the true values. The loss functions measure the difference between the predicted output and the actual target values. Common loss functions include Mean Squared Error (MSE), and Cross-Entropy Loss.
- **Backpropagation:** An algorithm that computes the gradient of the loss function with respect to each weight by applying the chain rule of calculus. This gradient informs how to adjust the weights to reduce the loss.
- **Optimization:** Methods such as gradient descent and its variants (e.g., Adam, RMSprop) are used to update the weights and biases to minimize the loss function.

3. DEEP LEARNING ARCHITECTURES

Deep learning has emerged as a transformative technology, enabling significant advancements across various fields such as computer vision, natural language processing, and robotics. At the core of deep learning are various neural network architectures, each designed to handle specific types of data and tasks. This section delves into the key types of deep learning architectures, exploring their structures, functionalities, and applications.

3.1. Feedforward Neural Networks (FNNs)

Feedforward Neural Networks (FNNs) are the simplest form of neural networks where information moves in one direction—from the input layer to the output layer—without cycles or loops. They consist of an input layer, one or more hidden layers, and an output layer. FNNs are Suitable for straightforward classification and regression tasks.

Figure 1. Feedforward neural network architecture

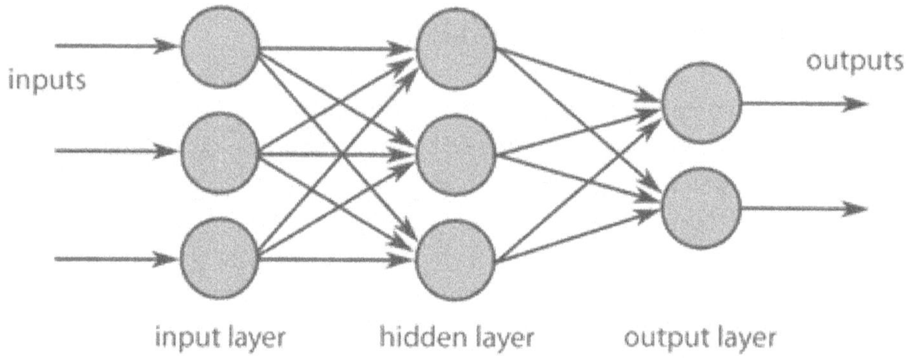

3.1.1. Components

- **Input Layer:** This layer receives the raw data. Each neuron in this layer represents a feature of the input data.
- **Hidden Layers:** These intermediate layers perform transformations on the input data. Each neuron in these layers applies a linear transformation followed by a non-linear activation function. These layers are usually used to extract complex relations within the data. Increase in the number of these layers helps in extracting more complex relations which in turn cause high computation power requirements.
- **Output Layer:** The final layer produces the model's prediction or classification result. The number of neurons in this layer is equal to the number of classes.

3.1.2. Training and Activation Functions

FNNs are trained using the backpropagation algorithm, which adjusts weights based on the error between the predicted and actual output. Common activation functions used in FNNs include:

- **Sigmoid:** Maps input values to a range between 0 and 1, useful for binary classification tasks.
- **Tanh (Hyperbolic Tangent):** Maps input values to a range between -1 and 1, often used for hidden layers to center data.
- **ReLU (Rectified Linear Unit):** Applies a non-linear transformation where values less than zero are set to zero, helping to mitigate the vanishing gradient problem.

3.1.3. Applications

FNNs are utilized for a range of tasks including simple classification problems, regression tasks, and basic pattern recognition. They are often the starting point for more complex architectures and serve as a foundational element in deep learning.

3.2. Convolutional Neural Networks (CNNs)

Convolutional Neural Networks (CNNs) are designed for processing grid-like data, such as images and spatial data. They leverage convolutional layers to automatically and adaptively learn spatial hierarchies of features from input data.

Figure 2. Typical CNN architecture

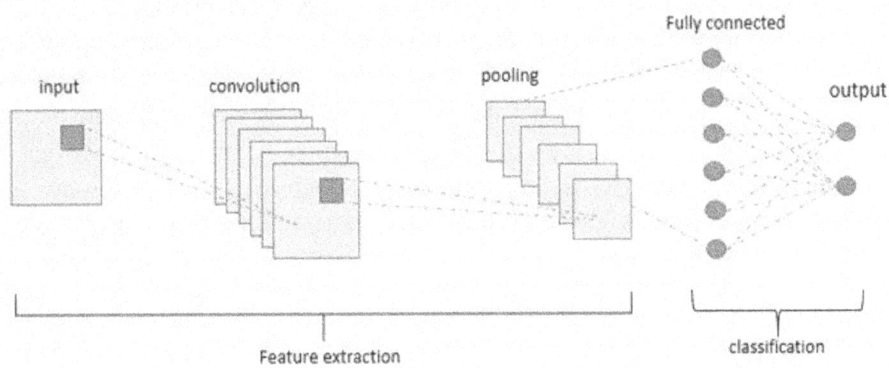

3.2.1. Components

- **Convolutional Layers:** Apply convolutional filters (kernels) to input data to produce feature maps. This process captures local patterns and spatial relationships within the data.
- **Activation Layers:** Typically use ReLU to introduce non-linearity and enhance the model's ability to learn complex patterns.
- **Pooling Layers:** Reduce the dimensionality of feature maps and retain the most important features. Common pooling operations include max pooling and average pooling.
- **Fully Connected Layers:** Flatten the pooled feature maps and connect them to fully connected layers to produce the final output.

3.2.2. Key CNN Architectures

Prominent CNN architectures are:

- **LeNet:** One of the earliest CNN architectures, developed for handwritten digit recognition. LeNet was the beginning of CNNs in deep learning. It consists of multiple convolutional and pooling layers, followed by a fully connected layer. The model has five convolution layers (for feature extraction) followed by two fully connected layers.
- **AlexNet:** Achieved significant improvements in image classification and won the ImageNet competition in 2012, introducing concepts like ReLU and dropout to CNNs. Also, it increases the number of feature extraction stages (convolutional layers) to seven. It was designed to be used with large-scale image datasets and it achieved state-of-the-art results at the time of its publication.
- **VGGNet:** VGGNet or "VGG16" stands for "Visual Geometry Group 16". The "16" in the name indicates that the model contains 16 layers that have weights; this includes convolutional layers as well as fully connected layers. Known for its simplicity and depth, VGGNet uses small 3x3 convolutional filters and achieved state-of-the-art performance on image classification tasks. However, it uses up to 95 million parameters and trained on over one billion images (1000 classes). It can take large input images of 224 x 224-pixel size for which it has 4096 convolutional features. CNNs with such large filters are expensive to train and require a lot of data, which is the main reason why it is not popular.
- **ResNet:** ResNet is the CNN architecture having 152 layers and over one million parameters. It introduces residual connections (skip connections) to address the vanishing gradient problem in very deep networks, enabling the

training of networks with hundreds of layers. CNNs are mostly used for image classification tasks with 1000 classes, but ResNet proves that CNNs can also be used successfully to solve natural language processing problems like sentence completion or machine comprehension.

3.2.3. Applications

CNNs are extensively used in image and video recognition, object detection, facial recognition, and medical image analysis. They excel at capturing spatial hierarchies and local patterns, making them ideal for visual data.

3.3. Recurrent Neural Networks (RNNs)

Recurrent Neural Networks (RNNs) are designed for sequential data, where the order of data points is crucial. They use feedback loops to maintain context and learn temporal dependencies. Features derived from earlier input are fed back into the network which gives them an ability to memorize. These interactive networks are dynamic due to the ever-changing state until they reach an equilibrium point. These networks are mainly used in sequential autocorrelative data like time series.

Figure 3. Standard RNN architecture

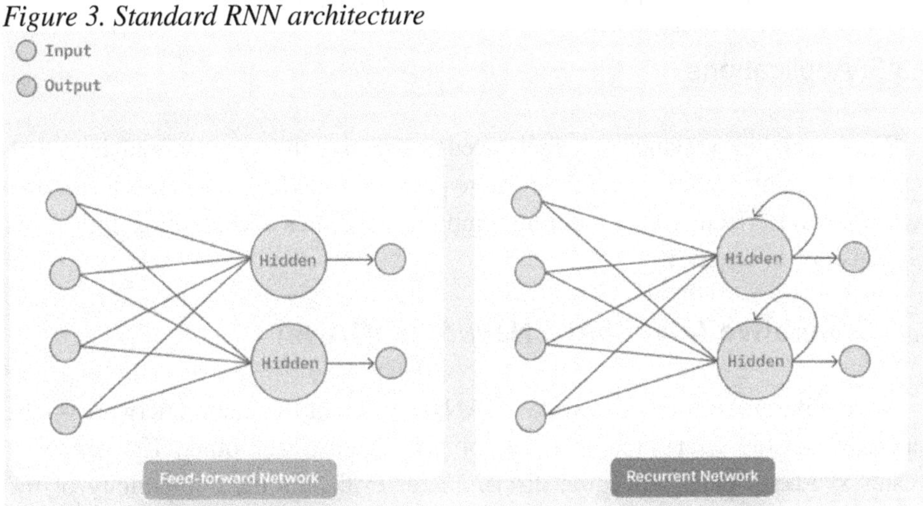

3.3.1. Components

- **Recurrent Layers:** Process sequences by passing information from previous time steps to subsequent ones. Each time step produces an output and updates a hidden state that carries information through the sequence.
- **Hidden State:** Represents the memory of the network, capturing information from previous time steps.

3.3.2. Variants of RNNs

- **Vanilla RNNs:** Basic RNN architecture with a single recurrent layer. Training of standard RNN models can be very difficult and time-consuming as compared to other Artificial Neural Networks. This model is also prone to issues like vanishing and exploding gradients.
- **Long Short-Term Memory (LSTM):** Addresses the vanishing gradient problem by using memory cells and gating mechanisms (input gate, forget gate, output gate) to manage long-term dependencies.
- **Gated Recurrent Unit (GRU):** A simplified version of LSTM with fewer parameters, combining the forget and input gates into a single update gate. It provides simplified structure and faster training than LSTM while retaining the capability of capturing long-term dependencies.

3.3.3. Applications

RNNs and their variants are widely used in tasks involving sequential data, such as time-series prediction, natural language processing (NLP), and speech recognition. They are effective for modeling temporal dynamics and learning contextual relationships in sequences.

3.4. Generative Adversarial Networks (GANs)

Generative Adversarial Networks (GANs) consist of two neural networks—the generator and the discriminator—that compete against each other. The generator creates synthetic data, while the discriminator evaluates the authenticity of the generated data.

Figure 4. GAN architecture

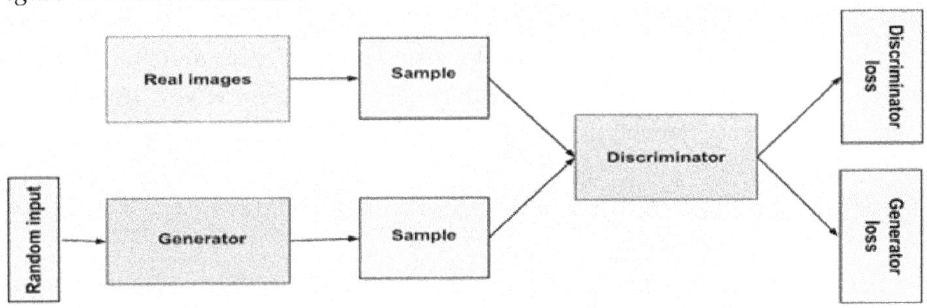

3.4.1. Components

- **Generator:** Takes random noise as input and produces synthetic data samples. Its goal is to generate data that is indistinguishable from real data.
- **Discriminator:** Takes both real and generated data as input and predicts whether the data is real or fake. It provides feedback to the generator to improve its outputs.

3.4.2. Training Process

The training process involves adversarial training where generator and discriminator are trained simultaneously, improving each other's performance over time:

- **Generator Training:** The generator aims to minimize the discriminator's ability to distinguish between real and fake data.
- **Discriminator Training:** The discriminator aims to maximize its accuracy in distinguishing real data from fake data.

3.4.3. Applications

GANs are used for various applications, including image generation, data augmentation, style transfer, and deepfake creation. They excel at producing high-quality, realistic data and are a powerful tool for creative and generative tasks.

3.5. Transformer Networks

Transformer Networks are designed for handling sequences and are known for their efficiency in processing long-range dependencies. Unlike RNNs, transformers do not use recurrent connections, relying instead on self-attention mechanisms.

3.5.1. Architectural components

- **Self-Attention Mechanism:** Computes attention scores to weigh the importance of different elements in the input sequence. This mechanism allows the model to focus on relevant parts of the sequence while processing each element.
- **Multi-Head Attention:** Utilizes multiple self-attention mechanisms in parallel to capture different types of relationships within the sequence.
- **Positional Encoding:** Adds positional information to input embeddings to retain the order of elements in the sequence.

3.5.2. Key Transformer Models

- **BERT (Bidirectional Encoder Representations from Transformers):** Pre-trained on large text corpora and fine-tuned for specific tasks, BERT excels in understanding context and semantics in natural language.
- **GPT (Generative Pre-trained Transformer):** Focuses on generative tasks, such as text completion and language modeling. GPT-4, the latest version, has advanced capabilities in generating coherent and contextually relevant text.
- **T5 (Text-To-Text Transfer Transformer):** Frames all NLP tasks as text-to-text problems, allowing a unified approach to various tasks like translation, summarization, and question-answering.

3.5.3. Applications

Transformers are widely used in natural language processing tasks, including machine translation, text generation, and sentiment analysis. Their ability to handle long-range dependencies and parallelized computations makes them highly effective for complex language tasks.

3.6. Autoencoders

Autoencoders are neural networks designed to learn efficient representations of data through unsupervised learning. They consist of an encoder and a decoder, trained to reconstruct input data from a compressed representation.

3.6.1. Components

- **Encoder:** Maps input data to a lower-dimensional latent space, capturing essential features while reducing dimensionality.
- **Decoder:** Reconstructs the original input data from the latent space representation, aiming to minimize the reconstruction error.

3.6.2. Variants of Autoencoders

- **Denoising Autoencoders:** Trained to reconstruct clean data from noisy inputs, improving robustness and feature extraction.
- **Variational Autoencoders (VAEs):** Introduce probabilistic modeling to the latent space, enabling generation of new data samples and smooth interpolation between data points.
- **Sparse Autoencoders:** Enforce sparsity constraints on the latent representation to capture more meaningful features.

3.6.3. Applications

Autoencoders are used for tasks such as dimensionality reduction, anomaly detection, data denoising, and generative modeling. They are valuable for learning compact representations of data and generating new samples.

Table 1 summarizes the most popular deep learning techniques used in cyber forensics investigation.

Table 1. Popular deep learning techniques used in cyber forensics

DL Algorithm	Pros	Cons	Applications
Autoencoders	• Based on Unsupervised Learning, no need of labeled data • Dimensionality Reduction	• Performance can be affected by the choice of architecture and hyperparameters. • The features learned by autoencoders are not always easy to interpret.	• Network Traffic Analysis • Anomaly Detection • Data Denoising • File Integrity Monitoring
Variational Autoencoders (VAEs)	• Probabilistic Approach helps in modeling uncertainty	• more complex than standard autoencoders. • produce less accurate reconstructions compared to standard autoencoders	• Anomaly Detection • Synthetic Data Generation
Convolutional Neural Networks (CNNs)	• Automatically extracts hierarchical features from data • High Accuracy	• Computationally Intensive • Risk of overfitting	• Image Forensic • Malware Analysis • Phishing detection
Recurrent Neural Networks (RNNs)	• Effective for Sequential Data Handling • Contextual Awareness	• Training Complexity • Vanishing Gradient Problem	• Network Traffic Analysis • Behavioral Analysis • Phishing detection
Long Short-Term Memory Networks (LSTMs)	• Improved Memory • Robust to Vanishing Gradient	• Complex Architecture • Resource Intensive	• Intrusion Detection Systems (IDS) • Anomaly Detection
Generative Adversarial Networks (GANs)	• Generate synthetic data for training or testing	• Training Instability • Complexity	• Image Forensics • Malware Analysis • Anomaly Detection
Graph Neural Networks (GNNs)	• Effective for analyzing complex relationships and dependencies • Can be applied to various types of graph data	• Scalability • Data Preparation may require additional preprocessing	• Network Forensics • Malware Behavior Analysis
Transformers	• Contextual Understanding • Scalability	• Requires significant computational power and memory • Can be difficult to interpret and tune due to their complexity	• Phishing Detection • Semantic Analysis

continued on following page

Table 1. Continued

DL Algorithm	Pros	Cons	Applications
Deep Reinforcement Learning (DRL)	• Adaptive Learning • Dynamic Decision-Making	• Requires extensive training and can be computationally intensive	• Automated Threat Response • Behavioral Analysis
Deep Belief Networks (DBNs)	• Hierarchical Feature Learning • Unsupervised Pretraining	• Training can be complex and time-consuming. • May not scale well to very large datasets	• Feature Extraction • Pattern Recognition

Deep learning algorithms offer powerful tools for cyber forensics, each with unique strengths and limitations. By leveraging these algorithms, forensic investigators can enhance their capabilities to detect, analyze, and respond to cyber threats. However, it is crucial to consider the specific needs of the investigation, available resources, and potential challenges when choosing and implementing these algorithms.

4. THE ROLE OF DEEP LEARNING IN CYBER FORENSICS

Deep learning has transformed cyber forensics by enabling the analysis of large datasets with unprecedented accuracy and efficiency. Traditional forensic methods often rely on manual analysis and rule-based systems, which can be time-consuming and prone to error. Deep learning automates and enhances various forensic processes, including data classification, anomaly detection, and pattern recognition (Husain, Khan, & Siddiqui, Big Data Concepts, Technologies, and Applications, 2023) (Husain, Faisal, Sadia, Ahmad, & Shukla, 2023) (Afaq, Husain, Bello, & Sadia, 2023).

4.1. Enhancing Data Recovery and Analysis

- **Data Extraction from Corrupted Files:** Deep learning models, especially those using convolutional neural networks (CNNs) and autoencoders, have shown significant potential in recovering data from corrupted files. Traditional methods for data recovery often struggle with incomplete or damaged files. Deep learning techniques can learn patterns and features from large datasets of corrupted and intact files, enabling models to predict and reconstruct missing or damaged parts. For instance, deep autoencoders can be trained to reconstruct corrupted images or documents, facilitating data recovery from damaged storage devices.
- **Automated Evidence Classification:** In digital forensics, classifying evidence—such as categorizing files, emails, or logs—can be a time-

consuming task. Deep learning models, particularly those using CNNs or recurrent neural networks (RNNs), can automate this process by learning from labeled training data to classify new evidence accurately. For example, deep learning-based classification systems can automatically identify and categorize types of digital evidence, such as distinguishing between different file formats or identifying malware versus benign files.

- **Advanced File Carving Techniques:** File carving is a technique used to recover files from a raw disk image when file system metadata is damaged or missing. Traditional file carving methods often rely on heuristics and are limited by predefined patterns. Deep learning approaches, however, can learn complex patterns from large datasets of file types and structures, enhancing the accuracy and efficiency of file carving. By training models on various file types, deep learning can help identify and reconstruct file fragments more effectively, even when traditional methods fail.

4.2. Improving Data Search and Retrieval

- **Semantic Search Capabilities:** Traditional search methods rely on exact matching or keyword-based searches, which can be limited in their ability to handle variations in data. Deep learning models, particularly those based on transformers and natural language processing (NLP) techniques, can significantly enhance search capabilities. These models understand and process the semantic meaning of data, allowing for more effective searches across large datasets. For example, BERT (Bidirectional Encoder Representations from Transformers) can be used to understand the context of documents and retrieve relevant information based on meaning rather than exact keyword matches.
- **Image and Video Analysis:** Deep learning has revolutionized image and video analysis, making it possible to automatically detect and analyze visual evidence. CNNs and their advanced variants, such as YOLO (You Only Look Once) and Faster R-CNN, are capable of object detection, facial recognition, and scene understanding. Deep learning models, such as FaceNet, have advanced facial recognition systems, aiding in suspect identification and verification. In digital forensics, these techniques can be applied to analyze surveillance footage, detect suspicious activities, and identify individuals or objects of interest. This capability not only speeds up the review process but also enhances the accuracy of identifying relevant evidence.
- **Textual Data Analysis and Anomaly Detection:** In forensic investigations involving textual data, deep learning models can analyze and detect anomalies within large volumes of text. Recurrent neural networks (RNNs)

and transformers can be used to detect unusual patterns or inconsistencies in documents, emails, or chat logs. RNNs and Transformer models, such as BERT (Bidirectional Encoder Representations from Transformers), excel at extracting information from unstructured text, including detecting cyberbullying, phishing attempts, or fraudulent documents. For instance, deep learning models can identify abnormal language patterns indicative of fraud or malicious activity, aiding in the investigation of financial crimes or insider threats. Deep learning models analyze sentiment and intent in text, which can be useful for understanding communications between suspects.

4.3. Enhancing Cybercrime Investigations

- **Malware Detection and Classification:** Malware detection and classification are critical aspects of digital forensics, and deep learning has significantly advanced these processes. Traditional signature-based methods are often insufficient against new and evolving threats. Deep learning models, particularly those using CNNs and deep autoencoders, can analyze and classify malware based on its behavior and code patterns. By training models on vast datasets of known malware and benign software, these systems can identify previously unknown threats and adapt to new variations of malware.
- **Network Traffic Analysis:** Deep learning can enhance the analysis of network traffic to detect and respond to cyber threats. Models such as deep neural networks (DNNs) and autoencoders can be used to identify anomalous network behavior that may indicate a security breach or attack. For example, deep learning techniques can be employed to analyze traffic patterns, detect unusual spikes in activity, and identify potential threats such as Distributed Denial of Service (DDoS) attacks or data exfiltration.
- **Fraud Detection:** Fraud detection is another area where deep learning is making a significant impact. By analyzing transaction data, user behavior, and communication patterns, deep learning models can identify suspicious activities and potential fraud. Techniques such as anomaly detection, using models like autoencoders or RNNs, can reveal deviations from normal behavior that may indicate fraudulent activities. This capability is valuable for financial institutions and organizations in preventing and investigating fraud.

  Recent work in forensics investigation using Deep Learning:

Deep learning algorithms have become increasingly significant in cyber forensics, providing advanced tools for analyzing and interpreting large volumes of data in a variety of contexts. Each deep learning algorithm brings unique strengths to cyber forensics, depending on the specific requirements of the investigation. By leveraging these algorithms, forensic investigators can enhance their ability to detect, analyze, and respond to cyber threats, though challenges such as computational demands, interpretability, and training complexity need to be addressed. Selecting the appropriate algorithm involves considering the specific nature of the data and the goals of the investigation. Table 2 summarizes the prominent work done in digital forensics using deep learning algorithms.

Table 2. Summary of prominent work in digital forensics investigation using DL

Forensic Purpose	Reference	Work objective	DL approach
Image Forensics	(Sabir, Jones, Liu, & Mbaziira, 2019)	Detect stealthy watermarks in various types of files	Multilayer Perceptron (MLP) algorithms
	(Rosli, et al., 2021)	Deep Fake Image detection	Convolutional Neural Network (CNN) variants with transfer learning
	(Wu, Wu, Lei, Li, & Tong, 2021)	Fingerprint Identification	CNN and Autoencoder
	(Miao, Tan, Chu, Yu, & Guo, 2022)	Propose a novel Hierarchical Frequency-assisted Interactive Networks (HFI-Net) to explore comprehensive frequency-related forgery cues for face manipulation detection.	CNN and transformer model for capturing local details with novel Frequency-based Feature Refinement (FFR) module
IoT Forensics	(Salih & Ibrahim, 2023)	Big Data analysis to identify potential sources of evidence, and construct predictive models to prevent future attacks	LSTM and RNN
Multimedia Forensics	(Neaimi, Hamadi, Yeun, & Zemerly, 2020)	Identifying corrupted files	CNN
Cyber forensics	(Bokolo, Chen, & Liu, 2023)	Cybercriminal profiling	DistilBert, LSTM, and BERT models
Network Forensic	(Mei, et al., 2024)	Identifying and tracking network attacks	Multi-Layer Perceptual Deep Neural Network (MLP DNN) model
	(Nowroozi, Mohammadi, Savaş, Mekdad, & Conti, 2023)	Improving the Security of Computer Networks Against Adversarial Attacks	Ensemble classifier combining the enhanced security of 1-Class classification with the high performance of conventional 2-Class classification
	(Zhao, et al., 2021)	Network Intrusion Detection (NID)	Lightweight Dynamic Autoencoder network (LDAN)
Multimodal Biometrics Forensics	(Talreja, Valenti, & Nasrabadi, 2020)	Integrating multimodal fusion (face & Iris), deep hashing, and biometric security	Deep Hashing

Deep learning offers powerful tools for cyber forensics, enhancing the ability to detect, analyze, and respond to cyber threats. However, careful consideration of the ethical and practical aspects of these technologies is essential to ensure effective and responsible use.

5. IMPLEMENTATION OF DEEP LEARNING IN DIGITAL FORENSICS

Implementing deep learning in cyber forensics involves applying sophisticated machine learning techniques to analyze and interpret data for investigative purposes. The goal is often to detect, prevent, or investigate cybercrimes and security incidents. Implementation of Deep Learning in Digital Forensics involves the following steps as shown in Figure 5.

- **Identify the Forensic Task and set objectives:** Determine the specific problem you want to address, such as malware detection, anomaly detection, network traffic analysis, or digital evidence classification. Define clear objectives, such as increasing accuracy in detecting malicious activity or reducing false positives in security alerts.

Figure 5. Key steps for deep learning implementation in cyber forensics

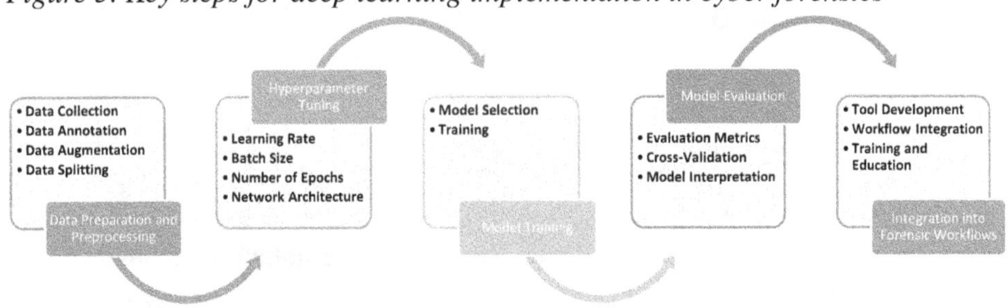

5.1. Data Preparation and Preprocessing

Effective implementation of deep learning requires high-quality data which needs meticulous data preparation:

- **Data Collection:** Gather diverse and representative datasets relevant to forensic tasks, such as images, text, or network logs.
- **Data Annotation:** Annotate data with relevant labels or metadata, often using manual or semi-automated tools.
- **Data Augmentation:** Enhance datasets with techniques like rotation, scaling, or noise addition to improve model robustness and generalization.
- **Data Splitting:** Divide the dataset into training, validation, and test sets to evaluate the model's generalization ability.

5.2. Architecture Design

Define the model's architecture, including the number of layers, types of layers (e.g., convolutional, recurrent), activation functions, and any regularization techniques. Deep Learning models have several hyperparameters that need tuning:

- **Learning Rate:** Controls the size of weight updates during training.
- **Batch Size:** The number of training samples processed before updating the model parameters.
- **Number of Epochs:** The number of times the entire dataset is passed through the network during training.
- **Network Architecture:** Includes the number of layers, types of layers, and the number of neurons in each layer.

5.3. Model Training

Training deep learning models involves:

- **Model Selection:** Choose appropriate architectures based on the forensic task, such as CNNs for image analysis or RNNs for text analysis.
- **Training:** Use labeled datasets to train models, employing techniques like transfer learning to leverage pre-trained models and improve performance.
    - o **Choosing a Loss Function:** Depending on the task, select a suitable loss function (e.g., cross-entropy for classification).
    - o **Optimization:** Apply optimization algorithms (e.g., Adam, SGD) to minimize the loss function.
    - o **Hyperparameter Tuning:** Adjust hyperparameters (e.g., learning rate, batch size) to improve model performance. Hyperparameter tuning can be performed using techniques like grid search, random search, or Bayesian optimization.

- **Validation:** Monitor model performance on the validation set to prevent overfitting and adjust training parameters as needed.

5.4. Model Evaluation

Evaluating the performance of deep learning models involves:

- **Evaluation Metrics:** Metrics such as accuracy, precision, recall, F1 score, and mean squared error are used to assess the model's performance.
- **Cross-Validation:** A technique that divides the dataset into multiple folds to ensure that the model's performance is consistent across different subsets of data.
- **Model Interpretation:** Techniques like SHAP (SHapley Additive exPlanations) and LIME (Local Interpretable Model-agnostic Explanations) help interpret the model's decisions and improve transparency.

5.5. Integration into Forensic Workflows

Integrating deep learning into forensic workflows includes:

- **Tool Development:** Create or customize forensic tools that incorporate deep learning models, ensuring compatibility with existing forensic software and hardware.
- **Workflow Integration:** Incorporate deep learning solutions into standard forensic procedures, such as evidence collection, analysis, and reporting.
- **Monitoring:** Continuously monitor the model's performance and make adjustments as necessary. This may include retraining the model with new data or updating its parameters.
- **Training and Education:** Provide training for forensic professionals on using deep learning tools and interpreting their results.

5.6. Maintain and Update

- **Model Maintenance:** Regularly update the model with new data to ensure it remains effective against evolving threats.
- **Continuous Learning:** Implement mechanisms for continuous learning and adaptation to new types of cyber threats.
- **Documentation:** Maintain thorough documentation of the model's design, training process, and performance metrics for transparency and reproducibility.

By following proper steps, deep learning techniques can effectively be implemented in cyber forensics to enhance the ability of the system to detect and analyze cyber threats and incidents.

6. CHALLENGES AND CONSIDERATIONS

6.1. Data Privacy and Security

Deep learning models require large amounts of high-quality data to train effectively. In cyber forensics, obtaining such datasets can be challenging due to data privacy issues, the sensitive nature of forensic data, and the often-proprietary nature of data sources. Ensuring that data is collected and used ethically is crucial for the responsible development of AI technologies.

- **Sensitive Information:** Forensic data often contains sensitive personal information, necessitating robust data protection measures.
- **Ethical Considerations:** Ensure that deep learning applications comply with ethical guidelines and legal standards when collecting and using data to avoid misuse.
- **Data Augmentation:** Techniques like synthetic data generation or augmentation can help in scenarios where real data is scarce.

6.2. Interpretability and Explainability

Deep learning models, especially those with complex architectures like deep neural networks, are often considered "black boxes" because their decision-making processes are not easily interpretable. In forensic investigations, understanding how a model arrives at its conclusions is crucial for validating findings and presenting evidence in court. Developing methods for explaining and interpreting deep learning models, such as using saliency maps or feature attribution techniques, is important for addressing this challenge.

- **Model Validation:** Due to Black-Box Nature, the internal workings of deep learning models are often opaque, making it difficult to understand how decisions are made. Regularly validate and test models with known outcomes to ensure reliability.
- **Explainability Tools:** Explainable AI (XAI) utilize techniques that enhance model interpretability, such as attention mechanisms or surrogate models, to provide insights into how decisions are made. Use of techniques like LIME

(Local Interpretable Model-agnostic Explanations) can enhance model interpretability and transparency.

6.3. Resource Requirements

Training deep learning models, particularly those with many layers and parameters, demands significant computational power and resources, which can be expensive and environmentally impactful. Advances in hardware and algorithms are needed to make deep learning more accessible and sustainable.

- **Resource Management:** Training deep learning models demands powerful GPUs or TPUs, which can be costly. Employ cloud-based solutions or distributed computing to handle large-scale computations.
- **Computational Time:** Training and fine-tuning models can be time-consuming, requiring careful management of computational resources. Use of techniques such as model pruning or quantization can reduce the computational demands of deep learning models.

6.4. Model Robustness and Generalization

Deep learning models are prone to overfitting, especially when trained on limited or non-representative datasets. Ensuring that deep learning models generalize well to new and unseen data is a key challenge. Techniques such as regularization, dropout, and data augmentation are employed to improve model robustness and reduce overfitting. Ensuring that models are robust and generalize well to new data is crucial.

- **Overfitting:** Avoid overfitting by using techniques such as regularization and dropout.
- **Generalization:** Use cross-validation techniques to validate models on diverse datasets to ensure they perform well across various scenarios.

6.5. Adversarial Attacks

Deep learning models can be vulnerable to adversarial attacks, where small, intentional perturbations to input data can cause the model to make incorrect predictions. In cyber forensics, this could undermine the reliability of forensic tools and analyses.

- **Robustness Testing:** Regularly test models against adversarial attacks and incorporate defenses such as adversarial training.

- **Continuous Monitoring:** Monitor models for potential vulnerabilities and update them as needed to address emerging threats.

6.6. Ethical and Legal Implications

The use of deep learning in cyber forensics raises ethical and legal concerns, such as privacy issues, consent for data use, and the potential for misuse of technology.

- **Compliance:** Ensure that all data handling and model deployment practices comply with relevant laws and regulations.
- **Ethical Guidelines:** Develop and adhere to ethical guidelines for the use of deep learning in forensic investigations to safeguard privacy and fairness.

6.7. Integration with Existing Forensic Tools

Integrating deep learning techniques with existing forensic tools and workflows can be complex. Forensic investigations often rely on established processes and tools, and incorporating deep learning may require significant changes to these workflows.

- **Interoperability:** Ensure that deep learning models and tools are compatible with existing forensic software and processes.
- **Training and Adaptation:** Provide training for forensic professionals to effectively use new deep learning tools and adapt workflows to incorporate these advanced techniques.

7. EXAMPLE CASE STUDIES

Deep learning, a subset of machine learning that involves neural networks with many layers, has significantly advanced digital forensics by enhancing capabilities in evidence analysis, anomaly detection, and data classification. Here are five detailed case study examples illustrating the application of deep learning in digital forensics:

- **Automated Malware Detection and Classification**

Malwarebytes Anti-Malware leverages deep learning to enhance its malware detection capabilities. The tool aims to address the challenge of identifying new and sophisticated malware variants that traditional signature-based antivirus systems might miss. Convolutional Neural Networks (CNNs) are implemented to analyze file structures and identify patterns indicative of malware. Recurrent Neural Networks (RNNs) are used for analyzing dynamic behaviors and sequences in executable files.

The use of deep learning improved the ability to detect both known and unknown malware, significantly enhancing the tool's effectiveness in protecting systems. Deep learning models achieved higher accuracy in distinguishing between benign and malicious files, reducing the occurrence of false positives.

Malwarebytes Anti-Malware's deep learning approach has led to more effective and timely identification of malware threats, improving endpoint security and reducing the risk of infections.

- **Forensic Analysis of Encrypted Data**

X1 Social Discovery utilizes deep learning techniques to analyze and extract data from encrypted and obfuscated social media content. The tool addresses the challenge of accessing and interpreting encrypted or protected forensic evidence. Autoencoders have been employed for feature extraction and dimensionality reduction to process and analyze encrypted data. Generative Adversarial Networks (GANs) were used to generate synthetic data for training and improving model performance. Deep learning models facilitated faster and more accurate decryption and extraction of relevant data from encrypted social media sources. Use of Deep Learning has enhanced the ability to interpret complex and obfuscated data, providing valuable insights for investigations.

X1 Social Discovery's integration of deep learning has advanced the capability to handle encrypted forensic evidence, aiding in the recovery and analysis of critical data.

- **Social Media Content Analysis**

Face++ is a facial recognition technology that uses deep learning to analyze and identify individuals in social media photos. This technology is applied in digital forensics to match suspects with images and track their online activities. Utilizing Deep Convolutional Neural Networks (DCNNs) for facial recognition and feature extraction from images and Deep learning models to create embeddings that represent facial features for accurate matching the system has achieved high accuracy in identifying and matching faces across different images and contexts. The system can be effective in improving the capability to trace individuals and gather evidence from social media platforms.

Face++'s deep learning-based facial recognition has enhanced forensic investigations by providing reliable tools for identifying and tracking suspects through online images.

- **Voice Authentication and Analysis**

Microsoft Azure Cognitive Services offers voice recognition and authentication services that leverage deep learning to analyze and verify voice samples. This technology is used in digital forensics to authenticate speakers and analyze audio evidence. Deep Neural Networks (DNNs) are applied for voice recognition and speaker identification. The system uses Recurrent Neural Networks (RNNs) for analyzing temporal patterns and sequences in speech. The model has achieved precise speaker identification and verification, even in noisy or variable conditions which can be very supportive in forensics investigations.

Microsoft Azure's deep learning-powered voice recognition services have advanced forensic audio analysis, providing robust tools for verifying and analyzing voice evidence.

- **Anomaly Detection in Network Traffic**

Darktrace's Enterprise Immune System employs deep learning to monitor and analyze network traffic for anomalies and potential threats. The system aims to detect unusual patterns that may indicate cyber-attacks or insider threats. Utilizes Autoencoders for anomaly detection by learning normal network behavior and identifying deviations. LSTM Networks (Long Short-Term Memory) are applied to analyze sequential network traffic data and detect anomalies over time. This deep learning model provides real-time alerts for unusual network activities, allowing for prompt investigation and response.

Darktrace's deep learning-based anomaly detection has enhanced network security by identifying and mitigating threats more effectively, reducing the risk of breaches and improving overall network resilience.

8. FUTURE DIRECTIONS

8.1. Advances in Deep Learning Techniques

The field of deep learning is continuously evolving, with new techniques and architectures continually emerging. Innovations such as attention mechanisms, self-supervised learning, and generative models hold promise for further enhancing digital forensics. For example, advancements in self-supervised learning could reduce the need for labeled data, making it easier to train models on large and diverse datasets. Similarly, generative models like GANs could be used for data augmentation, improving the robustness of forensic analyses.

Transformers based models like GPT-4 and other transformer-based architectures show promise in handling complex forensic tasks involving large-scale data and multiple modalities.

Few-Shot Learning techniques that enable models to learn from a few examples could improve performance in scenarios with limited training data.

8.2. Cross-Domain Applications

Deep learning has the potential to benefit from cross-domain applications:

- **Transfer Learning:** Leverage advancements from other fields, such as healthcare or finance, to enhance forensic techniques.
- **Multimodal Learning:** Integrate data from multiple sources (e.g., text, images, and network logs) for comprehensive forensic analysis.

8.3. Integration with Other Technologies

The integration of deep learning with other technologies, such as blockchain, edge computing, and the Internet of Things (IoT), has the potential to further transform digital forensics. Blockchain technology can provide tamper-proof records of digital evidence, while edge computing can enable real-time analysis of data collected from IoT devices. Combining these technologies with deep learning can enhance the efficiency and accuracy of forensic investigations.

8.4. Collaboration and Standardization

Collaboration between researchers, practitioners, and industry stakeholders is essential:

- **Standards and Protocols:** Develop and adhere to standards for deep learning applications in digital forensics to ensure consistency and reliability.
- **Knowledge Sharing:** Promote knowledge sharing and collaboration through conferences, workshops, and publications to advance the field.

9. SUMMARY

Deep learning is playing a transformative role in digital forensics, enhancing data recovery, analysis, search, and cybercrime investigations. By leveraging advanced neural network architectures, deep learning techniques offer improved accuracy, efficiency, and capabilities in handling complex and large-scale data. Despite challenges related to privacy, interpretability, and model generalization, the continued advancement of deep learning techniques and their integration with other technologies hold great promise for the future of digital forensics. As the field evolves, deep learning will likely become an even more integral part of forensic investigations, driving innovation and improving the effectiveness of digital evidence analysis.

REFERENCES

Afaq, S. A., Husain, M. S., Bello, A., & Sadia, H. (2023). A critical analysis of cyber threats and their global impact. In *Computational Intelligent Security in Wireless Communications* (pp. 201–220). CRC Press.

Ahmed, B., Gulliver, T. A., & alZahir, S. (2020). (1-12). Blind copy-move forgery detection using svd and ks test. *SN Applied Sciences.*

Ali, M., Shiaeles, S., Clarke, N., & Kontogeorgis, D. (2019). A proactive malicious software identification approach for digital forensic examiners. *Journal of Information Security and Applications*, 47, 139–155. DOI: 10.1016/j.jisa.2019.04.013

Balushi, Y. A., Shaker, H., & Kumar, B. (2023). The Use of Machine Learning in Digital Forensics: Review Paper. *International Conference on Innovation in Information Technology and Business* (pp. 96-113). Springer Nature. DOI: 10.2991/978-94-6463-110-4_9

Barni, M., Nowroozi, E., & Tondi, B. (2018). Detection of adaptive histogram equalization robust against jpeg compression. *International Workshop on Biometrics and Forensics (IWBF)* (pp. 1-8). IEEE. DOI: 10.1109/IWBF.2018.8401564

Barra, P., Bisogni, C., Nappi, M., Freire-Obreg'on, D., & Castrill'on-Santana, M. (2019). Gait analysis for gender classification in forensics. *International Conference on Dependability in Sensor, Cloud, and Big Data Systems and Applications* (pp. 180-190). Springer. DOI: 10.1007/978-981-15-1304-6_15

Bokolo, B. G., Chen, L., & Liu, Q. (2023). Deep Learning Assisted Cyber Criminal Profiling. *6th International Conference on Big Data and Artificial Intelligence (BDAI)*, (pp. 226-231).

Durall, R., Keuper, M., Pfreundt, F.-J., & Keuper, J. (2019). Unmasking deepfakes with simple features. *arXiv preprint arXiv:1911.*

Ferreira, S., Antunes, M., & Correia, M. E. (2021). Exposing manipulated photos and videos in digital forensics analysis. *Journal of Imaging*, 7(7), 102. DOI: 10.3390/jimaging7070102 PMID: 39080890

Hina, M., Ali, M., Javed, A. R., Srivastava, G., Gadekallu, T. R., & Jalil, Z. (2021). *Email classification and forensics analysis using machine learning. IEEE Smart-World, Ubiquitous Intelligence & Computing, Advanced & Trusted Computing, Scalable Computing & Communications, Internet of People and Smart City Innovation (Smart-World/SCALCOM/UIC/ATC/IOP/SCI).* IEEE.

Husain, M. S. (2023). Deep Learning. In *Big Data Concepts, Technologies, and Applications* (pp. 108-123). Taylor & Francis group, CRC Press. DOI: 10.1201/9781003441595-9

Husain, M. S., Faisal, M., Sadia, H., Ahmad, T., & Shukla, S. (2023). *Advances in Cyberology and the Advent of the Next-gen Information Revolution*. IGI Global. DOI: 10.4018/978-1-6684-8133-2

Husain, M. S., Khan, M. Z., & Siddiqui, T. (2023). *Big Data Concepts, Technologies, and Applications*. CRC Press. DOI: 10.1201/9781003441595

Islam, M. M., Karmakar, G., Kamruzzaman, J., Murshed, M., Kahandawa, G., & Parvin, N. (2018). *Detecting splicing and copymove attacks in color images. Digital Image Computing: Techniques and Applications (DICTA)*. IEEE.

Kachavimath, A. V., Nazare, S. V., & Akki, S. S. (2020). Distributed denial of service attack detection using na¨ıve bayes and k-nearest neighbor for network forensics. *2020 2nd International conference on innovative mechanisms for industry applications (ICIMIA)* (pp. 711-717). IEEE.

Li, H., Xi, B., Wu, S., Jiang, J., & Rao, Y. (2018). The application of association analysis in mobile phone forensics system. *International Conference on Intelligence Science* (pp. 126-133). Springer. DOI: 10.1007/978-3-030-01313-4_13

Mei, Y., Han, W., Li, S., Lin, K., Tian, Z., & Li, S. (2024). A Novel Network Forensic Framework for Advanced Persistent Threat Attack Attribution Through Deep Learning. *IEEE Transactions on Intelligent Transportation Systems*, 25(9), 12131–12140. DOI: 10.1109/TITS.2024.3360260

Miao, C., Tan, Z., Chu, Q., Yu, N., & Guo, G. (2022). Hierarchical Frequency-Assisted Interactive Networks for Face Manipulation Detection. *IEEE Transactions on Information Forensics and Security*, 17, 3008–3021. DOI: 10.1109/TIFS.2022.3198275

Neaimi, M. A., Hamadi, H. A., Yeun, C. Y., & Zemerly, M. J. (2020). Digital Forensic Analysis of Files Using Deep Learning. *3rd International Conference on Signal Processing and Information Security (ICSPIS)*, (pp. 1-4). DOI: 10.1109/ICSPIS51252.2020.9340141

Nowroozi, E., Mohammadi, M., Savaş, E., Mekdad, Y., & Conti, M. (2023). Employing Deep Ensemble Learning for Improving the Security of Computer Networks Against Adversarial Attacks. *IEEE Transactions on Network and Service Management*, 20(2), 2096–2105. DOI: 10.1109/TNSM.2023.3267831

Rosli, N. A., Abdullah, S. N., Zamani, A. N., Ghazvini, A., Othman, N. S., & Tajuddin, N. A. (2021). Comparison Multi Transfer Learning Models for Deep Fake Image Recognizer. *3rd International Cyber Resilience Conference (CRC)*, (pp. 1-6). DOI: 10.1109/CRC50527.2021.9392566

Roy, A., Dixit, R., Naskar, R., & Chakraborty, R. S. (2020). *Digital Image Forensics: Theory and Implementation*. Springer Link. DOI: 10.1007/978-981-10-7644-2

Ruriawan, M. F., Anggono, B., Siahaan, I. A., & Purwanto, Y. (2019). Development of digital evidence collector and file classification system with k-means algorithm. *Asia Pacific Conference on Wireless and Mobile (APWiMob)* (pp. 64-68). IEEE. DOI: 10.1109/APWiMob48441.2019.8964232

Sabir, M. F., Jones, J. H., Liu, H., & Mbaziira, A. V. (2019). Predicting Stealthy Watermarks in Files Using Deep Learning. *7th International Symposium on Digital Forensics and Security (ISDFS)* (pp. 1-6). IEEE. DOI: 10.1109/ISDFS.2019.8757538

Salih, K. M., & Ibrahim, N. B. (2023). Enhancing IoT Forensics through Deep Learning: Investigating Cyber-Attacks and Analyzing Big Data for Improved Security Measures. *4th International Conference on Big Data Analytics and Practices (IBDAP)* (pp. 1-8). IEEE. DOI: 10.1109/IBDAP58581.2023.10271950

Sudha, T. S., & Rupa, C. (2019). *Analysis and evaluation of integrated cyber crime offences. Innovations in Power and Advanced Computing Technologies (i-PACT)*. IEEE.

Talreja, V., Valenti, M. C., & Nasrabadi, N. M. (2020). Deep Hashing for Secure Multimodal Biometrics. *IEEE Transactions on Information Forensics and Security*, 16, 1306–1321. DOI: 10.1109/TIFS.2020.3033189

Tuncer, T., Ertam, F., & Dogan, S. (2021). Automated malware identification. *Multimedia Tools and Applications*, 80(7), 10881–10900. DOI: 10.1007/s11042-020-10317-6

Usman, N., Usman, S., Khan, F., Jan, M. A., Sajid, A., Alazab, M., & Watters, P. (2021). Intelligent dynamic malware detection using machine learning in ip reputation for forensics data analytics. *Future Generation Computer Systems*, 118, 124–141. DOI: 10.1016/j.future.2021.01.004

Wu, C., Wu, H., Lei, S., Li, X., & Tong, H. (2021). Deep Learning in Automatic Fingerprint Identification. *IEEE 6th International Conference on Smart Cloud (SmartCloud)*, (pp. 111-116).

Yudhana, A., Riadi, I., & Ridho, F. (2018). Ddos classification using neural network and na¨ıve bayes methods for network forensics. *International Journal of Advanced Computer Science and Applications*, 9(11). Advance online publication. DOI: 10.14569/IJACSA.2018.091125

Zhao, R., Yin, J., Xue, Z., Gui, G., Adebisi, B., Ohtsuki, T., Gacanin, H., & Sari, H. (2021). An Efficient Intrusion Detection Method Based on Dynamic Autoencoder. *IEEE Wireless Communications Letters*, 10(8), 1707–1711. DOI: 10.1109/LWC.2021.3077946

KEY TERMS AND DEFINITIONS

Accuracy: Accuracy is a metric used to evaluate the performance of a classification model. It measures the proportion of correctly classified instances out of the total number of instances. Essentially, it indicates how often the model makes correct predictions.

Distributed Denial of Service (DDoS): A Distributed Denial of Service (DDoS) attack is a type of cyberattack aimed at making a service, website, or network unavailable by overwhelming it with a flood of malicious traffic from multiple sources. The attack usually involves a coordinated effort from a network of compromised computers or devices, known as a botnet, which are controlled by the attacker.

F1 Score: The F1 score is the harmonic mean of precision and recall. It provides a single metric that balances both precision and recall, especially useful when the class distribution is imbalanced.

Interoperability: Interoperability refers to the ability of different systems, organizations, or technologies to work together and exchange information seamlessly. In a broader sense, it ensures that diverse systems or components can operate together effectively, even if they were designed by different manufacturers or for different purposes. Different aspects of interoperability are Technical Interoperability, Semantic Interoperability, Organizational Interoperability, and Syntactic Interoperability.

LIME: LIME, which stands for Local Interpretable Model-agnostic Explanations, is a technique used to interpret the predictions of machine learning models. It focuses on providing insights into why a model made a specific prediction for a given instance by approximating the model's behavior locally around that instance.

LSTM: LSTM stands for Long Short-Term Memory, which is a type of artificial recurrent neural network (RNN) architecture used in machine learning and deep learning. LSTMs are designed to model sequential data and can capture long-term dependencies in the data, which standard RNNs struggle with due to issues like vanishing gradients.

Mean Squared Error (MSE): Mean Squared Error measures the average squared difference between predicted values and actual values. It's used for regression tasks to quantify the prediction error.

Natural Language Processing (NLP): Natural Language Processing is a subfield of artificial intelligence (AI) focused on the interaction between computers and human language. The primary goal of NLP is to enable computers to understand, interpret, and generate human language in a way that is both meaningful and useful. This involves a range of tasks and techniques that aim to bridge the gap between human communication and computer understanding.

Precision: Precision measures the proportion of positive predictions that are actually correct. It reflects how many of the predicted positives are true positives.

Recall: Recall measures the proportion of actual positives that are correctly identified by the model. It reflects how many of the actual positives are captured by the model.

SHAP: SHapley Additive exPlanations (SHAP) is a framework used in machine learning to interpret the predictions of complex models. It provides a unified approach to explaining model outputs by attributing the contribution of each feature to a given prediction. SHAP combines concepts from game theory, specifically Shapley values, with machine learning interpretability.

Chapter 4
Blockchain Forensics

ABSTRACT

Blockchain technology, first introduced by Bitcoin in 2008, has since expanded far beyond its original scope. Its immutable ledger and decentralized nature have made it an attractive foundation for a wide range of applications, from cryptocurrencies to smart contracts and decentralized finance (DeFi). However, these same characteristics also introduce new challenges in the realm of digital forensics. Blockchain forensics involves the analysis and investigation of transactions and activities within blockchain networks to uncover fraudulent behavior, track illicit activities, and ensure compliance with regulations (Shukla, et al., 2024).

1. INTRODUCTION

Blockchain technology, first introduced by Bitcoin in 2008, has since expanded far beyond its original scope. Its immutable ledger and decentralized nature have made it an attractive foundation for a wide range of applications, from cryptocurrencies to smart contracts and decentralized finance (DeFi). However, these same characteristics also introduce new challenges in the realm of digital forensics. Blockchain forensics involves the analysis and investigation of transactions and activities within blockchain networks to uncover fraudulent behavior, track illicit activities, and ensure compliance with regulations (Shukla, et al., 2024).

This chapter provides an in-depth exploration of blockchain forensics, covering its foundational concepts, methodologies, tools, and applications. It aims to offer a comprehensive understanding of how blockchain forensics works, the challenges faced, and the strategies employed to address these challenges.

DOI: 10.4018/979-8-3693-2960-3.ch004

2. FUNDAMENTALS OF BLOCKCHAIN TECHNOLOGY

A blockchain is a decentralized, distributed ledger technology (DLT) that maintains a continuous chain of blocks, each containing a set of transactions. It is decentralized, meaning no single entity has control over the entire network. Key components include (Husain, Khan, & Siddiqui, 2023):

Figure 1. Structure of a block

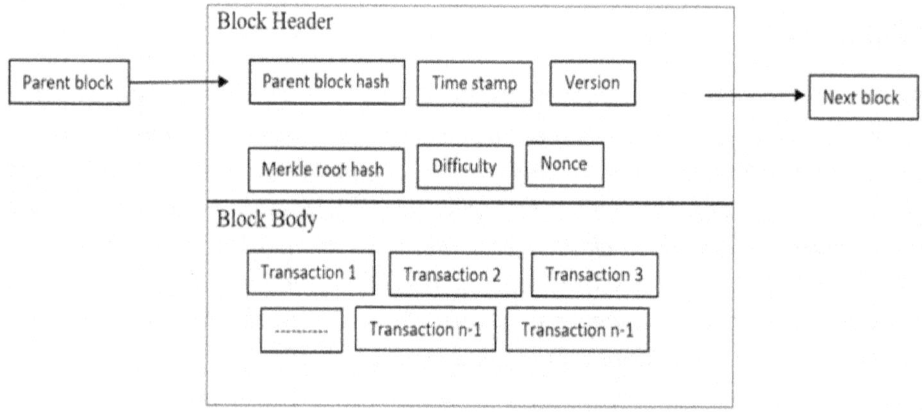

(Husain, Khan, & Siddiqui, 2023)

Figure 2. Structure of blockchain

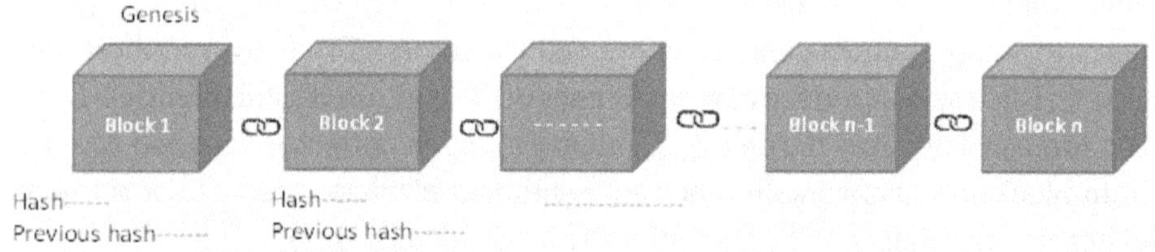

(Husain, Khan, & Siddiqui, 2023)

- **Blocks:** Individual units in the blockchain that store data about transactions, timestamps, and previous block references. This linkage creates a chain of blocks that extends back to the first block, known as the genesis block.

Components of a block:

- **Block Header**: Contains metadata about the block, including:
  - **Previous Block Hash**: The hash of the preceding block in the blockchain. This links blocks together and ensures immutability.
  - **Timestamp**: The time at which the block was created or added to the blockchain.
  - **Nonce**: A value used in Proof of Work (PoW) to find a valid hash for the block.
  - **Merkle Root**: A hash representing the root of the Merkle Tree (discussed below), summarizing all transactions in the block.
  - **Difficulty Target**: For PoW systems, it specifies the difficulty of the computational problem miners need to solve.
- **Block Body**: Contains the actual data, typically a list of transactions. Each transaction includes:
  - **Transaction ID**: A unique identifier for the transaction.
  - **Sender and Receiver**: Addresses of the parties involved.
  - **Amount**: The value being transferred.
  - **Signature**: Cryptographic proof of the transaction's authenticity.
    - **Chain:** Blocks are connected in a sequential order through cryptographic hashes forming a chain. Each block's hash is derived from the contents of the block and the hash of the previous block, ensuring the integrity of the data.
    - **Nodes:** Computers or participants in the network that validate and propagate transactions and blocks. Nodes ensure consensus and maintain the integrity of the blockchain.
    - **Decentralization:** Unlike traditional ledgers maintained by a single entity (like a bank), a blockchain is maintained by multiple nodes in a network. Each node has a copy of the entire blockchain, and changes to the blockchain must be agreed upon by the majority of nodes.
    - **Consensus Mechanisms:** Protocols used to achieve agreement on the blockchain's state among distributed nodes. Common mechanisms include Proof of Work (PoW) and Proof of Stake (PoS).
- **Proof of Work (PoW):** Nodes (miners) solve complex mathematical problems to validate transactions and add new blocks. Bitcoin uses PoW.
- **Proof of Stake (PoS):** Validators are chosen based on the number of tokens they hold and are willing to "stake" as collateral. Ethereum is transitioning to PoS.
- **Delegated Proof of Stake (DPoS)**: DPoS is a variation of the Proof of Stake (PoS) consensus mechanism designed to improve scalability and efficiency. In a DPoS system, stakeholders elect a small number of delegates (also called

witnesses or block producers) who are responsible for validating transactions and creating new blocks.

- o **Proof of Authority (PoA):** Proof of Authority (PoA) is a consensus mechanism that relies on a small number of pre-approved nodes (authorities) to validate transactions and produce blocks. Unlike PoW and PoS, PoA does not require extensive computational work or staking of tokens.
    - **Cryptographic Hashing:** Cryptographic hashing is used to secure data. Each block contains a unique hash, which is a fixed-size string generated from the block's data. This hash is produced by a hash function and is dependent on the block's content. If the content of the block changes, the hash changes, ensuring the integrity of the data.
    - **Immutability:** Once a block is added to the blockchain, it is nearly impossible to alter the data without changing all subsequent blocks. This is due to the cryptographic hash linking each block to the previous one. This immutability ensures the integrity and reliability of the data recorded on the blockchain.
    - **Smart Contracts:** Smart contracts are self-executing contracts with terms directly written into code. They automatically enforce and execute the terms of the contract when predefined conditions are met. This concept is primarily associated with Ethereum.

2.1. Types of Blockchains

The various types of blockchains offer different advantages and are suited to different use cases. Public blockchains provide transparency and decentralization, private blockchains offer control and privacy, consortium blockchains facilitate collaboration among multiple entities, hybrid blockchains combine elements of both public and private systems, sidechains improve scalability and experimentation, and federated blockchains enable controlled and efficient collaboration among selected organizations. Each type has its own set of features, benefits, and limitations depending on the needs of the users and the specific applications. Top of Form

2.1. Bottom of Form

Different types of block chain implementations are public blockchain, private blockchain, Consortium Blockchain, and Hybrid blockchain as depicted in figure 4.3:

- **Public Blockchains:** Open and permissionless, allowing anyone to participate in the network. Examples include Bitcoin and Ethereum. Public blockchains are highly transparent but can present challenges for privacy.

Features:

- o **Transparency:** All transactions are visible to everyone on the network.
- o **Decentralization:** Control is distributed across many nodes, enhancing security and reducing single points of failure.
- o **Security:** Transactions are secured through consensus mechanisms like Proof of Work (PoW) or Proof of Stake (PoS).

Examples: Bitcoin, Ethereum

- **Private Blockchains:** Restricted access and controlled by a single organization or consortium. They offer higher privacy and control but lack the same level of decentralization as public blockchains. Examples include Hyperledger Fabric and R3 Corda.

Features

- o **Access Control:** Only pre-approved entities can join and participate in the network.
- o **Efficiency:** Can offer faster transaction processing and lower costs compared to public blockchains due to fewer participants.
- o **Privacy:** Data is only visible to authorized users, enhancing confidentiality.

Examples: Hyperledger Fabric, R3 Corda

Figure 3. Main types of blockchain

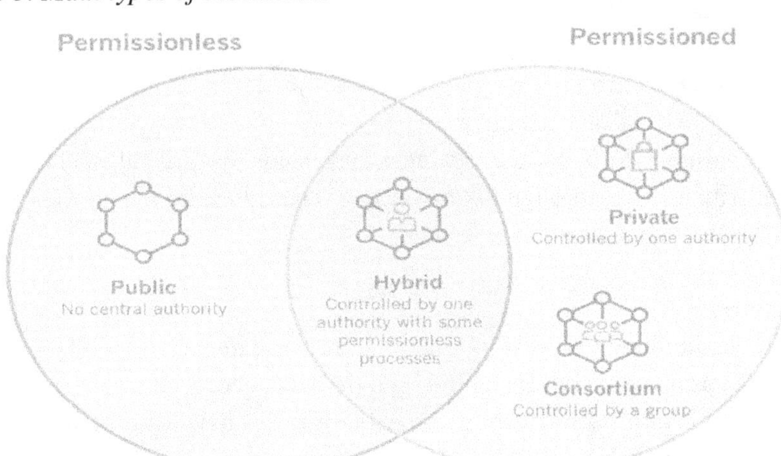

(Kathleen E., 2021)

• **Consortium Blockchains:** Operated and Controlled by a group of organizations with shared interests. They combine elements of public and private blockchains, offering a balance between transparency and control.

Features:

- o **Shared Control:** Governance is managed by a consortium of organizations, providing a balance between decentralization and control.
- o **Collaboration:** Useful for industries or sectors where multiple organizations need to work together and share data securely.
- o **Privacy:** Access is restricted to consortium members, while still maintaining some level of transparency within the group.

Examples: Enterprise Ethereum Alliance (EEA), Energy Web Chain

• **Hybrid blockchain:** Combinations of public and private blockchains are known as hybrid blockchain. Hybrid blockchain networks are private blockchains that allow special access for authorized individuals. It combines the privacy and permissioned features of Private Blockchains with the ease-of-use, flexibility, and transparency of Public Blockchains on a single platform.

Features:

- o **Selective Transparency:** Some data is public while other data remains private, based on the requirements of different stakeholders.
- o **Customizable Governance:** Allows for a mix of decentralized and centralized governance, depending on the use case.
- o **Interoperability:** Can interact with both public and private blockchains, facilitating data exchange.

Examples: Dragonchain, Quorum

Few other types of blockchain are:

• **Sidechains:** Sidechains are separate blockchains that are attached to a parent blockchain (mainchain) through a two-way peg. They allow for the transfer of assets between the mainchain and the sidechain.

Features:

- o **Scalability:** Offloads transactions from the mainchain to the sidechain, improving overall scalability and performance.
- o **Experimentation:** Allows developers to test new features and functionalities without affecting the primary chain.
- o **Customization:** Sidechains can have different consensus mechanisms and rules from the mainchain.

Examples: Liquid Network, RSK (Rootstock)

- **Federated Blockchains:** Federated blockchains are similar to consortium blockchains but are typically managed by a group of pre-selected organizations or institutions rather than a single entity.

Features:

- o **Controlled Access:** Only authorized participants can access and validate transactions.
- o **Consensus Mechanisms:** Often use more efficient consensus mechanisms compared to public blockchains, such as Practical Byzantine Fault Tolerance (PBFT).
- o **Interoperability:** Can interact with other federated or public blockchains.

Examples: IBM Food Trust, Corda Network

2.2. Blockchain Data Structures

Blockchain data structures are fundamental components that define how data is stored, organized, and maintained within a blockchain network. These structures ensure the integrity, security, and consistency of the blockchain. The key data structures used in blockchains are:

- **Transaction:** The fundamental unit of data in a blockchain, recording details such as sender, receiver, amount, and timestamp.

The components of transaction are:

- o **Transaction ID**: A unique identifier for the transaction.
- o **Inputs and Outputs**:
  - ▪ **Inputs**: Specify the source of the funds or data being transferred.
  - ▪ **Outputs**: Specify the destination of the funds or data.
- o **Digital Signatures**: Cryptographic signatures that validate the transaction's authenticity and ensure that the transaction is authorized by the owner of the funds or data.
- o **Metadata**: Additional data such as transaction fees, timestamps, and smart contract details (if applicable).
  - **Genesis Block:** The Genesis Block is the first block in a blockchain. It serves as the foundation for the entire blockchain and has unique characteristics. Genesis block Provides the initial reference point for the blockchain and establishes the initial state of the ledger.

Components of a Genesis Block are:

- o **Unique Header:** The Genesis Block has a distinct header and may have different rules or attributes compared to subsequent blocks.
- o **Predefined Data:** Often contains special or hardcoded data, such as an initial message or system parameters.

• **Merkle Tree:** Data structures that efficiently summarize and verify the integrity of transactions within a block. They enable quick verification of data without requiring access to the entire dataset. A Merkle Tree is a binary tree used to efficiently and securely verify the integrity of data within a block. It provides a way to hash multiple transactions into a single hash, known as the Merkle Root.

Components of a Merkle tree are:

- o **Leaf Nodes:** Hashes of individual transactions.
- o **Non-Leaf Nodes:** Hashes of concatenated pairs of child nodes, creating a hierarchy of hashes.
- o **Merkle Root:** The topmost hash of the tree, representing the aggregate of all transaction hashes in the block.

This data structure provides benefits such as:

- o **Efficiency:** Allows quick and efficient verification of the integrity of individual transactions without needing to check the entire block.
- o **Data Integrity:** Changes to any transaction would alter the Merkle Root, thus ensuring that data has not been tampered with.
  - **Hash Functions:** Cryptographic algorithms that produce a fixed-size output (hash) from variable-size input data, ensuring data integrity and security by creating unique identifiers for each block.
  - **Chain State:** The Chain State represents the current state of the blockchain, including the latest status of all accounts and smart contracts.

Components of chain state:

- o **Account Balances:** Current balances of all accounts in the blockchain.
- o **Smart Contract States:** The current state of all deployed smart contracts, including variables and execution results.
- o **Utxo Set:** In some blockchains like Bitcoin, the Unspent Transaction Output (UTXO) set represents the collection of all unspent transaction outputs that can be used in new transactions.

Benefits of chain state are:

- o **Snapshot of Current State:** Provides a real-time view of the blockchain's status, allowing participants to understand the latest state without processing the entire history.
- o **Efficiency:** Optimizes the performance of the blockchain by maintaining a concise representation of the current state.

2.3. Challenges in Blockchain implementation

Implementing blockchain technology presents several critical challenges that organizations and developers need to address to ensure successful deployment and operation. The key challenges in blockchain implementation are:

- **Scalability:** Many blockchain networks, particularly those using Proof of Work (PoW), face limitations in processing transactions quickly and efficiently. As the number of transactions increases, the network can become congested, leading to slower processing times and higher transaction fees.

Solutions like sharding, layer 2 scaling solutions (e.g., Lightning Network for Bitcoin, Rollups for Ethereum), and improved consensus mechanisms (e.g., Proof of Stake) are being explored to address scalability.

- **Energy Consumption:** PoW consensus mechanisms, used by cryptocurrencies like Bitcoin, require significant computational power and energy. This has led to concerns about the environmental impact and sustainability of blockchain technology.

Transitioning to more energy-efficient consensus mechanisms like Proof of Stake (PoS) or Proof of Authority (PoA) can help reduce energy consumption. Additionally, innovations in hardware and renewable energy sources are being explored.

- **Regulation and Compliance:** The regulatory environment for blockchain technology is evolving and varies significantly across jurisdictions. Unclear or inconsistent regulations can create legal and compliance challenges for businesses.

Engaging with regulators, staying informed about legal developments, and implementing robust compliance practices can help mitigate regulatory risks. Some organizations also advocate for clearer regulations to guide the industry.

- **Interoperability:** Different blockchain networks often operate in isolation, making it challenging to transfer data and value between them. This lack of interoperability can limit the utility and integration of blockchain solutions.

Developing cross-chain protocols and interoperability solutions, such as Polkadot and Cosmos, can facilitate communication and data exchange between different blockchains.

- **Security Vulnerabilities:** While blockchain is inherently secure, vulnerabilities can still arise due to coding errors, bugs in smart contracts, and attacks on network participants. These vulnerabilities can lead to significant financial losses or data breaches.

Implementing rigorous code audits, security testing, and using formal verification techniques for smart contracts can help enhance security. Regular updates and patches are also essential.

- **User Experience and Adoption:** Blockchain technology can be complex and difficult for non-technical users to understand and use. Poor user experience can hinder widespread adoption.

Improving the design and usability of blockchain applications, providing user-friendly interfaces, and offering educational resources can help make blockchain technology more accessible to a broader audience.

- **Data Privacy:** Public blockchains are transparent, meaning that transaction data is visible to all participants. This transparency can be a concern for applications that require confidentiality.

Privacy-focused solutions such as zero-knowledge proofs (e.g., zk-SNARKs) and private or permissioned blockchains can provide enhanced privacy while maintaining the integrity of the data.

- **Integration with Existing Systems:** Integrating blockchain technology with existing legacy systems and infrastructure can be challenging. Compatibility issues and the need for system redesign can create significant barriers.

Developing hybrid systems that combine blockchain with traditional technologies, using APIs and middleware, and ensuring thorough planning and testing can ease integration challenges.

- **Governance:** Effective governance of blockchain networks is crucial for decision-making, protocol upgrades, and conflict resolution. Poor governance structures can lead to inefficiencies and disputes within the network.

Implementing clear governance frameworks, involving diverse stakeholders, and using on-chain governance mechanisms can help ensure effective management and decision-making.

- **Scalability vs. Decentralization dilemma:** There is often a trade-off between scalability and decentralization. Increasing scalability can sometimes reduce the number of participating nodes, leading to centralization.

Balancing scalability and decentralization involve finding a suitable consensus mechanism, optimizing protocol parameters, and exploring innovations like layer 2 solutions that can help achieve both goals.

The implementation of blockchain technology faces several challenges, including scalability, energy consumption, regulation, interoperability, security, user experience, data privacy, integration with existing systems, governance, and the scalability-decentralization trade-off. Addressing these challenges requires a combination of technological innovation, regulatory compliance, and user-centric design to unlock the full potential of blockchain technology while minimizing its risks and limitations.

3. BLOCKCHAIN FORENSICS OVERVIEW

Blockchain forensics is the application of investigative techniques to analyze and interpret blockchain data. It aims to trace transactions, identify patterns, and uncover illicit activities, such as fraud, money laundering, and cybercrime. The scope of blockchain forensics includes:

- **Transaction Analysis:** Involves examining individual blockchain transactions to identify patterns, trace funds, their origin, destination, path through the network and detect anomalies. Different techniques and tools are used to visualize transaction flows, identify patterns, and associate addresses with known entities or activities. For instance, analyzing how a specific transaction is split across multiple addresses or how funds are moved between different wallets.
- **Wallet Analysis:** Investigating cryptocurrency wallets to understand their ownership, transactions, activities, and relationships with other wallets.

- **Smart Contract Auditing:** Reviewing smart contracts for vulnerabilities, compliance, and malicious activities. Smart contract auditing is a crucial process that involves reviewing and analyzing smart contracts to ensure they are secure, reliable, and functioning as intended. Smart contracts are self-executing contracts with the terms of the agreement directly written into code and deployed on a blockchain. Given their autonomous nature and the potential for financial transactions or sensitive data management, ensuring their integrity through thorough auditing is essential.

3.1. Transaction Analysis

Transaction analysis involves examining individual transactions and their relationships to identify suspicious activities and trace the flow of funds. Key techniques for transaction analysis includes:

- **Transaction Tracking:** Monitoring and following the path of individual transactions through the blockchain. Key techniques are:
  - **Transaction ID Lookup**: Using blockchain explorers to retrieve detailed information about specific transactions, including sender and receiver addresses, transaction amount, and timestamps.
  - **Flow Analysis**: Tracing how funds move between different addresses, often involving the creation of transaction graphs to visualize the movement of assets.
- **Pattern Recognition**: Identifying patterns or anomalies in transaction data. Key techniques are:
  - **Behavioral Patterns**: Analyzing recurring patterns, such as the frequency and size of transactions, to identify normal versus suspicious activities.
  - **Clustering**: Grouping transactions or addresses that exhibit similar behaviors to detect unusual patterns or networks.
- **Address Clustering:** Grouping addresses that are likely controlled by the same entity based on transaction patterns and behavioral analysis. Techniques such as heuristic analysis and machine learning can enhance clustering accuracy. Methods used for address clustering includes:
  - **Heuristic Analysis**: Using predefined rules and patterns to identify potential fraud or suspicious behavior. This method involves identifying known patterns of illicit behavior, such as large transactions or frequent small transactions.
  - **Cross-Referencing**: Combining blockchain data with external sources to corroborate address ownership and control.

- **Link Analysis**: Analyzing the relationships between different addresses and transactions to uncover networks or connections. Key methods for link analysis are:
    - o **Graph Visualization**: Visualizing and analyzing the network of transactions to identify connections, clusters, and patterns indicative of illicit activities. Tools such as Gephi and Cytoscape can help in creating and interpreting transaction graphs.
    - o **Social Network Analysis**: Applying techniques from social network analysis to understand the relationships between addresses and entities.
- **Anomaly Detection**: Identifying unusual or unexpected transaction behaviors that may indicate fraudulent or illicit activities. Methods for anomaly detection includes:
    - o **Statistical Methods**: Employing algorithms and statistical models to detect deviations from normal transaction patterns.
    - o **Machine Learning**: Using machine learning models to classify transactions as normal or suspicious based on historical data and features.
- **Forensic Tools**: Utilizing specialized software to assist in transaction analysis. Examples:
    - o **Chainalysis Reactor**: Provides comprehensive tools for tracking and analyzing cryptocurrency transactions.
    - o **Elliptic**: Offers solutions for identifying and investigating suspicious transactions.
    - o **CipherTrace**: Focuses on blockchain forensics and provides tools for analyzing transaction data and detecting illicit activities.

Transaction analysis involves examining blockchain transactions to uncover insights, detect anomalies, and provide evidence for various purposes. Key methods include transaction tracking, pattern recognition, address clustering, link analysis, and anomaly detection. Challenges such as anonymity, complex transactions, and large data volumes require sophisticated tools and techniques. Applications span criminal investigations, regulatory compliance, risk management, and market research. Effective transaction analysis helps in detecting fraudulent activities, ensuring compliance, recovering assets, and understanding market dynamics.

3.2. Wallet Analysis

Wallet analysis focuses on investigating cryptocurrency wallets to determine ownership and activity. Key techniques in wallet analysis include:

- **Address Lookup:** Identifying and verifying the owners of cryptocurrency addresses through public records, known addresses, and database queries. Services like WalletExplorer and BitcoinAbuse can assist in this process.
- **Transaction Tracking:** Analyzing the transaction history of wallets to uncover patterns, and connections. This analysis can help trace the origin and destination of funds and detect unusual activities and their potential connections to criminal activities.
- **Address Fingerprinting:** Creating unique identifiers for addresses based on transaction patterns, network interactions, and other characteristics. This technique helps in identifying and linking addresses associated with the same entity.
- **Behavioral Analysis:** Examining wallet behavior patterns to detect anomalies or unusual activities. Techniques for behavioral analysis are Analyzing spending patterns, transaction volumes, and interaction frequencies to identify potential red flags.
- **Cross-Referencing Data:** Comparing wallet data with external sources to enhance the accuracy of the analysis. Techniques are integrating data from exchanges, blockchain explorers, and other databases to build a more complete picture of wallet activities.
- **Forensic Tools:** Utilizing specialized software to conduct in-depth wallet analysis. Examples:
  - **Chainalysis Reactor:** Provides tools for tracking and analyzing cryptocurrency transactions, including wallet activities.
  - **Elliptic Lens:** Offers comprehensive analytics for identifying and investigating cryptocurrency transactions and wallets.
  - **CipherTrace:** Focuses on blockchain forensics and provides tools for tracing transactions and analyzing wallet activities.
- **Link Analysis:** Mapping the relationships between different wallets to identify clusters or networks of related addresses. Graph analysis is used to visualize connections between wallets and identify central nodes or suspicious networks.

Wallet analysis is a crucial aspect of blockchain forensics and cryptocurrency management, focusing on examining the activities, transactions, and relationships associated with cryptocurrency wallets. Key methods include transaction tracking, address attribution, link analysis, and behavioral analysis. Challenges such as anonymity, complex transactions, and evolving technology require sophisticated tools and techniques. Applications span criminal investigations, regulatory compliance, risk management, and market research. Effective wallet analysis helps in detecting fraudulent activities, ensuring compliance, recovering assets, and understanding market dynamics.

3.3. Smart Contract Auditing

Smart contracts are self-executing contracts with terms directly written into code. Auditing smart contracts involves:

- **Code Review:** Analyzing the smart contract's source code for vulnerabilities, errors, and malicious logic that could be exploited. Tools such as Mythril and Slither can assist in identifying security flaws.
- **Behavioral Analysis:** Observing how smart contracts interact with the blockchain and other contracts to detect unintended or malicious behavior.
- **Formal Verification:** Applying mathematical methods to ensure that the smart contract behaves as intended and adheres to specified properties. Formal verification techniques like using test cases based on the smart contract's specifications can provide guarantees about the correctness of smart contracts.
- **Security Testing:** Evaluating the smart contract for common security issues and vulnerabilities.
    - **Static Analysis:** Analyzing the code without executing it to find potential vulnerabilities and issues.
    - **Dynamic Analysis:** Executing the smart contract in a controlled environment to observe its behavior and identify issues during execution.
    - **Fuzz Testing:** Providing random or unexpected inputs to the smart contract to uncover potential vulnerabilities.

3.3.1. Challenges in Smart Contract Auditing

- **Complexity:** Smart contracts can be complex, making it challenging to thoroughly analyze and test all possible interactions and edge cases. Breaking down the contract into smaller, manageable components and using automated tools to aid in the analysis.
- **Evolving Standards:** Blockchain and smart contract technology evolve rapidly, leading to new vulnerabilities and best practices. Staying updated with the latest developments, tools, and techniques in smart contract auditing is very crucial.
- **Code Quality:** Inexperienced developers or poorly written code can introduce vulnerabilities or errors. Adopting best practices for coding standards and ensuring that experienced auditors conduct the review is recommended.

- **Human Error:** Manual code reviews can be prone to human error, potentially missing critical vulnerabilities. Combining manual reviews with automated tools and conducting multiple rounds of auditing can increase accuracy.
- **Resource Intensive:** Comprehensive auditing can be time-consuming and resource intensive. Prioritizing critical components for auditing and utilizing automated tools to streamline the process is recommended.

Smart contract auditing is a vital process that ensures the security, functionality, and efficiency of smart contracts deployed on a blockchain. It involves reviewing the code, testing for vulnerabilities, verifying functionality, and optimizing for performance. Challenges such as complexity, evolving standards, and resource intensity must be addressed through a combination of manual and automated techniques. Effective auditing supports secure deployments, regulatory compliance, and operational efficiency, ultimately enhancing trust in blockchain applications and their underlying smart contracts.

4. BLOCKCHAIN FORENSICS TOOLS AND TECHNIQUES

4.1. Blockchain Explorers

Blockchain explorers are web-based tools that provide a user-friendly interface for interacting with blockchain networks. They allow users to view and analyze blockchain data, such as transaction histories, block details, and address activities. These explorers are essential for transparency and facilitate the exploration of the decentralized and immutable data stored on blockchains.

Key Features of blockchain explorers are:

- **Transaction Tracking**: Users can search for and view details of specific transactions, including amounts, sending and receiving addresses, and transaction IDs. This helps in verifying transactions and understanding their status.
- **Block Information**: Explorers display details about individual blocks, such as block height, timestamp, miner information, and the list of transactions contained within the block. This is useful for verifying when a transaction was confirmed.
- **Address Analysis**: Users can input a blockchain address to view its transaction history, balance, and other related activities. This can help in tracking the movement of assets and understanding the behavior of specific addresses.

- **Network Statistics**: Many explorers provide real-time statistics about the blockchain network, such as hash rate, transaction volume, and network difficulty. This information is crucial for assessing the health and performance of the network.
- **Search and Filtering**: Explorers typically offer search and filtering capabilities to easily locate transactions, addresses, or blocks. This functionality enhances usability and aids in detailed blockchain analysis.

Examples of blockchain explorers include:

- **Etherscan:** Etherscan is one of the most popular and widely used blockchain explorers for the Ethereum network. It provides a comprehensive view of Ethereum blockchain data, including transaction details, smart contract interactions, and network statistics (Ethereum).
- **Blockchair:** Blockchair is a versatile blockchain explorer that supports multiple blockchain networks. It offers a unified interface for exploring data across different blockchains, making it a valuable tool for users interested in more than one network (Blockchair).
- **Blockchain.com Explorer:** A popular explorer for Bitcoin and Bitcoin Cash. It Provides insights into Bitcoin and Bitcoin Cash transactions, addresses, and blocks (Blockchain.com Explorer).
- **BscScan:** BscScan is the blockchain explorer specifically designed for the Binance Smart Chain. It offers features similar to Etherscan but tailored to the BSC network (Chain).
- **Solscan:** Solscan is a blockchain explorer for the Solana network. It provides insights into the fast and scalable transactions that Solana is known for, as well as detailed analytics (SOLSCAN).

4.2. Forensic Analysis Tools

Blockchain forensics tools are specialized software designed to analyze and investigate blockchain data for various purposes, including financial investigations, fraud detection, and compliance monitoring. These tools enable users to trace and interpret complex blockchain transactions, providing insights that are crucial for law enforcement, regulatory agencies, financial institutions, and blockchain enterprises.

Key Features

- **Transaction Tracing**: These tools allow users to follow the path of transactions across the blockchain. This includes tracking the flow of funds from one address to another, identifying transaction patterns, and mapping out the movement of assets.

- **Address Clustering**: Forensics tools can group addresses that are likely controlled by the same entity, which helps in understanding the behavior of particular actors and identifying potential sources of illicit activity.
- **Graph Visualization**: They provide graphical representations of blockchain transactions, showing the relationships between addresses and transactions. This visual approach aids in recognizing complex patterns and networks.
- **Entity Identification**: Some tools offer features for identifying and associating blockchain addresses with real-world entities, such as exchanges or known addresses, which is crucial for linking blockchain activity with identifiable individuals or organizations.
- **Risk Scoring**: Tools can assess the risk associated with addresses or transactions based on historical data and known patterns of illicit behavior. This helps in prioritizing investigations and managing compliance risks.
- **Reporting and Documentation**: Forensics tools often include features for generating detailed reports and documentation, which are useful for presenting findings to stakeholders, regulatory bodies, or in legal proceedings.

Several specialized tools are designed for blockchain forensics:

- **Chainalysis:** Provides comprehensive analytics and investigative tools for tracing cryptocurrency transactions and detecting illicit activities. Chainalysis Reactor provides advanced features for transaction graphing and entity identification and has played a crucial role in bringing transparency and compliance to the evolving cryptocurrency landscape (Chainalysis).
- **Elliptic:** Elliptic is a prominent blockchain analytics and forensics platform, recognized for its comprehensive tools designed to address the needs of financial institutions, law enforcement agencies, and cryptocurrency businesses. Elliptic offers tools for analyzing blockchain transactions and identifying connections to criminal entities. Elliptic Forensics offers insights into transaction flows and risk assessments (Elliptic).
- **Bitquery Coinpath API**: The Bitquery Coinpath API is a tool provided by Bitquery that allows developers to access detailed blockchain data. Specifically, it offers insights into the transaction paths of cryptocurrencies. This can include information on how transactions flow through different addresses, providing a way to trace the movement of assets and analyze transaction patterns across various blockchain networks (Bitquery).

- **CipherTrace:** CipherTrace provides blockchain forensics and cryptocurrency intelligence solutions that focuses on cryptocurrency transaction tracing, risk assessment, and anti-money laundering compliance. CipherTrace Trace helps in tracking and recovering stolen funds.

4.3. Data Visualization Tools

Blockchain data visualization tools are essential for interpreting and analyzing the complex and often voluminous data generated by blockchain networks. These tools help users understand blockchain activities, trends, and insights through graphical representations.

Key Features

Key features of blockchain data visualization tools are:

- **Interactive Dashboards:** Interactive dashboards provide a centralized view of blockchain data, allowing users to explore and interact with various metrics and data points. It provides features like Customizable widgets, real-time data updates, and drill-down capabilities for detailed insights.
- **Transaction Tracking:** This feature allows users to track individual transactions across the blockchain. This feature facilitates visualization of transaction flow, sender and receiver details, transaction status, and historical transaction data. Often includes search functionality by transaction ID, address, or other identifiers.
- **Network Analysis:** Analyzes the structure and behavior of the blockchain network, including nodes and connections. It provides features such as visual representations of node connections, transaction volume between nodes, and network topology. This feature is very useful for identifying key nodes and analyzing network health and performance.
- **Address and Wallet Analytics:** Through visualization of transaction history, balance changes, and activity patterns it provides insights into the activity of specific addresses or wallets. Often includes tools to track wallet interactions and identify high-value addresses.
- **Real-Time Data:** Displays Real-time updates of block production, transaction confirmations, and network statistics, allowing users to monitor current network activity. It is Essential for applications that require up-to-the-minute information.
- **Historical Data Analysis:** Allows users to analyze historical blockchain data through charts, trend lines, and comparative analysis over

different time periods to identify trends and patterns. This is useful for examining past performance and behavior of the blockchain.

- **Customizable Reports:** This feature enables users to generate, customize, and export reports with selected metrics, visualizations, and filters useful for auditing, compliance, and strategic decision-making.
- **Smart Contract Monitoring:** Monitors the execution and performance of smart contracts on the blockchain. It aids in visualization of smart contract interactions, execution status, and performance metrics to help in tracking contract deployments, function calls, and error rates.
- **Security and Compliance Insights:** Provides insights into the security and compliance aspects of blockchain transactions and network behavior. Features include Detection of suspicious activities, compliance with regulations, and security vulnerabilities. Often includes alerts and notifications for unusual behavior.
- **User-Friendly Interface:** Intuitive design, drag-and-drop functionalities, and clear visualizations ensure that the tool is accessible and easy to use for both technical and non-technical users. Features like tooltips, guides, and help sections assist users in navigating the tool effectively.
- **Integration Capabilities:** API support for data integration, compatibility with various blockchain networks, and ability to connect with external data sources like databases or third-party applications allows the visualization tool to integrate with other systems and data sources.
- **Scalability:** Support for large-scale data processing, efficient data handling, and optimization for performance ensures that the tool can handle increasing amounts of data as the blockchain grows.
- **Geospatial Visualization:** Provides geographical context to blockchain data useful for understanding regional distribution and activities by mapping of transactions or nodes to geographical locations.
- **Custom Alerts and Notifications:** Allows users to set up alerts based on specific criteria or thresholds to stay informed about critical events in real time. For example, notifications for high-value transactions, network anomalies, or contract failures.

Exampls:

Examples of data visualization tools offering unique capabilities for blockchain forensics includes:

- **GraphSense:** GraphSense is an open source blockchain analytics platform that provides advanced data visualization for cryptocurrency transactions. It is designed to help users understand complex transaction networks and detect suspicious activities (Haslhofer, Stütz, Romiti, & King, 2021).

- **Gephi:** An open-source network analysis and visualization tool used for visualizing transaction networks and identifying patterns (Bastian, Heymann, & Jacomy, 2009).
- **Chainalysis Reactor:** Chainalysis Reactor is a powerful tool provided by Chainalysis that combines blockchain data with advanced visualization features to assist in forensic investigations and compliance monitoring (McShane, 2023).
- **Graphistry:** Offers interactive graph analysis and visualization capabilities, allowing users to explore blockchain data and uncover connections (Graphistry, n.d.).

4.4. Machine Learning and AI

Machine learning and AI techniques are increasingly being used in blockchain forensics. The key purpose of AI and ML are:

- **Anomaly Detection:** Identifying unusual patterns or deviations in transaction data that may indicate fraudulent activities. Machine learning models can be trained on historical data to detect anomalies in real-time.
- **Predictive Analysis:** Using historical data to predict future transactions and identify potential risks. Predictive models can help in anticipating fraudulent activities and mitigating threats.

5. IMPORTANCE AND APPLICATIONS OF BLOCKCHAIN FORENSICS

Blockchain technology, initially designed to support cryptocurrencies like Bitcoin, has expanded into numerous sectors due to its transparency, immutability, and decentralization. However, these very features also introduce complexities in tracking and analyzing transactions, especially when it comes to illicit activities. Blockchain forensics has emerged as a critical field to address these challenges.

5.1. Importance of Blockchain Forensics

5.1.1. Ensuring Security and Integrity

Blockchain's inherent design promotes security and data integrity through its immutable ledger and decentralized validation mechanisms. However, these benefits also attract malicious actors seeking to exploit the technology for illicit purposes. Blockchain forensics is vital in maintaining the security and integrity of blockchain networks by:

By analyzing transaction patterns and wallet behaviors, forensics can uncover fraudulent schemes such as Ponzi schemes, phishing attacks, and fake ICOs. For example, through transaction analysis and address clustering, investigators can identify suspicious patterns indicative of fraudulent activities.

Blockchain forensics helps in detecting and preventing financial crimes such as money laundering and terrorist financing. Techniques like heuristic analysis and graph analysis can reveal suspicious transaction flows and connections between addresses.

5.1.2. Enhancing Regulatory Compliance

As blockchain technology becomes more mainstream, regulatory bodies have increased their focus on ensuring compliance with financial regulations, including anti-money laundering (AML) and know-your-customer (KYC) requirements. Blockchain forensics plays a crucial role in:

- **Monitoring and Reporting:** Forensic tools enable organizations to monitor blockchain transactions in real-time, providing timely reports on suspicious activities. This helps in adhering to AML and KYC regulations by ensuring that transactions are traceable and transparent.
- **Auditing and Verification:** Blockchain forensics supports the auditing process by verifying the legitimacy of transactions and identifying any non-compliant activities. Regular audits facilitated by forensic tools ensure that blockchain-based businesses operate within legal frameworks.

5.1.3. Supporting Law Enforcement and Legal Proceedings

Blockchain forensics aids law enforcement agencies and legal professionals in investigating and prosecuting crimes involving blockchain technology. Its importance in this domain includes:

In cases of theft, such as hacks on cryptocurrency exchanges, forensics can trace stolen assets through the blockchain. For instance, the analysis of transaction trails can help identify and recover stolen funds.

Forensic investigations provide evidence that can be used in legal proceedings. Detailed reports and analyses of transaction histories, wallet activities, and smart contract interactions can support cases in court.

5.1.4. Improving Trust and Transparency

The transparency of blockchain technology is one of its most significant advantages. Blockchain forensics reinforces this transparency by:

- **Building Trust in Blockchain Solutions:** By ensuring that blockchain applications are secure and compliant, forensics builds trust among users and stakeholders. This is essential for the adoption of blockchain technology in sensitive areas such as finance, healthcare, and supply chain management.
- **Promoting Accountability:** Forensics holds participants accountable for their actions within the blockchain ecosystem. It ensures that malicious actors are identified and dealt with, reinforcing the credibility of blockchain networks.

5.2. Applications of Blockchain Forensics

5.2.1. Financial Investigations

Blockchain forensics is extensively used in financial investigations to detect and analyze fraudulent activities, tracing stolen assets, and analyzing financial transactions. Applications include:

- **Fraud Detection:** Tools and techniques are employed to detect various types of financial fraud, including fake transactions, Ponzi schemes, and insider trading. Forensic analysis of transaction patterns can reveal anomalies and suspicious behavior.
- **Asset Recovery:** In cases of theft or misappropriation of funds, blockchain forensics helps trace and recover stolen assets. By following the trail of trans-

actions and analyzing wallet activities, investigators can locate and retrieve stolen cryptocurrencies.

- **Transparency and Immutability**: Blockchains offer a transparent and immutable ledger of all transactions, which can be invaluable for financial investigations. Each transaction is recorded on a public ledger, providing a traceable history that can be examined to uncover the flow of funds and identify suspicious activities.

5.2.2. Regulatory Compliance

Ensuring compliance with financial regulations is a critical application of blockchain forensics:

- **Anti-Money Laundering (AML) Compliance:** Financial institutions and cryptocurrency exchanges are required to comply with AML regulations designed to prevent money laundering and the financing of terrorism. Blockchain forensics tools enable these entities to monitor transactions for suspicious activities, identify high-risk addresses, and ensure that transactions align with AML requirements.
- **Know Your Customer (KYC) Requirements:** KYC regulations require businesses to verify the identity of their customers to prevent fraud and illicit activities. Blockchain forensics aids in verifying and cross-referencing customer information against transaction data to ensure that the entities involved in transactions are legitimate and meet KYC standards.
- **Transaction Monitoring:** Regulatory bodies mandate continuous monitoring of transactions to detect and report suspicious activities. Forensics tools provide real-time monitoring and analysis of blockchain transactions, allowing businesses to promptly identify and report activities that may indicate financial crimes or regulatory violations.
- **Reporting and Documentation:** Blockchain forensics tools generate detailed reports and documentation on transactions and activities. These reports are essential for regulatory audits, compliance checks, and reporting requirements. They help demonstrate adherence to regulations and provide evidence of due diligence and risk management practices.
- **Risk Management:** Forensics tools assess the risk associated with transactions and addresses based on historical data and known patterns of illicit behavior. This risk scoring helps businesses prioritize their compliance efforts, focus on high-risk areas, and implement appropriate measures to mitigate potential risks.

- **Audit and Verification:** Regular audits facilitated by forensic tools ensure that blockchain-based operations comply with regulatory standards. This includes verifying the authenticity of transactions and addressing any discrepancies or violations.

5.2.3. Cybercrime Investigation

Blockchain forensics plays a pivotal role in investigating cybercrimes involving cryptocurrencies and blockchain technology. Main aspects are identifying and prosecuting illegal activities, such as ransomware attacks and hacking.

- **Hacking and Theft Investigations:** Forensics helps track and analyze the movement of stolen assets following a hack or theft. Detailed analysis of blockchain transactions can uncover the identities of perpetrators and facilitate asset recovery.
- **Ransomware and Extortion:** In cases of ransomware attacks, blockchain forensics can trace ransom payments made through cryptocurrencies. This helps in identifying the attackers and understanding their operations.
- **Tracing Illicit Transactions:** One of the most significant advantages of blockchain technology is its transparent ledger. Each transaction is recorded on the blockchain and is publicly accessible, providing a permanent and traceable record. Blockchain forensics tools help investigators trace the flow of funds involved in cybercrimes, such as ransomware payments or stolen cryptocurrencies, across different addresses and networks.
- **Uncovering Criminal Networks:** Cybercriminals often use complex networks of addresses and transactions to obscure their activities. Forensic tools can analyze these networks to identify connections between addresses, reveal patterns of behavior, and uncover organized criminal networks. This is crucial for understanding how cybercriminals operate and linking different activities to a common source.
- **Asset Recovery:** In cases of theft or fraud involving cryptocurrencies, blockchain forensics plays a key role in asset recovery. By tracing the movement of stolen funds, investigators can identify where the assets have been transferred and potentially work towards recovering them. This process involves tracking the funds through various exchanges and addresses to their ultimate destination.
- **Evidence Collection and Documentation:** Forensic tools provide detailed documentation and reports on blockchain transactions, which are essential for building cases against cybercriminals. These reports can be used as ev-

idence in legal proceedings, helping to establish the facts of the case and support prosecution efforts.

5.2.4. Smart Contract Auditing

Smart contracts, which are self-executing agreements with terms written in code, require auditing to ensure their security and functionality:

- **Vulnerability Detection:** Forensic analysis of smart contracts involves reviewing code for vulnerabilities and potential exploits. This includes identifying bugs, security flaws, and malicious logic that could be exploited.
- **Compliance and Verification:** Ensuring that smart contracts comply with regulatory standards and operate as intended. This involves verifying that the contract's code aligns with its documented terms and conditions.

5.2.5. Supply Chain Management

Blockchain forensics is increasingly being applied to supply chain management to ensure transparency and traceability:

Forensics can track the movement of goods through the supply chain, verifying their authenticity and ensuring that transactions are recorded accurately on the blockchain.

Monitoring compliance with contractual agreements and regulatory requirements throughout the supply chain. Forensic tools can help identify any discrepancies or fraudulent activities.

5.2.6. Asset and Property Verification

Blockchain forensics is used for verifying the ownership and authenticity of digital and physical assets:

- **Digital Asset Verification:** Ensuring the legitimacy of digital assets such as NFTs (non-fungible tokens) and verifying their ownership through blockchain records.
- **Property Title Verification:** Using blockchain to track property titles and verify ownership, ensuring that property transactions are recorded accurately and transparently.

6. CHALLENGES IN BLOCKCHAIN FORENSICS

While blockchain forensics offers numerous benefits, it also faces several challenges:

- **Privacy and Anonymity:** While blockchain transactions are transparent, the identities behind addresses are often pseudonymous or anonymous. The pseudonymous nature of blockchain addresses makes it challenging to identify the real-world entities behind transactions. Techniques such as address clustering and behavioral analysis are required to overcome this challenge. These challenges include:
    - **Address Anonymity:** Determining the real-world identities behind cryptocurrency addresses can be difficult due to the lack of personal information associated with addresses.
    - **Mixing Services:** Services that obscure transaction histories by mixing funds from multiple sources, complicating traceability. Techniques such as CoinJoin and tumblers are used to enhance privacy but pose challenges for forensic investigations.
- **Data Volume and Complexity:** The vast volume of data generated by blockchains, and the complexity of transactions can overwhelm forensic tools and analysts. Advanced analytical techniques and powerful tools are needed to manage and interpret this data effectively. Issues include:
    - **Complexity:** Analyzing complex transaction patterns and smart contract interactions can be computationally intensive. Advanced analytical techniques and tools are required to manage this complexity.
    - **Data Storage:** Handling and storing large volumes of blockchain data requires significant resources and infrastructure.
- **Evolving Technology:** Blockchain technology is rapidly evolving, presenting challenges for forensic analysis. The rapid evolution of blockchain technology and its applications can outpace forensic methods and tools. Continuous updates and advancements are necessary to keep up with new developments and emerging threats.

Emerging blockchain protocols and consensus mechanisms may require new analytical techniques and tools. New types of smart contracts and decentralized applications introduce additional complexity, requiring updated forensic methods.

- **Regulatory Variability:** Different jurisdictions have varying regulations and compliance requirements. Adapting analysis methods to comply with local regulations and collaborating with international authorities as needed.

7. CASE STUDIES

- **Silk Road Investigation:** The Silk Road was an online dark web marketplace that facilitated illegal transactions using Bitcoin. Ross Ulbricht, the site's creator, was arrested in 2013. Key aspects of the investigation included (Case, 2018):
    - **Transaction Tracing:** Law enforcement used blockchain forensics to trace the flow of Bitcoin from the Silk Road marketplace to various addresses, uncovering the flow of funds.
    - **Address Analysis:** Analyzing Bitcoin addresses associated with the Silk Road to identify the operator and co-conspirators.

The investigation led to the arrest of Ross Ulbricht, the alleged operator of the Silk Road, and the seizure of Bitcoin assets. Blockchain forensics were instrumental in building the case against him.

- **Mt. Gox Exchange Hack:** Mt. Gox was a major cryptocurrency exchange that suffered a massive hack in 2014, resulting in the loss of approximately 850,000 Bitcoins valued at over $450 million at that time (The Story of Mt. Gox: Explained, 2024). Key aspects of the forensic investigation included:
    - **Funds Tracking:** Analyzing blockchain transactions to track the stolen Bitcoins and identify their current location. Analysis identified the use of mixing services to obfuscate the origin of the stolen BTC.
    - **Wallet Analysis:** Investigating the addresses associated with the stolen funds to trace their movement and identify suspects. Blockchain forensics tools grouped addresses likely controlled by the hacker, revealing patterns of behavior.

The investigation provided insights into the hack and contributed to legal actions against the perpetrators. Authorities identified suspects and linked stolen funds to addresses controlled by the suspects. Key individuals were arrested, and a portion of the stolen BTC was recovered.

- **Bitfinex Hack:** In 2016, Bitfinex, a major cryptocurrency exchange, was hacked, resulting in the theft of nearly 120,000 BTC (Team, 2023). Key aspects included:
    - **Transaction Analysis:** Tracing the stolen Bitcoins through various addresses and exchanges to uncover their whereabouts.
    - **Smart Contract Analysis:** Investigators examined smart contracts for potential clues or ties to the stolen funds.

- **Collaborative Efforts:** Working with exchanges and law enforcement agencies to track and recover the stolen funds.

The investigation led to the identification of suspects and recovery of a portion of the stolen Bitcoins. In 2022, the U.S. Department of Justice (DOJ) seized over $3.6 billion in BTC linked to the Bitfinex hack. The forensic analysis played a critical role in tracing the funds and identifying the culprits.

- **The PlusToken Scam:** PlusToken was a Ponzi scheme that defrauded investors of over $2 billion using cryptocurrency.
  - **Fund Flow Analysis:** Investigators tracked the movement of funds from PlusToken wallets to other addresses. They identified large transactions and exchanges involved.
  - **Network Analysis:** By analyzing the network of transactions, investigators could identify the flow of stolen assets and connections between addresses.

Chinese authorities arrested several key figures behind the PlusToken scam, and some of the stolen assets were recovered. Blockchain forensics helped in tracing and understanding the scale of the scam.

- **The Ronin Network Hack:** In 2022, Ronin Network, a sidechain for the Axie Infinity game, was hacked, resulting in the theft of $620 million in Ethereum and USDC.
  - **Token Tracking:** Blockchain forensics tools traced the stolen Ethereum and USDC across different addresses.
  - **Laundering Techniques:** Investigators identified methods used to launder the stolen assets, such as converting them into different cryptocurrencies and using decentralized exchanges.

The analysis led to the identification of the hackers and their methods. Although some funds were recovered, the case highlighted the vulnerabilities in decentralized finance (DeFi) platforms.

- **The Colonial Pipeline Ransomware Attack:** In 2021, Colonial Pipeline, a major U.S. fuel pipeline, was shut down by a ransomware attack demanding Bitcoin.
  - **Bitcoin Tracking:** After payment, the FBI used blockchain forensics to track the Bitcoin ransom to a specific address.

- o **Recovery Operations:** By monitoring the blockchain, authorities identified attempts to move or exchange the ransom, leading to the recovery of a significant portion of the funds.

The FBI successfully recovered a substantial amount of the ransom paid in Bitcoin. Blockchain forensics played a key role in tracing and recovering the stolen funds.

- **The Poly Network Hack:** In 2021, Poly Network, a cross-chain DeFi protocol, was exploited, resulting in a loss of over $600 million.
  - o **Cross-Chain Analysis:** Investigators traced the stolen assets across multiple blockchains, including Ethereum, Binance Smart Chain, and Polygon.
  - o **Transaction Patterns:** Forensics tools analyzed transaction patterns and identified the use of various decentralized exchanges to launder the stolen funds.

The hacker, who was later identified as a white-hat hacker, returned the majority of the stolen funds after a public plea from Poly Network. The investigation highlighted both the risks and capabilities of blockchain forensics in cross-chain environments.

8. FUTURE DIRECTIONS

- **Advances in Forensic Technology:** Emerging technologies and techniques are expected to enhance blockchain forensics, including:
  - o Developing more sophisticated algorithms and tools for analyzing complex blockchain data, including improvements in machine learning and AI techniques.
  - o Combining blockchain forensics with big data analytics, AI, machine learning, and other technologies to improve investigative capabilities and efficiency.
- **Legal and Regulatory Developments:** As blockchain technology evolves, legal and regulatory frameworks will need to adapt. Future directions include:
  - o Developing and implementing regulations that address the challenges of blockchain forensics, including AML and KYC requirements.
  - o Enhancing collaboration between jurisdictions to address cross-border issues in blockchain investigations and ensure effective enforcement.
- **Ethical Considerations:** Ethical considerations in blockchain forensics will become increasingly important, including:

- **Privacy Concerns:** Balancing forensic investigations with the need to protect individual privacy and rights. Developing guidelines for handling sensitive data responsibly.
- **Data Security:** Ensuring the secure handling and storage of forensic data to prevent unauthorized access and misuse.

9. SUMMARY

Blockchain forensics involves investigating and analyzing blockchain transactions and activities to uncover illicit behavior, trace financial flows, and provide evidence for legal and regulatory purposes. Key aspects include transaction analysis, address attribution, link analysis, anomaly detection, and the use of forensic tools. By leveraging advanced methodologies, tools, and techniques, forensic professionals can effectively analyze blockchain data, trace transactions, and uncover fraudulent behavior. Challenges include dealing with anonymity, large volumes of data, evolving technology, and global jurisdictional issues. Effective blockchain forensics requires specialized knowledge, tools, and methods to address the unique characteristics of blockchain technology. As blockchain technology continues to evolve, so will the field of blockchain forensics, requiring ongoing innovation, collaboration, and adaptation to meet emerging challenges and opportunities.

REFERENCES

Bastian, M., Heymann, S., & Jacomy, M. (2009). *Gephi: An Open Source Software for Exploring and Manipulating Networks. Proceedings of the international AAAI conference on web and social media. 3*. Association for the Advancement of Artificial Intelligence., Retrieved from https://gephi.org/

Bitquery. (n.d.). Bitquery Coinpath APIs. *Follow the money on blockchain with Coinpath® APIs*. Retrieved from https://bitquery.io/products/coinpath

Blockchain.com Explorer. (n.d.). blockchain.com. Retrieved from https://www.blockchain.com/explorer

Blockchair. (n.d.). Blockchain explorer, analytics and web services. Retrieved from https://blockchair.com/

Case, S. (2018). *Silk Road: The Dark Web's Most Infamous Marketplace*. Oxford University Press.

Chain, B. B. (n.d.). BNB Smart Chain Explorer. BNB Beacon Chain. Retrieved from https://bscscan.com/

Chainalysis. (n.d.). Retrieved from https://www.chainalysis.com/

Elliptic. (n.d.). Elliptic. Retrieved from https://www.elliptic.co/

Ethereum. (n.d.). The Ethereum Blockchain Explorer. Etherscan. Retrieved from https://etherscan.io/

Graphistry. (n.d.). Retrieved April 2024, from https://www.graphistry.com/

Haslhofer, B., Stütz, R., Romiti, M., & King, R. (2021). GraphSense: A General-Purpose Cryptoasset Analytics Platform. *Arxiv pre-print*. Retrieved from https://graphsense.org/

Husain, M. S., Khan, M. Z., & Siddiqui, T. (2023). Blockchain. In *Big Data Concepts, Technologies, and Applications* (pp. 124-136). Taylor and Francis group, CRC press.

Kathleen, E. W. E. (2021). *Types of Blockchain: Public, Private, or Something in Between*. Retrieved from https://www.foley.com: https://www.foley.com/en/insights/publications/2021/08/types-of-blockchain-public-private-between

McShane, J. J. (2023). *In-Depth Look at Chainalysis, Elliptic, and CipherTrace: Forensic Science in Blockchain Analysis*. The Truth about Forensic Science. Retrieved April 2024, from https://thetruthaboutforensicscience.com/in-depth-look-at-chainalysis-elliptic-and-ciphertrace-forensic-science-in-blockchain-analysis/

Shukla, a., Hussain, S., Irshad, R. R., Alattab, A. A., Thakur, S., Breslin, J. G., . . . Jameel, S. M. (2024). Network analysis in a peer-to-peer energy trading model using blockchain and machine learning. *Computer Standards & Interfaces, 88*, 103799.

SOLSCAN. (n.d.). Explore Solana Blockchain. Solana Blockchain. Retrieved from https://solscan.io/

Team, C. (2023). *Bitfinex Hack Money Launderers Plead Guilty.* Chainalysis. Retrieved from https://www.chainalysis.com/blog/bitfinex-hack-plea-july-2023/

KEY TERMS AND DEFINITIONS

Bitcoin: The first and most well-known public blockchain, primarily used for cryptocurrency transactions.

Corda Network: A federated blockchain used for financial transactions and business contracts.

Dragonchain: A hybrid blockchain platform that supports both public and private interactions.

Energy Web Chain: A blockchain platform designed for the energy sector, operated by a consortium of energy companies.

Enterprise Ethereum Alliance (EEA): A consortium of companies working on Ethereum-based solutions for enterprises.

Ethereum: Supports smart contracts and decentralized applications (DApps) in addition to cryptocurrency.

Hyperledger Fabric: A modular blockchain framework designed for enterprise use, allowing organizations to create their own private blockchains.

IBM Food Trust: A federated blockchain network for the food supply chain, involving multiple stakeholders like suppliers, retailers, and consumers.

Liquid Network: A sidechain of Bitcoin designed to facilitate faster transactions and confidential transactions.

Quorum: A version of Ethereum that allows for private transactions and contracts, with the ability to connect to public Ethereum for broader applications.

R3 Corda: A private blockchain platform tailored for financial institutions and enterprises.

RSK (Rootstock): A smart contract platform that operates as a sidechain to Bitcoin, enabling Ethereum-like smart contracts on the Bitcoin network.

Chapter 5
Incident Response in the Cloud Environment

ABSTRACT

The transition to cloud computing has revolutionized the way organizations manage their IT resources, offering unprecedented scalability, flexibility, and cost efficiency. However, this shift also introduces a new set of challenges, particularly in the realm of cybersecurity. As cloud environments become increasingly integral to business operations, the need for effective incident response strategies tailored to these environments has never been more critical. This chapter explores the intricacies of incident response in cloud environments, providing a comprehensive guide to developing and implementing effective strategies to handle security incidents.

1. INTRODUCTION

The transition to cloud computing has revolutionized the way organizations manage their IT resources, offering unprecedented scalability, flexibility, and cost efficiency. However, this shift also introduces a new set of challenges, particularly in the realm of cybersecurity. As cloud environments become increasingly integral to business operations, the need for effective incident response strategies tailored to these environments has never been more critical. This chapter explores the intricacies of incident response in cloud environments, providing a comprehensive guide to developing and implementing effective strategies to handle security incidents.

This chapter provides a foundational understanding of incident response in cloud environments, offering guidance on addressing the complexities and challenges associated with securing cloud-based resources. Through effective planning, detection, response, and recovery, organizations can navigate the evolving landscape of cloud security and ensure their operations remain protected against emerging threats.

DOI: 10.4018/979-8-3693-2960-3.ch005

2. UNDERSTANDING CLOUD ENVIRONMENTS

To effectively address incident response in cloud environments, it's essential to first understand the unique characteristics of these environments compared to traditional on-premises setups.

2.1. Cloud Computing Service Models

Cloud computing models define how computing resources are delivered and managed over the internet. These models offer different levels of control, flexibility, and management, catering to various needs and preferences of businesses and individuals. Cloud computing can be categorized into several models (Husain & Khanum, 2017), each with its own implications for incident response (Akbar, Suaib, Husain, & Shukla, 2020):

- **Infrastructure as a Service (IaaS):** Provides virtualized computing resources over the internet. Users can rent infrastructure components such as servers, storage, and networking without owning or managing physical hardware. Users have control over operating systems, applications, and storage but rely on the cloud provider for the underlying infrastructure. Examples of IaaS are Amazon Web Services (AWS), Microsoft Azure, Google Cloud Platform (GCP). Key features of Infrastructure as a Service (IaaS) includes:
    - **Scalability:** Easily scale resources up or down based on demand.
    - **Cost-Effective:** Pay-as-you-go pricing model reduces capital expenditure and aligns costs with usage.
    - **Flexibility:** Users have control over operating systems, applications, and storage, allowing for customization.
    - **Development and Testing:** Quickly set up and dismantle development environments.
    - **Backup and Recovery:** Store and manage backup data in a secure, scalable manner.
    - **Big Data Analysis:** Process large volumes of data using scalable compute resources.
- **Platform as a Service (PaaS):** PaaS offers a platform allowing customers to develop, run, and manage applications without dealing with the underlying infrastructure. It includes development tools, databases, and middleware. This model abstracts much of the infrastructure management. Examples of PaaS includes Heroku, Google App Engine, Microsoft Azure App Services. Key features provided by PaaS are:

- **Development Efficiency:** Build and deploy applications with minimal infrastructure management. Streamlined development with built-in tools and frameworks.
- **Automatic Updates:** Platforms often include automated updates and maintenance.
- **Integrated Development:** Tools and services are integrated to simplify the development process.
- **Application Development:**
- **Web App Hosting:** Host web applications with built-in scalability and reliability.
- **API Development:** Develop and manage APIs with support for integration and deployment.

- **Software as a Service (SaaS):** Delivers software applications over the internet, where users can access and use the software without managing the underlying infrastructure or platforms. The cloud provider handles everything from infrastructure to application maintenance. Examples of SaaS are Google Workspace (formerly G Suite), Microsoft Office 365, and Salesforce. Key features of SaaS are:
    - **Accessibility:** Accessible from any device with an internet connection.
    - **Automatic Maintenance:** Providers handle updates, patches, and maintenance.
    - **Subscription-Based:** Typically offered on a subscription basis, reducing upfront costs.
- **Function as a Service (FaaS) / Serverless Computing:** FaaS allows developers to run code in response to events without managing servers. It abstracts the infrastructure management away, letting users focus solely on code. Examples of FaaS are AWS Lambda, Google Cloud Functions, Microsoft Azure Functions. Key characteristics of FaaS are:
    - **Event-Driven Execution:** Code runs in response to specific events or triggers.
    - **Automatic Scaling:** Scales automatically based on the number of events.
    - **Cost Efficiency:** Pay only for the compute time used, reducing costs associated with idle resources.
    - **Real-Time Data Processing**: Process data streams or events in real-time.
    - **Microservices**: Build and deploy microservices architectures with minimal management.
    - **Automated Workflows**: Trigger workflows or automation tasks in response to specific events.

- **Container as a Service (CaaS):** CaaS provides container-based virtualization where users can deploy and manage containers in a cloud environment. It offers a higher level of abstraction than IaaS but more control than PaaS. Prime examples of CaaS includes Google Kubernetes Engine (GKE), Amazon Elastic Kubernetes Service (EKS), Azure Kubernetes Service (AKS). Key features provided by CaaS are:
    - **Isolation:** Containers provide isolated environments for running applications.
    - **Portability**: Applications run consistently across different environments.
    - **Scalability**: Easily scale containerized applications based on demand.
    - **Microservices Deployment**: Deploy and manage microservices using container orchestration.
    - **DevOps**: Implement continuous integration and continuous deployment (CI/CD) pipelines with containerized applications.
    - **Hybrid Cloud**: Run containerized applications across different cloud providers and on-premises environments.
- **Database as a Service (DBaaS):** DBaaS provides database management and operations over the cloud, allowing users to access and manage databases without handling the underlying infrastructure. Examples include Amazon RDS, Google Cloud SQL, Microsoft Azure SQL Database. Key features:
    - **Automated Management:** Includes backup, scaling, and maintenance.
    - **Accessibility**: Access databases from anywhere with an internet connection.
    - **Scalability**: Easily scale database resources as needed.
    - **Application Databases**: Manage databases for web and mobile applications without infrastructure concerns.
    - **Analytics**: Use cloud databases for big data analytics and reporting.
    - **Data Storage**: Store and manage large volumes of structured and unstructured data.

Choosing the right cloud computing model depends on the specific requirements for control, flexibility, and management. Each model provides distinct advantages and is designed to address different aspects of computing needs in a cloud environment.

2.2. Cloud Computing Deployment Models

Cloud environments can also be deployed in different ways (Mishra, Siddiqui, & Tripathi, 2015):

- **Public Cloud:** In a public cloud model, cloud services are offered over the internet and shared across multiple organizations or users. The cloud service provider owns and manages the infrastructure and resources. Security and incident response responsibilities are shared between the provider and the customer. Examples: Amazon Web Services (AWS), Microsoft Azure, Google Cloud Platform (GCP). Key features provided by public cloud are:
    - **Cost-Effective:** Pay-as-you-go pricing reduces capital expenditure as you only pay for what you use. No need for upfront investment in hardware.
    - **Scalability:** Easily scale resources up or down to meet changing demands.
    - **Maintenance-Free:** The provider handles maintenance, updates, and security.
    - **Accessibility:** Access from anywhere with an internet connection.

      Challenges in public cloud are:
    - **Limited Control:** Less control over the infrastructure compared to other models.
    - **Security Concerns:** Data is stored off-premises, which can raise security and compliance concerns.
- **Private Cloud:** A private cloud is a dedicated cloud environment used exclusively by one organization. It can be hosted on-premises or by a third-party provider but is not shared with other organizations. It offers greater control but requires the organization to handle more aspects of security and incident response. Examples: VMware Cloud Foundation, Microsoft Azure Stack, OpenStack. Key features include:
    - **Control:** Greater control over the infrastructure, including customization of hardware and software. Tailor the infrastructure to meet specific needs.
    - **Security:** Enhanced security and privacy as resources are not shared with others and dedicated to a single organization.
    - **Compliance:** Easier to meet regulatory and compliance requirements.

      Challenges in private cloud are:
    - **Higher Costs:** Typically involves higher upfront costs and maintenance expenses.
    - **Management Overhead:** Requires internal resources for management and maintenance.
- **Hybrid Cloud:** A hybrid cloud combines public and private clouds, allowing data and applications to be shared between them. It offers flexibility in managing workloads and data. However, this model adds complexity to incident response due to the need to manage security across multiple environments.

Examples of hybrid cloud include Microsoft Azure with Azure Stack, AWS Outposts, Google Anthos. Key features of hybrid cloud are:

- **Flexibility:** Leverage the benefits of both public and private clouds. Optimize resource use by balancing between private and public clouds.
- **Optimized Workloads:** Run sensitive or critical workloads in the private cloud while using the public cloud for scalability and cost efficiency.
- **Data Portability:** Easily move data and applications between private and public clouds.
- **Disaster Recovery:** Use the public cloud as a backup or disaster recovery solution for private cloud resources.
- **Data Sovereignty:** Meet data residency requirements by storing sensitive data in a private cloud while utilizing public cloud resources for other needs.

Challenges in implementing hybrid cloud are:

- **Complex Management:** Requires managing and integrating multiple cloud environments.
- **Data Security:** Ensuring consistent security policies across both public and private clouds.

- **Community Cloud:** A community cloud is shared among multiple organizations with common interests or requirements. It is managed by one or more of the participating organizations or by a third party. Examples of community cloud environments are Government clouds, industry-specific clouds for healthcare or finance. Key Features provided by community cloud are:
    - **Shared Resources:** Multiple organizations share the same infrastructure, which can be more cost-effective.
    - **Common Requirements:** Designed to meet the specific needs of the community it serves, such as regulatory compliance or industry standards.
    - **Governance:** Often governed by a consortium of the participating organizations.
    - **Cost Sharing**: Share the cost of infrastructure among multiple organizations.
    - **Custom Fit**: Tailored to the specific needs of the community.
    - **Shared Governance**: Collaborate on governance and management with other community members.

    Challenges:

    - **Complexity:** Coordination and management among multiple organizations can be complex.
    - **Security:** Shared infrastructure can raise security concerns among community members.

Choosing the right cloud deployment model depends on an organization's requirements for control, security, compliance, and cost. Each model offers distinct benefits and challenges, and the choice should align with the organization's strategic goals and operational needs.

Figure 1. Cloud deployment models

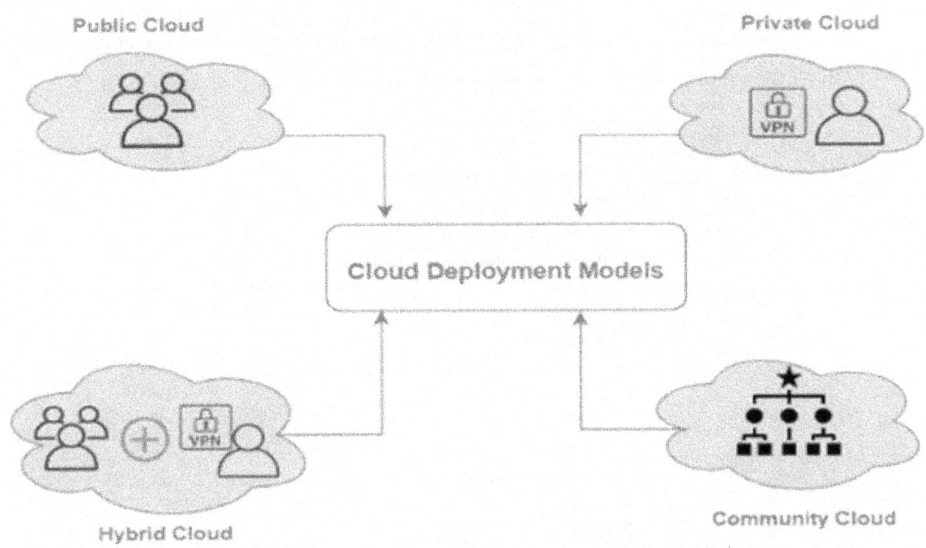

3. RECENT WORK IN CLOUD INCIDENT RESPONSE

Recent research in cloud incident response and forensics reflects a growing emphasis on addressing the unique challenges posed by cloud environments. The field of cloud incident response for forensics is rapidly evolving to address the complexities introduced by modern cloud environments. Ongoing research is focused on developing advanced tools, techniques, and frameworks to improve data collection, analysis, and response capabilities. By addressing challenges related to automation, multi-cloud environments, encryption, and legal considerations, researchers aim to enhance the overall effectiveness of forensic investigations in the cloud. Main aspects of research and development in cloud incident response are:

- Cloud-native Forensic Tools
- Data Integrity
- Automated Incident Detection and Response

- Interoperability
- Data Encryption
- Collaboration Models
- Post-Incident Analysis
- Container and Serverless Forensics
- Edge Computing

Table 1 provides a summary of prominent work done by the researchers in the field of incident response for forensics investigations in cloud environments.

Table 1. Notable work in cloud incident response

Reference	Objective	Approach
(P˘atra¸scu & Patriciu, 2013)	Monitoring and recreating user activity in cloud environments using a secure cloud forensic framework.	Creating a new module, the Cloud Forensic Module, implemented as a series of stand-alone kernel modules and user-space applications that can be activated or disabled at runtime to gather all forensic and log data from the virtual machines that are running inside the virtualization layer.
(Munke & Musuva, 2024)	Implementing Digital Forensics as a Service (DFaaS)	synthesized merge of the two industry best practice standards namely: ISO/IEC 27037 and NIST SP 800-101
(Mahajan, et al., 2023)	cloud security incident detection and response using AI	Decision Tree, random Forest, Neural Network
(Klinkhamhom & Boonyopakorn, 2022)	Analyze, track, and inspect incidents caused by the cyber-attack systematically and effectively	GRR rapid response framework
(Millán, 2021)	Examine different time-series predictions for network traffic analysis	Fourier transform and Multilayer Perceptron (MLP)
(Lotfollahi, Siavoshani, Zade, & Saberian, 2020)	Network traffic classification	Deep Neural Network (DNN)
(CHEN, YU, & ZHOU, 2021)	Intrusion detection	Random forest
(Tang, Gu, & Wang, 2021)	Intrusion detection	Deep Stacking Network model combining decision tree, k-nearest neighbors, deep neural network and random forests
(Shakeel, et al., 2021)	Detecting data scavenging attacks in virtualized resources (VRs).	blockchain technology for access log and control management. logistic regression (LR) for adversary event detection.

continued on following page

Table 1. Continued

Reference	Objective	Approach
(Mukherjee, Sahu, & Sahana, 2023)	Anomaly detection in IoT network	Logistic Regression (LR), Decision Tree (DT), Random Forest (RF), Naïve Bayes (NB), Artificial Neural Network (ANN)
(Abdel-Basset, Hawash, Chakrabortty, & Ryan, 2021)	Intrusions detection in IoT networks	A novel semi-supervised deep learning approach for intrusion detection (SS-Deep-ID)
(Gaurav, Gupta, Hsu, Peraković, & PEÑALVO, 2021)	Detection of DDoS attacks for cloud computing platforms	statistical approach using the concept of cluster entropy and packet score
(Alshammari & Aldribi, 2021)	Detect malicious network traffic in cloud computing	Decision Tree (DT), Neural Networks (NNs), K-nearest neighbor (KNN), Naïve Bayes (NB), Support Vector Machine (SVM), and Finally, Random Forest (RF).
(Sachdeva & Ali, 2021)	Attack detection in a cloud network environment	Analyzing web access log using K-nearest neighbor (KNN), and Multilayer Perceptron (MLP)
(Moustafa & Slay, 2017)	Evidence analysis	Real-time collaborative network Forensic scheme (RCNF) incorporating chi-square for feature selection and correntropy-variation for differentiating normal instance with attack.
(Radhakrishna & Majd, 2024)	Ransomware Detection	Random Forest (RF), Extreme Gradient Boost (XGB), and K-nearest neighbor (KNN)

4. KEY CHALLENGES IN CLOUD INCIDENT RESPONSE

Cloud computing has revolutionized how organizations manage and store data, providing scalable resources, flexibility, and cost-efficiency. However, as cloud adoption grows, so do the complexities associated with managing and securing cloud environments. One critical aspect of cloud security is incident response. Unlike traditional IT environments, cloud infrastructures present unique challenges that require tailored strategies for effective incident management. Incident response in cloud environments presents several challenges not typically encountered in traditional IT settings:

4.1. Dynamic and Elastic Environments

Cloud environments are characterized by their dynamic and elastic nature. Resources can be provisioned and decommissioned at a rapid pace, leading to challenges in tracking and managing these resources during an incident. The transient nature of cloud assets means that traditional methods of inventory and asset management become less effective. For instance, if an instance is terminated during an ongoing incident, critical evidence may be lost, complicating the investigation.

Implementing automated asset tracking tools and maintaining real-time visibility into cloud resources are crucial. Leveraging cloud-native monitoring and logging solutions can help maintain an up-to-date inventory and ensure that all relevant data is captured during an incident.

Figure 2. Major challenges in cloud incident response

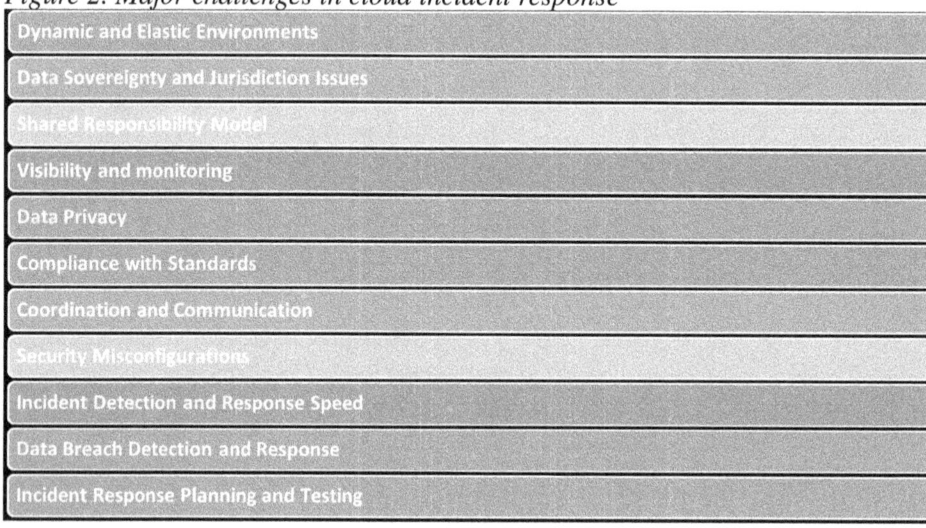

4.2. Data Sovereignty and Jurisdiction Issues

Data sovereignty refers to the concept that data is subject to the laws and regulations of the country in which it is stored. Cloud services often involve multiple jurisdictions due to the global nature of cloud providers. Data may reside in different countries, each with its own legal and regulatory requirements. This geographic dispersion complicates the process of data collection, legal compliance, and evidence preservation. Organizations must ensure that their incident response plans account for these legal requirements, which can vary significantly by jurisdiction.

Organizations should establish clear policies regarding data storage and processing locations. Additionally, understanding the legal requirements of each jurisdiction and working closely with legal teams can help ensure compliance during incident response efforts.

4.3. Shared Responsibility Model

In cloud computing, security is a shared responsibility between the cloud service provider (CSP) and the customer. The cloud service provider is responsible for securing the cloud infrastructure, while the customer is responsible for securing their data, applications, and operating systems. This division can lead to confusion and misalignment, particularly regarding who is accountable for certain aspects of security and incident response and complicated incident response.

When incidents occur, both CSP and customer may need to collaborate closely to address the incident, which can lead to delays if communication is not clear or if responsibilities are not well-defined. This collaboration is crucial for effective resolution, but it requires well-established protocols and understanding. Organizations should establish agreements with cloud providers regarding incident response protocols and ensure that their internal teams are well-versed in their responsibilities. Regular reviews and updates to these agreements can help address any evolving challenges.

4.4. Visibility and monitoring

Cloud environments often involve complex architectures with multiple interconnected services and resources such as virtual machines, containers, serverless functions, and managed services. Each component may be provided by different vendors and may have varying configurations and access controls. This complexity can make it difficult for security teams to gain comprehensive visibility into the environment, hindering the detection and response to incidents.

Cloud service providers (CSPs) manage the underlying infrastructure and often limit the level of access that customers have to these systems. This limitation can hinder an organization's ability to perform detailed forensic analysis or fully understand the scope of an incident. Monitoring tools available to customers may not always provide the depth of visibility needed for effective incident detection and response.

Implementing comprehensive monitoring and logging across all components of the cloud environment is crucial. Utilizing tools that provide end-to-end visibility and integrating security information and event management (SIEM) systems can enhance the ability to detect and respond to incidents effectively.

4.5. Data Privacy

Different cloud providers may store data in various geographic locations, each with their own data privacy laws and compliance requirements. This can create complications in managing and responding to incidents, particularly when data sovereignty issues are involved.

During incident response, handling sensitive data appropriately is critical to maintaining privacy and compliance with regulations such as GDPR or CCPA. The need to collect and analyze data for forensic purposes must be balanced with the need to protect personal and sensitive information.

Implementing data masking and encryption techniques can help protect sensitive information during incident response. Developing data handling policies that align with privacy regulations and ensuring that incident response procedures include privacy considerations can help address these concerns.

4.6. Compliance with Standards

Different industries and regions have specific compliance standards and requirements (e.g., GDPR, HIPAA, PCI-DSS). Incident response teams must ensure that their response actions align with these standards. This alignment often involves maintaining detailed documentation, conducting regular audits, and ensuring that response strategies are updated in accordance with evolving regulations.

4.7. Coordination and Communication

Incident response in a cloud environment often involves multiple stakeholders, including internal teams, cloud providers, and possibly third-party vendors. Effective coordination and communication are essential for a timely and successful response. Establishing a clear incident response plan that includes roles and responsibilities for all stakeholders is vital. Regularly conducting tabletop exercises and ensuring that communication channels are well-defined can help improve coordination during actual incidents.

Effective internal communication is essential for a successful incident response. During an incident, teams must coordinate across various departments, including IT, security, legal, and management. Ensuring that communication channels are clear and that roles are well-defined can help streamline the response process and reduce confusion.

Managing external communication, including notifications to customers, partners, and regulators, is also a critical aspect of incident response. Organizations must balance transparency with protecting sensitive information, which requires careful planning and coordination. Effective communication strategies can help maintain trust and manage the impact of an incident on stakeholders.

4.8. Security Misconfigurations

Cloud environments are susceptible to security misconfigurations due to the sheer number of configuration options and the potential for human error. Misconfigurations can lead to vulnerabilities that are exploited during incidents, exacerbating the impact and complexity of the response.

Implementing automated configuration management tools and conducting regular security assessments can help identify and rectify misconfigurations. Adopting a "security by design" approach and integrating security checks into the deployment pipeline can also reduce the risk of misconfigurations.

4.9. Incident Detection and Response Speed

The speed at which incidents are detected and responded to is critical in minimizing damage. Cloud environments can introduce latency in detection and response due to the distributed nature of resources and the potential delay in communicating between different services and regions.

Employing advanced threat detection solutions, such as behavioral analytics and machine learning-based systems, can improve the speed of incident detection. Automating response workflows and employing orchestration tools can also help reduce response times and mitigate the impact of incidents.

4.10. Data Breach Detection and Response

Detecting data breaches in cloud environments can be challenging due to the dynamic nature of cloud resources. The ability to detect and respond to breaches depends heavily on the effectiveness of monitoring tools and the ability to analyze vast amounts of data for anomalous behavior. Cloud environments may also experience increased data volumes and faster changes, complicating the detection process.

Once a breach is detected, containing and remediating the issue requires rapid action and coordination. In a cloud environment, the steps to contain a breach might include isolating compromised resources, applying security patches, or modifying access controls. The transient nature of cloud resources, combined with the potential involvement of multiple stakeholders, can make these tasks more complex and time-consuming.

4.11. Incident Response Planning and Testing

Developing an effective incident response plan for cloud environments requires an understanding of the specific risks and challenges associated with cloud computing. This includes defining roles and responsibilities, establishing communication protocols, and ensuring that the plan accounts for the unique aspects of cloud infrastructure. Plans must be comprehensive and adaptable to different types of incidents.

Regular testing of incident response plans is crucial for ensuring their effectiveness. However, testing cloud-specific scenarios can be more complex than traditional environments due to the dynamic nature of cloud resources and the involvement of external vendors. Organizations must conduct regular drills and simulations to test their response strategies and update them based on lessons learned from these exercises.

5. BUILDING AN EFFECTIVE CLOUD INCIDENT RESPONSE STRATEGY

An effective incident response strategy for cloud environments should encompass several key components as shown in Figure 3:

Figure 3. Steps in cloud incident response strategy

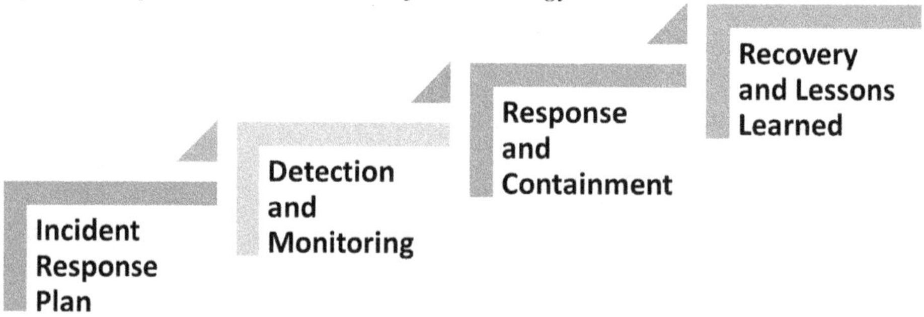

5.1. Incident Response Plan

Developing a robust incident response plan is fundamental to managing security incidents effectively. The plan should outline:

- **Roles and Responsibilities:** Clearly define the roles and responsibilities of internal teams and external partners, including the cloud provider.
- **Communication Protocols:** Establish communication protocols for internal teams, external stakeholders, and the cloud provider. This includes setting up escalation paths and communication channels.
- **Incident Classification and Prioritization:** Create a system for classifying and prioritizing incidents based on their impact and urgency. This helps in allocating resources and addressing the most critical issues first.

5.2. Detection and Monitoring

Effective detection and monitoring are crucial for identifying potential incidents in cloud environments (Khan, Shoaib, Husain, Nisa, & Quasim, 2024). Considerations include:

- **Cloud-native Tools:** Utilize cloud-native monitoring and logging tools provided by the cloud service provider. These tools can offer valuable insights into the health and security of cloud environments.
- **Third-party Solutions:** Integrate third-party security solutions to enhance visibility and detection capabilities. These tools can provide additional layers of protection and analytics.
- **Behavioral Analysis:** Implement behavioral analysis to detect anomalies and potential threats. Machine learning and artificial intelligence can be leveraged to identify unusual patterns that may indicate a security incident.

5.3. Response and Containment

Once an incident is detected, a well-defined response and containment strategy should be in place:

- **Incident Response Team:** Assemble a dedicated incident response team with the expertise needed to address cloud-specific challenges. This team should include members with knowledge of cloud architecture, security, and compliance.
- **Containment Strategies:** Develop strategies to contain and mitigate the impact of an incident. This may involve isolating affected resources, blocking malicious traffic, or rolling back changes.
- **Forensic Analysis:** Conduct forensic analysis to understand the root cause of the incident and gather evidence. This information is crucial for remediation and for preventing future incidents.

5.4. Recovery and Lessons Learned

After containment and resolution, focus on recovery and learning from the incident:

- **Recovery Procedures:** Implement recovery procedures to restore normal operations. This may involve restoring data from backups, reconfiguring systems, or applying patches.
- **Post-Incident Review:** Conduct a post-incident review to analyze the incident, assess the effectiveness of the response, and identify areas for improvement. Document lessons learned and updated the incident response plan accordingly.

6. CLOUD PROVIDER INTEGRATION

Effective incident response in the cloud requires close collaboration with the cloud provider. Key considerations include:

- **Service Level Agreements (SLAs):** Review and understand the SLAs provided by the cloud provider. SLAs typically outline the provider's responsibilities for security and incident response, including response times and remediation obligations.
- **Provider Communication:** Establish clear communication channels with the cloud provider. Ensure that the provider's support teams are aware of your incident response procedures and can provide timely assistance during an incident.
- **Provider Tools and Resources:** Leverage any tools and resources offered by the cloud provider to aid in incident response. This may include access to security logs, incident reporting mechanisms, and response assistance.

7. COMPLIANCE AND LEGAL CONSIDERATIONS

Compliance and legal considerations for incident response in a cloud environment are crucial due to the unique nature of cloud computing, which involves shared infrastructure and data across multiple jurisdictions. Effective incident response not only involves technical and procedural aspects but also must align with legal and regulatory requirements. Key regulatory and compliance requirements which can impact incident response and cloud environments must adhere to are:

- **Data Protection Regulations:** Ensure compliance with data protection regulations such as the General Data Protection Regulation (GDPR), Payment Card Industry Data Security Standard (PCI DSS), Sarbanes-Oxley Act (SOX), Federal Risk and Authorization Management Program (FedRAMP) or the Health Insurance Portability and Accountability Act (HIPAA). These regulations may impose specific requirements for data handling, reporting, and incident response.
- **Legal Obligations:** Understand and comply with any legal obligations related to incident reporting and response. This may include notifying affected parties, regulatory authorities, or law enforcement.
- **Data Residency and Jurisdiction:** Data residency refers to the physical or geographic location of data storage, while jurisdiction involves the legal authority over that data. Different countries have different laws regarding data storage and access, which can complicate incident response.

Ensure compliance with regulations governing the transfer of data across borders, such as GDPR's restrictions on data transfers outside the EU. Ensuring that cloud providers comply with local data residency requirements and restrictions.

- **Cloud Service Provider (CSP) Contracts and SLAs:** Service agreements with cloud providers, including contracts and Service Level Agreements (SLAs), outline responsibilities and obligations related to data security and incident response. These contracts should clearly define the division of security responsibilities between the organization and the CSP, often referred to as the "shared responsibility model."

Ensure that contracts clearly specify the CSP's obligations regarding incident response, data protection, and compliance. Periodically review and update agreements to reflect changes in regulations and business needs.

- **Incident Response Planning and Coordination:** Developing and implementing an incident response plan that addresses both technical and legal aspects of managing incidents in the cloud. The incident response plan defines a detailed plan outlining roles, responsibilities, procedures, and communication strategies for handling incidents. It also specifies how legal, and compliance teams will be involved in the incident response process to ensure adherence to regulations and manage legal risks.

Ensure that IT, legal, compliance, and communication teams work together effectively during an incident. Conduct regular drills and simulations to test the effectiveness of the incident response plan and update it based on lessons learned.

- **Data Breach Notification and Reporting:** Legal requirements for notifying affected parties and regulatory authorities in the event of a data breach.

Adhere to specific timelines for notifying affected individuals and regulators, which can vary by jurisdiction and regulation.

Provide clear and accurate information about the breach, including the nature of the data compromised and steps taken to address the incident.

Maintain detailed records of the breach and response actions to support regulatory reporting and potential legal proceedings.

Develop a communication strategy to manage public relations and mitigate reputational damage.

- **Data Retention and Forensics:** Proper handling of data during and after an incident, including retention, analysis, and forensic investigation.

Implement policies for retaining and managing data related to incidents, including logs, backups, and evidence. Conduct forensic analysis to determine the cause and impact of the incident, ensuring that findings are documented and preserved.

Maintain a documented chain of custody for evidence to support legal proceedings and ensure the integrity of forensic analysis and adhere to regulations governing data retention and forensic investigations.

- **Documentation and Reporting:** Maintain thorough documentation of incidents, including details of the response, remediation efforts, and communications. This documentation is essential for compliance, audits, and legal purposes. Submit required reports to regulatory bodies, if applicable, and address any compliance issues identified. Communicate findings and improvements to relevant stakeholders, including customers, partners, and regulators.

Compliance and legal considerations for incident response in a cloud environment involve understanding and adhering to relevant regulations, managing data residency and jurisdiction issues, ensuring clear agreements with cloud service providers, developing comprehensive incident response plans, and effectively handling breach notifications and forensic investigations. Organizations must coordinate efforts across technical, legal, and compliance teams to manage incidents effectively and minimize legal and reputational risks. Regular reviews and updates to policies and procedures are essential to maintain compliance and improve response capabilities.

8. BEST PRACTICES FOR CLOUD INCIDENT RESPONSE

Adopting best practices can significantly enhance the effectiveness of incident response in cloud environments:

Figure 4. Best practices for cloud incident response strategy

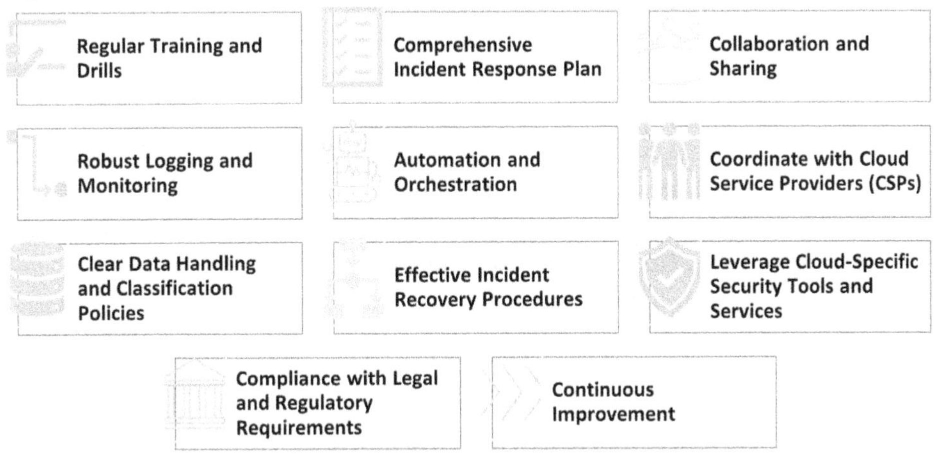

- **Regular Training and Drills:** Conduct regular training and simulation exercises for the incident response team. This helps ensure that team members are familiar with cloud-specific scenarios and response procedures.
    - o Provide training on the IRP, tools, and procedures for handling cloud incidents.
    - o Educate employees about phishing and social engineering attacks that could compromise cloud security.
    - o Conduct regular exercises and simulations to test readiness and improve response skills. Incorporate feedback from exercises and real incidents to continuously improve training programs.

- **Comprehensive Incident Response Plan:** A well-defined incident response plan (IRP) is crucial for managing cloud incidents effectively. This plan should include:
    - o Define who is responsible for different aspects of the response, including cloud service providers (CSPs) and internal teams.
    - o Outline categories of incidents (e.g., data breaches, service outages) and corresponding response protocols.
    - o Establish internal and external communication strategies, including notification requirements and public relations management.
    - o Regularly update and test the IRP to address new cloud services and evolving threats. Conduct tabletop exercises to ensure that all team members are familiar with their roles.
- **Collaboration and Sharing:** Engage in collaboration and information sharing with industry peers and security communities.
    - o Sharing insights and experiences can enhance threat intelligence and improve incident response capabilities.
- **Robust Logging and Monitoring:** Comprehensive logging and monitoring are essential for detecting and responding to incidents.
    - o Enable logging for all critical components, including virtual machines, databases, and network traffic.
    - o Aggregate logs from different sources to a centralized location for easier analysis and correlation.
    - o Implement real-time monitoring to detect anomalies and potential security breaches.
    - o Ensure logs are retained according to compliance requirements and regularly review logs for signs of unusual activity.
- **Automation and Orchestration:** Utilize automation and orchestration tools to streamline incident response processes. Automation can accelerate detection, containment, and remediation, reducing the time required to address incidents. Early detection is key to minimizing the impact of an incident.
    - o Integrate threat intelligence feeds to stay informed about emerging threats and vulnerabilities.
    - o Utilize machine learning and behavioral analytics to identify deviations from normal activity.
    - o Configure alerts for critical events to ensure timely detection and response.
    - o Continuously refine detection strategies based on evolving threats and past incident data.
- **Coordinate with Cloud Service Providers (CSPs):** Effective incident response often requires collaboration with CSPs.

- Review SLAs to understand the provider's responsibilities in incident response.
- Maintain updated contact information for CSP support teams and establish communication channels.
- Understand the shared responsibility model and clarify roles and responsibilities with the CSP.
- Develop a collaborative incident response plan with CSPs to ensure a coordinated approach during incidents.

- **Clear Data Handling and Classification Policies:** Data handling and classification are crucial for protecting sensitive information during an incident.
  - Categorize data based on sensitivity and importance (e.g., public, internal, confidential).
  - Implement strict access controls based on data classification to minimize exposure during an incident. Ensure that sensitive data is encrypted both in transit and at rest.
  - Regularly review and update data handling policies to reflect changes in data sensitivity and compliance requirements.
- **Effective Incident Recovery Procedures:** Recovery procedures are critical for restoring normal operations after an incident.
  - Ensure regular backups of critical data and test restore procedures to verify data integrity.
  - Develop and maintain a disaster recovery plan that includes cloud-specific recovery strategies.
  - Conduct post-incident reviews to identify lessons learned and areas for improvement.
  - Regularly test and update recovery procedures to ensure they are effective and aligned with current cloud infrastructure.
- **Leverage Cloud-Specific Security Tools and Services:** Cloud providers offer various security tools and services to aid in incident detection and response. Utilize these tools to enhance your security posture.
  - Security Information and Event Management (SIEM): Integrate cloud-native SIEM solutions for real-time monitoring and alerting.
  - Implement Cloud Access Security Brokers (CASBs) to monitor and enforce security policies across cloud services.
  - Use automated response capabilities to handle predefined scenarios and reduce response time.
  - Regularly review and configure these tools to ensure they are optimized for your cloud environment and aligned with your security policies.
- **Compliance with Legal and Regulatory Requirements:** Compliance is crucial for managing legal and regulatory aspects of cloud incidents.

- Understand and comply with data privacy laws such as GDPR, CCPA, and HIPAA. Follow regulatory requirements for incident reporting and notification.
  - Maintain detailed documentation of incidents for compliance audits and legal proceedings.
  - Regularly review and update compliance requirements to reflect changes in regulations and industry standards.
- **Continuous Improvement:** Continuously review and improve incident response procedures based on lessons learned from past incidents and evolving threats.
  - Analyze incidents to identify root causes, response effectiveness, and areas for improvement.
  - Track and report metrics related to incident detection, response times, and recovery efforts.
  - Incorporate feedback from incident response teams and stakeholders to enhance the IRP and security posture.
  - Regularly update the incident response plan to address new challenges and incorporate emerging best practices.

9. SUMMARY

Incident response in cloud environments presents unique challenges that require tailored strategies and practices. By understanding the characteristics of cloud computing, addressing key challenges, and implementing a comprehensive incident response strategy, organizations can effectively manage and mitigate security incidents. Collaboration with cloud providers, adherence to compliance requirements, and continuous improvement are essential components of a robust incident response approach. As cloud technologies continue to evolve, staying informed about emerging threats and best practices will be crucial for maintaining a secure and resilient cloud environment.

REFRENCES

Abdel-Basset, M., Hawash, H., Chakrabortty, R. K., & Ryan, M. J. (2021). Semi-supervised spatiotemporal deep learning for intrusions detection in IoT networks. *IEEE Internet of Things Journal*, 8(15), 12251–12265. DOI: 10.1109/JIOT.2021.3060878

Akbar, M., Suaib, M., Husain, M. S., & Shukla, S. (2020). A Compendium of Cloud Forensics. In *Critical Concepts, Standards, and Techniques in Cyber Forensics* (pp. 215-227). IGI Global. DOI: 10.4018/978-1-7998-1558-7.ch012

Alshammari, A., & Aldribi, A. (2021). Apply machine learning techniques to detect malicious network traffic in cloud computing. *Journal of Big Data*, 8(1), 90. DOI: 10.1186/s40537-021-00475-1

CHEN., Z., YU, W., & ZHOU, L. (2021). ADASYN-Random Forest Based Intrusion Detection Model. *4th International Conference on Signal Processing and Machine Learning*, (pp. 152-159).

Gaurav, A., Gupta, B. B., Hsu, C.-H., & Peraković, D., & PEÑALVO, F. J. (2021). Filtering of Distributed Denial of Services (DDoS) Attacks in Cloud Computing Environment. *IEEE International Conference on Communications Workshops (ICC Workshops)*, (pp. 1-6). DOI: 10.1109/ICCWorkshops50388.2021.9473886

Husain, M. S., & Khanum, M. A. (2017). Cloud computing in E-governance: Indian perspective. In *Securing government information and data in developing countries* (pp. 104–114). IGI Global. DOI: 10.4018/978-1-5225-1703-0.ch006

Khan, M. Z., Shoaib, M., Husain, M. S., Nisa, K. U., & Quasim, M. T. (2024). Enhanced mechanism to prioritize the cloud data privacy factors using AHP and TOPSIS: A hybrid approach. *Journal of Cloud Computing (Heidelberg, Germany)*, 13(1), 42. DOI: 10.1186/s13677-024-00606-y

Klinkhamhom, C., & Boonyopakorn, P. (2022). Threat Hunting for Digital Forensic Using GRR Rapid Response with NIST Framework. *37th International Technical Conference on Circuits/Systems, Computers and Communications (ITC-CSCC)*, (pp. 177-180). DOI: 10.1109/ITC-CSCC55581.2022.9894977

Lotfollahi, M., Siavoshani, M. J., Zade, R. S., & Saberian, M. (2020). Deep packet: A novel approach for encrypted traffic classification using deep learning. *Soft Computing*, 24(3), 1999–2012. DOI: 10.1007/s00500-019-04030-2

Mahajan, K., Madhavidevi, B., Supreeth, B. R., Lakshmi, N. V., Joshi, K., & Bavankumar, S. (2023). Detecting and Responding to Cloud Security Incidents based on AI and Forensic Approach. *International Conference on Innovative Computing, Intelligent Communication and Smart Electrical Systems (ICSES)*, (pp. 1-6). DOI: 10.1109/ICSES60034.2023.10465380

Millán, G. (2021). Traffic flows analysis in high-speed computer networks using time series. *arXiv preprint arXiv:2103.03984.*

Mishra, N., Siddiqui, S., & Tripathi, J. P. (2015). A compendium over cloud computing cryptographic algorithms and security issues. *International Journal of Information Technology : an Official Journal of Bharati Vidyapeeth's Institute of Computer Applications and Management*, 7(1), 810–814.

Moustafa, N., & Slay, J. (2017). RCNF: Real-time collaborative network forensic scheme for evidence analysis. *arXiv preprint arXiv:1711.02824.*

Mukherjee, I., Sahu, N. K., & Sahana, S. K. (2023). Simulation and modeling for anomaly detection in IoT network using machine learning. *International Journal of Wireless Information Networks*, 30(2), 173–189. DOI: 10.1007/s10776-021-00542-7

Munke, E., & Musuva, P. M. (2024). *Digital Forensics as a Service Implementation: A Scalable Solution for Cyber Incident Response. IST-Africa Conference*. IST-Africa.

P˘atra¸scu, A., & Patriciu, V.-V. (2013). Beyond Digital Forensics. A Cloud Computing Perspective Over Incident Response and Reporting. *International Symposium on Applied Computational Intelligence and Informatics*, (pp. 455-460). DOI: 10.1109/SACI.2013.6609018

Radhakrishna, T., & Majd, N. E. (2024). Edge Computing Ransomware Detection in IoT using Machine Learning. *Workshop on Computing, Networking and Communications (CNC)*, (pp. 244-248). DOI: 10.1109/ICNC59896.2024.10556351

Sachdeva, S., & Ali, A. (2021). A Hybrid approach using digital forensics for attack detection in a cloud network environment. *International Journal of Future Generation Communication and Networking*, 1536-1546.

Shakeel, P. M., Baskar, S., Fouad, H., Manogaran, G., Saravanan, V., & Montenegro-Marin, C. E. (2021). Internet of things forensic data analysis using machine learning to identify roots of data scavenging. *Future Generation Computer Systems*, 115, 756–768. DOI: 10.1016/j.future.2020.10.001

Tang, Y., Gu, L., & Wang, L. (2021). Deep Stacking Network for Intrusion Detection. *sensors.*

ADDITIONAL READING

Husain, M. S. (2023). Deep Learning. In Big Data Concepts, Technologies, and Applications (pp. 108-123). Taylor & Francis group, CRC Press. DOI: 10.1201/9781003441595-9

Husain, M. S., Faisal, M., Sadia, H., Ahmad, T., & Shukla, S. (2023). *Advances in Cyberology and the Advent of the Next-gen Information Revolution*. IGI Global. DOI: 10.4018/978-1-6684-8133-2

Husain, M. S., & Khan, M. Z. (2019). *Critical Concepts, Standards, and Techniques in Cyber Forensics*. IGI Global.

Iqbal, S., & Alharbi, S. A. (2020). Advancing automation in digital forensic investigations using machine learning forensics. Digital Forensic Science, 3.

Javed, N., Ahmed, T., Faisal, M., Sadia, H., & Sidaine-Daumiller, E. Z. (2023). Workplace cyberbullying in the remote-work era: a new dimension of cyberology. In *Advances in Cyberology and the Advent of the Next-Gen Information Revolution* (pp. 166–177). IGI Global. DOI: 10.4018/978-1-6684-8133-2.ch009

Khan, M. Z., Husain, M. S., & Shoaib, M. (2020). Introduction to email, web, and message forensics. In *Critical concepts, standards, and techniques in cyber forensics* (pp. 174–186). IGI Global. DOI: 10.4018/978-1-7998-1558-7.ch010

Shahid, H. M., Adnan, M. H., Khan, M. Z., Shukla, S., & Khan, F. U. (2022). *Pervasive Healthcare*. Springer International Publishing.

Suaib, M., Akbar, M., & Husain, M. S. (2020). Digital forensics and data mining. In *Critical concepts, standards, and techniques in cyber forensics* (pp. 240–247). IGI Global. DOI: 10.4018/978-1-7998-1558-7.ch014

Wu, C., Wu, H., Lei, S., Li, X., & Tong, H. (2021). Deep Learning in Automatic Fingerprint Identification. IEEE 6th International Conference on Smart Cloud (SmartCloud), (pp. 111-116). DOI: 10.1109/SmartCloud52277.2021.00027

KEY TERMS AND DEFINITIONS

Cloud Access Security Brokers (CASBs): Cloud Access Security Broker (CASB) are security solutions or services that provide visibility and control over an organization's cloud services and applications. They act as intermediaries between users and cloud service providers to enhance security, compliance, and data protection. CASBs offer a range of features designed to address the security challenges associated with cloud computing.

CSP: A Cloud Service Provider (CSP) is a company or organization that offers cloud computing services and resources over the internet. These services typically include infrastructure, platforms, or software that can be used by individuals or businesses without the need to manage physical hardware or software. CSPs provide scalable and on-demand access to various computing resources, such as servers, storage, databases, networking, software applications, and more.

Federal Risk and Authorization Management Program (FedRAMP): Provides a standardized approach to security assessment and authorization for cloud services used by U.S. federal agencies.

General Data Protection Regulation (GDPR): Governs data protection and privacy for individuals in the European Union (EU). It includes requirements for breach notification and data protection impact assessments.

Health Insurance Portability and Accountability Act (HIPAA): Applies to healthcare organizations in the U.S., setting standards for protecting health information and breach notification.

Payment Card Industry Data Security Standard (PCI DSS): Applies to organizations handling credit card information, requiring measures for data protection and breach response.

Sarbanes-Oxley Act (SOX): U.S. law focused on financial reporting and data integrity, which impacts incident response in financial institutions.

SLA: A Service Level Agreement (SLA) is a formal contract or agreement between a service provider (such as a Cloud Service Provider) and a customer that defines the expected level of service. It outlines specific performance metrics, quality standards, and responsibilities that the provider agrees to meet. SLAs serve to set clear expectations and provide a basis for measuring service performance and ensuring accountability.

Section 2
Current Trends in Cyber Forensics

Chapter 6
Social Media Forensics

ABSTRACT

In the digital age, social media has become a central facet of daily life, with billions of users across various platforms. Social media platforms such as Facebook, Twitter, Instagram, LinkedIn, and TikTok have revolutionized how people communicate, share information, and interact (Husain, Khan, & Siddiqui, 2023). While social media provides a rich source of information and connectivity, it also introduces unique challenges for forensic investigation. Social media platforms have become crucial sources of evidence in both criminal and civil investigations. Social media forensics is the specialized field dedicated to uncovering, preserving, and analyzing digital evidence from social media platforms. Given the increasing role of social media in both personal and professional spheres, the need for specialized forensic tools and methodologies is critical. This chapter explores social media forensics, covering its historical development, methodologies, legal and ethical considerations, tools and technologies, and case studies.

1. INTRODUCTION

In the digital age, social media has become a central facet of daily life, with billions of users across various platforms. Social media platforms such as Facebook, Twitter, Instagram, LinkedIn, and TikTok have revolutionized how people communicate, share information, and interact (Husain, Khan, & Siddiqui, 2023). While social media provides a rich source of information and connectivity, it also introduces unique challenges for forensic investigation. Social media platforms have become crucial sources of evidence in both criminal and civil investigations. Social media forensics is the specialized field dedicated to uncovering, preserving, and analyzing digital evidence from social media platforms. Given the increasing role of social media in both personal and professional spheres, the need for specialized forensic tools and methodologies is critical. This chapter explores social media

DOI: 10.4018/979-8-3693-2960-3.ch006

forensics, covering its historical development, methodologies, legal and ethical considerations, tools and technologies, and case studies.

2. EVOLUTION OF SOCIAL MEDIA FORENSICS

- **Early Digital Forensics:** The origins of digital forensics trace back to the early days of computer technology, focusing initially on hard drives and traditional computing devices. Early digital forensic investigations involved recovering data from hard drives, floppy disks, and other physical media. The field was primarily concerned with ensuring the integrity and authenticity of data, which laid the foundation for contemporary forensic practices.
- **Advent of social media:** As the internet evolved, so did the scope of digital forensics, eventually encompassing a wide range of online activities and platforms. Social media began to gain prominence in the early 2000s with platforms such as Friendster, MySpace, and later Facebook and Twitter. These platforms introduced new types of digital evidence, including user-generated content, social interactions, and metadata. The proliferation of social media created a new paradigm for digital forensics, necessitating the development of specialized techniques for handling and analyzing data from these platforms (Husain M. S., 2019).
- **Defining Social Media Forensics:** Social media forensics involves the application of forensic principles to recover, analyze, and present evidence from social media platforms. It encompasses the identification, preservation, and examination of data originating from sites such as Facebook, Twitter, Instagram, and LinkedIn. The goal is to extract reliable and admissible evidence that can support investigations or legal proceedings (Khan, Husain, & Khan, 2018) (Adnan, Ariffin, Hanafi, Husain, & Panessai, 2021).
    - **Goals of Social Media Forensics:**

As shown in Figure 1 the main objectives of social media forensics are: reconstruction of past events, identifying criminal activities, locating hidden networks, and analyzing public sentiments regarding an event/policy (Bokolo & Liu, 2024).

Figure 1. Goals of social media forensics

Reconstruction of past events	Thoroughly analyzing user activities and social media interactions. forensics timelines helps in reconstructing events related to cyber attacks, fake news dissemination or illegal activities.
Identifying criminal activities	Forensics analysis of Social media can help the investigators in collecting proof and tracking illegal activities like online fraud, cyberbullying, and online harassment.
Locating hidden networks	Examining social media connections can uncover communication and association patterns, supporting investigations into organized crime, terrorist groups, and other criminal networks.
Analyzing public sentiments	Business organizations, and governments are making use of huge volume of data available in the form of social media posts to gain valuable insights into public opinion and sentiments on various topics to understand societal trends and make informed decisions.

- **Evolution of Social Media Forensics:** As social media platforms evolved, so did the field of social media forensics. The introduction of mobile apps, real-time updates, and multimedia content added complexity to forensic investigations. Social media forensics had to adapt to handle the diverse types of data generated by these platforms, including text posts, images, videos, and geolocation data (Yadav, 2020). The field continues to evolve with advancements in technology and changes in social media usage patterns.
    - Advanced Data Analysis: As social media usage expanded, forensic techniques became more advanced. Analysts started employing sophisticated methods to examine metadata, timestamps, and geolocation data, allowing them to create detailed profiles and timelines of user activities (Pasquini, Amerini, & Boato, 2021). Investigators began to focus on collecting not only public content but also private messages, metadata, and deleted posts. Advanced software allowed law enforcement and forensic experts to extract and preserve evidence from various platforms, including Instagram, Snapchat, and LinkedIn.
    - Integration of AI and Machine Learning for Big Data Analysis: With the explosion of data on platforms like Facebook, Twitter, TikTok, and YouTube, social media forensics entered an era of big data analysis. Investigators now use advanced algorithms, machine learning, and artificial intelligence to sift through massive amounts of data for relevant

evidence. This includes identifying trends, mapping connections between individuals, uncovering hidden networks, detecting anomalies and potential manipulations in multimedia content. These technologies also allow for more efficient analysis of multimedia content, such as images, videos, and live streams.

- Deepfake Detection: With the rise of deepfake technology, forensic analysts developed specialized tools to detect and analyze manipulated videos and images. This became crucial in maintaining the integrity of digital evidence (Fakiha, 2020).
- Cross-Platform Analysis: Modern social media forensics involves cross-platform analysis, where data from multiple social media sites is aggregated and analyzed together. This helps in understanding the broader context and connections between different pieces of evidence (Josephine, Shekar, Meghana, Rao, & Rajesh, 2019).
- Legal and Ethical Considerations: The rapid pace of change, encryption technologies, and privacy concerns make it more difficult to extract data without violating users' rights. Legal and ethical issues surrounding the collection and use of social media data also pose significant challenges, requiring investigators to navigate complex laws around privacy and consent. Ensuring the privacy and rights of individuals while conducting forensic investigations became a critical concern (Fakiha, 2020).

The evolution of social media forensics reflects broader trends in technology and society. From simple data collection to the application of advanced analytics and AI, social media forensics has become a powerful tool in modern criminal investigations, although it continues to face challenges related to privacy, security, and legal frameworks.

3. SOCIAL MEDIA DATA FOR CYBER FORENSICS

Social media platforms generate a diverse range of data. In the context of forensic analysis, social media data is a critical component for investigating and understanding digital evidence. The various types of social media data are textual data, multimedia, metadata, and user interactions. Analysis of this data provides different layers of information that can be crucial in forensic investigations.

3.1. Textual Data

Textual data refers to the written content shared on social media platforms. This includes status updates, tweets, posts, comments, replies, and messages. It encompasses any form of written communication or textual expression provided by users. Textual data is used to understand user sentiments, opinions, and interactions, and can provide insights into trends, behaviors, or events. Key aspects of textual data are:

- **Posts:** Short or long-form text shared on platforms like Facebook or LinkedIn.
- **Tweets:** Concise messages or updates posted on Twitter, often limited to a specific character count.
- **Comments and Replies:** Textual responses or feedback on posts or other content.
- **Messages:** Private or direct messages exchanged between users Posts, comments, direct messages.
  - **Role of textual data from social media in Forensic Analysis:**
- **Evidence of Communication:** Textual data, such as posts, comments, and messages, can provide direct evidence of communication between individuals, revealing their thoughts, intentions, and interactions.
- **Context and Intent:** Analyzing the content of posts and messages can help investigators understand the context of events and the intent behind certain actions or statements. This is particularly useful in cases involving harassment, threats, or conspiracy.
- **Timeline Construction:** Textual data can be used to reconstruct timelines of events based on timestamps and content, which is crucial for understanding the sequence of actions and verifying alibis.

3.2. Multimedia

Multimedia refers to any non-textual content shared on social media platforms, including images, videos, audio files, and other media formats. This type of data adds visual or auditory elements to the text and can enhance communication or provide entertainment. Multimedia can provide context to textual data, illustrate events, capture user experiences, and convey emotions or messages in a more engaging way. Key aspects of multimedia are:

- **Images:** Photos or graphics shared in posts, comments, or messages.
- **Videos:** Clips or full-length videos uploaded or shared on platforms like YouTube, Instagram, or TikTok.

- o **Audio Files:** Sound recordings, such as podcasts or voice messages, shared on social media.
- o **Infographics:** Visual representations of data or information.
  - **Role of multimedia from social media in Forensic Analysis:**
- o **Visual Evidence:** Images and videos can serve as direct evidence of events, locations, and individuals. For example, photos of a crime scene or video footage of an incident can provide critical visual evidence.
- o **Verification and Authentication:** Multimedia content can be analyzed to verify its authenticity using techniques like forensic image analysis or video integrity checks. This helps confirm whether the content has been altered or is genuine.
- o **Contextual Analysis:** Multimedia can provide context to textual data, helping to illustrate or corroborate written statements. For example, a photo tagged with a location can support claims made in a post.

3.3. Metadata

Metadata refers to the data that describes and provides context about other data. In the social media context, metadata includes information about the content, such as timestamps, geolocation, file formats, and user data. Metadata helps to contextualize and verify the authenticity of content, track the origin and timing of posts, and support investigations by providing additional information. Key aspects of metadata are:

- o **Timestamps:** The date and time when a post, comment, or multimedia file was created or shared.
- o **Geolocation:** Information about the physical location where the content was created or accessed.
- o **File Attributes:** Details about file size, type, and resolution for multimedia content.
- o **User Information:** Data about the user who created or interacted with the content, including user IDs and usernames.
  - **Role of metadata from social media in Forensic Analysis:**
- o **Authentication and Verification:** Metadata such as timestamps, geolocation data, and file attributes provide essential details for verifying the authenticity of content and establishing its context. For example, timestamps can help confirm when an image or post was created.
- o **Timeline Reconstruction:** Metadata helps build accurate timelines of events by providing precise information about when and where content was created or modified.

- **Linkage of Evidence:** Metadata can link different pieces of evidence by showing connections between various data points, such as user locations and interaction times.

3.4. User Interactions

User interactions encompass all forms of engagement between users and content on social media platforms. This includes actions such as likes, shares, comments, mentions, and follows. User interactions reflect the level of engagement with content, help gauge the popularity or impact of posts and can provide insights into social dynamics and relationships on the platform. Key aspects of user interaction are:

- **Likes/Reactions:** Indicators of approval or emotional response to content, such as thumbs up, heart, or other reaction buttons.
- **Shares/Retweets:** Actions where users distribute or amplify content to their own followers or networks.
- **Comments:** User responses or feedback on posts, providing additional context or opinions.
- **Mentions/Tags:** Instances where users reference or tag other users in their posts or comments.
- **Follows/Subscribes:** Actions where users choose to receive updates from other users or content creators.
  - **Role of user interaction from social media in Forensic Analysis:**
- **Behavioral Patterns:** Analyzing user interactions, such as likes, shares, and comments, can reveal patterns of behavior and social connections. This is useful for understanding relationships and influence networks.
- **Engagement Evidence:** Interactions with content can provide evidence of a user's engagement with specific topics or individuals, which can be relevant in cases involving online communities or coordinated activities.
- **Corroboration of Evidence:** User interactions can corroborate other forms of evidence by showing support or opposition to specific content or actions, helping to validate findings.

Social media data provides valuable insights and evidence in forensic investigations. Each data type on social media platforms presents unique challenges for forensic analysis, necessitating specialized tools to handle the volume, variety, and veracity of information. By understanding and effectively utilizing textual data, multimedia, metadata, and user interactions, forensic experts can uncover crucial information, build accurate case narratives, and support legal proceedings.

4. METHODOLOGIES IN SOCIAL MEDIA FORENSICS

Social media forensics consist of following steps:

Figure 2. Steps in social media forensics

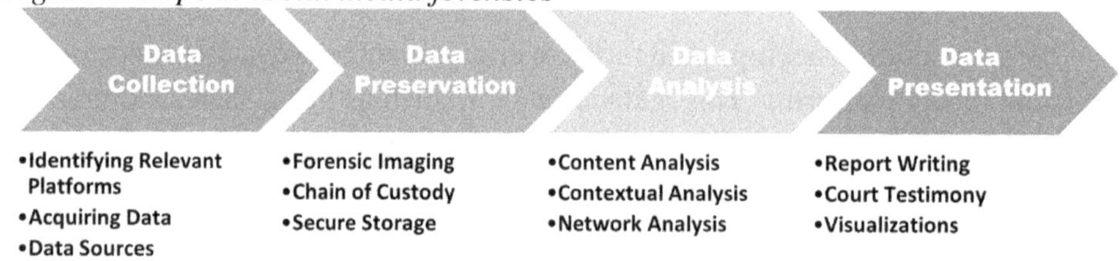

4.1. Data Collection

Data collection is a critical first step in social media forensics and involves several key processes:

- **Identifying Relevant Platforms**: Investigators must determine which social media platforms may contain relevant evidence. This involves understanding the types of data available on each platform and assessing the potential value of the data.
- **Acquiring Data**: Data acquisition involves capturing data, which may include posts, messages, photos, videos, and metadata from social media platforms in a manner that preserves its integrity. Techniques for data acquisition include using platform APIs, web scraping tools, and forensic imaging software.
- **Data Sources**: Social media data can be sourced directly from user accounts, public profiles, or through third-party tools, or APIs that provide access to historical data. Investigators must consider the scope and limitations of each data source.

4.2. Data Preservation

Preservation involves ensuring that collected data remains intact and unaltered. Techniques include:

- **Forensic Imaging:** Creating exact copies of digital evidence to ensure that the original data remains unaltered. Forensic imaging tools capture bit-for-bit copies of data, preserving all content and metadata.

- **Chain of Custody:** Documenting the handling of evidence to maintain its credibility. The chain of custody involves tracking who has accessed or handled the evidence and ensuring that it has not been tampered with.
- **Secure Storage:** Storing evidence in a secure environment to prevent unauthorized access. This includes using encryption and access controls to protect data from being altered or accessed by unauthorized individuals.

4.3. Data Analysis

Data analysis involves examining and interpreting social media data to extract relevant information. Key aspects of data analysis include:

- **Content Analysis:** Examining posts, messages, and other content to identify relevant evidence. This may involve analyzing textual content, images, and videos to determine their significance.
- **Contextual Analysis:** Understanding the context in which data was created or shared. This includes examining timestamps, geolocation data, and the relationship between users to gain insight into the meaning and relevance of the content.
- **Network Analysis:** Analyzing social connections and interactions between users. Network analysis can reveal patterns, relationships, and associations that are relevant to the investigation.

4.4. Data Presentation

Data presentation involves communicating forensic findings in a clear and understandable manner. Key aspects of data presentation include:

- **Report Writing:** Creating comprehensive reports that detail the forensic process, findings, and interpretations. Reports should be clear, concise, and well-organized to support legal proceedings.
- **Court Testimony:** Providing expert testimony in court to explain the forensic process and the significance of the evidence. Forensic experts must be prepared to answer questions and clarify their findings for judges and juries.
- **Visualizations:** Using charts, graphs, and other visual aids to illustrate key findings and connections. Visualizations can help convey complex information and highlight important connections and patterns.

5. RECENT WORK

Recent research in social media forensics has evolved to address the complex challenges posed by the ever-expanding scope of social media platforms and the increasing sophistication of digital evidence. This field continues to advance as new technologies emerge and social media usage grows. Key aspects of the research are:

- Automated Evidence Collection and Analysis
- Enhancing Data Privacy
- Metadata Extraction
- Maintaining Metadata Integrity
- Metadata Analysis
- Cross-Platform Forensics
- Counter Interoperability Challenges
- Digital Evidence Authenticity and Integrity
- Behavioral Analysis and Sentiment Analysis
- Integration of Forensic and Legal Standards

Table 1 provides a summary of notable work done by the researchers in the field of social media forensics analysis.

Table 1. Notable work in social media forensics

Reference	Objective	Approach
(Grigaliūnas, Brūzgienė, & Venčkauskas, 2023)	User profiling and evidence linking	Ontology model
(Theophilo, Giot, & Rocha, 2023)	Authorship Attribution of social media messages	Deep Neural Network (DNN)
(Ibrahim, Essameldin, & Saad, 2024)	Hate Speech Detection for cyberbullying	Neutrosophic Logic within the Multi-Layer Perceptron (MLP) model
(Daradkeh, 2023)	Identifying link between Privacy and Disclosure Behavior in Social Networks	composite reliability (CR), and average variance extracted (AVE)
(Javed, Ahmed, Faisal, Sadia, & Sidaine-Daumiller, 2023)	Discovering Workplace Cyberbullying in the Remote-Work Era	Providing a detailed survey exhibiting the danger of cyberbullying
(Akbar, Suaib, & Hussain, 2023)	Detecting Deepfake on social media using ML	Linear Regression, Decision Tree, K-Means, Random Forest, Generative Adversarial Networks (Gans)
(Koru & Uluyol, 2024)	Fake news detection on social media	BERT deep learning model

continued on following page

Table 1. Continued

Reference	Objective	Approach
(Hu, Liao, Wang, & Qin, 2022)	Deepfake video detection	Convolutional Neural Network (CNN)
(Qiao, et al., 2024)	Detecting Synthesized Fake Images	Deep Neural Network (DNN)
(Padilha, et al., 2022)	Content-Aware Detection of timestamp manipulation	Convolutional Neural Network (CNN)
(Madhusudhanan, Jose, Sahoo, & Malekian, 2023)	Privacy-Preservation	Pattern identification in Locale of Users with Mining (PLUM) tree for pattern mining and Genetic Algorithm (GA)
(Sharrab, Al-Fraihat, & Alsmirat, 2023)	Detection of suspicious text on social media	Long Short-Term Memory (LSTM)
(Gazeau, Gupta, & An, 2024)	Social Media Data Collection for Digital Forensic Investigations	Web parser
(Shullani, Baracchi, Iuliani, & Piva, 2022)	Social Network Identification of Laundered Videos	DCT (Discrete cosine transform) coefficient
(Rafique, Nawaz, Kibriya, & Masood, 2021)	DeepFake Detection	convolution neural network (CNN) models: Alex Net and Shuffle Net
(Kraetzer, Siegel, Seidlitz, & Dittmann, 2022)	Modelling of media for forensic detection of DeepFake videos	Process-Driven Modelling based on established guidelines

6. TOOLS AND TECHNOLOGIES IN SOCIAL MEDIA FORENSICS

A wide array of tools is available for social media forensics, each designed to address specific aspects of data collection and analysis. These tools can be broadly categorized into:

6.1. Forensic Software

Forensic software tools are essential for capturing, analyzing, and presenting social media data. Various software tools are available for social media forensics, including:

- **X1 Social Discovery:** A specialized tool for searching, capturing, and analyzing social media data. It offers advanced search capabilities and the ability to capture and analyze large volumes of social media data from sources like Facebook, websites, Tumblr, Instagram, YouTube, and IMAP email.

X1 Social Discovery collects social media in a legally defensible manner, preserves the chain of custody, and uses the same court-accepted digital hashing algorithm used by digital forensics and eDiscovery professionals to validate and authenticate their data (DISCOVERY)

- **FTK Imager:** A forensic imaging tool that can capture data from social media platforms and create exact copies of digital evidence. FTK features powerful file filtering and search functionality and is recognized as the leading forensic tool for e-mail analysis. FTK Imager is a free data preview and imaging tool used to acquire electronic evidence in a forensically sound manner by creating copies of computer data without making changes to the original evidence. FTK Imager is widely used and trusted tool for preserving the integrity of data (Exterro).
- **Paraben E3:** Provides tools for data extraction, analysis, and reporting. Paraben E3 supports a wide range of digital evidence sources, including social media platforms. E3 Platform is a comprehensive digital forensic tool designed to handle more data, effectively and efficiently (Corporation).
- **Cellebrite UFED:** A leading mobile forensics tool that also supports extraction from social media apps. It allows investigators to extract, decode, and analyze data from a variety of sources. Cellebrite UFED is a cost-effective, flexible, and convenient software that follow industry Standard for Lawfully Accessing and Collecting Digital Data (Cellebrite).

6.2. Data Extraction Tools

Data extraction tools assist in obtaining data from social media platforms. Key tools include:

- **Web Scraper:** Automated tools that Extract data from complex and dynamic web pages or web sites. Web scrapers can be customized to extract specific types of information from social media sites (Web scraper).
- **API Access:** API access Interact with and utilize the functionalities provided by an Application Programming Interface (API). These tools allow mobile apps, developers' frameworks, and software applications to access and use data from a given API. Properly manage interactions with an API ensure authorized access to structured data and allow for automated data collection while protecting sensitive data and maintaining system integrity.
- **Browser Extensions:** Add-ons that facilitate data extraction from social media sites. Browser extensions can be used to capture content from web-based platforms.

6.3. Data Analysis Tools

Tools for analyzing social media data include:

- **Social Network Analysis (SNA) Tools:** Tools for mapping and analyzing social relationships and interactions among peoples, groups or organizations. SNA tools help identify connections and patterns within social networks using graph models where Nodes represent network members, like people, organizations, or computers. Meanwhile, Edges are their direct connections, showing interactions. Popular SNA tools include Gephi, UCINET (UCI Network), and NodeXL.
- **Text Analysis Software:** Text analysis software helps users gain insights from both structured and unstructured text data. These tools are used for analyzing textual data, including sentiment or emotion analysis and keyword extraction. Text analysis software can reveal insights from written content. Amazon Comprehend, Google Cloud Natural Language, IBM Watson Natural Language Understanding, and Microsoft Azure Text Analytics are some popular text analysis software.
- **Maltego:** This tool is used for link analysis and visualization. It helps investigators map out relationships and connections between social media accounts, assisting in identifying networks and patterns.
- **Social Links:** Focuses on open-source intelligence (OSINT) and social media investigations. It provides data aggregation and visualization capabilities, which are crucial for analyzing complex social media interactions.
- **EnCase Forensic:** A comprehensive digital forensic tool that supports a wide range of data sources, including social media. It is used for in-depth analysis and evidence presentation.

6.4. Data Preservation Tools

- **Preservica:** Provides long-term digital preservation solutions, ensuring that social media evidence remains accessible and unaltered over time.
- **CaseGuard:** Offers tools for redacting sensitive information in social media evidence while preserving the original data's integrity.

6.5. Emerging Technologies

- **Artificial Intelligence (AI) and Machine Learning:** AI and machine learning technologies are increasingly integrated into forensic tools to enhance

data analysis capabilities. These technologies can automate pattern recognition, sentiment analysis, and anomaly detection.
- **Blockchain Technology:** Used to ensure the integrity and authenticity of digital evidence. Blockchain provides a tamper-proof ledger for tracking changes and access to social media data.

7. LEGAL AND ETHICAL CONSIDERATIONS IN SOCIAL MEDIA FORENSICS

7.1. Legal Framework

The legal framework for social media forensics is multifaceted, involving various regulations and laws that govern the collection, preservation, and use of digital evidence. Key legal considerations include:

- **Privacy Laws:** Privacy regulations such as the General Data Protection Regulation (GDPR) in Europe and the California Consumer Privacy Act (CCPA) in the United States impose restrictions on the collection and processing of personal data. Forensic investigators must navigate these laws to ensure compliance while conducting investigations.
- **Search and Seizure:** Traditional legal principles governing search and seizure apply to digital evidence. Law enforcement agencies often need to obtain warrants or subpoenas to access social media data. The legal process for obtaining these orders can vary by jurisdiction and may require demonstrating probable cause.
- **Admissibility of Evidence:** Forensic evidence must meet legal standards for admissibility in court. This includes demonstrating the authenticity and reliability of the evidence, as well as ensuring that the evidence was obtained through lawful means.

7.2. Ethical Issues

Ethical considerations in social media forensics are crucial to maintaining the integrity of the investigative process. Key ethical issues include:

- **Informed Consent:** Obtaining informed consent from individuals whose data is being accessed is an important ethical consideration. While consent may not always be required in legal investigations, ethical guidelines advocate for transparency and respect for individuals' privacy.

- **Privacy:** Balancing the need for evidence with respect for individual privacy is a central ethical challenge. Forensic investigators must ensure that data is accessed and used in a manner that minimizes invasion of privacy and avoids unnecessary exposure of sensitive information.
- **Data Integrity:** Ensuring the integrity and authenticity of digital evidence is critical to maintaining its credibility. Forensic investigators must employ rigorous procedures to preserve the authenticity of data and avoid contamination or tampering.

8. CHALLENGES AND LIMITATIONS IN SOCIAL MEDIA FORENSICS

While the tools and technologies available are powerful, several challenges persist in social media forensics:

- **Data Volatility:** Social media data is highly dynamic. Posts, comments, and profiles can be deleted or modified by users, making it difficult to recover original content and leading to gaps in the evidence. This volatility poses challenges for preservation and recovery, requiring forensic investigators to act quickly and employ techniques for capturing data before it changes. Ensuring timely collection and preservation is crucial to maintaining evidence integrity.

Use of tools to take snapshots or archival copies of social media content and implementation of continuous monitoring to capture data before it changes or disappears is highly recommended.

- **Platform Variability:** Different social media platforms have varying data structures, privacy settings, APIs, user interfaces and access mechanisms. This variability complicates the forensic process, requiring investigators to adapt their methods for each platform. Data formats and access methods vary between platforms, requiring specialized tools and techniques. Platform APIs may have limitations on data access or functionality.

To mitigate these issues, using or developing forensic tools tailored to the specific requirements of each platform and developing expertise, or partnerships with forensic professionals who specialize in specific social media platforms are advised.

- **Encryption and Privacy Features:** The increasing use of encryption and privacy features on social media platforms can hinder access to data. Forensic investigators may need to use specialized techniques or tools to bypass or work around these protections (Mohammad, 2023). Encrypted messages or posts may be inaccessible without decryption keys. User privacy settings can limit the visibility of content and complicate data collection.

Seeking legal avenues to access encrypted or restricted content when necessary and working with social media platforms to obtain data that is subject to privacy controls can help in countering these challenges.

- **Legal and Ethical Issues:** Accessing and using social media data raises significant privacy and legal concerns, especially regarding user consent and data protection laws. Navigating legal and jurisdictional issues can be complex, especially when dealing with international platforms and laws. Investigators must be aware of and comply with legal requirements in different jurisdictions. Balancing the need for investigation with respect for individual privacy is a critical concern. Obtaining the necessary legal permissions to access and use social media data can be challenging.

Key challenges involved are Ensuring that collected data is used appropriately and not exploited for unintended purposes, following established ethical guidelines and standards for social media forensics, and Maintaining transparency about the methods and purposes of data collection and analysis.

Working with legal professionals to ensure compliance with relevant privacy and data protection laws and obtaining appropriate warrants or permissions before accessing private social media content can help in resolving these issues.

- **Data Complexity:** The vast amount of data and the complexity of data generated on social media social media interactions can overwhelm forensic tools making it challenging to identify relevant information. Storing and managing large datasets requires substantial resources. Also filtering through vast amounts of data to find pertinent details can be time-consuming and complex. Effective analysis requires sophisticated algorithms and human expertise to interpret results accurately.

Implementing machine learning and AI tools to assist with data processing and pattern recognition and utilizing advanced search and filtering tools to narrow down relevant information can mitigate these challenges.

- **Platform-Specific Challenges:** Different social media platforms have unique data structures and security measures. Forensic tools must be adaptable to handle variations in data formats and access methods.

Social media platforms frequently update their features, interfaces, and policies, which can impact forensic analysis. New features or changes to existing ones can alter how data is stored and accessed. Updates to platform policies may affect data retention and availability.

Keeping abreast of platform changes and their potential impact on forensic processes and regularly updating forensic tools and methods to accommodate changes in social media platforms can help in dealing with dynamic nature of social media platforms.

- **Data Integrity and Authenticity:** Ensuring the integrity and authenticity of social media data is crucial for forensic investigations. Data can be manipulated or fabricated. The presence of fake profiles and misleading information can compromise the credibility of the data. Verifying the authenticity of the data and its source can be difficult.

Maintaining a detailed chain of custody for all collected data and cross-reference social media data with other sources to confirm authenticity is recommended.

- **Contextual Interpretation:** Social media content often lacks context, which can make interpreting its meaning and relevance challenging. Out-of-context posts or messages can lead to misinterpretation of their intent or significance. Understanding regional slang, idioms, and cultural references is crucial for accurate interpretation.

Considering the broader context of social media interactions and content and engaging with cultural and linguistic experts to ensure accurate interpretation can resolve these issues.

- **Data Ownership and Access Issues:** Issues related to data ownership and access rights can arise when dealing with social media data. Disagreements over who owns the data or has the right to access it can delay investigations. Gaining access to private accounts or data may be restricted by platform policies.

To counter these challenges the key is to establish clear policies and agreements regarding data ownership and access. Also, seeking legal assistance to resolve disputes over data access and ownership can help in mitigating data access issues.

9. CASE STUDIES IN SOCIAL MEDIA FORENSICS

Social media forensics is applied across various domains, including law enforcement, corporate investigations, and cybersecurity. Companies use social media forensics to monitor brand reputation, investigate employee misconduct, and ensure compliance with regulations. Data analysis tools help in detecting fraudulent activities and assessing risks. In cybersecurity, social media forensics is employed to identify and mitigate threats, such as phishing attacks and social engineering schemes. Analyzing social media data helps in understanding attack vectors and developing countermeasures.

Some notable case study examples include:

- **Criminal Investigation Case example:** A case study involving a criminal investigation illustrates the application of social media forensics in real-world scenarios. Social media forensics helps law enforcement agencies in tracking suspects, gathering evidence, and establishing timelines. Tools are used to analyze communications, identify criminal networks, and recover deleted data. For instance, a murder investigation may use social media data to establish timelines, identify suspects, or uncover motives:
  - **Establish Timelines:** Analyze posts and messages to establish a timeline of events leading up to the crime.
  - **Identify Suspects:** Examine interactions and connections to identify potential suspects or witnesses.
  - **Uncover Motives:** Investigate content and communications to uncover possible motives or conflicts.
- **Civil Litigation Case example:** Social media forensics can also play a role in civil court cases such as defamation or employment disputes. In these cases, forensic analysis might reveal evidence of harassment, false statements, or violations of company policies. For example, a defamation case may involve:
  - **Gathering Evidence:** Collecting posts, comments, and messages related to the alleged defamation.
  - **Analyzing Impact:** Assessing the impact of the defamatory content on the plaintiff's reputation and seeking evidence of harm.
  - **Supporting Claims:** Using forensic analysis to support claims of false statements or harassment.

- **The Social Media Fraud Scandal:** Several fraud schemes have exploited social media platforms to deceive individuals and organizations, including investment scams and phishing attacks.

Analysts examined social media profiles and communications to identify fraudulent activities and perpetrators. Investigators reviewed phishing schemes to trace the source and methods used by scammers. Social media was used to alert potential victims and gather information about the scope of the fraud.

Social media forensics has been instrumental in uncovering and prosecuting fraudulent schemes. The approach to detecting and mitigating social media fraud continues to evolve as scammers develop new tactics.

- **The NXIVM Cult Investigation:** NXIVM was a self-help organization led by Keith Raniere, which was exposed as a criminal cult involved in sex trafficking and other illegal activities.

Social media posts and communications were analyzed to document the activities of cult members and their interactions. Investigators examined how the cult used social media to recruit new members and maintain control. Social media content was used as evidence in court to illustrate the cult's operations and abuse.

The investigation led to the arrest and conviction of key figures, including Raniere. Social media forensics provided crucial evidence of the cult's practices and the manipulation of victims.

- **The Boston Marathon Bombing:** The Boston Marathon bombing on April 15, 2013, was a tragic event in which two homemade bombs were detonated, killing three people and injuring hundreds.

Authorities used social media to gather information and identify potential suspects. Images and videos posted by bystanders were analyzed to locate the bombers. Social media platforms were used to request assistance from the public to identify suspects. This led to the identification of Tamerlan and Dzhokhar Tsarnaev. Social media profiles and communications were examined to track the suspects' activities and connections.

The Tsarnaev brothers were identified and apprehended. Social media played a crucial role in the initial investigation and public engagement. The case demonstrated the power of social media in rapidly disseminating information and gathering evidence.

- **The Capitol Riot:** On January 6, 2021, a mob stormed the U.S. Capitol in Washington, D.C., leading to multiple arrests and extensive damage.

Investigators analyzed social media posts, live streams, and photos shared by participants to identify individuals involved in the riot. Social media activity was correlated with physical evidence and security footage to build cases against suspects. Social media was used to understand the organization and coordination of the riot.

Numerous individuals were arrested and charged based on social media evidence. The case highlighted the ability of social media to provide real-time evidence of criminal activity and the importance of cross-referencing digital and physical evidence.

- **The Jeffrey Epstein Case:** Jeffrey Epstein, a financier and convicted sex offender, was arrested in 2019 on charges of sex trafficking minors.

Social media was used to trace Epstein's network of associates and identify potential victims. Posts, messages, and connections on social media helped corroborate testimonies and link Epstein to various individuals. Social media campaigns were employed to encourage other victims to come forward. Epstein's arrest and subsequent death in custody highlighted the role of social media in investigating high-profile criminal cases and gathering evidence of criminal networks.

- **The Christchurch Mosque Shootings:** On March 15, 2019, a gunman attacked two mosques in Christchurch, New Zealand, resulting in 51 deaths and numerous injuries.

The attacker live-streamed the attack on Facebook. Investigators analyzed the live stream and associated posts to understand the attacker's actions and motivations. The shooter's social media accounts were scrutinized to uncover extremist views, connections with radical groups, and planning details. Platforms and authorities worked together to quickly remove the video and related content to prevent further dissemination.

The investigation revealed the shooter's radicalization process and connections with extremist ideologies. The case highlighted the challenges of managing live-streamed content and the need for rapid response to prevent the spread of harmful material.

- **The Gabby Petito Case:** Gabby Petito, a 22-year-old van-life blogger, was reported missing in September 2021. Her body was later found in Wyoming, and her fiancé, Brian Laundrie, was a person of interest.

Petito's social media posts, including photos and videos, were analyzed for geolocation data, which helped narrow down the search area. Investigators reviewed social media interactions and posts for potential clues about relationship dynamics and possible motives. Social media was used to spread awareness and solicit tips from the public.

The investigation utilized social media extensively to trace Petito's last movements and gather information about her relationship with Laundrie. Laundrie's eventual death and the discovery of Petito's body underscored the role of social media in missing persons' cases.

- **The Cambridge Analytica Scandal:** Cambridge Analytica was a political consulting firm accused of improperly harvesting personal data from millions of Facebook users to influence elections.

Investigators analyzed how data was collected and used by Cambridge Analytica, including examining social media APIs and data handling practices. Social media platforms were scrutinized to understand the scope and impact of the data misuse. Social media evidence played a key role in legal actions against the company and its affiliates.

The scandal exposed significant issues with data privacy and social media practices. It led to regulatory changes and greater scrutiny of how social media data is used by political and commercial entities.

10. BEST PRACTICES FOR SOCIAL MEDIA FORENSICS

Social media forensics is a specialized area within digital forensics focused on collecting, analyzing, and preserving evidence from social media platforms. Given the dynamic and vast nature of social media, practitioners need to adhere to best practices to ensure the integrity, accuracy, and legality of the forensic process. Here are best practices for social media forensics:

- **Understand Platform-Specific Features:** Each platform has its own methods for data storage, presentation, and privacy settings, which can affect how evidence is accessed and interpreted. Gain familiarity with the specific features, data structures, and data retrieval methods of the social media platforms involved in the investigation (e.g., Facebook, Twitter, Instagram).
- **Preserve Evidence Properly:** Evidence preservation is crucial to prevent alteration or loss of data. Proper methods ensure that the evidence remains admissible in court. Use tools and techniques that preserve the integrity of digital evidence, such as taking screenshots, exporting data through official APIs, or using forensic tools designed for social media.

- **Document All Procedures:** Documentation provides a clear audit trail, which is essential for verifying the process and ensuring that evidence handling adheres to legal standards. Maintain thorough documentation of every step taken during the forensic process, including data collection methods, tools used, and chain of custody.
- **Obtain Proper Authorization:** Unauthorized access or collection of data can violate privacy laws and render the evidence inadmissible in legal proceedings. Ensure that all data collection and investigation activities are conducted with proper legal authorization, such as search warrants or consent forms.
- **Use Reliable Forensic Tools:** Reliable tools help ensure accurate data extraction and analysis while minimizing the risk of data corruption or loss. Employ reputable and validated forensic tools that are designed to handle social media data and are regularly updated to address new features or changes on platforms.
- **Analyze Metadata Carefully:** Metadata provides context and can help validate the authenticity of the content, establish timelines, and corroborate evidence. Examine and analyze metadata associated with social media posts, including timestamps, geolocation data, and user interactions.
- **Preserve User Privacy:** Preserving user privacy is important for legal compliance and ethical considerations, particularly when dealing with sensitive or private information. Handle personal and sensitive information with care, ensuring that any data collected is necessary for the investigation and is protected against unauthorized access.
- **Verify and Corroborate Evidence:** Corroborating evidence helps establish a more comprehensive understanding of the case and strengthens the overall validity of the findings. Cross-check social media evidence with other sources of information, such as phone records, emails, or physical evidence, to verify its authenticity and reliability.
- **Stay Updated with Platform Changes:** Social media platforms frequently update their features and security practices, which can impact data collection and forensic analysis. Staying informed ensures that your forensic practices remain effective and relevant. Keep up-to-date with changes and updates to social media platforms, including new features, data formats, and security measures.
- **Follow Legal and Ethical Guidelines:** Compliance with legal and ethical standards is crucial to ensuring that forensic practices are legitimate, and evidence is admissible and ethically obtained. Adhere to relevant legal standards and ethical guidelines for digital forensics, including respecting user rights, privacy laws, and data protection regulations.

- **Conduct Comprehensive Training:** Well-trained personnel are crucial for conducting effective and reliable forensic investigations. Ensure that all personnel involved in social media forensics are properly trained in forensic techniques, legal considerations, and platform-specific features.
- **Review and Validate Findings:** Validation helps detect potential errors or oversights and enhances the credibility of the findings. Regularly review and validate forensic findings with peer reviews or secondary analysis to ensure accuracy and completeness.
- **Prepare for Expert Testimony:** Clear and accurate testimony is essential for ensuring that the forensic findings are understood and considered in legal proceedings. Be prepared to present and explain your forensic findings in court, including the methodologies used, the reliability of tools, and the validity of the evidence.

By following these best practices, forensic experts can ensure that their investigations into social media evidence are thorough, accurate, and legally sound. Proper understanding of platform features, meticulous documentation, secure evidence handling, and adherence to legal and ethical standards are all essential components of effective social media forensics.

11. FUTURE DIRECTIONS

The field of social media forensics is poised for continued evolution. Future developments may include:

- **Enhanced AI Capabilities:** Advancements in AI and machine learning will further automate and refine data analysis processes, improving accuracy and efficiency.
- **Integration of Blockchain:** Blockchain technology could become more prevalent in ensuring the authenticity and integrity of digital evidence, providing an immutable record of social media data.
- **Improved Data Extraction Techniques:** Ongoing research and development will likely yield new methods for extracting and preserving data from social media platforms, addressing current limitations and challenges.
- **Collaboration and Standardization:** Increased collaboration among forensic experts, platform providers, and regulatory bodies may lead to standardized practices and improved interoperability among tools.

12. SUMMARY

Social media forensics is a rapidly evolving field that plays a critical role in modern investigations and legal proceedings. As social media platforms continue to develop and expand, forensic experts must adapt to new technologies, challenges, and legal considerations. By employing advanced methodologies, tools, and ethical practices, forensic professionals can effectively uncover and analyze digital evidence from social media platforms, supporting justice and accountability in the digital age.

This chapter provides a comprehensive overview of social media forensics, highlighting its historical development, methodologies, legal and ethical considerations, tools and technologies, and case studies. As the field continues to advance, ongoing research and development will be essential to address emerging issues and ensure that forensic practices remain effective and reliable.

REFERENCES

Abdel-Basset, M., Hawash, H., Chakrabortty, R. K., & Ryan, M. J. (2021). Semi-supervised spatiotemporal deep learning for intrusions detection in IoT networks. *IEEE Internet of Things Journal*, 8(15), 12251–12265. DOI: 10.1109/JIOT.2021.3060878

Adnan, M. H., Ariffin, S. A., Hanafi, H. F., Husain, M. S., & Panessai, I. Y. (2021). A social media analytics framework to increase prospective students' interests in STEM and TVET education. *Asian Journal of University Education*, 16(4), 82–90. DOI: 10.24191/ajue.v16i4.11945

Akbar, M., Suaib, M., & Hussain, M. (2023). The Rise of Deepfake Technology: Issues, Challenges, and Countermeasures. In *Advances in Cyberology and the Advent of the Next-Gen Information Revolution* (pp. 178–201). IGI Global. DOI: 10.4018/978-1-6684-8133-2.ch010

Alshammari, A., & Aldribi, A. (2021). Apply machine learning techniques to detect malicious network traffic in cloud computing. *Journal of Big Data*, 8(1), 90. DOI: 10.1186/s40537-021-00475-1

Bokolo, B. G., & Liu, Q. (2024). Artificial Intelligence in Social Media Forensics: A Comprehensive Survey and Analysis. *Electronics (Basel)*, 13(9), 1671. DOI: 10.3390/electronics13091671

Cellebrite. (n.d.). Cellebrite UFED. Retrieved from https://cellebrite.com/en/ufed/

Chen, Z., Zhou, L., & Yu, W. (2021, August). ADASYN− Random forest based intrusion detection model. In *Proceedings of the 2021 4th International Conference on Signal Processing and Machine Learning* (pp. 152-159).

Corporation, P. (n.d.). Paraben E3. Retrieved from https://paraben.com/paraben-e3-forensic-platform/

Daradkeh, M. (2023). The Link Between Privacy and Disclosure Behavior in Social Networks. In *Advances in Cyberology and the Advent of the Next-Gen Information Revolution* (pp. 38–61). IGI Global. DOI: 10.4018/978-1-6684-8133-2.ch003

Exterro. (n.d.). FTK Imager. Retrieved from https://www.exterro.com/ftk-product-downloads/ftk-imager-version-4-7-1

Fakiha, B. (2020). Digital Forensics: Crimes and Challenges in Online Social Networks Forensics. *Journal of the Arab American University*.

Gaurav, A., Gupta, B. B., Hsu, C. H., Peraković, D., & Penalvo, F. J. G. (2021, June). Filtering of distributed denial of services (DDoS) attacks in cloud computing environment. In 2021 IEEE International Conference on Communications Workshops (ICC Workshops) (pp. 1-6). IEEE.

Gazeau, V., Gupta, K., & An, M. K. (2024). Enhancing Social Media Data Collection for Digital Forensic Investigations: A Web Parser Approach. *International Conference on Computer, Information and Telecommunication Systems (CITS)*, (pp. 1-7). DOI: 10.1109/CITS61189.2024.10607983

Grigaliūnas, Š., Brūzgienė, R., & Venčkauskas, A. (2023). Ontology-Driven Digital Profiling for Identification and Linking Evidence Across Social Media Platform. *IEEE Access : Practical Innovations, Open Solutions*, 11, 111672–111691. DOI: 10.1109/ACCESS.2023.3322162

Hu, J., Liao, X., Wang, W., & Qin, Z. (2022). Detecting Compressed Deepfake Videos in Social Networks Using Frame-Temporality Two-Stream Convolutional Network. *EEE Transactions on Circuits and Systems for Video Technology*, 1089-1102.

Husain, M. S. (2019). Social media analytics to predict depression level in the users. In *Early detection of neurological disorders using machine learning systems* (pp. 199–215). IGI Global. DOI: 10.4018/978-1-5225-8567-1.ch011

Husain, M. S., Khan, M. Z., & Siddiqui, T. (2023). *Big Data Concepts, Technologies, and Applications*. CRC Press. DOI: 10.1201/9781003441595

Ibrahim, Y. M., Essameldin, R., & Saad, S. M. (2024). Social Media Forensics: An Adaptive Cyberbullying-Related Hate Speech Detection Approach Based on Neural Networks With Uncertainty. *IEEE Access : Practical Innovations, Open Solutions*, 12, 59474–59484. DOI: 10.1109/ACCESS.2024.3393295

Javed, N., Ahmed, T., Faisal, M., Sadia, H., & Sidaine-Daumiller, E. Z. (2023). Workplace cyberbullying in the remote-work era: a new dimension of cyberology. In *Advances in Cyberology and the Advent of the Next-Gen Information Revolution* (pp. 166–177). IGI Global. DOI: 10.4018/978-1-6684-8133-2.ch009

Josephine, B. M., Shekar, K. V., Meghana, G., Rao, K. R., & Rajesh, C. (2019). Forensic Analysis of Social Media Apps. *International Journal of Innovative Technology and Exploring Engineering*, 9(1), 2302–2305. DOI: 10.35940/ijitee.A5205.119119

Khan, A., Husain, M. S., & Khan, A. (2018). Analysis of mental state of users using social media to predict depression! a survey. *International Journal of Advanced Research in Computer Science*, 9(2), 100–106.

Klinkhamhom, C., & Boonyopakorn, P. (2022). Threat Hunting for Digital Forensic Using GRR Rapid Response with NIST Framework. *37th International Technical Conference on Circuits/Systems, Computers and Communications (ITC-CSCC)*, (pp. 177-180). DOI: 10.1109/ITC-CSCC55581.2022.9894977

Koru, G. K., & Uluyol, Ç. (2024). Detection of Turkish Fake News From Tweets With BERT Models. *IEEE Access : Practical Innovations, Open Solutions*, 12, 14918–14931. DOI: 10.1109/ACCESS.2024.3354165

Kraetzer, C., Siegel, D., Seidlitz, S., & Dittmann, J. (2022). Process-driven modelling of media forensic investigations-considerations on the example of deepfake detection. *Sensors (Basel)*, 22(9), 3137. DOI: 10.3390/s22093137 PMID: 35590827

Lotfollahi, M., Siavoshani, M. J., Zade, R. S., & Saberian, M. (2020). Deep packet: A novel approach for encrypted traffic classification using deep learning. *Soft Computing*, 24(3), 1999–2012. DOI: 10.1007/s00500-019-04030-2

Madhusudhanan, S., Jose, A. C., Sahoo, J., & Malekian, R. (2023). PRIMϵ: Novel Privacy-Preservation Model With Pattern Mining and Genetic Algorithm. *IEEE Transactions on Information Forensics and Security*, •••, 571–585.

Mahajan, K., Madhavidevi, B., Supreeth, B. R., Lakshmi, N. V., Joshi, K., & Bavankumar, S. (2023). Detecting and Responding to Cloud Security Incidents based on AI and Forensic Approach. *International Conference on Innovative Computing, Intelligent Communication and Smart Electrical Systems (ICSES)*, (pp. 1-6). DOI: 10.1109/ICSES60034.2023.10465380

Millán, G. (2021). Traffic flows analysis in high-speed computer networks using time series. *arXiv preprint arXiv:2103.03984.*

Mohammad, D. (2023). The Link Between Privacy and Disclosure Behavior in Social Networks. In *Advances in Cyberology and the Advent of the Next-Gen Information Revolution* (pp. 38–61). IGI Global.

Moustafa, N., & Slay, J. (2017). RCNF: Real-time collaborative network forensic scheme for evidence analysis. *arXiv preprint arXiv:1711.02824.*

Mukherjee, I., Sahu, N. K., & Sahana, S. K. (2023). Simulation and modeling for anomaly detection in IoT network using machine learning. *International Journal of Wireless Information Networks*, 30(2), 173–189. DOI: 10.1007/s10776-021-00542-7

Munke, E., & Musuva, P. M. (2024). *Digital Forensics as a Service Implementation: A Scalable Solution for Cyber Incident Response. IST-Africa Conference*. IST-Africa.

Padilha, R., Salem, T., Workman, S., Andaló, F. A., Rocha, A., & Jacobs, N. (2022). Content-Aware Detection of Temporal Metadata Manipulation. *IEEE Transactions on Information Forensics and Security*, 17, 1316–1327. DOI: 10.1109/TIFS.2022.3159154

Pasquini, C., Amerini, I., & Boato, G. (2021). Media forensics on social media platforms: A survey. *EURASIP Journal on Information Security*, 2021(1), 4. DOI: 10.1186/s13635-021-00117-2

P˘atra¸scu, A., & Patriciu, V.-V. (2013). Beyond Digital Forensics. A Cloud Computing Perspective Over Incident Response and Reporting. *International Symposium on Applied Computational Intelligence and Informatics*, (pp. 455-460). DOI: 10.1109/SACI.2013.6609018

Qiao, T., Chen, Y., Zhou, X., Shi, R., Shao, H., Shen, K., & Luo, X. (2024). CSC-Net: Cross-Color Spatial Co-Occurrence Matrix Network for Detecting Synthesized Fake Images. *IEEE Transactions on Cognitive and Developmental Systems*, 16(1), 369–379. DOI: 10.1109/TCDS.2023.3274450

Radhakrishna, T., & Majd, N. E. (2024). Edge Computing Ransomware Detection in IoT using Machine Learning. *Workshop on Computing, Networking and Communications (CNC)*, (pp. 244-248). DOI: 10.1109/ICNC59896.2024.10556351

Rafique, R., Nawaz, M., Kibriya, H., & Masood, M. (2021). DeepFake Detection Using Error Level Analysis and Deep Learning. *4th International Conference on Computing & Information Sciences (ICCIS)*, (pp. 1-4). DOI: 10.1109/ICCIS54243.2021.9676375

Sachdeva, S., & Ali, A. (2021). A Hybrid approach using digital forensics for attack detection in a cloud network environment. *International Journal of Future Generation Communication and Networking*, 1536-1546.

Shakeel, P. M., Baskar, S., Fouad, H., Manogaran, G., Saravanan, V., & Montenegro-Marin, C. E. (2021). Internet of things forensic data analysis using machine learning to identify roots of data scavenging. *Future Generation Computer Systems*, 115, 756–768. DOI: 10.1016/j.future.2020.10.001

Sharrab, Y., Al-Fraihat, D., & Alsmirat, M. (2023). Deep Neural Networks in Social Media Forensics: Unveiling Suspicious Patterns and Advancing Investigations on Twitter. *3rd Intelligent Cybersecurity Conference (ICSC)*, (pp. 95-102). DOI: 10.1109/ICSC60084.2023.10349985

Shullani, D., Baracchi, D., Iuliani, M., & Piva, A. (2022). Social Network Identification of Laundered Videos Based on DCT Coefficient Analysis. *IEEE Signal Processing Letters*, 29, 1112–1116. DOI: 10.1109/LSP.2022.3167631

Tang, Y., Gu, L., & Wang, L. (2021). Deep Stacking Network for Intrusion Detection. *sensors*.

Theophilo, A., Giot, R., & Rocha, A. (2023). Authorship Attribution of Social Media Messages. *IEEE Transactions on Computational Social Systems*, 10(1), 10–23. DOI: 10.1109/TCSS.2021.3123895

Yadav, S. (2020). Cyber Forensics: Its Importance, Cyber Forensics Techniques, and Tools. In Husain, M. S., & Khan, M. Z. (Eds.), *Critical Concepts, Standards, and Techniques in Cyber Forensics* (pp. 1–15). IGI Global. DOI: 10.4018/978-1-7998-1558-7.ch001

KEY TERMS AND DEFINITIONS

API: An Application Programming Interface (API) is a set of rules, protocols, and tools that allows different software applications to communicate and interact with each other. APIs define the methods and data formats that applications can use to request and exchange information, enabling developers to integrate and utilize functionalities from other services or platforms without needing to understand their internal workings.

Social Network Analysis (SNA): Social Network Analysis (SNA) is a methodological approach used to study and analyze the relationships and interactions among individuals, groups, or organizations within a network. It involves mapping and examining the structure and dynamics of social relationships to understand how they influence behaviors, communication, and the flow of information within the network.

Chapter 7
AI-Powered Behavioral Analysis in Digital Investigations

ABSTRACT

Behavior analysis, a discipline traditionally associated with psychology and criminology, involves studying patterns in behavior to understand and predict actions. In the realm of digital forensics, behavior analysis has gained significant traction due to the increasing complexity of cybercrimes and the vast amounts of data involved. This chapter delves into the role of AI-powered behavioral analysis in digital investigations, exploring its methodologies, applications, and implications for cybersecurity and forensic science.

1. INTRODUCTION

The exponential growth of digital data and the complexity of cyber threats have necessitated advanced tools and methodologies in digital investigations. Traditional methods of forensic analysis often fall short when faced with large-scale, dynamic, and multifaceted digital environments. To bridge this gap, Artificial Intelligence (AI) has emerged as a transformative force, particularly in the realm of behavioral analysis.

Behavior analysis, a discipline traditionally associated with psychology and criminology, involves studying patterns in behavior to understand and predict actions. In the realm of digital forensics, behavior analysis has gained significant traction due to the increasing complexity of cybercrimes and the vast amounts of data involved. This chapter delves into the role of AI-powered behavioral analysis

DOI: 10.4018/979-8-3693-2960-3.ch007

in digital investigations, exploring its methodologies, applications, and implications for cybersecurity and forensic science.

2. EVOLUTION OF DIGITAL INVESTIGATIONS

Digital investigations have evolved significantly since the early days of computer forensics. Initially focused on data recovery and system reconstruction, the field has expanded to address complex cybercrimes and sophisticated attacks. The advent of AI has further revolutionized this domain, offering new paradigms for analyzing and interpreting vast amounts of digital evidence.

- **From Manual Analysis to Automation:** Traditional digital investigations were labor-intensive and required forensic experts to manually sift through data. This process was slow and prone to human error, limiting the ability to handle large datasets or respond in real-time. These methods are typically reactive, focusing on evidence recovery and analysis after an incident has occurred. The introduction of automated tools and scripts represented a significant leap forward, allowing for more efficient data processing and analysis. However, these tools were still limited by their reliance on predefined patterns and rules.
- **The Role of AI in Transforming Investigations:** AI has revolutionized digital investigations by introducing advanced capabilities for analyzing large volumes of data, identifying patterns, and predicting future behavior. Unlike traditional methods that rely heavily on human intervention, AI-powered systems can process and analyze data at large scale, uncovering insights that would be challenging or impossible to detect manually.

AI-enhanced techniques provide proactive capabilities, enabling real-time monitoring, threat detection, and predictive analytics.

- **Integration of Behavior Analysis and Digital Forensics:** Integrating behavior analysis with digital forensics offers a deeper understanding of the motives and actions behind digital crimes. By analyzing patterns of behavior, investigators can gain insights into the intentions of cybercriminals, identify potential threats, and improve the accuracy of forensic investigations. This integration enhances the ability to interpret digital evidence and link it to specific behaviors and intentions.

3. UNDERSTANDING BEHAVIOR ANALYSIS

Behavior analysis is the systematic study of observable behaviors and the factors influencing them. It focuses on understanding why people behave the way they do, how behavior can be changed, and how certain behaviors can be prevented. Behavior analysis is grounded in the principles of behaviorism, which emphasize that behavior can be understood and modified through observable interactions with the environment. Behavior analysis is often used in mental health treatment to help people overcome problem behaviors (Tripathi, Haroon, Khan, & Husain, 2022), (Adnan, Ariffin, Hanafi, Husain, & Panessai, 2021), (Husain, 2019), (Shahid, Adnan, Khan, Shukla, & Khan., 2022). It can also be helpful in organizational settings to enhance employee performance. The basic principles of behavior analysis are often adapted for use in educational settings for optimal learning and classroom management.

In digital forensics, behavior analysis focuses on examining patterns and anomalies in digital activities to uncover insights about potential criminal actions or breaches.

3.1. Core Concepts of Behavior Analysis

- **Behavior Patterns:** Recurrent activities or actions that can be observed and measured. In digital forensics, this includes user actions, access logs, and interaction patterns with digital systems.
- **Behavioral Triggers:** Events or conditions that prompt specific behaviors. For instance, unusual login attempts might trigger a behavioral analysis to determine if they are indicative of malicious activity.
- **Anomalies:** Deviations from established patterns that may suggest an underlying issue or threat. Anomalies in behavior are often the focal point in digital forensic investigations.

3.2. Psychological Theories Relevant to Behavior Analysis

Several psychological theories contribute to understanding behavior in the context of digital forensics:

- **Social Learning Theory:** Proposed by Albert Bandura, this theory emphasizes learning through observation and imitation. It is relevant for understanding how individuals may emulate behaviors observed in digital environments.
- **Cognitive Behavioral Theory:** This theory explores the relationship between thoughts, feelings, and behaviors. It helps in understanding how cognitive processes influence actions and decisions.

- **Motivational Theory:** This theory focuses on understanding the factors that drive individuals to engage in certain behaviors. It is useful for analyzing the motives behind digital crimes.

3.3. Methods of Behavior Analysis

Behavior analysis employs various methods to study and understand behavior:

- **Observation:** Directly observing individuals in different settings provides insights into their actions and interactions. In digital forensics, this can involve analyzing user interactions with digital systems.
- **Experimental Methods:** Conducting controlled experiments to test hypotheses about behavior. This method helps determine the impact of specific variables on behavior.
- **Data Analysis:** Analyzing data collected from various sources to identify patterns and trends in behavior. In digital forensics, this includes examining logs, communication records, and other digital artifacts.

3.4. Behavior Analysis vs. Traditional Forensics

Traditional digital forensics often focuses on the recovery and examination of digital evidence without necessarily analyzing the behavior behind the evidence. While traditional methods might involve identifying files, timestamps, and system logs, behavior analysis adds a layer of understanding by interpreting how and why certain activities occurred.

The Need for Behavioral Analysis: As cyber threats become more advanced, understanding the behavior of attackers has become crucial. Behavioral analysis focuses on identifying patterns, anomalies, and deviations in digital activities that may indicate malicious intent. This approach goes beyond mere data retrieval, offering insights into the motives, strategies, and techniques of cybercriminals.

4. BEHAVIOR ANALYSIS IN CYBER FORENSICS

Applying Behavior Analysis to cyber forensics involves understanding how behavioral principles can be used to investigate and interpret digital behaviors, patterns, and activities. Cyber forensics deals with the recovery, analysis, and presentation of digital evidence from electronic devices and networks, and behavior analysis can enhance this process by providing insights into user actions, motivations, and patterns.

4.1. Core Concepts of Behavior Analysis in Cyber Forensics

Behavioral analysis principles such as behavior, reinforcement, punishment, antecedents, consequences, shaping, functional analysis, behavioral assessment, generalization, and maintenance are leveraged in the field of cyber forensics to enhance investigative efforts and address cyber threats effectively.

- **Behavior:** In cyber forensics, behavior refers to any observable actions or activities performed by users on digital platforms. This includes actions such as accessing files, sending emails, using applications, or engaging in online communication. Analyzing behavior helps in identifying unusual or suspicious behavior patterns that may indicate malicious activities or security breaches.
- **Reinforcement:** Reinforcement in cyber forensics pertains to understanding what motivates users to perform certain actions. This includes identifying what types of rewards or consequences influence user behavior in a digital context. Reinforcement analysis helps in creating profiles based on reinforcement patterns to predict potential future actions or identify the underlying motivations behind cybercrimes. It also helps in understanding the motivation behind any activity, i.e. determining what drives certain behaviors, such as the desire for financial gain leading to fraudulent activities or the pursuit of prestige driving hacking attempts.
- **Punishment:** Punishment involves identifying and analyzing the consequences that deter or discourage certain behaviors. In cyber contexts, this might include the identification of actions that were taken to avoid detection or consequences. It helps in understanding how the threat of punitive measures might affect the behavior of individuals involved in cyber incidents and examining how cybercriminals react to potential punishments or legal consequences and how these reactions influence their behavior.
- **Antecedents:** Antecedents are the events or conditions that precede and influence digital behavior. In the cyber realm, this includes triggers or conditions that lead to specific user actions or decisions. It helps in identifying conditions or events that prompted specific actions, such as security alerts or system vulnerabilities. It also aids in understanding the environmental or situational factors that contributed to the occurrence of certain behaviors, such as exploiting a known vulnerability.
- **Consequences:** Consequences are the outcomes or responses that follow a user's actions. Analyzing these helps in understanding how specific behaviors are reinforced or punished. This characteristic aids in evaluating the ef-

fects of a user's actions, such as data breaches or unauthorized access, and how these consequences influence further behavior.

- **Behavioral Shaping:** Behavioral shaping involves gradually guiding behavior through successive approximations. In cyber forensics, this concept can be applied to understand how cybercriminals might incrementally escalate their activities. This helps in identifying how cybercriminals progressively increase the complexity or scale of their attacks over time and developing strategies to counteract and mitigate these cyber-attacks.
- **Functional Analysis:** Functional analysis in cyber forensics refers to identifying the functions or purposes of specific behaviors by analyzing their causes and effects. Functional analysis is used to determine the purpose of certain actions, such as why a hacker might choose a specific method for breaching a system (e.g., financial gain, data theft). This helps in tailoring investigative efforts based on the identified functions of behaviors to more effectively address and resolve cyber incidents.
- **Behavioral Assessment:** Behavioral assessment involves evaluating user behavior through various methods to understand its nature and underlying causes. Assessing user logs, communication records, and system interactions to identify patterns of behavior helps in developing risk profiles based on behavioral assessments to predict potential security threats and vulnerabilities.
- **Generalization:** Generalization involves understanding how behaviors observed in one context may apply to different contexts or systems. Using knowledge of general behavior patterns to model and predict potential threats across different environments. For example recognizing how a cybercriminal's tactics in one attack might be applied to other systems or targets.
- **Maintenance:** Maintenance refers to the persistence of certain behaviors over time. In cyber forensics, this involves understanding how long-term behaviors or strategies are sustained by individuals or groups. Analyzing how cybercriminals maintain their activities over time, including the continued exploitation of vulnerabilities or persistent access to compromised systems aids in implementing monitoring systems to detect ongoing or recurring malicious behaviors and ensure continued security.

Core concepts of behavior analysis, when applied to cyber forensics, provide a framework for understanding and investigating digital behaviors and patterns. By examining behavior, reinforcement, punishment, antecedents, consequences, shaping, functional analysis, and other key concepts, forensic investigators can gain deeper insights into the motivations, actions, and strategies of individuals involved in cyber incidents. This approach enhances the ability to analyze, interpret, and address cyber threats and criminal activities effectively.

5. ROLE OF BEHAVIOR ANALYSIS IN DIGITAL FORENSICS

Behavior analysis is increasingly important in digital forensics due to the growing sophistication of cyber threats and the sheer volume of data involved in investigations. Here's why behavior analysis is significant:

Figure 1. Role of behavior analysis in digital forensics

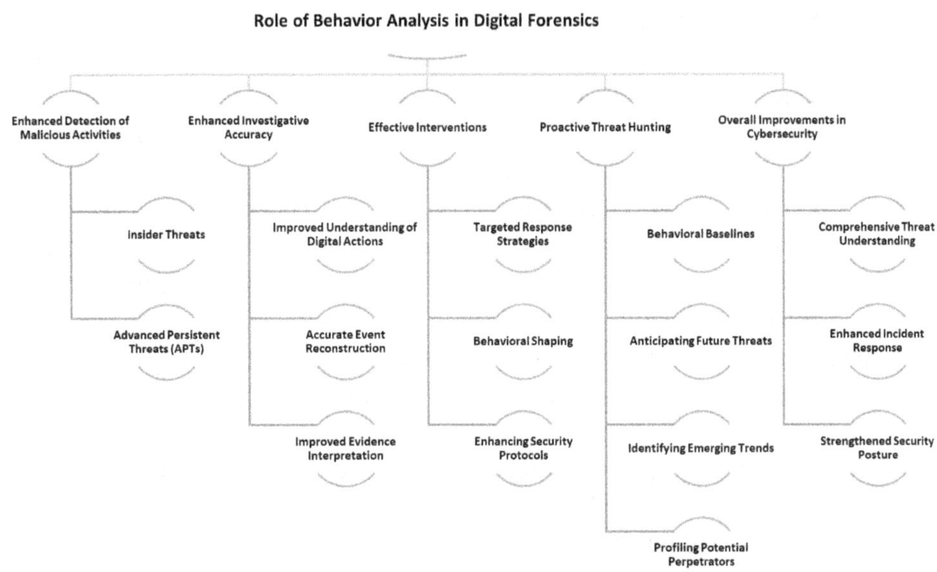

5.1. Enhanced Detection of Malicious Activities

Behavior analysis helps in identifying and understanding complex cyber threats by examining deviations from normal patterns of behavior. For example:

- **Insider Threats:** Analyzing patterns of user behavior can help detect potential insider threats by identifying unusual activities, such as accessing sensitive data not required for their role or attempting to exfiltrate large amounts of data.
- **Advanced Persistent Threats (APTs):** APTs are often characterized by prolonged and sophisticated attack strategies. By analyzing behavior over time, forensic investigators can identify subtle indicators of APTs that may not be apparent through conventional methods.

5.2. Enhanced Investigative Accuracy

Behavior analysis principles can be applied in digital forensics to enhance understanding, improve investigations, and address cyber threats effectively.

- **Improved Understanding of Digital Actions:** Behavior analysis provides a structured approach to understanding and interpreting digital behaviors by focusing on observable actions and their context.
  - **Detailed Activity Tracking:** Analyzing user activity logs, system interactions, and network traffic allows forensic experts to reconstruct the sequence of events accurately. For instance, tracking login times, file access, and communication patterns helps in creating a comprehensive timeline of actions leading to an incident.
  - **Pattern Recognition:** Behavior analysis aids in identifying patterns and anomalies in digital behavior. For example, detecting unusual access patterns or unauthorized data transfers can highlight potential security breaches or malicious activities.
- **Accurate Event Reconstruction:** Reconstructing events involves piecing together actions and interactions to understand the full scope of an incident. By examining the antecedents (triggers) and consequences (outcomes) of digital actions, forensic experts can reconstruct events with greater accuracy. For example, identifying the conditions leading to a data breach helps in understanding how and why the breach occurred.

Behavior analysis helps in creating profiles of users based on their actions, which can be used to reconstruct the behavior of suspects and understand their motives.

- **Improved Evidence Interpretation:** Interpreting evidence involves analyzing digital data to draw meaningful conclusions about an incident. Understanding the reinforcement and punishment mechanisms behind user actions provides insights into their motivations. For instance, analyzing why a hacker targeted specific data can reveal underlying motives such as financial gain or competitive advantage.

5.3. Effective Interventions

Behavior analysis enables more effective and timely incident response by providing insights into the nature and scope of an attack. For instance:

- **Targeted Response Strategies:** Targeted response strategies involve developing specific measures to address identified threats and vulnerabilities. Understanding the underlying causes of behaviors, such as motivations and triggers, allows for the development of targeted response strategies. For example, if financial gain is identified as a primary motivation for a cybercriminal, responses can focus on disrupting financial incentives.

Behavior analysis enables the creation of customized solutions based on the specific behaviors and patterns observed. For example, tailored security measures can address specific vulnerabilities identified through behavioral analysis.

- **Behavioral Shaping:** Behavioral shaping involves influencing and modifying behaviors through reinforcement and other techniques. By applying principles of behavioral shaping, forensic experts can design interventions to modify undesirable behaviors. For example, modifying the behavior of users who exhibit risky online behavior through training and awareness programs.

Behavioral shaping techniques can be used to develop preventive measures, such as implementing policies and procedures that discourage risky behaviors.

- **Enhancing Security Protocols:** Enhancing security protocols involves improving existing security measures based on behavioral insights. Developing security protocols that are informed by behavioral analysis ensures that they address the specific behaviors and tactics of cybercriminals. For example, implementing multi-factor authentication to address observed patterns of unauthorized access. Behavior analysis allows for the continuous improvement of security protocols by regularly updating them based on new behavioral insights and emerging threats.

5.4. Proactive Threat Hunting

Behavioral analysis allows for proactive threat hunting, where investigators actively seek out potential threats before they cause significant damage. This involves:

- **Behavioral Baselines:** Establishing normal behavior patterns for users, systems, and networks, which can be used to detect deviations and potential threats early. Using AI and machine learning to detect anomalies in behavior that may indicate emerging threats, such as new malware strains or novel attack vectors.

- **Anticipating Future Threats:** Predicting future threats involves using behavioral insights to anticipate potential cyber risks and criminal activities. By applying principles of behavior analysis, forensic experts can model potential threats based on observed patterns and behaviors. For example, recognizing how attackers have previously escalated their tactics helps in anticipating future attack strategies.

Predictive capabilities allow organizations to implement proactive security measures. For example, if certain behavior patterns indicate a high risk of data exfiltration, preventive measures can be put in place to mitigate this risk.

- **Identifying Emerging Trends:** Identifying emerging trends involves recognizing new patterns or changes in cybercriminal behavior. Behavior analysis helps in identifying emerging trends in cybercrime, such as new attack vectors or techniques. For instance, analyzing recent incidents can reveal a shift towards more sophisticated phishing attacks. Understanding emerging trends allows organizations to adapt their security strategies and defenses, accordingly, staying ahead of evolving threats.
- **Profiling Potential Perpetrators:** Profiling potential perpetrators involves creating profiles based on behavioral patterns and motivations. By analyzing past behaviors, forensic experts can create profiles of potential attackers. For example, profiling based on past criminal behavior can help in identifying individuals who might be involved in similar activities. Behavioral profiling aids in predicting the actions and motives of potential perpetrators, allowing for targeted prevention and response strategies.

5.5. Overall Improvements in Cybersecurity

Behavior analysis offers significant benefits to digital forensics by enhancing investigative accuracy, predictive capabilities, and intervention effectiveness. This approach improves threat detection, response strategies, and overall cybersecurity.

- **Comprehensive Threat Understanding:** Comprehensive threat understanding involves gaining a holistic view of cyber threats and vulnerabilities. Behavior analysis provides a comprehensive understanding of cyber threats by examining both user actions and system interactions. This holistic approach improves the ability to detect and address complex threats. A thorough understanding of threats enables the development of integrated defense strategies that address multiple facets of

- **Enhanced Incident Response:** Enhanced incident response involves improving the effectiveness and efficiency of responding to cyber incidents. By applying behavior analysis, forensic experts can respond more swiftly and effectively to incidents. For example, identifying the cause of a breach through behavioral insights allows for a quicker resolution. Enhanced incident response leads to better coordination among forensic teams, security personnel, and other stakeholders, ensuring a more effective resolution of incidents.
- **Strengthened Security Posture:** Strengthened security posture involves improving an organization's overall security measures and defenses. Behavior analysis informs the development of strategies that strengthen an organization's security posture by addressing specific behaviors and vulnerabilities. For example, implementing user training programs based on observed risky behaviors.

Strengthening security protocols and response strategies based on behavioral insights enhances an organization's resilience against cyber threats.

6. METHODOLOGIES IN BEHAVIOR ANALYSIS FOR DIGITAL FORENSICS

Effective behavior analysis in digital forensics involves different aspects including:

- **Data Collection and Preparation:** Collecting and analyzing system logs, application logs, and network traffic logs to identify unusual or suspicious activities. This includes examining login attempts, file access records, and communication patterns.

Analyzing metadata associated with files, emails, and documents to gain insights into the creation, modification, and access history of digital artifacts.

- **Pattern Recognition:** Identifying and analyzing recurring patterns in user and system behavior to detect normal versus anomalous activities.

Applying machine learning algorithms to identify patterns and anomalies in large datasets (Suaib, Akbar, & Husain, 240-247). Techniques such as clustering, classification, and anomaly detection can be used to analyze behavioral data.

- **Anomaly Detection:** Using statistical methods to detect deviations from established norms. This includes techniques such as standard deviation analysis and z-score calculation.

Implementing advanced AI and machine learning models to detect subtle anomalies and evolving threats. These models can be trained on historical data to identify patterns indicative of malicious activities.

A variety of methodologies and tools are incorporated in behavioral analysis for digital forensics. These methodologies are designed to analyze and interpret digital behaviors comprehensively.

6.1. Functional Behavioral Assessment (FBA)

Functional Behavioral Assessment (FBA) is a systematic approach used to understand the causes and functions of behavior. In digital forensics, FBA involves analyzing digital behaviors to determine their underlying motivations and triggers.

Functional Behavioral Assessment (FBA) can be used to analyze incidents by identifying the triggers and consequences of cyber behaviors. For example, understanding the conditions leading to a data breach can help in addressing vulnerabilities. FBA helps in creating profiles of individuals based on their digital behaviors, which can be used to predict future actions and motives.

Key Components of functional Behavioral assessment are:

- **Behavior Identification:** Identifying specific behaviors of interest, such as unauthorized data access or suspicious communication.
- **Antecedent Analysis:** Examining conditions or events that precede the behavior.
- **Consequence Analysis:** Analyzing the outcomes or consequences that follow the behavior.
- **Function Determination:** Identifying the purpose or function of the behavior, such as financial gain or revenge.

6.2. User Behavior Analysis (UBA)

User Behavior Analysis (UBA) involves monitoring and analyzing how users interact with digital systems. Key components include:

- **Activity Monitoring:** Tracking user actions, such as login times, file access, and network activity. This helps in identifying deviations from normal behavior.

- **Behavioral Baselines:** Establishing a baseline of normal behavior for comparison. Significant deviations from this baseline can indicate potential security threats or suspicious activities.
- **Anomaly Detection:** Identifying unusual patterns of behavior that may suggest malicious intent or unauthorized access. UBA tools often use algorithms and machine learning to detect anomalies.

6.3. Behavioral Mapping

Behavioral Mapping involves creating visual representations of behavior patterns and their relationships. In digital forensics, this technique helps in visualizing and analyzing digital interactions and connections. Behavioral mapping can be used to visualize network traffic and identify suspicious patterns. For example, mapping data flow can help detect abnormal data exfiltration activities. Creating maps of user interactions with systems and applications helps in understanding behavior patterns and identifying potential threats.

Key Components of behavioral mapping are:

- **Data Collection:** Gathering data on user activities, system interactions, and network communications.
- **Pattern Identification:** Identifying patterns and relationships among behaviors.
- **Mapping:** Creating visual maps to represent behavior patterns and their connections.

6.4. Psychological Profiling

Psychological profiling involves creating profiles of individuals based on their behavior and communication patterns. In digital forensics, this technique is used to understand the motives, tactics, and characteristics of cybercriminals. Psychological profiling helps in identifying potential suspects based on their digital activities and profiles. For example, profiling based on access patterns and communication can narrow down suspects in a cybercrime investigation.

Analyzing behavioral profiles provides insights into the motives behind cybercrimes. For example, understanding that a cybercriminal is motivated by financial gain can inform investigative strategies. Key elements of psychological profiling include:

- **Behavioral Patterns:** Analyzing patterns in user behavior to identify characteristics of potential suspects. This includes examining communication styles, decision-making processes, and digital footprints.
- **Motivation Analysis:** Understanding the psychological motivations behind certain actions. Profiling helps in identifying the reasons why individuals engage in specific behaviors.
- **Profile Creation:** Developing profiles based on observed behaviors and interactions.
- **Risk Assessment:** Evaluating the likelihood of future actions based on observed behaviors. This helps in predicting potential threats and planning appropriate responses.

6.5. Threat Modeling

Threat Modeling is a structured approach to identifying and analyzing potential threats and vulnerabilities within a system. In behavior analysis, this methodology focuses on understanding the behaviors and tactics used by cybercriminals to exploit weaknesses.

Threat modeling helps in predicting potential attack scenarios and developing preventive measures. For example, modeling potential attack vectors can inform the implementation of targeted security controls. Understanding potential threats and vulnerabilities helps in developing effective incident response plans. For example, identifying common attack techniques informs response strategies and mitigation measures.

Key Components of threat modeling are:

- **Asset Identification:** Identifying valuable assets and information that need protection.
- **Threat Identification:** Recognizing potential threats and attack vectors.
- **Vulnerability Analysis:** Analyzing vulnerabilities that could be exploited by threats.
- **Impact Assessment:** Assessing the potential impact of threats on assets and systems.

6.6. Predictive Analysis

Predictive Analysis involves using historical data and behavioral patterns to forecast future events and behaviors. In digital forensics, this methodology helps in anticipating potential cyber threats and incidents.

Predictive analysis helps in anticipating potential cyber threats and attack vectors. For example, analyzing trends in ransomware attacks can inform the development of preventive measures. Predictive models can assess the likelihood of specific threats and vulnerabilities. For example, forecasting the potential impact of emerging threats helps in prioritizing security measures.

Key Components of predictive analysis are:

- **Data Collection:** Gathering historical data on cyber incidents and behaviors.
- **Pattern Analysis:** Analyzing patterns and trends in historical data.
- **Forecasting:** Using predictive models to anticipate future threats and behaviors.

6.7. Behavioral Data Analytics

Behavioral Data Analytics involves analyzing large datasets to identify patterns and insights related to behavior. In digital forensics, this technique is used to analyze and interpret vast amounts of digital data. Behavioral data analytics helps in detecting anomalies and suspicious activities. For example, analyzing login patterns to identify unusual access attempts. Analyzing trends in digital behavior to understand emerging threats and patterns. For example, identifying trends in malware distribution and propagation.

Key Components of behavioral data analytics are:

- **Data Collection:** Gathering data from various digital sources, such as logs, communications, and transactions.
- **Pattern Analysis:** Using analytics tools to identify patterns and anomalies in the data.
- **Insight Generation:** Extracting meaningful insights and conclusions from the analyzed data.

6.8. Forensic Linguistics

Forensic linguistics involves analyzing language and communication patterns to understand the context and motives behind digital interactions. Key components include:

- **Language Analysis:** Examining the language used in digital communications, such as emails and chat logs, to identify linguistic features and patterns.
- **Communication Style:** Understanding the communication style of individuals to gain insights into their psychological state and intentions.
- **Contextual Interpretation:** Interpreting the context of communications to provide a clearer understanding of the interactions and potential motives behind them.

6.9. Social Network Analysis (SNA)

Social Network Analysis (SNA) involves analyzing relationships and interactions within a social network. In digital forensics, SNA is used to understand the connections and dynamics between individuals and entities. Analyzing social networks provides insights into the dynamics and motivations of individuals within the network. For example, understanding the role of a key figure in a cybercriminal organization.

SNA helps in mapping connections between suspects, victims, and other entities. For example, visualizing connections between individuals involved in a cybercrime network.

Key Components of social network analysis are:

- **Network Mapping:** Creating visual representations of relationships and interactions within a network.
- **Relationship Analysis:** Examining the nature and strength of connections between individuals and entities.
- **Influence Assessment:** Assessing the influence and impact of individuals within the network.

6.10. Behavioral Experimentation

Behavioral Experimentation involves conducting controlled experiments to study behavior and its effects. In digital forensics, this technique is used to test hypotheses and evaluate the impact of different variables on digital behavior. Behavioral experimentation helps in testing hypotheses about cyber behaviors and their triggers. For example, experimenting with different security measures to evaluate their effectiveness. Behavioral experimentation helps in evaluating the impact of interventions and changes on digital behavior. For example, assessing the effectiveness of new security policies on user behavior.

Key Components of Behavioral experimentation are:

- **Hypothesis Development:** Formulating hypotheses about digital behavior and its causes.
- **Experiment Design:** Designing controlled experiments to test hypotheses and collect data.
- **Data Analysis:** Analyzing experimental data to draw conclusions and insights.

7. AI-POWERED BEHAVIORAL ANALYSIS

Artificial Intelligence (AI) has revolutionized numerous fields, including cyber forensics. AI-powered behavioral analysis involves using machine learning (ML) and other AI techniques to examine digital behaviors and identify anomalies or patterns indicative of malicious activity. This section explores the core components and methodologies involved in AI-powered behavioral analysis.

7.1. Machine Learning Algorithms

Machine learning (ML) and deep learning (DL) are at the core of AI-powered behavioral analysis. ML algorithms can be trained to recognize patterns in large datasets, making them invaluable for identifying unusual behaviors in digital investigations. These algorithms learn from historical data to identify patterns and make predictions about future behaviors. Supervised learning involves training the model on labeled data, while unsupervised learning allows the model to identify patterns without predefined labels. Deep learning, a subset of ML, uses neural networks with multiple layers to analyze complex data structures. Common ML algorithms used in behavioral analysis include:

- **Supervised Learning:** This technique involves training models on labeled datasets where the outcomes are known. Supervised learning algorithms, such as decision trees, random forests, and support vector machines, classify and predict behaviors based on historical data. For example, a supervised learning model might be trained to detect fraudulent transactions by learning from previously labeled examples of fraudulent and legitimate transactions.
- **Unsupervised Learning:** Unlike supervised learning, unsupervised learning works with unlabeled data to uncover hidden patterns and structures. Clustering algorithms like k-means and hierarchical clustering are used to group similar behaviors together, which can help identify anomalous activities. For instance, unsupervised learning might reveal new patterns of cyber-attacks that were not previously recognized.

- **Reinforcement Learning:** Reinforcement learning involves training models to make decisions based on feedback from their environment. In digital investigations, reinforcement learning can be used to adapt detection strategies based on evolving threats. For example, an AI system might continuously adjust its detection algorithms in response to new types of malware or attack techniques.

Applications in Cyber Forensics:

- **Anomaly Detection:** ML algorithms can detect deviations from normal behavior, such as unusual login patterns or data access activities.
- **Threat Prediction:** ML models can predict potential threats based on historical data and observed patterns.
- **User Behavior Profiling:** SVM and Random Forests can classify user behaviors as normal or suspicious based on historical data.
- **Malicious Activity Detection:** Neural networks can learn patterns associated with malicious activities, such as data exfiltration or privilege escalation.
- **Adaptive Security Policies:** Reinforcement learning can optimize security policies based on feedback from interactions with simulated attacks or real-world data.
- **Intrusion Detection Systems (IDS):** Machine learning algorithms enhance IDS by analyzing network traffic in real time and identifying deviations from normal behavior.
- **Fraud Detection:** Behavioral analysis using machine learning helps detect fraudulent activities by identifying unusual patterns in financial transactions.

Despite challenges related to data privacy, model accuracy, and integration, the continued advancement of machine learning technologies holds significant promise for enhancing cyber forensics practices. Future developments in ML will further shape and improve the field, offering new opportunities for innovation and effectiveness in cybersecurity.

7.2. Natural Language Processing (NLP)

Natural Language Processing (NLP) is crucial for analyzing and interpreting textual data, such as emails, chat logs, and social media posts. NLP techniques enable AI systems to extract meaningful information from unstructured text, helping investigators understand communication patterns, sentiment, and potential malicious intent. Techniques like sentiment analysis can help determine the emotional tone of a message, while entity recognition can identify key individuals and organizations mentioned in the text. Key NLP techniques include:

- **Tokenization and Parsing:** Tokenization involves breaking down text into smaller units, such as words or phrases, while parsing analyzes the grammatical structure. These techniques help AI systems understand the context and content of textual data.
- **Named Entity Recognition (NER):** NER identifies and categorizes entities such as names, dates, and locations within text. This can be useful for tracking interactions between individuals and identifying relevant events.
- **Text Classification:** Categorizing text into predefined categories, such as spam or legitimate based on its content. This can be used to classify communication as malicious or benign.
- **Sentiment Analysis:** Sentiment analysis assesses the emotional tone of text, which can provide insights into the intent and mood of the author. For example, analyzing the sentiment of messages in a phishing campaign can help determine the level of urgency or threat perceived by the attackers.
- **Topic Modeling:** Topic modeling involves identifying the underlying topics present in a collection of text documents. It uncovers themes and patterns within textual data.

Applications in Cyber Forensics:

- **Content Analysis:** NLP can analyze email content, social media posts, and chat logs to identify potential threats or malicious intent.
- **Contextual Understanding:** NLP helps in understanding the context and nuances of communication, which is crucial for detecting sophisticated social engineering attacks.
- **Threat Categorization:** Identifying and categorizing threats based on textual descriptions or communication patterns.
- **Information Extraction:** Extracting and identifying key entities from communications or documents for further analysis.
- **Threat Intelligence:** Identifying mentions of specific individuals, organizations, or locations in threat communications.
- **Anomaly Detection:** Detecting unusual topics or content in user communications that may indicate malicious behavior.
- **Phishing Detection:** NLP techniques are used to identify phishing attempts by analyzing the content and context of emails, messages, or web pages.
- **Insider Threat Detection:** NLP techniques analyze employee communications and behaviors to detect potential insider threats.

- **Fraud Detection:** NLP techniques are used to detect fraudulent activities by analyzing textual data related to transactions, communications, and user interactions.

7.3. Pattern Recognition and Anomaly Detection

Pattern recognition and Anomaly detection is a key component of behavioral analysis, focusing on identifying deviations from normal behavior (established patterns or norms). In digital investigations, this can include unusual login times, unexpected file access patterns, or irregular network traffic. This approach is valuable for detecting unusual activities that may indicate a security breach or other malicious actions. Anomaly detection algorithms, such as isolation forests and autoencoders, help flag potentially malicious activities that deviate from normal behavior. For example, an anomaly detection algorithm might flag an unusual login attempt from a different geographic location, prompting further investigation.

- **Statistical Methods:** Statistical anomaly detection involves defining normal behavior based on statistical models and identifying deviations. Techniques such as z-score analysis and probabilistic models can help detect outliers.
- **Machine Learning Approaches:** Machine learning-based anomaly detection methods, such as isolation forests and autoencoders, learn from historical data to identify deviations. These methods can adapt to new patterns and evolving threats, improving the accuracy of anomaly detection.

Using algorithms to analyze data and identify patterns that may not be immediately apparent. This includes detecting trends, correlations, and anomalies in digital evidence.

Applying machine learning models to predict future behavior based on historical data. This helps in anticipating potential threats and planning preventative measures.

Utilizing automated tools to streamline the analysis process and improve efficiency. Machine learning models can be trained to recognize specific patterns and behaviors relevant to digital forensics.

- **Deep Learning Techniques:** Deep learning techniques use neural networks with multiple layers to identify complex patterns and relationships in data. For example Convolutional Neural Networks (CNNs) are used for pattern recognition in image and video data, Recurrent Neural Networks (RNNs) are suitable for analyzing sequential data, such as log files or network traffic and Autoencoders are useful for anomaly detection by learning compressed representations of data.

- **Time Series Analysis:** Time series analysis involves analyzing data points collected over time to identify patterns, trends, and anomalies. Techniques used for time series analysis are: Moving Averages, Autoregressive Integrated Moving Average (ARIMA), and LSTM.
- **Pattern Matching Techniques:** Pattern matching involves identifying specific patterns or signatures within data. For example, Regular Expressions are used to identify specific text patterns in logs or communications, Signature-Based Detection identifies known patterns or signatures of malware or attacks, and Sequence Matching aids in identifying patterns in sequences of events or data.

Applications in Cyber Forensics:

- **Intrusion Detection:** Identifying unusual network traffic or access patterns that may indicate a breach.
- **Fraud Detection:** Detecting anomalous financial transactions that could signify fraudulent activity by analyzing patterns of transactions.
- **Anomaly Detection:** Identifying deviations from normal network traffic or user behavior.
- **Network Traffic Analysis:** Deep learning models analyze network traffic to identify patterns indicative of attacks.
- **Log Analysis:** RNNs analyze log data to detect unusual sequences or behaviors.
- **Malware Detection:** Pattern recognition techniques are applied to analyze and detect malware by identifying specific patterns or signatures in files or network traffic.
- **Threat Detection:** Matching known attack patterns in system logs or communications.

7.4. Behavioral Clustering

Behavioral Clustering involves grouping similar behaviors to identify patterns and trends. In cyber forensics, clustering algorithms can be used to group similar cyber activities and detect emerging threats. Key Techniques used for behavioral clustering are:

- **K-Means Clustering:** A popular clustering algorithm that partitions data into k clusters based on similarity.
- **Hierarchical Clustering:** Groups data into a hierarchy of clusters, allowing for detailed analysis of behavior patterns. Hierarchical clustering creates a

tree-like structure of clusters by either successively merging smaller clusters (agglomerative) or splitting larger clusters (divisive).

- **DBSCAN (Density-Based Spatial Clustering of Applications with Noise):** DBSCAN is a density-based clustering algorithm that groups together data points that are closely packed while marking points in low-density regions as outliers.
- **Gaussian Mixture Models (GMM):** Gaussian Mixture Models are probabilistic models that assume data is generated from a mixture of several Gaussian distributions. They estimate the parameters of these distributions to identify clusters.

Applications in Cyber Forensics:

- **Threat Identification:** Clustering similar attack vectors or behaviors to identify new or emerging threats.
- **User Behavior Analysis:** Grouping similar user behaviors to detect abnormal patterns or potential threats.
- **Network Traffic Analysis:** Grouping network traffic patterns to identify normal and suspicious activities.
- **Fraud Detection:** Clustering financial transactions and user activities to identify patterns and outliers that may indicate fraudulent behavior.
- **Intrusion Detection Systems (IDS):** Behavioral clustering enhances IDS by grouping network traffic patterns to identify normal versus suspicious activities.
- **Malware Analysis:** Behavioral clustering is used to analyze malware behaviors and classify them into categories based on their similarities.
- **Insider Threat Detection:** Clustering user activities to identify unusual behaviors that may indicate insider threats. Behavioral clustering is applied to identify potential insider threats by analyzing user activities and detecting deviations from normal patterns.

8. APPLICATIONS OF AI-POWERED BEHAVIORAL ANALYSIS

AI-powered behavioral analysis has a broad range of applications in digital investigations, from detecting and responding to cyber threats to uncovering criminal activities and fraud. By leveraging advanced AI techniques, organizations can enhance their capabilities in threat detection, fraud prevention, and digital forensics.

8.1. Threat Detection and Prevention

AI-powered behavioral analysis plays a critical role in detecting and preventing cyber threats. By analyzing network traffic, user behavior, and system logs, AI systems can identify signs of malicious activity, such as unusual access patterns or data exfiltration attempts. Key applications include:

- **Intrusion Detection Systems (IDS):** AI-enhanced IDS use machine learning and anomaly detection to monitor and analyze network traffic and identify suspicious activities. These systems can detect unauthorized access attempts, data breaches, and other security incidents in real-time.
- **Endpoint Protection:** AI algorithms monitor and analyze endpoint behaviors to detect anomalies, such as unusual file modifications or unauthorized software installations. This helps in identifying potential threats and preventing malware infections.
- **Threat Intelligence:** AI systems aggregate and analyze threat intelligence data from various sources, including open-source data, dark web forums, and industry reports. This provides organizations with timely and actionable information about emerging threats and vulnerabilities.

8.2. Insider Threat Detection

Behavior analysis is essential for detecting insider threats within organizations:

- **Unusual Access Patterns:** Identifying unusual patterns of data access or system usage by employees. This includes monitoring access to sensitive information and detecting deviations from normal behavior.
- **Policy Violations:** Analyzing behavior to identify potential violations of organizational policies. This helps in detecting activities that may indicate malicious intent or policy breaches.
- **Employee Monitoring:** Implementing monitoring systems to track employee behavior and detect signs of potential insider threats. Behavior analysis helps in distinguishing between legitimate and suspicious activities.

8.3. Fraud Detection

Fraud detection is another critical application of AI-powered behavioral analysis. Financial institutions, e-commerce platforms, and other organizations use AI to identify fraudulent activities by analyzing transaction patterns and user behaviors to identify fraudulent activities and protect against financial losses. Key techniques include:

- **Transaction Monitoring:** AI systems analyze transaction patterns to detect anomalies, such as unusual spending behaviors or rapid changes in transaction amounts, which may indicate fraudulent activities.
- **Identity Theft:** Monitoring behaviors associated with identity theft, such as unauthorized access to personal information and account manipulation.
- **User Behavior Analysis:** By examining user interactions and behaviors, AI can detect deviations that may indicate account compromise or fraudulent activities. For example, AI systems can flag unusual login patterns or suspicious changes in account settings.
- **Fraudulent Schemes:** Identifying patterns in fraudulent schemes, such as Ponzi schemes and investment scams. Behavioral analysis helps in detecting red flags and preventing fraudulent activities.

8.4. Cybercrime Investigations

In digital forensics, AI-powered behavioral analysis assists investigators in reconstructing events, identifying perpetrators, and understanding the scope of cyber incidents by analyzing digital evidence. Key applications include:

- **Data Correlation:** AI systems correlate data from multiple sources, such as emails, files, and logs, to reconstruct the sequence of events and establish connections between individuals and activities. This helps investigators build a comprehensive picture of the incident.
- **Hacking and Unauthorized Access:** Analyzing behavior patterns related to hacking attempts and unauthorized access. This includes examining login patterns, IP addresses, and access logs to identify potential perpetrators.
- **Malware and Virus Distribution:** Understanding the behavior of malware and virus creators. Behavioral analysis helps in tracking the spread of malicious software and identifying the methods used for distribution.
- **Online Fraud:** Analyzing behaviors associated with online fraud, such as phishing schemes and financial scams. Behavioral insights help in detecting fraudulent activities and identifying the perpetrators.
- **Pattern Recognition:** AI algorithms identify patterns and trends in digital evidence, helping investigators uncover hidden relationships and motives. For example, pattern recognition can reveal connections between different cyberattacks or identify common tactics used by attackers.

- **Predictive Analytics:** AI can analyze historical data to predict potential future actions of suspects, aiding in proactive investigation and prevention. For example, predictive analytics can help anticipate the next move of an attacker based on their previous behaviors.

8.5. Incident Response

Behavior analysis enhances the effectiveness of incident response by providing insights into the actions of attackers:

- **Attack Analysis:** Understanding the behavior of attackers during a cyber incident. This includes analyzing their methods, tactics, and objectives to respond effectively.
- **Response Planning:** Using behavioral insights to plan and execute appropriate response strategies. This helps in addressing the specific actions and motives of the attackers.
- **Post-Incident Review:** Analyzing behavior post-incident to evaluate the effectiveness of the response and identify areas for improvement. This includes reviewing how the attackers' behavior influenced the incident and response.

8.6. Proactive Threat Hunting

Behavioral analysis is used in proactive threat hunting to identify potential threats before they materialize:

- **Threat Detection:** Using behavior-based approaches to detect signs of potential threats. This includes analyzing network traffic, user activity, and system logs for suspicious behavior.
- **Proactive Search:** Conducting proactive searches for indicators of compromise and potential threats. Behavioral insights help in identifying emerging threats and vulnerabilities.
- **Continuous Monitoring:** Implementing continuous monitoring systems to track behavior and detect anomalies in real-time. This helps in maintaining an up-to-date understanding of potential threats.

9. CHALLENGES AND LIMITATIONS

Despite its potential, AI-powered behavioral analysis faces several challenges and limitations. Addressing these issues is essential for maximizing the effectiveness of AI in digital investigations.

- **Algorithmic Bias:** AI algorithms can inherit biases from the data they are trained on, leading to skewed results and potentially unfair or inaccurate conclusions. For example, if an AI model is trained on biased data, it may disproportionately flag certain behaviors or individuals as suspicious. To mitigate algorithmic bias, it is essential to use diverse and representative datasets, regularly evaluate and update AI models, and implement fairness and transparency measures.
- **Data Privacy and Security:** The use of AI in digital investigations raises concerns about data privacy and security. Analyzing behavioral data can raise privacy issues, especially when dealing with personal or sensitive information. Forensic investigators must ensure that AI systems adhere to data protection regulations, such as the General Data Protection Regulation (GDPR) and the California Consumer Privacy Act (CCPA) and implement robust security measures to safeguard privacy and integrity. Investigators should obtain proper authorization and respect privacy rights while analyzing personal data.
- **Interpretability and Transparency:** AI systems, particularly deep learning models, can be complex and opaque, making it challenging to understand how they arrive at their conclusions. This lack of interpretability can be a barrier to trust and acceptance in forensic investigations. Efforts to improve the transparency and explainability of AI models, such as developing explainable AI (XAI) techniques, are crucial for addressing these concerns.
- **Evolving Threats:** Cyber threats are constantly evolving, and AI systems must adapt to new attack techniques and tactics. Continuous training and updating of AI models are necessary to keep pace with emerging threats and maintain the effectiveness of behavioral analysis. This requires ongoing investment in research, development, and collaboration with industry stakeholders.
- **Data Volume and Complexity:** The sheer volume of data generated in digital environments can be overwhelming. Behavior analysis requires robust data management and processing capabilities to handle and analyze large datasets effectively.
- **False Positives and False Negatives:** Behavior analysis can sometimes produce false positives (benign activities flagged as malicious) or false negatives

(malicious activities not detected). Fine-tuning algorithms and continuously updating behavioral baselines are essential to minimize these issues.

- **Behavioral Variability:** Human behavior is complex and varies widely, making it challenging to establish reliable patterns. Behavioral patterns may vary based on personal characteristics, experiences, and contexts. The investigators should account for individual differences in behavior and responses. Understanding the impact of contextual factors on behavior is key. This includes considering environmental, social, and situational influences on actions.

10. CASE STUDIES FOR BEHAVIORAL ANALYSIS IN DIGITAL INVESTIGATIONS

Examining real-world cases where behavior analysis played a pivotal role in digital forensics can illustrate its effectiveness and applications.

- **Insider Threat Detection:** A notable case involved a financial institution where unusual access patterns were detected through behavior analysis. By examining login times, file access frequencies, and data transfers, investigators identified an employee accessing sensitive information outside their job scope. The analysis led to the discovery of data exfiltration activities and the prevention of further breaches.
- **Advanced Persistent Threats (APTs):** In a case involving a sophisticated APT, behavior analysis helped trace the attackers' activities over several months. By analyzing network traffic, file access patterns, and user interactions, investigators uncovered a complex attack infrastructure and identified the attackers' methods, ultimately leading to their mitigation and improved defenses.
- **Fraud Detection:** In an e-commerce fraud case, behavior analysis identified unusual purchasing patterns and account activities. By analyzing transaction histories and user behavior, investigators detected a fraudulent scheme involving stolen credit card information, leading to the arrest of the perpetrators and the recovery of stolen funds.
- **The Boston Marathon Bombing:** Behavior analysis played a crucial role in the investigation of the Boston Marathon bombing. Social media posts and videos were analyzed to understand the behavior of the attackers. The analysis helped in identifying the suspects and providing insights into their methods and motives.

- **The Christchurch Mosque Shootings:** The Christchurch Mosque shootings involved live-streaming of the attack on Facebook. Behavior analysis was used to examine the shooter's online activity and communication patterns. The analysis provided insights into the attacker's motivations and helped in coordinating the response to the incident.
- **The Gabby Petito Case:** In the case of Gabby Petito, behavior analysis was used to trace her movements and interactions through social media. Analyzing posts and communications helped investigators understand the dynamics of her relationship and locate her last known whereabouts, leading to the resolution of the case.
- **The Cambridge Analytica Scandal:** The Cambridge Analytica scandal involved the misuse of personal data from millions of Facebook users. Behavior analysis was employed to understand how the data was harvested and used for political manipulation. The analysis revealed the extent of the misuse and led to regulatory changes and increased scrutiny of data practices.
- **The NXIVM Cult Investigation:** The NXIVM cult investigation utilized behavior analysis to understand the cult's operations and abuse. Analyzing communication patterns and behavioral interactions revealed the methods used for recruitment and control. The analysis provided crucial evidence for legal action against the cult's leaders.

11. FUTURE DIRECTIONS

The field of AI-powered behavioral analysis is rapidly advancing, with several emerging trends and future directions that promise to further enhance digital investigations.

- **Integration with Other Technologies:** AI-powered behavioral analysis is increasingly being integrated with other technologies, such as blockchain and Internet of Things (IoT) devices. These integrations can provide additional layers of data and context, improving the accuracy and effectiveness of digital investigations. For example, blockchain technology can offer immutable records of transactions, while IoT devices can provide valuable data on user interactions and environmental conditions.
- **Advances in Explainable AI (XAI):** The development of explainable AI (XAI) is addressing the need for greater transparency and interpretability in AI systems. XAI techniques aim to make AI models more understandable and accountable, improving their usability in forensic investigations. Advances in

XAI can help bridge the gap between complex AI algorithms and human decision-making, enhancing trust and acceptance in digital investigations.

- **Enhanced Collaboration and Data Sharing:** Collaboration and data sharing between organizations, law enforcement agencies, and cybersecurity firms can enhance the effectiveness of AI-powered behavioral analysis. By sharing threat intelligence, insights, and best practices, organizations can improve their collective ability to detect and respond to cyber threats. Collaborative efforts can also lead to the development of more robust AI models and detection techniques.
- **Enhanced Privacy and Security Measures:** Developing and implementing privacy-preserving techniques and robust security measures will be crucial in addressing privacy concerns associated with behavior analysis. Techniques such as data anonymization and encryption will play a key role in protecting sensitive information.
- **Ethical Considerations and Regulations:** As AI continues to evolve, ethical considerations and regulatory frameworks will play a crucial role in guiding its use in digital investigations. Developing and adhering to ethical guidelines and regulations will help ensure that AI is used responsibly and effectively. Key areas of focus include data privacy, algorithmic fairness, and the responsible use of AI in investigative processes.
- **Evolving Behavioral Models:** Adapting behavioral models to reflect changes in cybercriminal tactics and techniques to effectively address new and emerging threats. Incorporating continuous learning approaches to refine and improve behavioral analysis methods.

12. SUMMARY

AI-powered behavioral analysis represents a significant advancement in digital investigations, offering new capabilities and insights for detecting, preventing, and understanding cyber threats. By leveraging machine learning, natural language processing, and anomaly detection, AI systems can analyze and interpret complex digital behaviors, providing valuable support to investigators and cybersecurity professionals.

While AI-powered behavioral analysis offers many benefits, it also presents challenges related to data privacy, algorithmic bias, and interpretability. Addressing these challenges and staying abreast of emerging trends will be crucial for maximizing the benefits of AI in digital investigations and ensuring its continued effectiveness in the fight against cybercrime.

As the field of digital investigations continues to evolve, AI-powered behavioral analysis will play an increasingly central role, shaping the future of cybersecurity and forensic science. By embracing AI and addressing its challenges, organizations can enhance their capabilities, respond more effectively to cyber threats, and ultimately protect their digital assets and interests.

REFERENCES

Adnan, M. H., Ariffin, S. A., Hanafi, H. F., Husain, M. S., & Panessai, I. Y. (2021). A social media analytics framework to increase prospective students' interests in STEM and TVET education. *Asian Journal of University Education*, 16(4), 82–90. DOI: 10.24191/ajue.v16i4.11945

Husain, M. S. (2019). Social media analytics to predict depression level in the users. In *Early detection of neurological disorders using machine learning systems* (pp. 199–215). IGI Global. DOI: 10.4018/978-1-5225-8567-1.ch011

Khan, A., Husain, M. S., & Khan, A. (2018). Analysis of mental state of users using social media to predict depression! a survey. *International Journal of Advanced Research in Computer Science*, 100-106.

Shahid, H. M., Adnan, M. H., Khan, M. Z., Shukla, S., & Khan, F. U. (2022). *Pervasive Healthcare*. Springer International Publishing.

Suaib, M., Akbar, M., & Husain, M. S. (240-247). Digital forensics and data mining. In *Critical concepts, standards, and techniques in cyber forensics* (pp. 240–247). IGI Global.

Tripathi, M. M., Haroon, M., Khan, Z., & Husain, S. (2022). Security in digital healthcare system. In *Pervasive Healthcare: A Compendium of Critical Factors for Success* (pp. 217–231). Springer. DOI: 10.1007/978-3-030-77746-3_15

ADDITIONAL READING

Gazeau, V., Gupta, K., & An, M. K. (2024). Enhancing Social Media Data Collection for Digital Forensic Investigations: A Web Parser Approach. *International Conference on Computer, Information and Telecommunication Systems (CITS)*, (pp. 1-7). DOI: 10.1109/CITS61189.2024.10607983

Grigaliūnas, Š., Brūzgienė, R., & Venčkauskas, A. (2023). Ontology-Driven Digital Profiling for Identification and Linking Evidence Across Social Media Platform. *IEEE Access : Practical Innovations, Open Solutions*, 11, 111672–111691. DOI: 10.1109/ACCESS.2023.3322162

Hina, M., Ali, M., Javed, A. R., Srivastava, G., Gadekallu, T. R., & Jalil, Z. (2021). *Email classification and forensics analysis using machine learning. IEEE SmartWorld, Ubiquitous Intelligence & Computing, Advanced & Trusted Computing, Scalable Computing & Communications, Internet of People and Smart City Innovation (Smart-World/SCALCOM/UIC/ATC/IOP/SCI)*. IEEE.

Javed, N., Ahmed, T., Faisal, M., Sadia, H., & Sidaine-Daumiller, E. Z. (2023). Workplace cyberbullying in the remote-work era: a new dimension of cyberology. In *Advances in Cyberology and the Advent of the Next-Gen Information Revolution* (pp. 166–177). IGI Global. DOI: 10.4018/978-1-6684-8133-2.ch009

Khan, M. Z., Husain, M. S., & Shoaib, M. (2020). Introduction to email, web, and message forensics. In *Critical concepts, standards, and techniques in cyber forensics* (pp. 174–186). IGI Global. DOI: 10.4018/978-1-7998-1558-7.ch010

Khan, M. Z., Shoaib, M., Husain, M. S., Nisa, K., & Quasim, M. T. (2024). Enhanced mechanism to prioritize the cloud data privacy factors using AHP and TOPSIS: a hybrid approach. Journal of Cloud Computing, 13(1), 42., 13(1).

Madhusudhanan, S., Jose, A. C., Sahoo, J., & Malekian, R. (2023). PRIMϵ: Novel Privacy-Preservation Model with Pattern Mining and Genetic Algorithm. *IEEE Transactions on Information Forensics and Security*, •••, 571–585.

Mohammad, D. (2023). The Link Between Privacy and Disclosure Behavior in Social Networks. In Advances in Cyberology and the Advent of the Next-Gen Information Revolution (pp. 38-61). IGI Global.

Moustafa, N., & Slay, J. (2017). RCNF: Real-time collaborative network forensic scheme for evidence analysis. arXiv preprint arXiv:1711.02824.

Shahid, H. M., Adnan, M. H., Khan, M. Z., Shukla, S., & Khan, F. U. (2022). *Pervasive Healthcare*. Springer International Publishing.

Sharrab, Y., Al-Fraihat, D., & Alsmirat, M. (2023). Deep Neural Networks in Social Media Forensics: Unveiling Suspicious Patterns and Advancing Investigations on Twitter. *3rd Intelligent Cybersecurity Conference (ICSC)*, (pp. 95-102). DOI: 10.1109/ICSC60084.2023.10349985

Shukla, a., Hussain, S., Irshad, R. R., Alattab, A. A., Thakur, S., Breslin, J. G., . . . Jameel, S. M. (2024). Network analysis in a peer-to-peer energy trading model using blockchain and machine learning. Computer Standards & Interfaces, 88, 103799.

Siddiqui, M. Z., Yadav, S., & Husain, M. S. (2018). Application of artificial intelligence in fighting against cyber crimes: A review. *Int. J. Adv. Res. Comput. Sci.*, 9(2), 118–122.

Sudha, T. S., & Rupa, C. (2019). *Analysis and evaluation of integrated cyber crime offences. Innovations in Power and Advanced Computing Technologies (i-PACT).* IEEE.

Vaccari, C., & Chadwick, A. (2020). Deepfakes and disinformation: Exploring the impact of synthetic political video on deception, uncertainty, and trust in news. *Social Media + Society*, 6(1), 2056305120903408. DOI: 10.1177/2056305120903408

Yadav, S. (2020). Cyber Forensics: Its Importance, Cyber Forensics Techniques, and Tools. In Husain, M. S., & Khan, M. Z. (Eds.), *Critical Concepts, Standards, and Techniques in Cyber Forensics* (pp. 1–15). IGI Global. DOI: 10.4018/978-1-7998-1558-7.ch001

KEY TERMS AND DEFINITIONS

Autoregressive Integrated Moving Average (ARIMA): Autoregressive Integrated Moving Average models time series data to predict future values and identify anomalies. ARIMA is a statistical model used for analyzing and forecasting time series data. The ARIMA model combines three key components to capture various aspects of the data's temporal structure: autoregression, differencing (integration), and moving averages.

Long Short-Term Memory (LSTM) Networks: A type of RNN specifically designed to model sequential data and capture long-term dependencies used for analyzing and forecasting time series data. LSTMs are well-suited for tasks involving time series data, natural language processing, and other applications where the context from previous data points is crucial for understanding the current data.

Moving Averages: Moving Averages are statistical methods used to smooth time series data by creating an average of data points over a specified period. This technique helps in identifying trends and patterns by reducing noise and fluctuations in the data.

RNN: Recurrent Neural Network (RNN) is a class of artificial neural networks designed for processing and analyzing sequential data by maintaining a form of memory across different time steps. Unlike traditional feedforward neural networks, RNNs have connections that form directed cycles, allowing information to persist and be used across sequential steps.

Chapter 8
Forensic Analysis of AI-Generated Content

ABSTRACT

The emergence of artificial intelligence (AI) technologies has revolutionized various aspects of human endeavor, including content creation. AI-generated content, spanning from text and images to audio and video, has evolved from simple automated responses to sophisticated and realistic outputs that can closely mimic human creativity, making it challenging to distinguish between human and machine-generated outputs. The field continues to evolve, and staying informed about advancements in AI and forensic methodologies will be crucial for addressing future challenges and ensuring the authenticity of digital content. This chapter explores the forensic analysis of AI-generated content, focusing on techniques, methodologies, and implications for authenticity and integrity in digital media.

1. INTRODUCTION

The emergence of artificial intelligence (AI) technologies has revolutionized various aspects of human endeavor, including content creation. AI-generated content, spanning from text and images to audio and video, has evolved from simple automated responses to sophisticated and realistic outputs that can closely mimic human creativity, making it challenging to distinguish between human and machine-generated outputs. The field continues to evolve, and staying informed about advancements in AI and forensic methodologies will be crucial for addressing future challenges and ensuring the authenticity of digital content. This chapter explores the forensic analysis of AI-generated content, focusing on techniques, methodologies, and implications for authenticity and integrity in digital media.

DOI: 10.4018/979-8-3693-2960-3.ch008

2. AI-GENERATED CONTENT

AI-generated content refers to any digital material produced or manipulated by artificial intelligence technologies. AI-generated content encompasses a diverse range of digital materials. As AI technologies advance, they produce various types of content that can be utilized for legitimate purposes or exploited for malicious activities. Each type of content involves different techniques and technologies, offering various capabilities and presenting unique challenges in the context of cyber forensic investigations.

These types of content are generated using sophisticated AI models that learn patterns from vast amounts of data and then use these patterns to create new, seemingly authentic digital artifacts.

Different types of AI-generated content are:

2.1. AI-Generated Text

Automatically generated articles, reports, social media posts, and other written material created using models like Jasper AI, and GPT-4. AI-generated text is used in various applications, including content creation, customer service, translation, and even creative writing. It can help generate articles, answer questions, and provide recommendations.

- **Automated Articles and Reports:** Automated text generation refers to AI systems creating written content such as news articles, reports, and summaries. Models like OpenAI's GPT series can generate coherent, contextually relevant text that resembles human writing.

Forensics Significance:

- o **Authenticity Verification:** Automated text can be used to create fake news, misleading reports, or to fabricate evidence complicating the investigation of information spread and digital misinformation. Forensics investigators must verify the authenticity of such content by examining metadata, verifying the source of the text, checking for consistency with known facts, and using digital footprint analysis to trace the origins of the content.
- o **Detection of Misuse:** AI-generated reports or articles might be employed in financial fraud, phishing schemes, or defamation. Investigators need to evaluate the content's intent and cross-reference with reliable sources to ascertain authenticity.

- **Tool Utilization:** Tools designed to detect AI-generated text, such as those that analyze linguistic patterns or compare content with known datasets, are essential. Techniques include scrutinizing writing style, grammar consistency, and contextual anomalies.
    - **Chatbot Conversations:** AI-driven chatbots engage in automated dialogues with users, generating responses based on pre-trained models. These conversations can be used in customer service, but they may also be exploited in phishing or social engineering attacks.

Forensics Significance:

- **Interaction Analysis:** Analyzing chatbot logs involves examining timestamps, user interaction patterns, and the AI's response consistency. Forensic experts must determine if chatbots were used in scams, unauthorized data collection, or to impersonate individuals.
- **Integrity Verification:** Chatbot logs may be manipulated. Forensic analysis involves checking logs for consistency, verifying the authenticity of the chat logs, checking for signs of tampering, and evaluating whether the bot was used to impersonate individuals or extract sensitive information.
    - **Social Media Posts and Reviews:** AI-generated social media posts and reviews can be used to manipulate public opinion or create false perceptions. AI can generate or alter content to influence social discourse or perform reputation management.

Forensics Significance:

- **Pattern Detection:** Identifying AI-generated or manipulated posts involves recognizing unusual posting patterns such as unnatural frequency or timing, and repetitive content. Analyzing linguistic patterns and using tools to detect synthetic content are crucial.
- **Verification:** Cross-referencing posts with known legitimate sources and verifying the authorship and origin of content help in determining authenticity. Investigators may use digital forensics tools to trace the origins of the posts and validate their legitimacy.

2.2. AI-Generated Images

Photographs and artworks produced by generative adversarial networks (GANs) or similar technologies.

- **Deepfake Images:** Deepfake images are AI-generated visuals that manipulate or create faces and scenes to falsely represent individuals or situations and mislead viewers. These images can be used for defamation, misinformation, or unauthorized identity representation.

Forensics Significance:

- o **Artifact Detection:** Detecting deepfake images involves analyzing inconsistencies in visual artifacts, such as lighting mismatches, shadows, pixel anomalies and unnatural facial expressions. Tools and algorithms designed to detect deepfakes and image manipulation are crucial for validating image authenticity.
- o **Source Verification:** Investigators must determine the origin of the images and whether they were used in malicious contexts. Techniques include examining metadata, tracking image distribution, and using image forensics tools to verify authenticity.
  - **Synthetic Faces:** Synthetic faces are AI-generated images of individuals that do not exist or are altered from real faces. They may be used for fraudulent purposes, such as creating fake profiles or identities.

Forensics Significance:

- o **Identity Verification:** Investigators must assess whether synthetic faces are being used to impersonate individuals or create fake identities. Techniques include examining facial attributes, comparing with known databases, and using forensic tools to analyze image generation techniques.
- o **Manipulation Detection:** Investigators need to assess whether synthetic faces have been used to mislead or deceive. This involves examining image creation processes and detecting any alterations or manipulations.
  - **Image Manipulation and Alteration:** AI tools can modify existing images by changing backgrounds, combining different elements, or enhancing features, potentially leading to fabricated evidence or mislead viewers.

Forensics Significance:

- o **Alteration Detection:** Detecting image manipulations involves examining visual anomalies, such as inconsistent pixel patterns or metadata discrepancies. Techniques include pixel analysis and the use of image integrity verification tools.

- **Integrity Verification:** Ensuring the integrity of the original image requires examining the content for signs of tampering, such as inconsistencies in visual elements or discrepancies in image metadata.

2.3. AI-Generated Videos

Synthetic videos, including deepfakes, which are manipulated or wholly generated using advanced algorithms.

- **Deepfake Videos:** Deepfake videos are AI-generated or manipulated videos that can create realistic but fake footage of people, potentially used for disinformation, blackmail, or fraud.

Forensics Significance:

- **Artifact Identification:** Detecting deepfake videos involves detecting subtle artifacts and inconsistencies in video frames, such as unnatural movements or synchronization issues. Video forensics tools and deepfake detection algorithms are essential for accurate analysis.
- **Content Validation:** Verifying the authenticity of video content requires assessing the video's metadata, comparing it with known sources, and using specialized detection tools to identify synthetic elements.
    - **Synthetic Video Content:** Synthetic videos are entirely generated by AI, including simulated events, animations, or fabricated scenes that might be used for misleading purposes or to create false evidence.

Forensics Significance:

- **Content Validation:** Verifying synthetic videos involves determining the origin and intent behind synthetic videos by examining the video creation process, checking for inconsistencies, assessing its purpose and using forensic tools to assess authenticity. Techniques include metadata analysis and understanding the context in which the video was generated.
- **Detection Tools:** Forensic tools and algorithms designed to detect synthetic video content are essential for analyzing the video's authenticity and identifying any signs of manipulation or fabrication.
    - **Video Editing and Enhancement:** AI tools can enhance or alter video content, potentially used to cover up illicit activities or manipulate evidence.

Forensics Significance:

- o **Editing Detection:** Identifying signs of video editing involves analyzing changes in video quality, frame inconsistencies, and compression artifacts. Forensic analysis includes examining the video for evidence of tampering or unauthorized modifications.
- o **Evidence Integrity:** Ensuring the integrity of video evidence requires verifying its original state and detecting any alterations made during or after the creation process. Techniques include video forensics tools and frame-by-frame analysis.

2.4. AI-Generated Audio

Synthetic speech and manipulated audio files created through neural networks and other AI techniques.

- **Synthetic Voices:** Synthetic voices are AI-generated audio that mimics real human speech, potentially used in scams, identity theft, or misleading communications.

Forensics Significance:

- o **Voice Analysis:** Detecting synthetic voices involves analyzing speech features for anomalies or inconsistencies, such as unnatural inflections or speech patterns. Tools for voice recognition and analysis are used to identify synthetic content.
- o **Source Verification:** Investigators need to determine whether synthetic voices were used in fraudulent or malicious activities. Techniques include comparing the synthetic voice with known samples and assessing its authenticity.
  - **Audio Deepfakes:** Audio deepfakes involve AI-generated or manipulated audio that can convincingly mimic real voices, used for deception or fraud.

Forensics Significance:

- o **Anomaly Detection:** Identifying audio deepfakes requires analyzing speech patterns, voice characteristics like pitch or modulation, and potential artifacts introduced by AI generation. Forensic audio tools and algorithms help in detecting synthetic audio content.

- **Contextual Analysis:** Assessing the context and purpose of the audio deepfake involves understanding its usage and verifying its authenticity. Techniques include examining the audio's origin and comparing it with known legitimate sources.
  - **Audio Manipulation:** AI tools can alter existing audio recordings, potentially used to create misleading evidence or modify original content.

Forensics Significance:

- **Alteration Detection:** Detecting audio manipulations involves analyzing sound quality, consistency, and potential changes introduced by AI tools. Techniques include spectral analysis and waveform examination.
- **Evidence Integrity:** Ensuring the integrity of audio evidence requires verifying its original state and detecting any unauthorized modifications. Forensic analysis includes using audio forensics tools to validate the content.

2.5. AI-Generated Code

AI is useful to automatically generate codes or programs based on some triggers. These codes can be used for enhancing productivity or can also be used for malicious activities.

- **Automated Code Generation:** AI systems can generate or suggest programming code, which can be used to create or modify software, including potentially malicious code.

Forensic Significance:

- **Code Review:** Analyzing AI-generated code involves understanding its origin, functionality, and potential impact. Forensic experts must assess whether the code was used for legitimate or malicious purposes, including malware development.
- **Malware Detection:** Identifying AI-generated code involved in malicious activities requires examining code behavior, patterns, and integration with existing systems. Techniques include reverse engineering and malware analysis.
  - **Code Debugging and Modification:** AI tools assist in debugging and modifying code, which may be used to hide malicious functionality or alter software behavior.

Forensic Significance:

- o **Tampering Detection:** Detecting unauthorized code modifications involves reviewing changes for signs of tampering or malicious intent. Forensic analysis includes code comparison, integrity checks, and reverse engineering.
- o **Code Integrity:** Ensuring the integrity of software code requires verifying its original state and detecting any changes made during or after its creation. Techniques include code audits and forensic analysis.

Forensic experts must employ specialized tools and techniques to handle the complexities introduced by AI-generated text, images, videos, audio, and code. Understanding these types of content and their forensic implications is crucial for maintaining the integrity and reliability of digital investigations in an increasingly AI-driven world. As AI technology continues to advance, forensic professionals must stay updated on new developments and adapt their methods to effectively address emerging challenges.

3. EVOLUTION OF AI-GENERATED CONTENT

3.1. Historical Context

AI-generated content is not a recent phenomenon; its roots trace back to the early days of computational linguistics and natural language processing (NLP). Early AI models, such as ELIZA in the 1960s, demonstrated rudimentary conversational abilities. However, it was not until the development of more advanced models, such as GPT-3 by OpenAI, that AI-generated content began to exhibit human-like qualities. Contemporary AI models, including GPT-4, DALL-E, and Stable Diffusion, represent significant advancements. These models leverage vast datasets and complex algorithms to generate coherent and contextually relevant content. GPT-4, for instance, is capable of producing highly nuanced text, while DALL-E can create detailed and imaginative images from textual descriptions. The sophistication of these models necessitates advanced forensic techniques to discern the nature and origin of the content they generate.

- **Early Computational Models:** The genesis of AI-generated content can be traced back to early computational models developed in the mid-20th century. One of the pioneering systems was ELIZA, created by Joseph Weizenbaum in the 1960s. ELIZA simulated a Rogerian psychotherapist and could engage in basic conversational exchanges. Although rudimentary, ELIZA's ability to generate coherent responses marked the inception of AI-driven dialogue systems.

- **Rule-Based Systems and Expert Systems:** Following ELIZA, the development of rule-based systems and expert systems in the 1970s and 1980s expanded the scope of AI-generated content. These systems operated based on predefined rules and knowledge bases to generate text and solve specific problems. For example, MYCIN, an early expert system for medical diagnosis, used a set of rules to generate diagnostic suggestions based on user inputs. While limited in flexibility, these systems laid the groundwork for more advanced AI-generated content by demonstrating the potential of automated reasoning.
- **The Emergence of Statistical Methods and Natural Language Processing (NLP):** The 1990s and early 2000s saw significant advances in natural language processing (NLP), driven by statistical methods and large-scale data analysis. The advent of probabilistic models, such as Hidden Markov Models (HMMs) and n-gram models, enabled more sophisticated text generation. These models could predict word sequences based on statistical patterns in large text corpora, leading to improvements in machine translation, text summarization, and speech recognition.
- **The Rise of Deep Learning:** The true transformation in AI-generated content began with the rise of deep learning in the 2010s. Deep learning models, particularly neural networks with multiple layers, achieved remarkable improvements in NLP tasks. The introduction of word embeddings, such as Word2Vec and GloVe, allowed for more nuanced representations of words based on their contextual relationships. This era also saw the development of sequence-to-sequence models, which greatly enhanced machine translation and text generation capabilities.

3.2. Breakthroughs in AI Content Generation

- **The Advent of Transformer Models:** The introduction of the Transformer architecture in 2017 by Vaswani et al. marked a pivotal moment in AI content generation. Transformers, with their self-attention mechanisms, enabled more effective handling of long-range dependencies in text. This architecture paved the way for the development of large-scale language models like BERT (Bidirectional Encoder Representations from Transformers) and GPT (Generative Pre-trained Transformer).
- **GPT-3 and Large-Scale Language Models:** GPT-3, released by OpenAI in 2020, represents a significant leap in AI-generated content. With 175 billion parameters, GPT-3 demonstrated unprecedented capabilities in generating

coherent and contextually relevant text. Its ability to perform a wide range of language tasks, from creative writing to coding, highlighted the potential of large-scale language models to produce human-like content. The success of GPT-3 underscored the importance of scale and data diversity in advancing AI content generation.

- **AI-Generated Art and Multimedia:** The evolution of AI-generated content extends beyond text to include images, audio, and video. The development of Generative Adversarial Networks (GANs) in 2014 by Ian Goodfellow introduced a new approach to content creation. GANs consist of two neural networks—generator and discriminator—that work adversarially to produce realistic images. Technologies like DeepArt and DALL-E leverage GANs to create artistic images and visuals from textual descriptions, showcasing the potential of AI in creative domains.
- **Deepfakes and Synthetic Media:** Deepfakes represent another significant advancement in AI-generated content, utilizing deep learning techniques to create highly realistic synthetic media. Deepfake technology can generate convincing videos by superimposing or altering facial features and voices. While this technology has potential applications in entertainment and education, it also raises concerns about misinformation and privacy (Akbar, Suaib, & Hussain, The Rise of Deepfake Technology: Issues, Challenges, and Countermeasures, 2023), (Akbar, Suaib, & Hussain, Analysis of Deep-Fake Technology Impacting Digital World Credibility: A Comprehensive Literature Review, 2022). The ability to create hyper-realistic content underscores the need for robust detection mechanisms and ethical guidelines.

4. IMPLICATIONS AND CHALLENGES OF AI GENERATED CONTENT

As AI-generated content becomes more prevalent, the need for forensic analysis grows. Ensuring the integrity and authenticity of such content is crucial for various applications, including legal investigations, media verification, and security assessments. Effective forensic analysis can help detect manipulations, attribute content to specific sources, and ensure that AI-generated materials are used ethically and responsibly.

- **Difficulty in Verifying Authenticity**
    - **Challenge:** AI-generated content, such as deepfake videos synthetic text, and altered media can be highly realistic and difficult to distinguish

from genuine material. This challenges forensic experts to verify the authenticity of digital evidence.

  - **Implication:** Forensic experts must develop and employ advanced detection techniques to distinguish between real and synthetic content, which can be resource-intensive and complex. Traditional methods may not be sufficient, requiring sophisticated tools and methods for accurate verification.

- **Increased Risk of Misinformation and Disinformation**
  - **Challenge:** AI-generated content can be used to create misleading or false information like fabricated news articles, fake social media profiles, and manipulated multimedia content contributing to misinformation and manipulating public opinion.
  - **Implication:** Forensic investigations must account for the possibility that digital evidence could be part of a broader attempt to deceive or manipulate public opinion. This requires additional layers of scrutiny and verification to ensure the accuracy of evidence and prevent the dissemination of false information.
- **Detection of Manipulated Evidence**
  - **Challenge:** Advanced AI tools can create realistic manipulations of images, audio, and video, making it challenging to detect alterations or tampering. Deepfake technology, for example, can produce videos where individuals appear to say or do things they never did.
  - **Implication:** Traditional forensic methods may not be sufficient to identify subtle alterations. Detecting these sophisticated manipulations requires specialized forensic tools and methods, which may not be readily available or fully developed. The challenge is exacerbated by the continuous evolution of AI technologies, making it difficult to keep pace with new forms of manipulation.
- **Complexity of Evidence Analysis**
  - **Challenge:** The complexity of AI-generated content adds layers of difficulty to the forensic analysis process. Forensic experts must analyze not just the content itself but also the methods and tools used to generate or manipulate it.
  - **Implication:** This complexity can slow down the investigative process and increase the risk of errors. Forensic experts must consider the potential for sophisticated manipulations and ensure that their analysis methods are capable of addressing these complexities. Forensic professionals need advanced analytical tools and expertise to effectively handle and interpret AI-generated content.
- **Impact on Evidence Integrity**

- **Challenge:** The ability to create realistic synthetic content raises concerns about the integrity of digital evidence. AI-generated content can be used to fabricate or alter evidence, potentially compromising the reliability of forensic findings.
- **Implication:** Ensuring the integrity of digital evidence requires rigorous verification processes and the use of advanced forensic tools to detect and address potential fabrications.

- **Ethical and Privacy Considerations:**
  - **Challenge:** The creation and use of AI-generated content, such as realistic synthetic images or voices, raises several ethical and privacy concerns, particularly when used to create synthetic representations of individuals or manipulate personal data. This includes issues related to consent, the potential for misuse in creating deceptive or harmful content, such as deepfakes and fake news, and the impact on individuals' reputations.
  - **Implication:** The potential for misuse of AI-generated content necessitates a careful examination of the ethical implications of AI technologies. Forensic investigations must address these concerns by adhering to ethical guidelines and ensuring that AI tools are used in ways that respect individual privacy rights and legal boundaries. Forensic analysis must traverse issues related to the unauthorized use of personal data and the potential for deepfakes to invade individuals' privacy. Ensuring responsible usage and developing ethical guidelines are critical to addressing these concerns. Legal frameworks need to evolve to address these concerns and protect individuals from AI-generated content misuse.
- **Impact on Creative Industries:** AI-generated content has the potential to transform creative industries, including writing, art, and entertainment. While AI can augment human creativity and automate certain tasks, it also poses challenges related to authorship, originality, and intellectual property. The integration of AI into creative processes requires a reevaluation of traditional concepts of creativity and ownership.
- **Technical Concerns**
  - **Challenge:** The rapid advancement of AI-generated content presents technical challenges related to detection and verification. As AI-generated content becomes more sophisticated, distinguishing between genuine and synthetic content becomes increasingly difficult. Addressing these challenges requires the development of advanced detection algorithms and the implementation of strategies to ensure content authenticity.

- o **Implication**: Forensic professionals face ongoing challenges in keeping up with the latest AI developments and ensuring that their tools and techniques remain effective. This requires a proactive approach to monitoring technological advancements and updating forensic practices accordingly.

- **Increased Resource and Expertise Requirements:**
  - o **Challenge:** The integration of AI-generated content into forensic investigations requires specialized tools, training, and expertise. Keeping up with rapid advancements in AI technology demands significant resources and continuous professional development.
  - o **Implication:** Forensic professionals need to stay updated on the latest AI technologies and methods, which may necessitate specialized training and investment in advanced tools. This can increase the cost and complexity of forensic investigations and may limit access to cutting-edge forensic methods and tools for some organizations or jurisdictions.
- **Potential for New Forms of Cybercrime:**
  - o **Challenge:** AI-generated content opens the door to new forms of cybercrime, such as creating realistic phishing attacks, fraudulent identity documents, or convincing social engineering schemes.
  - o **Implication:** Forensic professionals must adapt their investigative techniques to address these emerging threats and develop strategies to detect and counteract new forms of AI-driven cybercriminal activities. This includes staying informed about evolving cybercrime tactics and incorporating relevant detection techniques.
- **Legal Frameworks and Regulation**
  - o **Challenge:** The legal system may struggle with the admissibility of AI-generated content as evidence. Questions about the authenticity, reliability, and source of AI-generated evidence can lead to legal challenges and disputes.

    The legal landscape surrounding AI-generated content is still evolving. Existing laws may not adequately address the complexities of AI-generated content, necessitating new regulations and guidelines.
  - o **Implication:** Forensic professionals must ensure that AI-generated evidence meets legal standards for admissibility, which may involve additional documentation and validation processes. This can affect the overall success of legal proceedings and the outcome of cases.

Forensic experts should contribute to the development of legal frameworks by providing insights into the technical aspects of AI-generated content and its implications for authenticity and integrity.

The critical challenges and implications posed by AI-generated content in cyber forensics underscore the need for advanced detection tools, rigorous verification processes, and ongoing professional development. Addressing these challenges requires a multi-faceted approach that incorporates technological innovation, ethical considerations, and legal expertise to ensure the integrity and effectiveness of digital investigations. As AI technology continues to evolve, forensic professionals must remain vigilant and adaptable to effectively manage the complexities introduced by AI-generated content.

5. FORENSIC ANALYSIS TECHNIQUES FOR AI GENERATED CONTENT

Different techniques used for forensics analysis of AI generated content can be categorized based on the type of the content to be analyzed. These approaches are summarized in Figure 1.

Figure 1. Forensic analysis techniques for AI generated content

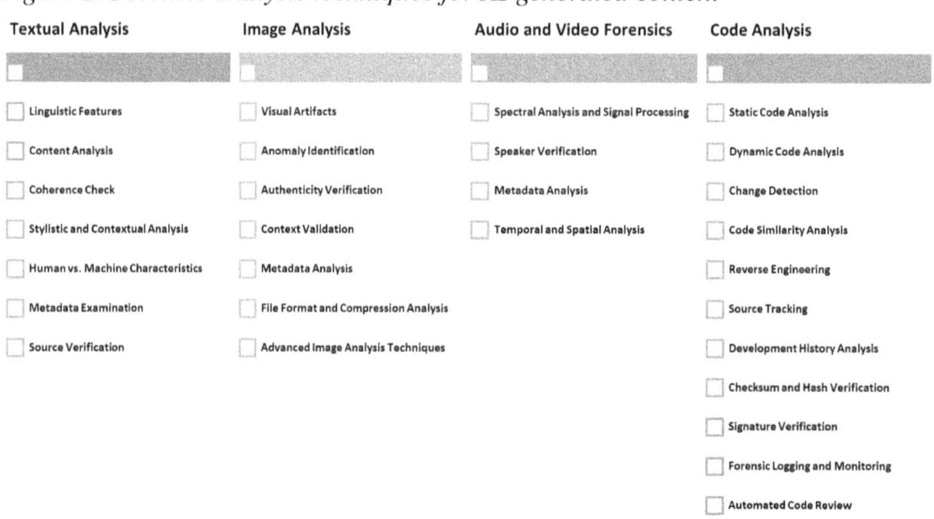

5.1. Textual Analysis

Textual analysis of AI-generated content is a dynamic and essential area of forensic investigation. By employing a combination of NLP, machine learning, deep learning, and stylometric analysis, forensic experts can effectively identify and analyze synthetic text. Textual analysis of AI-generated content involves examining various aspects of the text produced by AI models, such as language, coherence, style, and the accuracy of information. With AI technologies increasingly used to produce human-like text for various applications, from news articles to social media posts, the ability to discern between genuine and synthetic content is essential for maintaining information integrity. Textual analysis of AI-generated content involves several approaches to determine its origin and authenticity:

- **Linguistic Features:** AI-generated text often exhibits distinct linguistic patterns, such as repetitive phrases or unnatural coherence. Forensic linguists analyze these patterns to identify whether the content deviates from typical human writing styles. Techniques include statistical analysis of word frequency, sentence structure, and syntactic complexity.
- **Content Analysis:** Content analysis involves verifying the accuracy and credibility of the information presented in the text. AI-generated text may include inaccurate or fabricated information. Fact-checking tools can validate the accuracy of claims and statements.
- **Coherence Check:** AI-generated text may exhibit structural anomalies, such as abrupt topic shifts or lack of logical flow. Analyzing the structure of the text helps identify such issues.
- **Stylistic and Contextual Analysis:** AI-generated content may lack the depth of personal experiences and emotional nuance found in human writing. Forensic experts assess stylistic elements, such as tone, voice, and contextual relevance, to determine the likelihood of AI authorship. Discrepancies in style and context can signal AI involvement. Also check if the style and tone are appropriate for the intended audience or purpose of the content.
- **Human vs. Machine Characteristics:** Consider aspects that might reveal the AI nature of the content, such as unnatural phrasing or repetitive patterns. Be aware of common limitations of AI, such as difficulty with nuanced understanding or generating contextually appropriate responses.
- **Metadata Examination:** Metadata embedded in digital documents can provide information about the creation and modification history of the text, helping to verify its authenticity.
- **Source Verification:** Cross-referencing text with reliable sources helps identify any discrepancies or false information. Tracking the source and develop-

ment history of the text can reveal whether it was generated by an AI system and identify the tools used.

5.1.1. Tools and Techniques for Text Analysis

Common tools and techniques used for text analysis during cyber forensics investigation includes:

- **Stylometric Analysis:** Tools like JStylo (PSAL - The Privacy, 2011) or LIWC (Linguistic Inquiry and Word Count) (Pennebaker, 1993) analyze writing style and linguistic features.
- **Contextual Analysis Tools:** Text analysis software that evaluates coherence and context, such as Coh-Metrix (Graesser & McNamara, 2004), can help detect inconsistencies.
- **Metadata Analyzers:** Tools like ExifTool (Harvey, 2024) or Document Metadata Analyzer can extract and analyze metadata.
- **Provenance Tracking Tools:** Systems like Provenance Aware Storage Systems (PASS) (Muniswamy-Reddy, Kiran-Kumar, Holland, Braun, & Seltzer, 2006) can track the origin and modifications of digital content.
- **Fact-Checking Services:** Platforms like FactCheck.org or Snopes can be used to verify the accuracy of text content.
- **Content Verification Tools:** Tools such as IBM Watson Discovery or Google Fact Check Tools can assist in content analysis.
- **Text Analysis Software:** Tools like OpenAI's GPT-3 or Hugging Face's Transformers can be used to analyze text coherence and structure.
- **Structural Analysis Tools:** Software like AntConc or Voyant Tools can help analyze text structure and consistency.
- **Source Verification Platforms:** Services like SourceCred or Trustpilot can assess the credibility of sources.
- **Validation Methods:** Methods such as digital forensics or blockchain-based verification can validate the source of the text.

Forensic analysis of AI-generated text requires a multi-faceted approach that combines traditional text analysis methods with advanced AI detection techniques. By employing a range of tools and methods, including linguistic analysis, machine learning models, metadata examination, and expert consultation, forensic experts can effectively investigate and verify AI-generated text. Adapting to the evolving capabilities of AI and integrating specialized forensic techniques are essential for maintaining the accuracy and reliability of digital content investigations.

5.1.2. Best Practices

Cyber forensics analysis of AI-generated text involves a range of practices to ensure accuracy, reliability, and comprehensiveness. Few best practices to follow are:

- **Understand the AI Model and Its Capabilities:** Gain a thorough understanding of the AI model or tool used to generate the text. Different models (e.g., GPT-4, BERT) have different architectures, training data, and capabilities. Identify the specific version and any parameters or configurations used, as these can impact the text output and analysis.

Recognize the common behaviors, biases, and limitations of the AI model to better interpret its outputs.

- **Establish a Baseline for Normal Text Patterns:** Analyze the typical text patterns and styles generated by the AI based on its training data. This helps in identifying deviations or anomalies. Document the common characteristics of AI-generated text, such as linguistic style, coherence, and repetition patterns.
- **Use Forensic Tools and Techniques:** Employ specialized forensic tools designed for text analysis, such as text comparison and anomaly detection software.

Check for metadata associated with the text files, such as creation dates, authorship details, and editing history, which might provide insights into the text's origin.

- **Verify the Source of AI-Generated Text:** Trace the source of the AI-generated text to determine the specific tool or platform used. Cross-check the text against known outputs from the AI model to confirm authenticity.
- **Conduct Comparative Analysis:** Compare the AI-generated text with a dataset of known outputs from the same or similar models to identify patterns or anomalies. Analyze differences between AI-generated text and human-generated text to spot potential discrepancies.
- **Preserve Evidence Integrity:** Ensure that all AI-generated text and related evidence are stored securely to prevent tampering or loss. Maintain a detailed chain of custody documentation to track the handling and transfer of evidence.
- **Apply Contextual Analysis:** Interpret the AI-generated text in the context of the case or investigation. Understanding the context helps in determining the relevance and intent behind the text. Look for contextual clues that may indi-

cate the purpose or origin of the text, such as specific references or language style.

- **Document the Analysis Process:** Keep comprehensive records of the analysis process, including methods, tools used, and findings.

  Prepare clear and detailed reports summarizing the analysis, findings, and conclusions, which are crucial for legal and investigative purposes.
- **Consult with Experts:** Collaborate with AI and text analysis experts to gain deeper insights or validate findings. Engage with professionals from different fields (e.g., linguistics, AI research) to enhance the analysis.
- **Stay Updated with Evolving AI Technologies:** Stay informed about advancements in AI and machine learning to understand emerging trends and capabilities. Regularly update forensic tools and techniques to keep pace with new developments in AI technology.

5.2. Image Analysis

In the realm of cyber forensics, image and video analysis plays a crucial role in investigating digital evidence. As digital media becomes increasingly prevalent in evidence collection, forensic experts must employ specialized techniques to authenticate, analyze, and interpret images and videos. AI-generated images and videos, created through technologies like Generative Adversarial Networks (GANs) present unique challenges.

- **Visual Artifacts:** AI-generated images may exhibit artifacts or inconsistencies, such as unnatural textures, distortions, inconsistent lighting, or improbable details. Forensic analysts use image processing tools to detect these anomalies. Techniques include examining pixel-level inconsistencies and employing deep learning models trained to identify synthetic imagery.
- **Anomaly Identification:** Unusual patterns or inconsistencies in fine details, such as facial features or textures, can signal manipulation or AI generation.
- **Authenticity Verification:** Techniques like visual coherence checks and consistency analysis ensure the image aligns with real-world expectations.
- **Context Validation:** Cross-referencing the image with known events, locations, or subjects helps verify its authenticity and context. Evaluating the source of the image and its relevance to the context can reveal whether it is AI-generated.
- **Metadata Analysis:** Metadata refers to the data embedded within an image file, such as creation date, camera settings, and location information. Metadata associated with digital content can provide clues about its origin and modification history. Forensic experts analyze metadata, such as creation

timestamps and software information, to identify discrepancies that might indicate AI involvement.

- **File Format and Compression Analysis:** File format and compression analysis involve examining the encoding and compression techniques used in an image file. AI-generated images might exhibit compression artifacts that differ from those found in naturally captured images. Examining the file format and compression methods can reveal inconsistencies or signs of artificial generation.
- **Advanced Image Analysis Techniques:** Deep learning and AI detection models use machine learning algorithms to identify patterns and features characteristic of AI-generated images. Models trained on datasets of AI-generated and real images can identify subtle differences and detect synthetic content. Machine learning algorithms analyze image features and anomalies that may not be visible to the naked eye.

5.2.1. Tools and Techniques for Image Analysis

Forensic investigator can use different tools or techniques for image analysis during investigation such as:

- **Image Editing Software:** Tools like Adobe Photoshop or GIMP can be used to zoom in and analyze fine details and anomalies.
- **Artifact Detection Software:** Specialized forensic tools can highlight and analyze potential artifacts in images.
- **ELA Tools:** Software like FotoForensics provides ELA capabilities to visualize and analyze error levels in images.
- **Metadata Extractors:** Tools like ExifTool or Adobe Bridge can extract and analyze metadata from image files.
- **Compression Analyzers:** Tools like JPEGsnoop or ImageMagick can analyze image compression and file formats.
- **AI Detection Tools:** Software like DeepFake Detection or GANalyze can identify AI-generated images.
- **Forensic Analysis Software:** Tools like Amped FIVE or FotoForensics provide advanced forensic analysis capabilities.
- **Contextual Verification Tools:** Platforms like Google Reverse Image Search or TinEye can assist in cross-referencing images with known sources.
- **Similarity Detection Tools:** Software that identifies similar images or patterns can assist in cross-referencing analysis.
- **Custom ML Models:** Developing custom machine learning models for specific types of AI-generated content can enhance detection accuracy.

Forensic analysis of AI-generated images involves a combination of traditional forensic techniques and advanced tools designed to address the unique challenges posed by AI technologies. By employing a range of methods, including visual inspection, metadata analysis, deep learning models, and contextual validation, forensic experts can effectively investigate and verify AI-generated images. Staying current with technological advancements and integrating specialized forensic techniques are crucial for maintaining the accuracy and reliability of digital content investigations.

5.2.2. Best Practices

Analyzing AI-generated images in cyber forensics requires meticulous attention to detail and specialized techniques due to the unique challenges posed by these images. Best practices for conducting a thorough and effective image analysis are:

- **Understand the AI Model and Techniques Used:** Gain a deep understanding of the specific AI model or technique used to generate the image (e.g., GANs, diffusion models). Learn about the dataset used to train the AI system, as it can influence the types of images it generates and the patterns you might observe.
- **Establish a Baseline for Normal Image Characteristics:** Review typical outputs from the AI model to establish a baseline for normal image characteristics. This includes style, common artifacts, and quality. Use known AI-generated images as benchmarks to compare and identify deviations or anomalies in the image under investigation.
- **Conduct Detailed Image Analysis:** Look for common artifacts of AI-generated images, such as unnatural textures, blending issues, or inconsistencies in lighting and shadows.

Utilize image forensics tools to detect signs of manipulation or generation. Tools like JPEGsnoop, FotoForensics, or deep learning-based detectors can help identify anomalies.

- **Examine Metadata and File Information:** Check the image file's metadata for details such as creation date, software used, and modification history. Metadata can sometimes reveal information about the AI tool or platform used.

Analyze the file structure and compression artifacts to gain insights into the image's origin and potential modifications.

- **Perform Comparative Analysis:** Compare the image with a database of known AI-generated images to identify similarities or patterns that might suggest the same model was used. Compare the image with known human-generated content to detect subtle differences that may indicate AI generation.
- **Verify Image Authenticity and Source:** Trace the image's source to determine the specific AI tool or platform used for generation. This may involve examining the distribution channels or platforms where the image appeared. Validate the content of the image against known sources or references to confirm its authenticity.
- **Analyze the Context and Purpose:** Analyze the context in which the image was found or used. Understanding the context can provide insights into the intent behind its creation and use.

Assess the purpose of the AI-generated image i.e. whether it's for artistic, fraudulent, or other specific uses. This can guide the investigation and interpretation.

- **Document the Analysis Process Thoroughly:** Maintain detailed documentation of the analysis process, including tools used, methods applied, and findings. This documentation is crucial for reproducibility and legal purposes.

Prepare comprehensive reports that include the analysis methodology, findings, and any conclusions drawn. Clear and accurate reporting is essential for legal and investigative clarity.

- **Consult with Experts:** Engage with digital forensics and AI experts for their insights, especially when dealing with sophisticated or novel AI-generated images. Collaborate with professionals from different fields (e.g., computer science, visual arts) to gain a broader perspective and enhance forensics analysis.
- **Stay Informed on Advances in AI and Forensics:** Keep up with the latest developments in AI image generation technologies and forensic analysis techniques. AI technologies evolve rapidly, and staying informed is crucial for effective analysis.

Regularly update forensic tools and techniques to adapt to new challenges and advancements in AI-generated image detection.

5.3. Audio and Video Forensics

Forensic analysis of AI-generated audio and video presents unique challenges due to the sophisticated nature of AI technologies like Deepfakes that can create highly realistic synthetic content. These challenges require specialized techniques to detect manipulations, verify authenticity, and understand the context of the content.

- **Spectral Analysis and Signal Processing:** AI-generated audio may exhibit unnatural spectral patterns or artifacts that differ from natural recordings. Spectral analysis examines the frequency components of audio signals to detect anomalies or artifacts that may indicate manipulation. Signal processing techniques can also identify patterns and distortions that are not typical in natural recordings. Tools like Audacity or Adobe Audition can perform spectral analysis to identify such anomalies.
- **Speaker Verification:** AI-generated voices might not accurately replicate the unique vocal traits of a specific individual. Voice biometrics involves analyzing the unique characteristics of a speaker's voice to verify authenticity. Speaker verification compares the AI-generated voice with known samples to assess whether it matches the claimed speaker.
- **Metadata Analysis:** Metadata analysis examines embedded information and timestamps for clues about the audio's origin and integrity. Analysis of metadata can reveal information about the creation and modification history of the audio file.
- **Temporal and Spatial Analysis:** Temporal and spatial inconsistencies, such as unnatural movement patterns or synchronization issues, can signal AI-generated content. AI-generated videos might have mismatched audio and visual elements, such as lip movements not matching spoken words. Forensic techniques involve analyzing frame-by-frame video content and audio-visual synchronization to identify potential fakes.

5.3.1. Tools and Techniques for Audio and Video Forensics

Audio and Video Forensics investigation can make use of different tools and techniques available such as:

- **Spectral Analyzers:** Software such as iZotope RX or Adobe Audition provides spectral views to analyze and detect anomalies.
- **Signal Processing Libraries:** Libraries like LibROSA for Python can assist in detailed signal analysis and feature extraction.

- **Voice Biometrics Systems:** Tools like Nuance or Pindrop can be used for speaker verification and comparison.
- **Acoustic Models:** Machine learning models trained on voice data can detect deviations from natural vocal patterns.
- **Metadata Analyzers:** Tools like ExifTool or MediaInfo can be used to examine and interpret metadata.
- **Deepfake Detection Tools:** Software such as Deepware Scanner or Microsoft Video Authenticator helps identify deepfake content.
- **Frame Analysis Software:** Tools like Adobe Premiere Pro or FFmpeg allow detailed frame-by-frame inspection.
- **Compression Analysis Software:** Software such as JPEGsnoop or VideoSpec provides insights into video compression techniques and artifacts.
- **Source Verification Methods:** Techniques such as digital fingerprinting or blockchain-based verification can provide insights into the video's origin.
- **Forensic Suites:** Integrated forensic tools that offer a range of analysis capabilities, such as FTK Imager or EnCase, can provide a comprehensive analysis.

Forensic analysis of AI-generated audio and video requires a multi-faceted approach that combines traditional forensic techniques with specialized tools designed to address the unique challenges posed by AI technologies. By employing a range of methods, from spectral and frame-by-frame analysis to metadata examination and synchronization checks, forensic experts can effectively detect manipulations and verify the authenticity of AI-generated content. Staying updated with the latest developments in AI and forensic technology is crucial for maintaining the accuracy and reliability of digital investigations.

5.3.2. Best Practices

Conducting forensic analysis of AI-generated audio and video involves unique challenges due to the sophisticated capabilities of modern AI technologies. Best practices to ensure thorough and accurate forensic analysis of AI-generated audio and video content are:

- **Understand the AI Technology and Model:** Familiarize yourself with the specific AI models used for generating or manipulating audio and video, such as deepfake technologies, voice synthesis models, or video enhancement algorithms. Knowing how these models work helps in recognizing their output characteristics.

Understand the datasets used to train these models, as they influence the style and potential artifacts in the generated content.

- **Establish a Baseline for Normal Media Characteristics:** Review and document the usual output characteristics of the AI models involved. This includes typical artifacts, compression patterns, or unnatural features that may be present in generated content. Use known AI-generated audio and video samples as benchmarks to identify deviations or anomalies in the media being analyzed.
- **Conduct Detailed Analysis for Audio Content:** Analyze audio for signs of AI generation or manipulation, such as unnatural intonation, inconsistent speech patterns, or anomalies in acoustic features. Tools like deepfake audio detectors or phonetic analysis software can be useful.

Use spectral analysis tools to examine the frequency domain of the audio. AI-generated audio might exhibit distinct patterns or artifacts not typical of natural recordings.

- **Conduct Detailed Analysis for Video Content:** Analyze video content frame by frame to detect artifacts like inconsistent lighting, unnatural motion, or irregularities in facial expressions and body movements. Tools like video forensics software can assist in this analysis.

Examine pixel-level data for anomalies that may indicate manipulation or generation, such as blending errors or mismatched textures.

- **Examine Metadata and File Information:** Check the metadata associated with audio and video files for creation dates, software used, and other relevant information. Analyze file structure and compression artifacts to detect signs of editing or generation. Tools like ExifTool can help examine metadata and file integrity.
- **Perform Comparative Analysis:** Compare the audio and video with a database of known AI-generated and manipulated media to identify similarities and differences. Analyze the content against natural, human-generated media to detect discrepancies or inconsistencies that might indicate AI involvement.
- **Verify Authenticity and Source:** Validate the content against known, reliable sources to verify its authenticity. Trace the origin of the media to determine if it was generated or manipulated using specific AI tools or platforms.

- **Analyze the Context and Intent:** Examine the context in which the audio or video was found or used to interpret the intent behind the creation and use of the content.
- **Document the Analysis Process Thoroughly:** Keep detailed records of the forensic analysis process, including methodologies, tools used, and findings. Accurate reporting is crucial for legal and investigative purposes.

5.4. Code Analysis

Forensic analysis of AI-generated code involves specialized techniques to address the unique challenges posed by code produced or altered through artificial intelligence. AI-generated code can be used for various purposes, including developing sophisticated malware or automating repetitive coding tasks. Analyzing such code requires advanced methods to ensure its integrity and detect any malicious or unauthorized modifications.

- **Static Code Analysis:** Static code analysis involves examining the code without executing it. This method uses automated tools to inspect the code for patterns, vulnerabilities, and adherence to coding standards.

Static analysis tools can flag potential security vulnerabilities or malicious code patterns embedded within the AI-generated code.

Techniques such as code obfuscation or encryption, often used to hide the true nature of code, can be identified through static analysis, revealing attempts to obscure malicious intentions.

- **Dynamic Code Analysis:** Dynamic code analysis involves executing the code in a controlled environment (sandbox) to observe its behavior and interactions.

By running the code in a sandbox, forensic analysts can monitor its runtime behavior, interactions with the operating system, and network activity to detect malicious actions or unintended consequences. Analyzing how the code performs under various conditions can reveal unusual or harmful behavior that may not be apparent from static analysis alone.

- **Change Detection:** By comparing AI-generated code with previous versions or reference implementations, analysts can detect unauthorized changes or additions that might indicate malicious intent.

- **Code Similarity Analysis:** Comparing the AI-generated code with known malicious code or code from similar AI tools can help identify patterns and similarities that may reveal hidden threats.
- **Reverse Engineering:** Reverse engineering involves deconstructing compiled or obfuscated code to understand its functionality and uncover any hidden components.

If the AI-generated code is compiled, decompiling it can help forensic analysts understand its logic and identify any embedded malicious code. Techniques used to obfuscate code can be reversed to reveal the true nature of the code, helping analysts detect hidden threats.

- **Source Tracking:** Identifying the source of the AI-generated code and its development environment can help determine its legitimacy and detect any unauthorized or malicious modifications.
- **Development History Analysis:** Analyzing the development history and version control logs can provide insights into the evolution of the code and identify any suspicious changes.
- **Checksum and Hash Verification:** Calculating and comparing checksums or cryptographic hashes of the code can help ensure its integrity and detect any unauthorized modifications.
- **Signature Verification:** Validating digital signatures or code certificates can confirm the authenticity of the code and its source.
- **Forensic Logging and Monitoring:** Forensic logging and monitoring involves capturing and analyzing logs and system activity related to the execution and modification of code. Monitoring logs related to the execution of AI-generated code can provide insights into its behavior and any anomalies or suspicious activities. Tracking changes to the codebase can help identify unauthorized modifications or tampering.
- **Automated Code Review:** Automated code review involves using AI and machine learning algorithms to analyze and review code for potential issues or malicious patterns. Automated reviews can identify deviations from typical coding practices or known code patterns that may indicate malicious intent. Machine learning models can be trained to recognize patterns indicative of malicious code or vulnerabilities in AI-generated code.

5.4.1. Tools and Techniques for Code Analysis

- **Linters and Code Quality Tools:** Tools like ESLint, SonarQube, or CodeClimate can identify common errors and style issues.

- **Security Scanners:** Tools such as Checkmarx or Fortify can detect vulnerabilities and potential security risks.
- **Sandbox Environments:** Tools such as Cuckoo Sandbox or Any.Run can create controlled environments to execute and analyze the behavior of AI-generated code.
- **Behavior Analysis Tools:** Tools like Process Monitor or Wireshark can help track system and network activity generated by the code.
- **Diff Tools:** Tools like Beyond Compare or WinMerge can be used to compare different versions of code.
- **Similarity Detection Tools:** Tools such as MOSS (Measure of Software Similarity) can identify similarities between code snippets.
- **Decompilers:** Tools like IDA Pro or Ghidra can decompile and analyze binary code.
- **Obfuscation Tools:** Tools like JStill or ProGuard can help analyze and deobfuscate Java code.
- **Version Control Systems:** Tools like Git or SVN can track changes and contributions to the codebase.
- **Provenance Tracking Tools:** Tools such as CodeTrace can help track the origin and history of code.
- **AI-Based Review Tools:** Tools such as DeepCode or CodeGuru can provide automated insights into code quality and security.
- **Machine Learning Models:** Custom machine learning models can be trained to detect specific types of malicious code or vulnerabilities.
- **Hashing Tools:** Tools like SHA-256 or MD5 can calculate and verify checksums or hashes.
- **Code Signing Tools:** Tools like OpenSSL or SignTool can validate digital signatures and certificates.
- **Logging Tools:** Tools like Splunk or ELK Stack can capture and analyze logs from various sources.
- **Monitoring Tools:** Tools such as Nagios or Zabbix can provide real-time monitoring of system activity and performance.
- **Code Quality Analyzers:** Tools such as SonarQube or CodeClimate can evaluate code quality and adherence to standards.

Forensic analysis of AI-generated code requires a combination of traditional and advanced techniques to address the unique challenges posed by AI technologies. By employing a range of methods, from static and dynamic analysis to reverse engineering and automated reviews, forensic experts can effectively investigate and manage AI-generated code. Adapting to the evolving landscape of AI technology and incorporating specialized tools and expertise are essential for ensuring accurate and reliable forensic analysis.

5.4.2. Best Practices

Forensic analysis of AI-generated code requires specialized techniques and practices due to the unique nature of AI technologies and their outputs. Best practices for conducting a thorough and accurate forensic analysis of AI-generated code are:

- **Understand the AI Model and Its Capabilities:** Gain a comprehensive understanding of the AI model used to generate the code, including its architecture, training data, and capabilities. Identify the type of AI model (e.g., neural network, decision tree) and understand its functionality and limitations. Investigate the nature of the data used to train the model, as it influences the behavior of the generated code.
- **Implement Specialized Code Analysis Tools:** Utilize tools specifically designed for analyzing AI-generated code, which may differ from traditional code analysis tools due to the unique characteristics of AI algorithms. Develop custom scripts or tools to handle unique aspects of AI code, such as model integration or proprietary algorithms.
- **Conduct Thorough Static and Dynamic Analysis:** Apply both static and dynamic analysis techniques to gain a complete understanding of AI-generated code, covering both the code's structure and its runtime behavior. Static Analysis like code review identify obfuscation, structural issues, complex patterns, or potentially malicious instructions in the code without executing it. Dynamic Analysis is done by executing the code in a controlled environment to observe its behavior and interactions with the system like system resource usage, network activity, and behavior.
- **Assess Integration and Interaction with AI Models:** Examine how the AI model is embedded in the code and how it communicates with other modules. Assess the impact of the AI model on the overall functionality and behavior of the code.
- **Cross-Reference Findings with Known Threats:** Validate your findings by comparing them with databases of known malware and vulnerabilities. Check findings against current threat intelligence and previous incidents to ensure relevance and accuracy.
- **Document and Report findings effectively:** Maintain detailed documentation of every step of the analysis, including methodologies, tools used, and results. Prepare clear and comprehensive report of the findings that are accessible to both technical and non-technical audiences.

- **Implement and Test Remediation Measures:** Based on the findings, apply appropriate remediation measures and test them to ensure that identified issues are effectively addressed. Develop and apply patches or updates to fix vulnerabilities or address malicious components.

6. CASE STUDIES

Forensics analysis of AI generated content is very crucial. Few real time examples of how AI generated content plays an important role in Forensics investigation are given below:

- **Textual Analysis Case Study:** A notable example of forensic analysis in textual content involves the detection of AI-generated fake news. In this case, forensic linguists analyzed linguistic features and stylistic elements to determine that the content was produced by an AI model. The investigation approach involves:
    - Content Analysis using natural language processing (NLP) techniques to identify patterns typical of AI-generated text, such as repetitive phrases or unnatural syntax.
    - Cross-referenced the information with reliable news sources and fact-checking databases to verify the authenticity of the content.
    - Applying machine learning models to detect linguistic features and statistical patterns indicative of synthetic text.

The analysis identified several articles with anomalous language patterns and repetitive content characteristic of AI-generated text. Verification against trusted sources confirmed that the articles were fabricated.

- **Image Forensics Case Study:** In an investigation involving AI-generated imagery, forensic experts identified a synthetic image used in a fraudulent scheme. The investigation involves:
    - Analyzing visual artifacts and metadata associated with the digital artwork to determine its creation date and software used.
    - Compared the artwork to known styles and patterns produced by AI systems to confirm its synthetic nature.
    - Cross-referenced the artwork's characteristics with AI model outputs to trace its origin.

Metadata revealed that the artwork was created using a known AI art generation tool incorporating GAN technology. Style analysis confirmed that the piece matched typical outputs of the AI system, impacting copyright claims and ownership disputes

This case highlighted the importance of combining multiple forensic techniques to confirm the authenticity of digital content.

- **Audio and Video Forensics Case Study:** Deepfake technology, which uses Generative Adversarial Networks (GANs) to create hyper-realistic but fake videos, has been used to produce fake videos of celebrities, leading to misinformation and reputational damage. A high-profile case involved the use of Deepfake technology to manipulate video content for political propaganda. Forensic analysts employed voice biometrics and facial recognition algorithms to expose the video as a forgery. The investigation underscored the need for advanced forensic techniques to address the challenges posed by AI-generated audio and video content. The forensics analysis involved the following aspects:
    - Analysts employed deep learning algorithms to detect inconsistencies in facial expressions, eye movements, and lighting. These anomalies are often present in deepfake videos.
    - Examined the synchronization between audio and video to identify signs of manipulation.
    - Traced the origin of the deepfake through metadata and reverse image searches to identify the creators.

The forensic team identified subtle inconsistencies in lip synchronization and facial movements that were indicative of deepfake technology. Metadata analysis revealed the use of known deepfake software, leading to the identification of the source.

- **AI-Generated Audio in Phishing Scams:** AI-generated voice recordings were used in phishing scams to impersonate executives and deceive employees into disclosing sensitive information. The investigation steps involved:
    - Voice Forensics; Analyzing the acoustic properties of the audio, including pitch, tone, and cadence, to identify anomalies inconsistent with human speech patterns.
    - Applied machine learning techniques to detect synthetic audio features and compare them with known voice samples.
    - Examine the context in which the audio was used to understand the scam's impact and identify the perpetrators.

The audio analysis revealed synthetic characteristics and inconsistencies in vocal features. Contextual information and acoustic analysis led to the identification of the AI tools used and the perpetrators behind the phishing scam.

- **AI-Generated Social Media Influencer Posts:** AI was used to create posts for fake social media influencers, designed to manipulate public opinion and promote products fraudulently. The steps followed during forensics investigation are:
    - o Content Analysis; Review the posts for unnatural patterns, including repetitive hashtags and unnatural engagement metrics.
    - o User Profile Examination; Analyze the fake influencer's profile for signs of automated creation, such as inconsistencies in follower interactions and posting patterns. Utilize tools to detect automated bot activity and fake user engagement.

Forensic analysis identified irregular posting patterns and engagement metrics typical of automated systems. Analysis confirmed that the influencer profiles were generated using AI, leading to actions against fraudulent marketing practices

- **AI-Generated Fake Medical Images:** AI was used to create fake medical images for fraudulent purposes, including fake diagnoses and treatment recommendations. The steps followed during forensics investigation to check the integrity of the medical image are:
    - o Image Analysis; Conduct a detailed examination of medical images for anomalies, such as unusual patterns or artifacts characteristic of AI generation. Identify the AI tools and models used to generate fake images through forensic analysis.
    - o Contextual Verification; Compared the images with legitimate medical imaging standards and protocols.

Forensic analysis identified visual anomalies and artifacts consistent with AI-generated content. Contextual verification confirmed that the images were fabricated, impacting medical diagnostics and patient safety

7. FUTURE DIRECTIONS

- **Advances in Forensic Technology:** The future of AI-generated content will likely see continued advancements in technology. Emerging techniques, such as few-shot and zero-shot learning, may further enhance the capabilities of AI models in generating diverse and contextually relevant content. Additionally, the integration of AI with other technologies, such as augmented reality (AR) and virtual reality (VR), may open new avenues for content creation and interaction.

As AI technology continues to evolve, forensic techniques must also advance. Future developments may include more sophisticated algorithms for detecting AI-generated content and improved methods for analyzing emerging content types. Researchers and practitioners must stay abreast of technological advancements to effectively address new challenges in forensic analysis.

- **Collaboration and Cross-Disciplinary Approaches:** The forensic analysis of AI-generated content requires collaboration between various disciplines, including computer science, linguistics, and law. Cross-disciplinary approaches can enhance the effectiveness of forensic techniques and contribute to a more comprehensive understanding of AI-generated content.
- **Public Awareness and Education:** Increasing public awareness and education about AI-generated content is crucial for mitigating its potential risks and ensuring responsible usage. Forensic experts and educators should work together to promote understanding of AI technologies and their implications for digital content. Public awareness initiatives can help individuals recognize and critically evaluate AI-generated content, fostering a more informed and discerning digital society.
- **Regulation and Policy:** As AI-generated content becomes more pervasive, the development of regulatory frameworks and policies will be essential. Governments and organizations will need to establish guidelines to address issues related to content authenticity, intellectual property, and ethical use of AI technologies. Collaboration between stakeholders, including policymakers, technologists, and content creators, will be crucial in shaping effective regulations.

8. SUMMARY

The forensic analysis of AI-generated content is a dynamic and evolving field that addresses the challenges posed by increasingly sophisticated AI technologies. By employing advanced techniques and methodologies, forensic experts play a critical role in ensuring the authenticity and integrity of digital content. Through these case studies, it is evident that forensic experts must adapt to new technologies and develop innovative techniques to detect, authenticate, and analyze AI-generated content. Image and video analysis is an essential component of cyber forensics, providing valuable insights and evidence for investigations. By employing a range of techniques, including metadata examination, digital forensics tools, and advanced analysis methods, forensic experts can effectively authenticate, analyze, and interpret digital media. Addressing challenges such as high-quality manipulations and metadata alteration, while adhering to best practices, ensures the integrity and reliability of digital evidence. As AI continues to advance, ongoing research, collaboration, and education will be essential for effectively addressing the challenges and implications of AI-generated content in the digital age.

REFERENCES

Akbar, M., Suaib, M., & Hussain, M. S. (2022). Analysis of Deep-Fake Technology Impacting Digital World Credibility: A Comprehensive Literature Review. *International Journal of Computer and Information Technology*, 11(2). Advance online publication. DOI: 10.24203/ijcit.v11i2.282

Akbar, M., Suaib, M., & Hussain, M. S. (2023). The Rise of Deepfake Technology: Issues, Challenges, and Countermeasures. In *Advances in Cyberology and the Advent of the Next-Gen Information Revolution* (pp. 178–201). IGI Global. DOI: 10.4018/978-1-6684-8133-2.ch010

Graesser, A. C., & McNamara, D. S. (2004). *Coh-Metrix.* Retrieved from soletlab.asu.edu: https://soletlab.asu.edu/coh-metrix/

Harvey, P. (2024). *ExifTool by Phil Harvey.* Retrieved from exiftool.org: https://www.exiftool.org/

Muniswamy-Reddy. Kiran-Kumar, Holland, D. A., Braun, U., & Seltzer, a. M. (2006). *PASS: Provenance-Aware Storage Systems.* Retrieved from https://syrah.eecs.harvard.edu/: https://syrah.eecs.harvard.edu/pass

Pennebaker, J. W. (1993). *LIWC.* Retrieved from receptiviti.com: https://docs.receptiviti.com/frameworks/liwc

PSAL - The Privacy. S. a. (2011). *jstylo- Authorship recognition analysis tool.* Retrieved from github.com: https://github.com/psal/jstylo

Vaccari, C., & Chadwick, A. (2020). Exploring the impact of synthetic political video on deception, uncertainty, and trust in news. *Social Media + Society*, 6(1), 2056305120903408. DOI: 10.1177/2056305120903408

ADDITIONAL READING

Grigaliūnas, Š., Brūzgienė, R., & Venčkauskas, A. (2023). Ontology-Driven Digital Profiling for Identification and Linking Evidence Across Social Media Platform. *IEEE Access : Practical Innovations, Open Solutions*, 11, 111672–111691. DOI: 10.1109/ACCESS.2023.3322162

Hu, J., Liao, X., Wang, W., & Qin, Z. (2022). Detecting Compressed Deepfake Videos in Social Networks Using Frame-Temporality Two-Stream Convolutional Network. EEE Transactions on Circuits and Systems for Video Technology, 1089-1102.

Husain, M. S., Faisal, M., Sadia, H., Ahmad, T., & Shukla, S. (2023). *Advances in Cyberology and the Advent of the Next-gen Information Revolution*. IGI Global. DOI: 10.4018/978-1-6684-8133-2

Husain, M. S., & Khan, M. Z. (2019). *Critical Concepts, Standards, and Techniques in Cyber Forensics*. IGI Global.

Ibrahim, Y. M., Essameldin, R., & Saad, S. M. (2024). Social Media Forensics: An Adaptive Cyberbullying-Related Hate Speech Detection Approach Based on Neural Networks With Uncertainty. *IEEE Access : Practical Innovations, Open Solutions*, 12, 59474–59484. DOI: 10.1109/ACCESS.2024.3393295

Koru, G. K., & Uluyol, Ç. (2024). Detection of Turkish Fake News From Tweets With BERT Models. *IEEE Access : Practical Innovations, Open Solutions*, 12, 14918–14931. DOI: 10.1109/ACCESS.2024.3354165

Padilha, R., Salem, T., Workman, S., Andaló, F. A., Rocha, A., & Jacobs, N. (2022). Content-Aware Detection of Temporal Metadata Manipulation. *IEEE Transactions on Information Forensics and Security*, 17, 1316–1327. DOI: 10.1109/TIFS.2022.3159154

Raymer, E., MacDermott, Á., & Akinbi, A. (2023). Virtual reality forensics: Forensic analysis of Meta Quest 2. *Forensic Science International Digital Investigation*, 47, 47. DOI: 10.1016/j.fsidi.2023.301658

Sabir, M. F., Jones, J. H., Liu, H., & Mbaziira, A. V. (2019). Predicting Stealthy Watermarks in Files Using Deep Learning. *7th International Symposium on Digital Forensics and Security (ISDFS)* (pp. 1-6). IEEE. DOI: 10.1109/ISDFS.2019.8757538

Sharrab, Y., Al-Fraihat, D., & Alsmirat, M. (2023). Deep Neural Networks in Social Media Forensics: Unveiling Suspicious Patterns and Advancing Investigations on Twitter. *3rd Intelligent Cybersecurity Conference (ICSC)*, (pp. 95-102). DOI: 10.1109/ICSC60084.2023.10349985

Sieberth, T., Dobay, A., Affolter, R., & Ebert, L. C. (2018). Applying virtual reality in forensics – a virtual scene walkthrough. *Forensic Science, Medicine, and Pathology*, 15(1), 41–47. DOI: 10.1007/s12024-018-0058-8 PMID: 30519987

Suaib, M., Akbar, M., & Husain, M. S. (2020). Digital forensics and data mining. In *Critical concepts, standards, and techniques in cyber forensics* (pp. 240–247). IGI Global. DOI: 10.4018/978-1-7998-1558-7.ch014

Theophilo, A., Giot, R., & Rocha, A. (2023). Authorship Attribution of Social Media Messages. *IEEE Transactions on Computational Social Systems*, 10(1), 10–23. DOI: 10.1109/TCSS.2021.3123895

KEY TERMS AND DEFINITIONS

Artifact: An artifact is any residual data or piece of evidence that is left behind as a result of user actions, system processes, or interactions within a digital environment. Artifacts can be used to reconstruct events, validate claims, or understand system behavior by providing information about what occurred on a device or within a system.

Disinformation: Disinformation refers to false or misleading information that is deliberately spread with the intent to deceive or manipulate the audience. Unlike misinformation, which may be incorrect or misleading but not intentionally spread.

Generative Adversarial Networks (GANs): Generative Adversarial Networks (GANs) is a type of neural network architecture consisting of two networks i.e. the generator and the discriminator, that are trained simultaneously in a competitive process. The generator creates synthetic data samples, while the discriminator evaluates them against real data, providing feedback to improve the generator's output.

Malicious: The term "malicious" refers to actions, behaviors, or intent that are intended to cause harm, damage, or injury. In the context of cybersecurity, malicious typically describes activities or software that are designed to compromise, damage, or exploit systems, networks, or data for harmful purposes.

Malware: Malware, short for malicious software, refers to any software intentionally designed to cause harm, exploit, or otherwise compromise the functionality, integrity, or security of a computer system, network, or device.

Natural Language Processing (NLP): Natural Language Processing (NLP) is a branch of artificial intelligence that focuses on enabling computers to understand, interpret, and generate human language. It involves the use of computational techniques to analyze and model natural language data, facilitating tasks such as text processing, language understanding, and human-computer interaction.

Chapter 9
Forensic Challenges in Augmented Reality (AR) and Virtual Reality (VR)

ABSTRACT

Augmented Reality (AR) has revolutionized various sectors by overlaying digital information onto the real world, creating immersive and interactive experiences. Its applications span from entertainment and education to healthcare and military training. Virtual Reality (VR) technology, which immerses users in a completely simulated environment, has seen rapid advancements and widespread adoption across various sectors. In the realm of forensics, VR holds promise for revolutionizing crime scene investigation, evidence analysis, and legal presentations. By creating detailed, interactive simulations, VR can enhance understanding and visualization of complex scenarios. However, the rapid adoption and integration of AR technologies and VCR into forensic practices brings forth a range of forensic challenges that need to be addressed. These challenges span the realms of data integrity, evidence preservation, authentication, and legal considerations.

1. INTRODUCTION

Augmented Reality (AR) has revolutionized various sectors by overlaying digital information onto the real world, creating immersive and interactive experiences. Its applications span from entertainment and education to healthcare and military training. Virtual Reality (VR) technology, which immerses users in a completely simulated environment, has seen rapid advancements and widespread adoption across various sectors. In the realm of forensics, VR holds promise for revolutionizing crime scene investigation, evidence analysis, and legal presentations. By creating

DOI: 10.4018/979-8-3693-2960-3.ch009

detailed, interactive simulations, VR can enhance understanding and visualization of complex scenarios. However, the rapid adoption and integration of AR and VR technologies into forensic practices brings forth a range of forensic challenges that need to be addressed. These challenges span the realms of data integrity, evidence preservation, authentication, and legal considerations.

This chapter explores these challenges in depth, providing insights into how they impact forensic investigations and offering potential solutions. By understanding and addressing these challenges, forensic professionals can better leverage AR and VR to enhance investigative processes and ensure the integrity and validity of evidence.

2. OVERVIEW AND SIGNIFICANCE OF AR AND VR IN CYBER FORENSICS

2.1. Overview of Augmented Reality (AR) and Virtual Reality (VR)

> **Augmented Reality**: enhances the user's perception of their environment by superimposing digital information, such as graphics, sounds, and text, onto the physical world. Unlike Virtual Reality (VR), which immerses users in a completely virtual environment, AR maintains a connection to the real world, making it particularly useful for applications requiring interaction with real-world elements.
>
> **Virtual Reality (VR)**: immerses users in a computer-generated environment that can simulate real-world or fantastical scenarios. Unlike Augmented Reality (AR), which overlays digital information onto the physical world, VR creates an entirely virtual space that users can interact with. VR systems typically involve headsets, motion controllers, and sometimes additional sensory equipment to provide a fully immersive experience.

Augmented Reality (AR) and Virtual Reality (VR) are both immersive technologies, but they have distinct differences in how they interact with and alter our perception of the real world. The key differences between them are summarized in Table 1.

Table 1. Summary of AR and VR

Parameter	Augmented Reality	Virtual Reality
User Experience	Offers a more blended experience, where users interact with digital enhancements while remaining connected to their real-world surroundings. This can lead to a more integrated experience in daily activities.	Provides a more immersive experience where users are completely absorbed in a simulated environment, which can lead to a more intense and often more focused engagement with the content.
User Interaction	Interaction methods can include touchscreens, voice commands, or gestures, depending on the device.	Interaction occurs entirely within the virtual space, often using VR controllers or hand tracking. Users manipulate objects and navigate the environment using these inputs.
Environment Interaction	Augmented Reality overlays digital information onto the real world. Users see and interact with both the physical environment and digital content simultaneously. For example, AR apps can project navigation directions onto the real-world view through a smartphone or AR glasses.	Virtual Reality creates a completely virtual environment that replaces the real world. Users are fully immersed in a digital environment and cannot see the real world around them. For instance, VR headsets transport users to a simulated space like a video game world or a virtual conference room.
Social Interaction	Enables users to interact with digital content and other people within their physical space. It allows for social activities that blend real-world and virtual elements, such as collaborative AR games or interactive exhibits.	Facilitates social interaction within a fully virtual space. Users can meet and interact with others in a shared virtual environment, often using avatars or virtual representations.
Immersion Level	Provides partial immersion, as it enhances the real world without completely replacing it. Users remain aware of their surroundings and can engage with physical objects and people.	Offers full immersion, as it entirely replaces the real world with a simulated one. Users are enclosed within the virtual environment, which can affect their sense of presence and spatial awareness.
Content Creation	Content is designed to be integrated with the real world. Developers create digital objects that can interact with physical environments, often requiring sophisticated tracking and spatial recognition technology.	Content is entirely digital and designed to create a believable virtual space. Developers build entire 3D environments and scenarios, focusing on creating an immersive experience from scratch.
Hardware Requirements	Typically requires devices with cameras and sensors to capture the real world and display the augmented content. Common AR devices include smartphones, tablets, and AR glasses like Microsoft HoloLens or Google Glass.	Requires more specialized hardware such as VR headsets (e.g., Oculus Rift, HTC Vive) and often motion controllers. VR setups might also involve external sensors or cameras to track user movements.
Development Challenges	Developers need to address challenges related to tracking and overlaying digital content onto dynamic real-world environments. This requires robust computer vision and spatial mapping technologies.	Developers focus on creating convincing and engaging virtual worlds with realistic graphics, physics, and interactions. The challenge lies in ensuring smooth and immersive experiences within the simulated environment.

continued on following page

Table 1. Continued

Parameter	Augmented Reality	Virtual Reality
User Training	Users often require minimal training to use AR applications, as they interact with digital content in a familiar real-world context.	Users may need more extensive training or orientation to navigate and interact within a fully virtual environment. The learning curve can be steeper due to the novel and immersive nature of VR experiences.
Application Use Cases	Commonly used for applications that enhance real-world experiences, such as navigation aids, educational tools, gaming apps (like Pokémon GO), and interactive advertising	Often used for applications that require full immersion, including video games, training simulations (e.g., military or medical training), virtual tours, and immersive storytelling.

2.2. Augmented Reality and Virtual Reality in Forensic Contexts

In forensic investigations, AR can be employed for various purposes, including crime scene reconstruction, virtual evidence analysis, and real-time data visualization. For instance, AR can help investigators visualize bullet trajectories, simulate crime scenarios, or even assist in the reconstruction of accidents. The integration of AR into forensic practices promises to enhance investigative capabilities and improve the accuracy of evidence interpretation (Golomingi, Dobay, Franckenberg, Ebert, & Sieberth, 2023).

In forensic contexts, VR offers significant benefits, including the ability to recreate crime scenes, simulate events, and analyze evidence in a virtual space. VR can facilitate a deeper understanding of spatial relationships, object interactions, and event sequences, which can be invaluable for investigators, legal professionals, and juries (Sieberth, Dobay, Affolter, & Ebert, 2018). Examples of VR applications in forensics include crime scene reconstruction, accident simulation, and virtual walkthroughs for courtroom presentations.

3. APPLICATIONS OF AR AND VR IN FORENSICS

Augmented Reality (AR) and Virtual Reality (VR) are transformative technologies that are increasingly being explored for their potential in the field of cyber forensics. These technologies can enhance various aspects of cyber forensic investigations, from evidence visualization and analysis to training and courtroom presentations. Cyber Forensics investigators can enhance the accuracy of the investigation by using augmented reality and virtual reality in different ways as shown in below Figure 1.

Figure 1. Applications of AR and VR in forensics

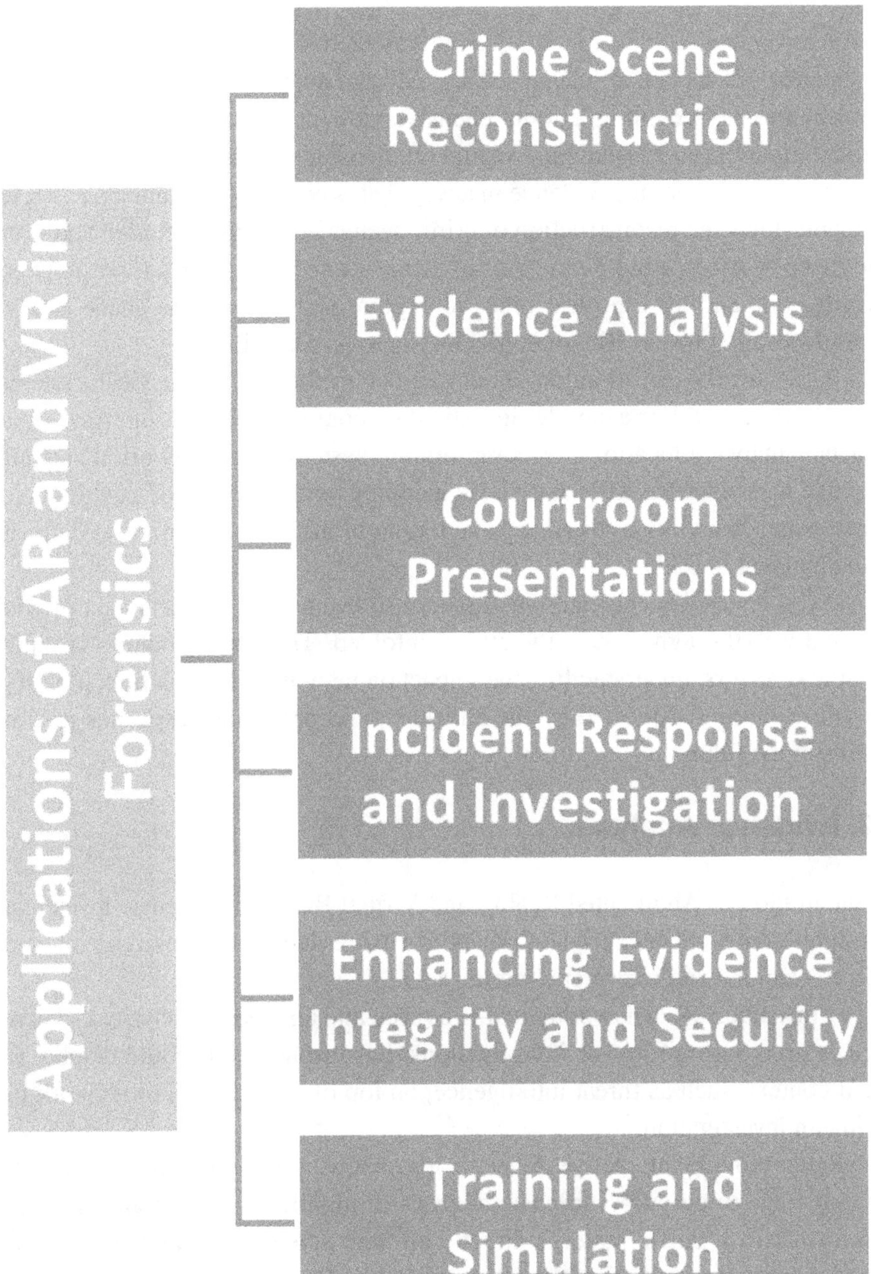

3.1. Crime Scene Reconstruction

AR technology allows for detailed and interactive crime scene reconstructions. By creating 3D models of crime scenes, AR can overlay digital information onto physical spaces, providing a comprehensive view of the scene. This capability is particularly useful for visualizing spatial relationships, understanding the sequence of events, and presenting evidence in a way that is easily understandable. VR technology enables the reconstruction of crime scenes in a highly detailed and immersive manner. By creating 3D models of crime scenes, VR allows forensic experts, investigators, and legal professionals to explore and analyze the scene as if they were physically present (Raymer, MacDermott, & Akinbi, 2023).

AR can overlay information about a cyber incident onto physical systems or network diagrams. For example, investigators could use AR to superimpose data breaches, malware locations, or compromised systems onto network maps during an active investigation. AR can assist in mapping out the impact of a cyber incident in real time, providing a visual representation of affected systems and data flows as the incident unfolds.

VR can be used to recreate the sequence of events in a cyber-attack, providing a virtual walkthrough of how the attack unfolded. This could include visualizing the attack vectors, understanding the impact on network infrastructure, identifying the vulnerabilities exploited by the attackers, and preparing responses to similar attacks in the future.

3.2. Evidence Analysis

Integration of Augmented Reality and Virtual Reality in forensic investigation can significantly enhance the analysis of forensic evidence by providing interactive tools to examine and interpret complex data.

For instance, AR can overlay real-time data and analysis on physical screens or devices used during forensic investigations. For instance, AR could display additional context, such as threat intelligence, on top of system logs or network maps during an investigation.

AR can provide interactive elements for reviewing digital evidence. For example, AR tools might allow forensic analysts to highlight and annotate suspicious code or network traffic patterns directly on their screens, enhancing their ability to collaborate and share findings. Augmented reality helps Investigators to document crime scenes more interactively, capturing detailed information and creating immersive records that can be revisited and analyzed later (Raffael, Akos, Sabine, Lars, & Sieberth, 2023).

VR can create immersive environments where forensic experts can explore and interact with complex datasets, network architectures, or system logs. For example, a VR environment might allow investigators to visualize and interact with network traffic data or malware behavior in a 3D space, helping them in understanding the flow of data, identifying bottlenecks, patterns and anomalies more effectively. This immersive approach can make it easier to trace the movement of data and pinpoint potential points of compromise. VR allows forensic experts to investigate crime scenes remotely, reducing the need for physical presence and enabling access to scenes that might be otherwise inaccessible. Remote investigations using VR can be conducted more quickly and efficiently, saving time and resources (ADF-Solutions, 2023).

3.3. Courtroom Presentations

In the courtroom, use of VR technology and AR technology can enhance courtroom presentations by creating immersive and engaging visualizations of evidence and crime scenes. The interactive nature of AR and VR can capture the attention of the courtroom and provide a more engaging way to present evidence, potentially increasing the impact of the presentation.

AR can enhance courtroom exhibits by overlaying additional information or explanations on physical evidence. For instance, AR can be used to show the relationships between different pieces of evidence or to highlight key aspects of digital evidence. During legal proceedings, AR can provide real-time annotations and explanations of complex technical details, helping the court to better understand the nuances of the cyber forensic evidence.

VR can create detailed 3D reconstructions of cybercrime scenes or attack scenarios for courtroom presentations. This immersive approach helps jurors and judges understand the complexity and impact of the cyber incident, making it easier to grasp the evidence and arguments presented.

In VR, legal teams can demonstrate how cyber-attacks were executed and how evidence was gathered, providing a more engaging and interactive experience for the court. This can help juries and judges better understand complex cases and visualize the evidence in a more impactful way.

3.4. Incident Response and Investigation

AR can assist forensic investigators in the field by overlaying real-time data, instructions, or contextual information onto their view of the evidence or systems being analyzed. This can improve the efficiency and accuracy of investigations. AR tools can visualize real-time data and alerts during investigations, helping forensic professionals quickly identify and respond to emerging threats or anomalies.

VR can create virtual incident response rooms where forensic teams can collaborate and analyze evidence in a shared virtual space, regardless of their physical locations. This facilitates better coordination and faster decision-making during investigations. VR allows forensic teams to test different response strategies and scenarios in a virtual environment, helping them prepare for and effectively manage real-world cyber incidents.

3.5. Enhancing Evidence Integrity and Security

AR can be used to monitor and manage the security of evidence during forensic investigations by overlaying alerts and status updates on physical evidence storage or handling areas. AR can help maintain the chain of custody by providing real-time documentation and verification of evidence handling processes, ensuring that all interactions with the evidence are accurately recorded.

VR can provide controlled access to sensitive evidence, allowing forensic teams to review and analyze data in a secure, virtual environment without compromising the integrity of the evidence.

3.6. Training and Simulation

AR can provide real-time guidance and support during cyber forensic investigations. For example, AR can display step-by-step procedures or best practices for forensic analysis directly on a user's screen as they perform tasks.

VR offers immersive training environments for cybersecurity professionals. Trainees can engage in simulated cyber-attacks such as data breaches or advanced persistent threats (APTs), practice incident response strategies, and learn how to handle various cyber threats in a controlled, virtual setting.

3.7. Case Studies

The application of Augmented Reality (AR) and Virtual Reality (VR) in cyber forensics offers innovative ways to enhance investigations, training, evidence analysis, and courtroom presentations. By leveraging these technologies, forensic professionals can gain deeper insights, improve collaboration, and present complex information more effectively. As AR and VR technologies continue to advance, their integration into cyber forensics is likely to become even more impactful, providing new tools and methods for tackling the challenges of modern cybercrime.

- In a murder investigation, AR and/or VR was used to reconstruct the crime scene, based on witness testimonies and physical evidence. This virtual reconstruction allowed investigators to visualize the positions of the victim and suspects at the time of the crime. This simulation aids the forensics investigators in the identification of inconsistencies in witness statements and helps to formulate a clearer understanding of the events.
- During an arson investigation, AR was employed to overlay heat maps and burn patterns onto the physical evidence, allowing investigators to analyze the spread of the fire and identify potential points of origin more effectively.
- During an accident investigation, VR was employed to recreate the scene and overlay data such as vehicle speeds, impact angles, and collision points. This facilitated a more detailed analysis of the accident dynamics and helped determine the cause of the collision.
- In a high-profile robbery case, AR and /or VR were used to recreate the sequence of events and simulate the crime scene, allowing the jury to experience the scenario firsthand from multiple perspectives. This immersive presentation helped clarify key aspects of the case to support the overall narrative presented by the prosecution and contributed to the jury's understanding.

4. FORENSIC CHALLENGES IN AUGMENTED REALITY

Forensic challenges in augmented reality (AR) are multifaceted due to the unique nature of AR technology, which blends digital information with physical environments. These challenges include:

4.1. Data Integrity and Authenticity

One of the primary challenges in AR forensics is ensuring the integrity and authenticity of AR-generated data. AR systems often create and manipulate data in real-time, which can be difficult to capture and maintain in its original form. The dynamic and interactive nature of data generated through AR raises concerns about the potential for data tampering or corruption. Forensic investigators must develop methods to validate the accuracy of AR data and establish its authenticity.

Challenges:

- **Data Tampering:** AR data can be altered or manipulated, either intentionally or unintentionally, raising questions about its reliability as evidence.

- **Real-Time Data Processing:** The dynamic nature of AR systems means that data is constantly changing, making it difficult to capture and preserve accurate snapshots of the evidence.

Solutions:

- **Blockchain Technology:** Implementing blockchain technology to create immutable records of AR data can enhance data integrity.
- **Digital Signatures:** Utilizing cryptographic digital signatures to validate AR data can ensure its authenticity and prevent unauthorized alterations.
- **Data Capture Techniques:** Developing advanced techniques for capturing and storing AR data in a way that preserves its original state is crucial.
- **Validation Methods:** Implementing methods to validate the authenticity of AR data, such as digital signatures or blockchain technology, can help ensure data integrity.

4.2. Evidence Preservation

Preserving AR evidence involves capturing and storing the digital information generated by AR systems. Given the ephemeral nature of AR experiences, preserving this data in a way that maintains its original context and relevance is crucial.

Challenges:

- **Data Volatility:** AR environments are often transient, with data disappearing once the AR session ends, complicating evidence preservation.
- **Storage Formats:** AR data may be stored in proprietary formats, such as local storage, cloud-based systems, or network servers that are not easily accessible or interpretable by forensic tools. Ensuring that all relevant data, including digital overlays and user interactions, is preserved accurately and securely is vital.

Solutions:

- **Enhanced Data Capture:** Developing advanced data capture methods that can record the entire AR experience, including all digital overlays and interactions, can aid in preserving evidence.
- **Standardization:** Creating standardized formats for AR data storage can facilitate better preservation and accessibility of evidence.

4.3. Complex Data Structures

AR systems generate complex data structures that include spatial information, user interactions, and real-time updates. Analyzing and interpreting this data can be intricate.

Challenges:

- **Overlay Data:** AR systems often overlay digital information onto the real world, requiring forensic experts to distinguish between real and virtual elements.
- **Metadata:** AR applications generate extensive metadata, such as timestamps and location data. Extracting and correlating this metadata with other evidence requires specialized analytical techniques.
- **Spatial and Interaction Data:** AR systems involve complex data structures that include spatial coordinates, digital overlays, and user interactions. Analyzing and interpreting this data requires sophisticated techniques.
- **Temporal Data:** AR data may include time-sensitive information, such as timestamps and real-time updates, which must be accurately reconstructed and correlated.

Solutions:

- **Advanced Frameworks:** Developing analytical frameworks and tools that can handle and interpret complex AR data structures is crucial. This may involve spatial analysis software, interaction tracking systems, and data visualization tools. Techniques for isolating and analyzing digital overlays from physical environments can help.
- **Temporal Correlation:** Implement methods for accurate temporal correlation of data, such as synchronizing timestamps from different data sources to reconstruct the sequence of events.
- **Data Integration:** Develop methods for integrating spatial, temporal, and interaction data to create a coherent and comprehensive forensic analysis.

4.4. Authentication and Verification of AR Evidence

Authentication and verification of AR evidence involve confirming that the evidence presented is genuine and accurately represents the AR experience as it occurred. This process can be challenging due to the complexity and variability of AR systems.

Challenges:

- **System Variability:** Different AR systems and platforms may produce varying outputs, complicating the verification process.
- **Forensic Tools:** Traditional forensic tools may not be directly applicable to AR devices. Developing or adapting tools to handle AR-specific data and formats is essential.
- **Lack of Standards:** The absence of standardized procedures for verifying AR evidence can lead to inconsistencies and difficulties in ensuring its accuracy.

Solutions:

- **Forensic Protocols:** Establishing forensic protocols specifically tailored for AR environments can provide guidelines for data handling and evidence verification ensuring consistency and reliability.
- **Cross-Platform Verification:** Implementing methods for cross-platform verification can help validate AR evidence across different systems and devices.

4.5. Chain of Custody

Maintaining a clear chain of custody is essential for ensuring that AR evidence remains unaltered and credible. This involves documenting every step in the handling and analysis of AR evidence.

Challenges:

- **Digital Chain of Custody:** Ensuring a secure digital chain of custody for AR evidence can be challenging due to the potential for data breaches or unauthorized access.
- **Complex Evidence Handling:** The complexity of AR data and interactions can complicate the documentation of the chain of custody.

Solutions:

- **Digital Forensic Tools:** Utilizing digital forensic tools designed for managing and tracking AR evidence can enhance chain of custody management.
- **Detailed Documentation:** Implementing comprehensive documentation practices, including detailed records of evidence handling and analysis, can support the chain of custody.

4.6. Synchronization and Correlation

AR systems often involve data from multiple sources, such as GPS, sensors, and cameras. Synchronizing and correlating this data to reconstruct events accurately is challenging.

Challenges:

- **Multi-source Data:** Integrating data from various sensors and sources requires advanced techniques to create a coherent picture of the events.
- **Real-time Data:** Capturing and correlating real-time data without altering its context is crucial for accurate forensic analysis.

Solutions:

- **Data Fusion Techniques:** Implementing advanced data integration and correlation techniques can help in reconstructing events from multi-source AR data. Use data fusion techniques to integrate data from various sources is recommended. This involves combining spatial, temporal, and sensor data to create a comprehensive view of the events.
- **Real-time Data Capture:** Ensuring accurate time synchronization between different data sources is also important. Implement real-time data capture methods that preserve the context and accuracy of the data. This may involve using specialized hardware or software that can handle live data streams.
- **Synchronization Protocols:** Develop protocols for synchronizing data from different sources to ensure that all relevant information is accurately correlated and integrated.

4.7. Technical Expertise

Forensic analysis of AR data requires specialized knowledge of AR technology and its implications.

Challenges:

- **Specialized Knowledge:** Forensic experts need to understand how AR systems operate and generate data to effectively analyze it.
- **Evolving Technology:** The rapid advancement of AR technology means that forensic methodologies must continually evolve to keep pace with new developments.

Solutions:

- **Training programs:** Providing ongoing training and education for forensic professionals on AR technology is crucial.

- **Collaboration:** Collaborating with AR developers and researchers to stay updated on technological advancements can also be beneficial.
- **Research and Development:** Invest in research and development to create new forensic methodologies and tools that keep pace with advancements in AR technology.

4.8. Legal Considerations in AR Forensics

The admissibility of AR evidence in court requires that it meets established legal standards for evidence. This involves demonstrating that AR evidence is relevant, reliable, and obtained through lawful means.

Challenges:

- **Legal Precedents:** The lack of legal precedents specifically addressing AR evidence can create uncertainties about its admissibility.
- **Technical Complexity:** The technical complexity of AR systems may pose challenges in explaining and validating AR evidence in a legal context.

Solutions:

- **Legal Frameworks:** Developing legal frameworks and guidelines specifically for AR evidence can provide clarity on its admissibility.
- **Expert Testimony:** Engaging technical experts to explain the workings of AR systems and the validity of AR evidence can support its admissibility in court.

4.9. Privacy and Ethical Issues

The use of AR in forensics raises privacy and ethical concerns, particularly regarding the collection and use of personal data. Ensuring that AR practices respect privacy rights and adhere to ethical standards is crucial.

Challenges:

- **Informed Consent:** Obtaining informed consent from individuals whose data is captured by AR systems can be challenging.
- **Data Privacy:** Ensuring the protection of personal data collected during AR investigations is essential to prevent misuse or unauthorized access.

Solutions:

- **Privacy Policies:** Implementing robust privacy policies and procedures for AR data collection and use can address privacy concerns.

- **Ethical Guidelines:** Developing ethical guidelines for the use of AR in forensics can help ensure that practices align with legal and ethical standards.

Addressing the forensic challenges in augmented reality requires a multidisciplinary approach, combining expertise in technology, legal standards, and forensic methods. As AR technology continues to evolve, developing and refining forensic practices to handle its unique data characteristics will be crucial for effective investigation and analysis.

5. FORENSIC CHALLENGES IN VIRTUAL REALITY

Virtual Reality (VR) technology creates immersive digital environments that can simulate real-world scenarios. While VR has many applications, including gaming, training, and therapy, it also poses unique forensic challenges when it comes to investigating incidents or crimes that occur within these virtual spaces. Forensic challenges associated with VR includes:

5.1. Data Integrity and Authenticity

Ensuring the integrity and authenticity of VR data is crucial, as VR environments can be dynamically altered, and data can be manipulated. Maintaining the original state of VR evidence is essential for its validity in forensic investigations.

Challenges:

- **Dynamic Nature of VR:** VR environments are often interactive and can change based on user inputs, complicating efforts to capture and preserve a static record of the environment.
- **Data Manipulation:** There is a risk of intentional or unintentional manipulation of VR data, which could affect its reliability as evidence.

Solutions:

- **Version Control Systems:** Implementing version control systems for VR environments can help track changes and ensure the preservation of original data.
- **Advanced Data Capture:** Implementing advanced data capture techniques that record the entire VR environment, including all relevant data, such as environment settings, user interactions, and logs, can aid in preserving evidence accurately. Write-blockers should be employed to prevent any modification during imaging.

- **Validation Measures:** Using digital signatures, blockchain technology, or other validation methods can help ensure the authenticity and integrity of VR data.
- **Digital Watermarking:** Applying digital watermarks to VR data can help verify their authenticity and detect unauthorized alterations.
- **Data Preservation Protocols:** Establish protocols that specify how VR data should be captured and preserved, including regular snapshots of data at various points during an investigation.
- **Use of Non-intrusive Methods:** Implement non-intrusive methods to log interactions and changes within the VR environment without altering the ongoing experience for users.

5.2. Evidence Preservation

Preserving VR evidence involves capturing and storing the entire virtual environment, including its state, interactions, and any modifications. Given the complex nature of VR data, this task presents several challenges.

Challenges:

- **Data Complexity:** VR environments consist of numerous components, including 3D models, textures, and interactions, which can be difficult to capture and store comprehensively.
- **Storage Requirements:** High-resolution VR data can require significant storage capacity, raising issues related to data management and preservation.
- **Temporal Dynamics:** VR interactions are often time-sensitive, making it essential to accurately document the sequence of events.

Solutions:

- **Comprehensive Data Capture:** Utilizing advanced data capture techniques that record the entire VR environment, including all interactions and modifications, can aid in evidence preservation.
- **Temporal Documentation:** Develop systems for documenting timestamps and sequences of user actions within the VR environment, ensuring that forensic analysts can reconstruct events accurately.
- **Data Visualization:** Use data visualization techniques to create representations of interactions within the VR space, aiding in analysis and presentation of findings.
- **Cloud Storage Solutions:** Leveraging cloud storage solutions with robust security measures can provide scalable and secure storage for large volumes of VR data.

5.3. Synchronization and Correlation

Challenges:

- **Multi-source Data Integration:** VR environments often rely on data from various sensors and sources, such as motion trackers, cameras, and microphones. Integrating and correlating this data can be challenging.
- **Real-time Data Handling:** Capturing and correlating real-time data without altering its context is crucial for accurate forensic analysis.

Solutions:

- **Data Fusion Techniques:** Employ data fusion techniques to integrate information from multiple sources, ensuring that spatial, temporal, and sensor data are combined accurately for comprehensive analysis.
- **Real-time Logging:** Implement logging systems that capture real-time data in a way that preserves context. This may involve specialized software capable of recording interactions and environmental changes without interfering with user experiences.
- **Standardized Time Stamping:** Ensure that all data sources are time-synchronized to facilitate accurate correlation and integration during forensic analysis.

5.4. Authentication and Verification of VR Evidence

Verifying VR evidence involves confirming that the VR simulation accurately represents the events and environment in question. This process can be challenging due to the complex and dynamic nature of VR environments.

Challenges:

- **System Variability:** Different VR systems and platforms may produce varying outputs, making it difficult to verify the consistency and accuracy of VR evidence.
- **Technical Complexity:** Explaining and validating the technical aspects of VR simulations in a legal context can be challenging.

Solutions:

- **Standardized Protocols:** Developing standardized protocols for VR evidence verification can help ensure consistency and accuracy across different systems and platforms.
- **Expert Testimony:** Engaging technical experts who can explain the VR system and its output can support the verification process in legal proceedings.

5.5. Chain of Custody

Maintaining a clear chain of custody for VR evidence is essential for ensuring its integrity and reliability. This involves documenting every step in the handling, analysis, and presentation of VR evidence.

Challenges:

- **Digital Chain of Custody:** Ensuring a secure and tamper-proof digital chain of custody for VR evidence can be challenging due to the potential for data breaches or unauthorized access.
- **Complex Evidence Handling:** The intricate nature of VR data and interactions can complicate the documentation of the chain of custody.

Solutions:

- **Forensic Software Tools:** Using specialized forensic software tools designed for managing VR evidence can enhance chain of custody management.
- **Detailed Documentation:** Implementing rigorous documentation practices, including detailed logs of evidence handling and analysis, can support the chain of custody.

5.6. Legal Considerations in VR Forensics

The admissibility of VR evidence in court requires that it meets established legal standards for evidence, including relevance, reliability, and lawful acquisition. Demonstrating the credibility of VR evidence is crucial for its acceptance in legal proceedings.

Challenges:

- **Legal Precedents:** The evolving nature of VR technology means that legal precedents specifically addressing VR evidence may be limited or nonexistent.
- **Admissibility of Evidence:** The legal admissibility of VR evidence may be uncertain, as there may be limited legal precedents or guidelines addressing VR technology.
- **Technical Complexity:** The technical aspects of VR simulations can make it difficult to explain and validate the evidence in a legal context.

Solutions:

- **Legal Frameworks:** Developing legal frameworks and guidelines tailored to VR evidence can provide clarity on its admissibility and help ensure that it meets legal standards.

- **Expert Testimony:** Utilizing expert testimony to explain the VR system and the VR evidence can support its admissibility in court.

5.7. Privacy and Ethical Issues

The use of VR in forensics raises privacy and ethical concerns, particularly regarding the collection and use of personal data. Ensuring that VR practices respect privacy rights and adhere to ethical standards is crucial.

Challenges:

- **Privacy Concerns:** The use of VR to capture and analyze evidence may involve collecting sensitive or personal data, raising privacy concerns.
- **Informed Consent:** Obtaining informed consent from individuals whose data is captured in VR simulations can be challenging, especially in cases involving sensitive information.
- **Data Privacy:** Ensuring the protection of personal data collected during VR investigations is essential to prevent misuse or unauthorized access.

Solutions:

- **Privacy Policies:** Implementing comprehensive privacy policies and procedures for the collection and use of VR data can address privacy concerns and protect individuals' rights.
- **Ethical Guidelines:** Developing ethical guidelines for the use of VR in forensics can help ensure that practices align with legal and ethical standards.

5.8. Technical Complexity

The technical complexity of VR systems can pose challenges in forensic investigations. VR technology involves sophisticated hardware and software components, which require specialized knowledge and expertise to operate effectively.

Challenges:

- **System Variability:** Different VR systems and platforms may produce varying outputs, complicating the analysis and interpretation of VR evidence.
- **Expertise Requirements:** Forensic professionals may need additional training to effectively use VR technology and interpret its outputs.
- **Rapid Technological Changes:** The fast pace of technological advancement in VR necessitates continuous updates to forensic methodologies and tools.

Solutions:

- **Standardization:** Developing standardized protocols for VR systems and data handling can help ensure consistency and reliability across different platforms.
- **Training Programs:** Providing training and educational resources for forensic professionals on VR technology can enhance their ability to utilize VR effectively in investigations.
- **Interdisciplinary Collaboration:** Encourage collaboration between forensic experts and VR developers to share knowledge and best practices, facilitating a deeper understanding of VR systems.
- **Research Initiatives:** Invest in research and development to create new forensic methodologies and tools that keep pace with advancements in VR technology.

The forensic challenges in virtual reality require a comprehensive, multidisciplinary approach that integrates technology, legal standards, and advanced forensic techniques. As VR technology continues to evolve, it is essential to develop and refine forensic practices tailored to the unique characteristics of VR data. Collaboration with technology developers, legal experts, and forensic professionals is crucial to overcoming these challenges and ensuring that VR evidence can be effectively and reliably utilized in legal contexts. By implementing the solutions outlined above, forensic investigators can enhance their ability to analyze and interpret VR environments while upholding the integrity of the investigative process. Table 2 summarizes the forensics challenges in AR and VR.

Table 2. Summary of forensics challenges in AR and VR

Parameter	Augmented Reality		Virtual Reality	
	Challenges	Solutions	Challenges	Solutions
Data Integrity and Authenticity	Data Tampering, Real-Time Data Processing	Blockchain Technology, Digital Signatures, Data Capture Techniques, Validation Methods	Dynamic Nature of VR, Data Manipulation	Version Control Systems, Advanced Data Capture, Validation Measures, Digital Watermarking
Complex Data Structures	Overlay Data, Metadata, Spatial and Interaction Data, Temporal Data	Advanced Frameworks, Temporal Correlation, Data Integration	3D Models using hierarchical Structures, Spatial Data, User Interaction Logs, Sensor Data, Biometric Data, Spatial Audio, Video Streams, proprietary file formats	User Interaction Analysis, Network Data Analysis, Data Correlation, frame by frame Forensic Imaging
Evidence Preservation	Data Volatility, Storage Formats	Enhanced Data Capture, Standardization	Data Complexity, Storage Requirements	Comprehensive Data Capture, Cloud Storage Solutions
Authentication and Verification of Evidence	System Variability, Lack of Standards	Forensic Protocols, Cross-Platform Verification	System Variability, Technical Complexity	Standardized Protocols, Expert Testimony
Chain of Custody	Digital Chain of Custody, Complex Evidence Handling	Digital Forensic Tools, Detailed Documentation	Digital Chain of Custody, Complex Evidence Handling	Forensic Software Tools, Detailed Documentation
Legal Considerations	Legal Precedents, Technical Complexity	Legal Frameworks, Expert Testimony	Legal Precedents, Admissibility of Evidence, Technical Complexity	Legal Frameworks, Expert Testimony
Privacy and Ethical Issues	Informed Consent, Data Privacy	Privacy Policies, Ethical Guidelines	Privacy Concerns, Informed Consent, Data Privacy	Privacy Policies, Ethical Guidelines
Technical Complexity	System Variability, Technical Expertise	Standardization, Training Programs	System Variability, Expertise requirements	Standardization, Training Programs

6. EXAMPLE CASE STUDIES

6.1. AR in Cyber Forensics Investigation

Augmented Reality (AR) is increasingly being integrated into cyber forensics to enhance investigations, visualize data, and streamline evidence analysis. Some real-life case study examples where AR has been applied in the field of cyber forensics are:

- **Enron Financial Scandal:** During the investigation of the Enron scandal, forensic accountants and investigators used AR to overlay complex financial transactions onto physical documents. By using AR devices, they were able to visualize financial flows, detect anomalies, and trace the movement of funds in an interactive manner. The AR technology provided a clear visual representation of complex accounting maneuvers, helping forensic experts identify fraudulent activities and gain insights into the sophisticated financial schemes used by Enron executives.
- **Target Data Breach:** In the aftermath of the Target data breach, which exposed millions of customer records, AR was utilized to analyze the network's vulnerabilities. Forensic analysts employed AR to overlay a virtual map of Target's network infrastructure onto physical workspaces. This allowed them to visualize data flows, identify compromised systems, and track the breach's progression through the network. The AR visualizations facilitated a deeper understanding of the breach's impact and helped in implementing stronger security measures.
- **Sony PlayStation Network Outage:** Following the 2011 PlayStation Network (PSN) outage caused by a cyber-attack, forensic investigators used AR to analyze the incident's impact. AR technology was used to overlay digital attack vectors and compromised system states onto physical models of the PSN infrastructure. This interactive visualization helped investigators understand how the attackers' exploited vulnerabilities, the extent of the damage, and the recovery process, providing valuable insights into the attack's execution and aftermath.
- **Experian Data Breach Investigation:** After a significant data breach at Experian, forensic teams used AR to manage and analyze digital evidence. AR was employed to tag and categorize physical evidence, such as hard drives and servers, with digital overlays showing critical metadata and analysis results. This approach enabled investigators to efficiently track and manage large volumes of evidence, improving the accuracy and speed of the forensic investigation.

- **Law Enforcement Training Programs:** Various law enforcement agencies have implemented AR for training in cybercrime response. For instance, AR was used to create simulations of cyber-attack scenarios, including data breaches and ransomware attacks. Trainees interacted with virtual representations of compromised systems and digital evidence, allowing them to practice incident response strategies in a controlled, immersive environment. This hands-on training improved their skills in handling real-world cyber threats and investigations.

6.2. VR in Cyber Forensics Investigation

Virtual Reality (VR) is an innovative tool in cyber forensics, offering new ways to visualize, analyze, and present digital evidence. few real-life case study examples demonstrating how VR has been applied in the field of cyber forensics are:

- **The 2017 Equifax Data Breach:** Forensic experts used VR to reconstruct the Equifax data breach, which exposed sensitive information of over 145 million people. The VR simulation included a virtual model of Equifax's network and data flow. Analysts could interact with different components of the system, visualize the breach's progression, and explore how attackers moved through the network. This immersive approach provided deeper insights into the breach, helping to identify specific vulnerabilities and improve future security measures.
- **WannaCry Ransomware Attack:** During the WannaCry ransomware attack, cybersecurity professionals used VR to model and analyze the spread of the ransomware. The VR environment simulated how WannaCry propagated through networks, encrypted files, and demanded ransom payments. By interacting with this virtual model, analysts gained a clearer understanding of the ransomware's behavior, which aided in developing more effective decryption tools and countermeasures.
- **Silk Road Case:** In the trial of Ross Ulbricht, the creator of the Silk Road dark web marketplace, VR was used to present evidence. The VR simulation featured a virtual model of the Silk Road website, allowing jurors to interact with the digital marketplace and understand its operations. This approach made complex digital evidence more accessible and comprehensible, helping the court grasp the scale and functionality of the illicit platform.
- **Simulating Cyber Attacks on Critical Infrastructure:** A cybersecurity firm developed a VR simulation to model cyber-attacks on critical infrastructure, such as power grids and water systems. The VR environment allowed security professionals to interact with virtual representations of these systems

and observe the impact of simulated attacks. This training helped refine incident response strategies and identify vulnerabilities in a controlled, immersive setting.

- **Analysis of the Shadow Brokers Data Leak:** The Shadow Brokers' leak of NSA hacking tools was analyzed using VR to visualize how the tools were used for data exfiltration. The VR simulation depicted the flow of stolen data from compromised systems to external servers. Analysts could interact with this virtual model to understand the techniques used by the attackers and the pathways of the stolen information, enhancing their ability to trace and mitigate such threats.
- **VR Training for Cybercrime Units:** The FBI employed VR to train its cybercrime units in handling complex digital investigations. The VR simulations included scenarios such as ransomware attacks, data breaches, and hacking attempts. Trainees could navigate virtual crime scenes, interact with simulated evidence, and practice their response strategies. This immersive training improved officers' skills in real-world scenarios and enhanced their preparedness for actual cyber incidents.

7. FUTURE DIRECTIONS AND INNOVATIONS

As AR and VR technologies continue to advance and integrate into various aspects of daily life, the field of cyber forensics faces new challenges and opportunities. The evolution of these immersive technologies necessitates innovative approaches to forensic investigation, evidence handling, and legal considerations. potential future directions and innovations in cyber forensics with respect to AR and VR are:

7.1. Advancements in Technology

The future of AR and VR in forensics will likely involve advancements in AR technology and virtual reality. These advancements are likely to enhance capabilities and applications in forensics, including improved data capture, storage, higher-resolution simulations, and more interactive tools for evidence analysis. Emerging technologies such as Artificial Intelligence (AI) and Machine Learning (ML) may also play a role in enhancing AR forensic practices.

- **Custom Data Extraction Tools:** Development of software that can efficiently extract and analyze spatial data, user interactions, and metadata from AR and VR systems.

- **Real-Time Monitoring Solutions:** Tools that can monitor and log interactions in real time without interfering with user experiences, ensuring that all data is preserved accurately for forensic analysis.
- **Snapshot and Replay Systems:** Systems that can take snapshots of AR and VR environments at specific moments, enabling forensic analysts to "replay" events as they occurred in virtual space.
- **AI and ML Integration:** Artificial Intelligence (AI) and Machine Learning (ML) algorithms can be used to analyze AR and VR data more efficiently and detect anomalies or patterns that may be relevant to forensic investigations.
- **Enhanced AR and VR Devices:** Advances in AR devices, such as more accurate sensors and higher-resolution displays, can improve the quality and precision of AR evidence. Advances in VR hardware, such as higher-resolution displays, better sensory feedback, and more accurate motion tracking can improve the quality and precision of VR evidence.
- **Blockchain for Evidence Integrity:** Utilizing blockchain technology to create immutable records of data interactions and changes within AR and VR environments, ensuring the integrity and traceability of evidence.
- **3D Visualization Tools:** Creating advanced visualization tools that can represent spatial data in a more understandable format, assisting forensic analysts in interpreting complex data sets.
- **Unified Data Standards:** Collaboration among industry stakeholders to develop common standards for data storage, retrieval, and sharing across different AR and VR platforms, facilitating easier forensic analysis.
- **Interoperability Protocols:** Establishing protocols that ensure compatibility among various devices and systems, allowing forensic tools to work seamlessly across different environments.

7.2. Legal Frameworks and Ethical Guidelines

As AR and VR technologies evolve, the legal frameworks governing their use in forensic investigations also have to be evolved. Ethical considerations regarding data privacy and user rights will also need to be addressed.

- **Dynamic Legal Frameworks:** Developing adaptable legal frameworks that can respond to the rapid changes in AR and VR technology, ensuring that forensic practices remain compliant with existing laws.
- **Ethical Guidelines for Data Handling:** Establishing ethical guidelines that govern how data from AR and VR environments is collected, stored, and analyzed, protecting user privacy and rights.

7.3. Collaborative Efforts

Addressing the forensic challenges in AR and VR will require collaboration between technologists, forensic experts, legal professionals, and policymakers. Collaborative efforts can help develop standardized practices, legal frameworks, and technological solutions to enhance forensic investigations in AR (augmented reality) and VR (virtual reality) environment.

Collaborative Initiatives:

- **Industry Standards:** Collaborating with industry stakeholders to establish standards for AR and VR data handling and forensic practices can improve consistency and reliability. Creating networks that connect forensic experts, technologists, and legal professionals to share knowledge and best practices, fostering a holistic understanding of the implications of AR and VR in forensic investigations.
- **Training and Education:** Providing training and education for forensic professionals on AR technologies and forensic methodologies can enhance their ability to handle AR and VR evidence effectively.
- **Public Education Campaigns:** Initiatives to inform users about the data collected by AR and VR systems and the potential risks associated with their use.
- **Workshops and Seminars:** Organizing training sessions for law enforcement and forensic professionals to keep them updated on the latest developments in AR and VR technologies and their forensic implications.

The future of cyber forensics in the context of augmented reality and virtual reality is poised for significant innovation and transformation. By focusing on the development of specialized tools, standardization of data formats, advanced analytical techniques, and collaboration across disciplines, the forensic community can better address the unique challenges posed by these immersive technologies. Furthermore, establishing robust legal frameworks and ethical guidelines will be crucial in ensuring that the benefits of AR and VR are realized while protecting individual rights and maintaining the integrity of forensic investigations.

8. BEST PRACTICES

Integrating Augmented Reality (AR) and Virtual Reality (VR) into cyber forensics offers numerous advantages, but it requires careful implementation to be effective and secure. Here are some best practices for using AR and VR in cyber forensics:

- **Ensure Data Security and Privacy:** Given the sensitive nature of forensic investigations, protecting data security and privacy is crucial. When using AR and VR tools, ensure that all data, including evidence and personal information, is securely stored and transmitted. Implement strong encryption methods and access controls to prevent unauthorized access to sensitive information. Regularly update security protocols to address emerging threats and vulnerabilities.
- **Use of Standardize Tools and Protocols:** To ensure consistency and reliability, standardize the AR and VR tools and protocols used in cyber forensics. Develop guidelines for selecting and using specific AR/VR systems, and create standardized procedures for data collection, analysis, and presentation. This helps maintain quality and ensures that different teams and experts can effectively collaborate and share information.
- **Integration of AR/VR with Existing Forensic Tools:** Integrate AR and VR technologies with traditional forensic tools and methods to enhance their capabilities. Ensure that AR/VR systems can work seamlessly with other forensic software and hardware, such as digital evidence management systems, forensic analysis tools, and case management databases. This integration provides a comprehensive approach to investigations and maximizes the effectiveness of forensic operations.
- **Validate and Test AR/VR Systems:** Regularly validate and test AR and VR systems to ensure their accuracy and reliability. Conduct thorough testing of VR simulations and AR visualizations to verify that they accurately represent real-world scenarios and data. Perform regular quality assurance checks to identify and correct any issues before using these tools in critical investigations.
- **Training and Skill Development:** Invest in training programs for forensic professionals to effectively use AR and VR technologies. Ensure that team members are proficient in operating AR/VR systems, understanding their outputs, and integrating them into forensic workflows. Ongoing training and skill development are essential for keeping up with technological advancements and maintaining expertise in using these tools.
- **Comprehensive Documentation:** Document all AR and VR activities meticulously, including the setup, configuration, and results of forensic in-

vestigations. Maintain records of how AR/VR tools were used, the data visualizations created, and the outcomes of the analysis. Comprehensive documentation is crucial for ensuring the integrity of the investigation, providing transparency, and supporting legal proceedings.

- **Ensuring Legal and Ethical Compliance:** Adhere to legal and ethical standards when using AR and VR in cyber forensics. Ensure that the use of these technologies complies with relevant laws, regulations, and ethical guidelines. Obtain necessary permissions and warrants when required and handle all evidence and data in accordance with legal protocols to ensure its admissibility in court.
- **Strict User Access Controls:** Establish strict access controls for AR and VR systems to protect sensitive forensic data and ensure that only authorized personnel can use these tools. Implement role-based access controls, authentication mechanisms, and audit trails to monitor and manage access to AR/VR systems. This helps prevent unauthorized use and maintains the security of forensic investigations.
- **User-Friendly Interfaces:** Develop AR and VR interfaces that are intuitive and user-friendly to facilitate ease of use and effective interaction. User-friendly design enhances the efficiency of forensic analysis and reduces the risk of errors.
- **Regular Reviews and Updates:** Regularly review and update AR and VR technologies and practices to keep pace with advancements in technology and evolving forensic needs. Stay informed about new developments in AR/VR and incorporate relevant improvements into forensic workflows. Periodic reviews help ensure that the tools remain effective, secure, and aligned with best practices in cyber forensics.

By following these best practices, forensic professionals can effectively leverage AR and VR technologies to enhance their investigative capabilities, improve evidence analysis, and maintain the integrity and security of their work.

9. SUMMARY

The integration of Augmented Reality (AR) and Virtual Reality (VR) into forensic practices offers significant benefits, including enhanced visualization, interactive data analysis, and immersive crime scene reconstruction. However, it also presents a range of forensic challenges related to data integrity, evidence preservation, authentication, and legal considerations. Addressing these challenges requires a multi-faceted approach, involving advancements in technology, development of standardized practices, and collaboration among various stakeholders. As AR and VR technology continues to evolve, it is essential to remain vigilant and proactive in addressing these challenges to ensure that AR evidence is effectively and ethically utilized in forensic investigations.

REFERENCES

ADF-Solutions. (2023). *Digital Forensics in VR: Investigating Crimes & Analyzing Data*. Retrieved from adfsolutions.com: https://www.adfsolutions.com/adf-blog/digital-forensics-in-virtual-reality-investigating-crimes-and-analyzing-data-in-virtual-worlds-using-digital-forensic-software

Golomingi, R., Dobay, A., Franckenberg, S., Ebert, L., & Sieberth, T. (2023). Augmented reality in forensics and forensic medicine – Current status and future prospects. *Science & Justice*, 63(4), 451–455. DOI: 10.1016/j.scijus.2023.04.009 PMID: 37453776

Raffael, G., Akos, D., Sabine, F., Lars, E., & Sieberth, T. (2023). Augmented Reality in Forensics and Forensic Medicine- Current Status and Future Prospects. *Science & Justice*. PMID: 37453776

Raymer, E., MacDermott, Á., & Akinbi, A. (2023). Virtual reality forensics: Forensic analysis of Meta Quest 2. *Forensic Science International Digital Investigation*, 47, 47. DOI: 10.1016/j.fsidi.2023.301658

Sieberth, T., Dobay, A., Affolter, R., & Ebert, L. C. (2018). Applying virtual reality in forensics – a virtual scene walkthrough. *Forensic Science, Medicine, and Pathology*, 15(1), 41–47. DOI: 10.1007/s12024-018-0058-8 PMID: 30519987

ADDITIONAL READING

Abdel-Basset, M., Hawash, H., Chakrabortty, R. K., & Ryan, M. J. (2021). Semi-supervised spatiotemporal deep learning for intrusions detection in IoT networks. *IEEE Internet of Things Journal*, 8(15), 12251–12265. DOI: 10.1109/JIOT.2021.3060878

Ahmed, B., Gulliver, T. A., & alZahir, S. (2020). (1-12). Blind copy-move forgery detection using svd and ks test. *SN Applied Sciences*.

Akbar, M., Suaib, M., & Hussain, M. (2023). The Rise of Deepfake Technology: Issues, Challenges, and Countermeasures. In Advances in Cyberology and the Advent of the Next-Gen Information Revolution (pp. 178-201). IGI Global.

Akbar, M., Suaib, M., & Hussain, M. S. (2022). Analysis of Deep-Fake Technology Impacting Digital World Credibility: A Comprehensive Literature Review. *International Journal of Computer and Information Technology*, 11(2). Advance online publication. DOI: 10.24203/ijcit.v11i2.282

Balushi, Y. A., Shaker, H., & Kumar, B. (2023). The Use of Machine Learning in Digital Forensics: Review Paper. International Conference on Innovation in Information Technology and Business (pp. 96-113). Springer Nature.

Casey, P., Baggili, I., & Yarramreddy, A. (2019). Immersive virtual reality attacks and the human joystick. *IEEE Transactions on Dependable and Secure Computing*, 18(2), 550–562. DOI: 10.1109/TDSC.2019.2907942

Ferreira, S., Antunes, M., & Correia, M. E. (2021). Exposing manipulated photos and videos in digital forensics analysis. *Journal of Imaging*, 7(7), 102. DOI: 10.3390/jimaging7070102 PMID: 39080890

Halima, N. B., Alluhaidan, A. S., Khan, M. Z., Husain, M. S., & Khan, M. A. (2023). A service-categorized security scheme with physical unclonable functions for internet of vehicles. *Journal of Big Data*, 10(1), 178. DOI: 10.1186/s40537-023-00865-7

Haroon, M., Misra, D. K., Husain, M., Tripathi, M. M., & Khan, A. (2023). Security Issues in the Internet of Things for the Development of Smart Cities. In Husain, M. S., Faisal, M., Sadia, H., Ahmad, T., & Shukla, S. (Eds.), *Advances in Cyberology and the Advent of the Next-Gen Information Revolution* (pp. 123–137). IGI. DOI: 10.4018/978-1-6684-8133-2.ch007

Husain, M. S., Faisal, M., Sadia, H., Ahmad, T., & Shukla, S. (2023). *Advances in Cyberology and the Advent of the Next-gen Information Revolution*. IGI Global. DOI: 10.4018/978-1-6684-8133-2

Khalilia, W. M., Gombár, M., Palková, Z., Palko, M., Valiček, J., & Harničárová, M. (2022). Using virtual reality as support to the learning process of forensic scenarios. *IEEE Access : Practical Innovations, Open Solutions*, 10, 83297–83310. DOI: 10.1109/ACCESS.2022.3196471

Lohr, D., & Komogortsev, O. V. (2022). Eye know you too: Toward viable end-to-end eye movement biometrics for user authentication. *IEEE Transactions on Information Forensics and Security*, 17, 3151–3164. DOI: 10.1109/TIFS.2022.3201369

Lotfollahi, M., Siavoshani, M. J., Zade, R. S., & Saberian, M. (2020). Deep packet: A novel approach for encrypted traffic classification using deep learning. *Soft Computing*, 24(3), 1999–2012. DOI: 10.1007/s00500-019-04030-2

Mahajan, K., Madhavidevi, B., Supreeth, B. R., Lakshmi, N. V., Joshi, K., & Bavankumar, S. (2023). Detecting and Responding to Cloud Security Incidents based on AI and Forensic Approach. *International Conference on Innovative Computing, Intelligent Communication and Smart Electrical Systems (ICSES)*, (pp. 1-6). DOI: 10.1109/ICSES60034.2023.10465380

Maneli, M. A., & Isafiade, O. E. (2022). 3D forensic crime scene reconstruction involving immersive technology: A systematic literature review. *IEEE Access : Practical Innovations, Open Solutions*, 10, 88821–88857. DOI: 10.1109/ACCESS.2022.3199437

Meshal, A., Hoshang, K., Ramy, H., & Tanzila, S. (2023). Seamless Crime Scene Reconstruction in Mixed Reality for Investigation Training: A Design and Evaluation Study. *IEEE Transactions on Learning Technologies*.

Serrano-Vergel, R., Morillo, P., Casas-Yrurzum, S., & Cruz-Neira, C. (2023). Exploring the suitability of using virtual reality and augmented reality for anatomy training. *IEEE Transactions on Human-Machine Systems*, 53(2), 378–389. DOI: 10.1109/THMS.2023.3235250

KEY TERMS AND DEFINITIONS

Access Control: Access control refers to the set of policies, technologies, and procedures that determine who is allowed to access and use resources within a computing environment. It involves the process of identifying users, authenticating their identities, and authorizing their access to specific data, applications, or systems based on predefined permissions. Access control helps protect sensitive information from unauthorized access, misuse, or disclosure, ensuring that only authorized individuals can perform certain actions or access specific resources.

Data Volatility: Data volatility refers to the rate at which data changes over time. High data volatility means that the data is frequently changing, which can be challenging for systems that need to maintain consistency or perform accurate analysis. Conversely, low data volatility indicates that data remains relatively stable over time.

Chapter 10
Deepfake Detection and Analysis in Cyber Forensics

ABSTRACT

Deepfake technology, which involves the use of artificial intelligence (AI) to create highly realistic but fabricated media, has evolved rapidly over the past decade and poses a severe challenge in the realm of cyber forensics. Deepfake technology, which leverages advanced machine learning and deep learning algorithms to create highly realistic yet fabricated media, has emerged as a potent tool for disinformation, fraud, and other malicious activities. These synthetic media, which can involve altered images, audio, and video, pose risks to personal privacy, security, and the integrity of digital evidence.

1. INTRODUCTION

Deepfake technology, which involves the use of artificial intelligence (AI) to create highly realistic but fabricated media, has evolved rapidly over the past decade and poses a severe challenge in the realm of cyber forensics. Deepfake technology, which leverages advanced machine learning and deep learning algorithms to create highly realistic yet fabricated media, has emerged as a potent tool for disinformation, fraud, and other malicious activities. These synthetic media, which can involve altered images, audio, and video, pose risks to personal privacy, security, and the integrity of digital evidence.

This chapter delves into the profound implications of deepfakes for the field of cyber forensics, exploring their impact on digital evidence integrity, the challenges they pose, and the strategies for detection and mitigation. By examining the mul-

DOI: 10.4018/979-8-3693-2960-3.ch010

tifaceted significance of deepfakes, this chapter aims to provide a comprehensive understanding of how they affect forensic practices and what can be done to address these challenges to protect the authenticity of digital evidence and uphold justice.

2. DEEPFAKE TECHNOLOGY OVERVIEW

Deepfakes are synthetic media created using artificial intelligence (AI), machine learning algorithms, and deep learning algorithms, primarily Generative Adversarial Networks (GANs) and Variational Autoencoders (VAEs). These technologies enable the creation of highly convincing fake images, videos, and audio clips that can be manipulated to convey misleading or fabricated information. Deepfake models learn from large datasets of authentic content and then generate new, yet highly realistic, variations. Deepfakes began as a niche technology but have rapidly evolved, becoming increasingly sophisticated and accessible (Akbar, Suaib, & Hussain, 2023). The democratization of deepfake tools has broadened their use, from harmless novelty applications to potentially malicious purposes.

2.1. Applications of Deepfakes

Deepfake technology has a wide range of applications across various fields, each with unique benefits and challenges such as:

- **Entertainment**
  - **Special Effects:** Deepfakes are used to create realistic visual effects, such as de-aging actors or resurrecting deceased performers for new roles.
  - **Fan Creations:** Fans can use deepfake technology to produce mashups and alternate reality videos featuring their favorite characters or celebrities.
  - **Content Creation:** deepfakes have been employed in creative applications, such as generating synthetic voices for virtual characters, dubbing in different languages, and creating new audio content for entertainment purposes.
- **Social Media**
  - **Viral Content:** Deepfake content can quickly go viral, attracting millions of views. While some are harmless or humorous, others can be misleading or defamatory.
  - **Influencer Marketing:** Influencers may use deepfakes to create engaging content that blends their persona with popular culture.

- **Education and Training**
  - o **Medical Simulations:** Healthcare professionals can practice on hyper-realistic patient simulations, improving training and preparedness.
  - o **Language Learning:** Deepfake avatars can provide interactive language learning experiences, mimicking real-life conversations.
- **Gaming**
  - o **Character Creation:** Game developers can use deepfake technology to generate more lifelike NPCs (non-playable characters) and enhance player immersion.
  - o **Custom Content:** Players can create personalized avatars or experiences using deepfake technology.
- **Corporate Training and Development**
  - o **Role-Playing Scenarios:** Companies can create realistic training scenarios for employees, improving skills in customer service, sales, or crisis management.
  - o **Diversity and Inclusion Training:** Custom scenarios can be developed to simulate interactions and enhance understanding of diversity issues.
- **Art and Creative Projects**
  - o **Exploratory Art:** Artists are exploring deepfake technology to challenge notions of identity, authorship, and reality, creating installations or performances that provoke thought.
  - o **Virtual Reality:** Creating immersive environments that incorporate deepfake elements to enhance user experience.
- **Political and Social Commentary**
  - o **Misinformation:** Deepfakes can be created to manipulate public perception of political figures, often during election seasons, which can lead to misinformation and political unrest.
  - o **Satire and Parody:** Comedians and content creators use deepfake technology to produce humorous or critical takes on current events and personalities.
- **Research and Development**
  - o **Psychological Studies:** Researchers can create realistic scenarios to study human behavior and reactions, particularly in social psychology.
  - o **AI and Machine Learning:** Developing and refining AI models that can generate or detect deepfakes, advancing the field of artificial intelligence.
- **Personalization in Marketing**
  - o **Tailored Advertisements:** Brands can create personalized content featuring consumers' likenesses, enhancing engagement and relevance.
- **Cybersecurity and Fraud**

- **Identity Theft:** While this is a malicious application, deepfakes can be used for impersonation and fraud, such as creating convincing fake voice messages for financial scams, leading to potential financial loss and privacy breaches. The ability to replicate voices with high accuracy poses risks for security and personal privacy.
- **Manipulation of Security Systems:** Advanced deepfakes can trick biometric systems that rely on facial recognition.
- **Reputation Damage:** Malicious actors can create deepfake videos to defame individuals or organizations, leading to severe reputational harm.

While the applications of deepfake technology hold great potential for innovation and creativity, they also raise significant ethical and societal concerns. Responsible use and ongoing dialogue about the implications of this technology will be crucial as it continues to develop.

2.2. Technologies driving Deepfake

Deepfake technology is primarily driven by advances in artificial intelligence and machine learning, particularly through specific algorithms and models. The core technologies driving deepfakes are:

- **Generative Adversarial Networks (GANs):** GANs consist of two neural networks; the generator and the discriminator, that are trained in opposition to each other. The generator creates fake media, while the discriminator attempts to distinguish between real and fake. Following this adversarial process, through iterative training, the generator learns to produce increasingly realistic media that the discriminator struggles to differentiate from real content, GANs improve the quality of generated media over time.
- **Variational Autoencoders (VAEs):** VAEs are used for generating new samples from learned data distributions. They work by encoding input data into a lower-dimensional space and then decoding it back, with modifications, to produce new, synthetic content. They are particularly useful for generating high-quality images and videos by learning data distributions and creating realistic variations.
- **Neural Rendering:** Techniques in neural rendering combine traditional graphics methods with neural networks to create photorealistic visuals, enhancing the quality of deepfake outputs. Style Transfer allows for the blending of different artistic styles with realistic images, further refining the appearance of deepfakes.

- **Voice Synthesis:** Text-to-Speech (TTS) algorithms that convert text to realistic speech can be integrated into deepfake technologies to create convincing audio that matches the video content. Advanced machine learning models can mimic a person's voice, adding another layer of realism to deepfake videos.
- **Libraries and Tools:** Frameworks like TensorFlow, PyTorch, and Keras provide the infrastructure for building and training deep learning models, making it easier to implement GANs and autoencoders. Many developers use pre-trained models, which can save time and computational resources while achieving high-quality results.
- **Temporal Coherence:** Maintaining temporal coherence ensures that changes in facial expressions or movements are smooth and consistent over time in video sequences. Techniques like recurrent neural networks (RNNs) may be used to help maintain continuity.
- **Computer Vision:** Advanced image processing techniques are employed to refine the quality of deepfakes, enhancing details, lighting, and shadows to make the output more realistic. Motion Transfer algorithms can capture and replicate the subtle nuances of movement and expressions, contributing to a lifelike portrayal in videos.

The synergy of these core technologies enables the creation of increasingly convincing deepfakes. As these technologies evolve, the potential for both positive applications and misuse grows, necessitating ongoing research into detection and ethical considerations.

2.3. Types of Deepfakes

- **Images:** Deepfake technology can superimpose faces or alter facial expressions in images. Deepfake images are commonly used in creating fake profiles, altering photographs for malicious purposes or misleading visuals and can be challenging to detect without specialized tools.
- **Audio:** Deepfake audio involves synthesizing or modifying speech to imitate someone's voice. Audio deepfakes can be used for fraudulent activities such as impersonating individuals in financial transactions or creating misleading voice recordings and spreading false information.
- **Video:** Deepfake videos are more complex and involve manipulating facial expressions, lip movements, and audio synchronization to create realistic but fabricated video content. This type of deepfake is particularly dangerous due to its potential to create false evidence, defame individuals, spread misinformation or damage reputations.

3. DEEPFAKE TECHNOLOGY EVOLUTION

Deepfake technology has undergone a remarkable evolution since its inception, driven by advancements in artificial intelligence (AI) and machine learning. This technology, which creates highly realistic yet fabricated media by manipulating or generating synthetic content, has become both a powerful tool and a significant challenge in various domains, including cybersecurity, media, and law enforcement. Understanding the history and evolution of deepfake technology is crucial for appreciating its impact and implications across various domains, including cybersecurity, digital forensics, and media integrity. The rise of deepfakes presents significant challenges for cyber forensics, as these fabricated media can be used for various malicious purposes, including misinformation, identity theft, and fraud.

Early AI and Machine Learning Developments (1950s-1980s)

The foundation for deepfake technology can be traced back to early developments in artificial intelligence (AI) and machine learning (ML). In the 1950s and 1960s, researchers began exploring neural network architectures to mimic human cognitive processes. Early neural networks, such as the Perceptron developed by Frank Rosenblatt in 1958, were designed for pattern recognition and simple classification tasks. These initial models laid the groundwork for more complex neural network structures used in deepfake technology.

Development of Deep Learning (2000s)

The 2000s saw significant progress in deep learning, a subfield of machine learning focused on neural networks with many layers (deep networks). The resurgence of neural networks, known as deep learning, enabled the development of models capable of handling complex data and performing intricate tasks. Key innovations included the introduction of deep convolutional neural networks (CNNs) for image recognition and the development of algorithms to build systems that could learn from large datasets.

Advent of Generative Adversarial Networks (GANs) (2014)

The concept of generative models, which are central to deepfake technology, emerged in the 1990s with the development of algorithms designed to generate new data based on existing data. One of the early generative models was the Restricted Boltzmann Machine (RBM), which could learn and generate complex data distributions. A major milestone in deepfake technology was the introduction of

Generative Adversarial Networks (GANs) by Ian Goodfellow and his team in 2014. GANs consist of two neural networks: the generator and the discriminator. The generator creates synthetic data, while the discriminator evaluates its authenticity. Through adversarial training, the generator improves its ability to produce realistic data, while the discriminator becomes better at distinguishing between real and fake data. GANs revolutionized the field of generative models by enabling the creation of highly realistic synthetic images and videos.

Advances in GAN Architectures (2016-2018)

Following the introduction of GANs, researchers made several advancements in GAN architectures to improve the quality and realism of generated media. Notable developments include:

- **Deep Convolutional GANs (DCGANs):** Introduced in 2015, DCGANs use convolutional layers in the GAN architecture, enabling the generation of higher-quality images. DCGANs demonstrated improved stability and visual quality compared to earlier GAN models.
- **Progressive Growing GANs (PGGANs):** Proposed in 2017, PGGANs use a progressive training approach, starting with low-resolution images and gradually increasing the resolution. This technique results in high-resolution and photorealistic images, addressing limitations in image quality and realism.
- **StyleGAN:** Developed by NVIDIA, StyleGAN introduced in 2018, is a novel architecture that separates the generation of high-level features (styles) from low-level details. StyleGAN achieved impressive results in generating high-quality, photorealistic images with fine-grained control over visual attributes.

Rise of Deepfake (2017): The term "deepfake" emerged in 2017 when a Reddit user began posting manipulated videos using GANs. These early deepfakes demonstrated the ability to swap faces in videos with high realism, sparking widespread interest and concern. Deepfake quickly gained attention due to its potential for misuse, particularly in creating misleading or harmful content.

Development of Voice Synthesis Models (2017-2019): While deepfake technology initially focused on visual content, advancements in audio deepfakes also became notable:

- **WaveNet (2016):** Developed by DeepMind, WaveNet is a deep generative model for raw audio waveform synthesis. WaveNet achieved high-quality voice synthesis, enabling the creation of realistic and natural-sounding speech.

- **Tacotron and Tacotron 2 (2017-2018):** These models, developed by Google, use sequence-to-sequence learning to generate speech from text. Tacotron 2, in particular, achieved impressive results in producing high-quality and expressive speech, further advancing the capabilities of audio deepfakes.

Emergence of Deepfake Applications: As deepfake technology developed, several key techniques and advancements emerged:

- **Face Swapping:** One of the earliest and most recognizable applications of deepfake technology was face swapping. Using GANs and other techniques, researchers demonstrated the ability to superimpose one person's face onto another's in videos, creating convincing but fake footage. This application gained popularity in entertainment and social media but also raised ethical concerns about privacy and consent.
- **High-Resolution Deepfakes:** Early deepfakes were limited by resolution and quality. However, advancements in GAN architectures, such as Progressive Growing GANs and StyleGAN, enabled the generation of high-resolution and photorealistic images and videos, further enhancing the realism of deepfakes.
- **Deepfake Pornography:** The use of deepfake technology to create non-consensual explicit content emerged as a significant concern. Deepfake pornography involved inserting individuals' faces into pornographic videos, leading to discussions about privacy violations and legal implications.
- **Political and Social Manipulation:** Deepfakes began to be used for political and social manipulation, including the creation of fake speeches and videos attributed to public figures. This raised concerns about misinformation, election interference, and the potential impact on public trust.
- **Avatar Deepfakes:** This involves creating digital avatars that can realistically mimic human expressions and speech, often used in gaming and virtual environments. For example, virtual characters in a video game that behaves and reacts like real persons.
- **Lip Sync Deepfakes:** This application focuses on matching lip movements in a video with new audio to make it appear as though the person is saying something different. For example. video where a politician's lips match a speech they never delivered.
- **Meme Deepfakes:** Short videos or images designed for humor or satire, often involving exaggerated or absurd scenarios. For example, a deepfake video of a celebrity in a comedic skit, heavily edited for humor.
- **Interactive Deepfakes:** Real-time deepfake technology that allows users to interact with and manipulate deepfakes, often used in virtual reality or gam-

ing. For example, users can create a deepfake avatar of themselves to interact in a virtual environment.

Public Awareness and Controversy: The increasing sophistication of deepfake technology led to significant public awareness and controversy. Deepfakes began to be used in various malicious contexts, including misinformation campaigns, political manipulation, and defamation. High-profile cases of deepfake misuse, such as fake celebrity videos and fraudulent political content, highlighted the potential dangers of the technology.

4. TECHNIQUES FOR DEEPFAKE DETECTION

Several approaches have been developed to detect deepfakes, ranging from traditional image analysis to sophisticated machine learning methods.

4.1. Traditional Methods

In the case of deepfake audio, detection techniques analyze speech patterns, intonation, and synchronization with visual cues. These techniques include examining the frequency spectrum and comparing them with known voice characteristics to identify anomalies or inconsistencies in voice modulation. However, these methods are limited by the quality of the generated audio and the sophistication of the deepfake.

Early methods focused on identifying visual inconsistencies such as unnatural skin textures, irregular lighting, and irregular facial movements. While these methods can be useful, they often fall short against high-quality deepfakes that minimize such artifacts.

4.2. Machine Learning-Based Methods

Machine learning (ML) provides powerful tools for detecting deepfakes by analyzing various features and inconsistencies in digital content. Prominent ML-based methods used for deepfake detection are:

- **Convolutional Neural Networks (CNNs):** CNNs are particularly effective for image and video analysis due to their ability to capture spatial hierarchies and patterns. They operate by applying convolutional filters to input data, which helps in detecting edges, textures, and other visual features that are difficult for humans to detect.

CNNs automatically extract hierarchical features from images or frames of videos. This includes low-level features such as edges and textures and high-level features like facial expressions.

The extracted features are used to train a classifier that distinguishes between real and deepfake images or videos. CNNs are effective at spotting artifacts and inconsistencies that may be present in deepfakes, such as unnatural lighting or facial distortions.

- **Recurrent Neural Networks (RNNs):** RNNs, particularly Long Short-Term Memory (LSTM) networks, are designed to handle sequential data, making them suitable for analyzing video frames over time. LSTM networks are used to analyze temporal patterns in video sequences. They are effective in deepfake detection. By observing inconsistencies in facial expressions and lip movements.

RNNs and LSTMs analyze sequences of video frames to capture temporal dependencies and motion patterns. They can model how objects move and interact over time.

By analyzing the temporal consistency of motion and facial expressions, these networks can identify unnatural movements or synchronization issues often found in deepfakes.

- **Autoencoders:** Autoencoders are neural networks trained to reconstruct input data. They can learn to encode and decode media, capturing its essential features in the process.

Autoencoders are trained on real images or videos to learn a compressed representation of the data. They encode the data into a lower-dimensional space and then reconstruct it back to its original form.

When presented with deepfake content, the reconstruction error (difference between the input and reconstructed output) can reveal anomalies or artifacts indicative of manipulation.

- **Generative Adversarial Networks (GANs):** GANs consist of two networks: a generator that creates fake data and a discriminator that distinguishes between real and fake data.

During training, the generator creates synthetic media, while the discriminator learns to differentiate between real and fake content. This adversarial process improves both networks over time.

A trained GAN can be used as a discriminator to evaluate new media, identifying subtle artifacts or inconsistencies that indicate deepfake content.

- **Transformers:** Transformers are a type of neural network architecture designed for processing sequential data with self-attention mechanisms. They have shown success in various tasks, including natural language processing and image analysis.

Transformers use self-attention mechanisms to weigh the importance of different parts of the input data, allowing them to focus on relevant features. In deepfake detection, transformers analyze video sequences or image patches to identify inconsistencies or anomalies in the media, leveraging their ability to capture long-range dependencies.

- **Temporal Convolutional Networks (TCNs):** Temporal Convolutional Networks are designed to handle sequential data, similar to RNNs, but with convolutional layers instead of recurrent layers. TCNs use dilated convolutions to capture long-range dependencies in sequential data. In deepfake detection, TCNs analyze video sequences to identify temporal anomalies or artifacts.
- **Multi-Modal Approaches:** Multi-modal approaches integrate information from various sources, such as audio and visual data, to enhance detection.

The approach Combines features from different modalities, such as facial images and audio recordings, to create a comprehensive representation of the media. These models analyze the combined data to detect inconsistencies or anomalies across different modalities.

- **Ensemble Methods:** Combining multiple detection models into an ensemble can improve accuracy by leveraging the strengths of different algorithms. Ensemble methods aggregate predictions from various models and reduce the likelihood of false positives and false negatives to make a final decision. Different models, such as CNNs, RNNs, and GANs, are trained separately and their predictions are combined using techniques like voting or averaging.

Machine learning-based methods offer powerful tools for detecting deepfakes by analyzing various features and inconsistencies in digital media. Each method has its strengths and challenges which are summarized in table 10.1. The choice of method depends on the specific requirements of the detection task.

4.3. Emerging Techniques

- **Deep Learning Transfer Learning:** Transfer learning involves fine-tuning pre-trained models to specific deepfake detection tasks. This approach can improve detection performance with limited data by leveraging existing knowledge from general models.
- **Blockchain Verification:** Blockchain technology can be used to create immutable records of media authenticity. By verifying the provenance of media through a blockchain ledger, it becomes possible to verify whether media has been altered since its creation thus ensuring its integrity.
- **Biometric Analysis:** Techniques that analyze biometric features such as eye movements, facial micro-expressions, and voice characteristics offer promising avenues for detecting deepfakes. These methods exploit the subtle, often imperceptible cues that are difficult for deepfake algorithms to replicate accurately, enhancing the detection process.

Table 1. Summary of various ML methods for deepfake detection

Method	Advantage	Disadvantage
CNN	• Capable of learning complex patterns and features. • Effective for high-resolution images and videos.	• Requires a large amount of labeled data for training. • Computationally intensive.
RNN	• Effective at capturing temporal patterns and sequences. • Useful for detecting inconsistencies in video content.	• Training can be complex and requires significant computational resources. • May struggle with long sequences due to vanishing gradient problems, though LSTMs mitigate this issue.
Autoencoders	• Effective at learning features and detecting deviations from normal patterns. • Can handle complex data and detect subtle manipulations.	• May require fine-tuning to differentiate between real and fake content accurately. • Can be sensitive to overfitting if not properly regularized.
GAN	• Highly effective at detecting deepfakes due to the adversarial training process. • Can capture complex patterns and artifacts.	• Requires substantial computational resources for training. • Can be prone to instability and mode collapse during training.
Transformers	• Effective at capturing complex dependencies and relationships. • Can handle large datasets and long sequences.	• Requires significant computational resources. • May need extensive tuning to achieve optimal performance.

continued on following page

Table 1. Continued

Method	Advantage	Disadvantage
TCN	• Efficiently captures long-range dependencies in sequential data. • Can be more stable and easier to train than RNNs.	• May require extensive training data to achieve optimal performance. • Performance can vary based on the architecture and hyperparameters.
Multi-model approach	• Provides a more holistic view of the media, improving detection accuracy. • Can capture subtle manipulations that may be missed by single-modal approaches.	• Requires synchronization and alignment of multiple data sources. • Can be complex to implement and manage.
Ensemble methods	• Combines the strengths of different models for improved performance. • Reduces the risk of overfitting and improves generalization.	• Requires careful integration and management of multiple models. • Can be computationally intensive.

5. APPLICATIONS OF DEEPFAKE IN CYBER FORENSICS

Deepfake detection plays a critical role in various aspects of cyber forensics, including digital evidence gathering, legal proceedings, and security measures. These applications leverage the technology's capability to generate and manipulate media to aid in investigations and training. Some notable applications of deepfake technology in cyber forensics are shown in Figure 1:

Figure 1. Applications of deepfakes in cyber forensics

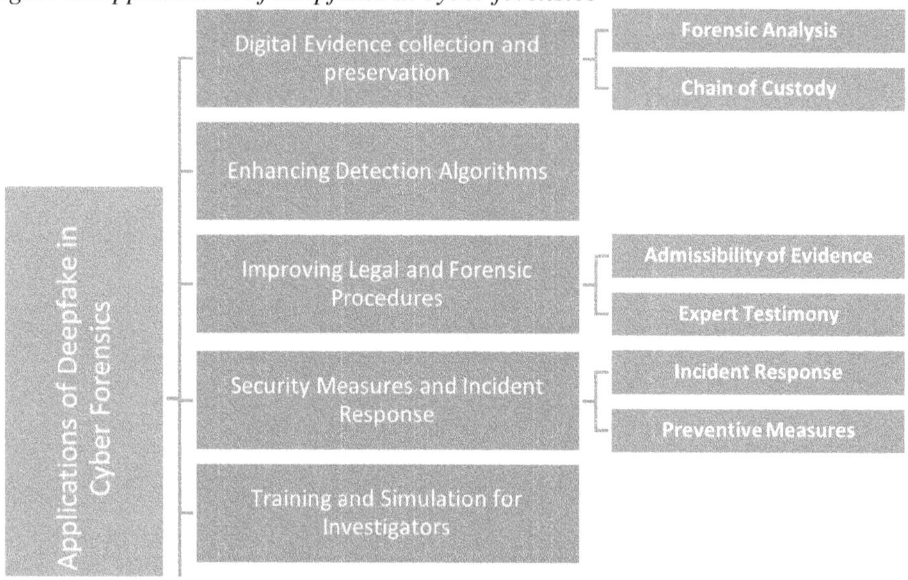

5.1. Digital Evidence collection and preservation

- **Forensic Analysis:** Deepfake detection tools are essential for forensic investigators to verify the authenticity of digital evidence. These tools help forensic investigators ensure that media used in legal proceedings is genuine and unaltered. This is crucial in cases involving cyber extortion, identity theft, and fraudulent activities.
- **Chain of Custody:** Ensuring the integrity of digital evidence is critical in forensic investigations. Detection tools assist in preserving the chain of custody and ensuring the credibility of the evidence by verifying that media has not been tampered with since its acquisition.

5.2. Enhancing Detection Algorithms

Deepfakes can be used to improve detection algorithms by providing diverse and challenging examples of manipulated media. Researchers can use these synthetic media to test and refine their detection methods, ensuring they can handle a wide range of deepfake techniques.

A deepfake dataset with various manipulation techniques can be used to train machine learning models for detecting deepfakes. By exposing the models to a broad spectrum of fake content, researchers can enhance the models' robustness and accuracy.

5.3. Improving Legal and Forensic Procedures

- **Admissibility of Evidence:** The credibility of digital evidence in court depends on its authenticity. Deepfake detection tools provide the necessary validation to ensure that media presented as evidence has not been manipulated and is genuine.
- **Expert Testimony:** Forensic experts use deepfake detection tools to provide testimony on the authenticity of digital evidence. Their analysis supports the credibility of the evidence and aids in judicial decision-making.

5.4. Security Measures and Incident Response

- **Incident Response:** Organizations employ deepfake detection tools as part of their incident response strategies to identify and mitigate the impact of deepfake-related attacks, such as fake news, fraudulent video contents, and other forms of malicious media.
- **Preventive Measures:** Early detection of deepfakes helps organizations protect their digital assets and reputation. Detecting deepfakes before they are used in attacks or disinformation campaigns helps in preventing potential harm. Implementing proactive measures and monitoring for deepfake activity is crucial for minimizing potential damage.

5.5. Training and Simulation for Investigators

Deepfake technology can be used to create realistic simulations for training purposes. By generating synthetic but plausible scenarios, forensic investigators can practice their skills in identifying manipulated media, understanding attack vectors, and responding to various cybercrime scenarios.

A deepfake simulation of a video call or public speech can be used to train law enforcement and cybersecurity professionals in recognizing signs of media manipulation. This helps them to better prepare for real-world situations where deepfakes might be used to deceive or manipulate.

5.6. Creating Controlled Test Environments

Deepfakes can be used to create controlled test environments for evaluating forensic tools and techniques. By generating specific types of deepfake content, forensic experts can assess how well their tools perform under various conditions. A controlled environment where deepfake videos are created with specific types of artifacts or manipulations can be used to test video forensic tools. This helps in identifying limitations and areas for improvement in existing technologies.

5.7. Enhancing Cybersecurity Awareness and Education

Deepfake technology can be used to raise awareness and educate individuals about the risks and implications of media manipulation. By demonstrating how deepfakes are created and their potential impact, organizations can improve cybersecurity awareness and training. Creating educational materials and demonstrations using deepfakes to show how easily media can be manipulated. This can be used in workshops, seminars, and training programs to inform individuals about the dangers of deepfakes and how to recognize and respond to them.

6. IMPLICATIONS OF DEEPFAKE IN CYBER FORENSICS

6.1. Threat to Digital Evidence Integrity

Deepfakes pose a serious threat to the integrity of digital evidence. Forensic investigations rely on the authenticity of digital media to support legal processes and decision-making. Deepfakes can be used to fabricate evidence, manipulate visual or auditory content, and produce misleading information. This compromises the credibility of evidence and can lead to wrongful convictions or acquittals.

- **Fabrication of Evidence:** Deepfakes can be used to create fabricated evidence, such as falsified videos or images, that can mislead investigations and legal proceedings. This can result in wrongful convictions or the dismissal of valid claims.
- **Manipulation of Evidence:** Existing media can be altered using deepfake technology to change its context or meaning. This manipulation can affect the outcome of legal cases and compromise the reliability of forensic evidence.

6.2. Potential for Misuse

- **Misinformation and Disinformation:** Deepfakes can be used to spread false information, create misleading narratives, and influence public opinion. This has implications for political elections, social unrest, and public trust.
- **Identity Theft and Fraud:** Deepfakes can facilitate identity theft and fraud by creating convincing fake identities or impersonating individuals. This can lead to financial losses and damage to personal and professional reputations.
- **Defamation and Harassment:** Malicious actors can use deepfakes to create defamatory or harassing content. This can have severe psychological and social impacts on individuals targeted by such attacks.

6.3. Enhancing Forensic Tools

The rise of deepfakes necessitates the development and integration of advanced forensic tools and techniques. Forensic professionals must adopt and refine cutting-edge detection technologies to address the challenges posed by deepfakes effectively. This includes investing in AI-powered analysis tools, leveraging multi-modal detection approaches, and continuously updating detection algorithms to address emerging threats.

- **Investing in AI-Powered Tools:** Leveraging AI-powered analysis tools can improve the accuracy and efficiency of deepfake detection. These tools are designed to handle the complexity and scale of modern deepfake technology.
- **Adopting Multi-Modal Detection Approaches:** Integrating visual, audio, and biometric analysis provides a more comprehensive detection strategy. Multi-modal approaches enhance the ability to detect and analyze deepfakes by considering various aspects of media.
- **Continuous Updates and Adaptation:** Forensic tools and methods must be regularly updated to keep pace with evolving deepfake techniques. Continuous adaptation ensures that detection strategies remain effective in the face of new challenges.

6.4. Legal and Ethical Considerations

- **Admissibility of Evidence:** Ensuring that digital evidence meets legal standards for admissibility is crucial. Forensic experts must validate that deepfake detection methods are reliable by meeting legal standards and can withstand scrutiny in judicial proceedings.
- **Privacy and Ethical Issues:** The use of deepfake detection technologies must balance effectiveness with privacy considerations. Ethical concerns arise regarding the extent of media analysis and potential intrusions into personal privacy. Establishing guidelines and protocols can help address these issues.
- **Psychological Impact:** The existence of realistic deepfakes can lead to anxiety and distrust, as people may question the authenticity of what they see in media and their social interactions.
- **Authenticity and Trust:** The proliferation of deepfake technology poses risks to public trust in the media. As deepfakes become more prevalent, distinguishing between real and manipulated content can become increasingly difficult.

6.5. Training and Awareness

- **Forensic Training:** Continuous training for forensic professionals is essential to stay updated on advancements in deepfake technology and detection techniques. Understanding the latest trends and tools is critical for effective forensic analysis. Training programs should cover the latest tools, methodologies, and best practices for handling deepfake-related cases.
- **Public Awareness:** Educating the public about deepfakes and their potential impact is crucial for mitigating risks. Awareness campaigns and educational initiatives can help individuals recognize and respond to deepfake-related threats, reducing the likelihood of falling victim to malicious media.

7. CHALLENGES IN DEEPFAKE DETECTION

Deepfake detection is fraught with challenges, largely due to the sophisticated nature of the technology and the rapid evolution of methods used to create deepfakes.

- **Technological Sophistication:** Deepfake technology is continuously improving. Advances in GANs and VAEs have led to deepfakes that are increasingly difficult to distinguish from real media. Improvements in resolution, synchronization, and the naturalness of artifacts make automated detection more challenging. The quality of deepfakes can make them difficult to detect, as subtle artifacts and inconsistencies may not be immediately apparent.

Deepfake creators continuously adapt their methods to bypass detection algorithms. They employ strategies such as adjusting the level of manipulation to match the quality of the original media, making detection more challenging. This cat-and-mouse game necessitates constant updates to detection techniques.

Detection models must constantly evolve to keep pace with new deepfake techniques, requiring ongoing research and development. Adapting detection methods to new deepfake technologies demands substantial computational resources and expertise.

- **Data Scarcity and Imbalanced Datasets:** High-quality datasets of both real and deepfake media are essential for training detection algorithms. However, creating and curating these datasets is resource-intensive, and the rapid evolution of deepfake techniques makes it difficult to maintain an up-to-date dataset.

Many available datasets are imbalanced, with more examples of real media than fake. This imbalance can lead to biased detection models that perform poorly in identifying deepfakes.

- **Resource Requirements and Computational Complexity:** Advanced deepfake detection methods, such as those based on deep learning, require significant computational resources. This can be a barrier to widespread implementation and accessibility, particularly in resource-constrained environments.

Forensic analysis often requires real-time or near-real-time processing of media. Ensuring that detection methods can operate efficiently under real time scenarios is a significant challenge.

- **Generalization Across Different Media Types:** Deepfake detection methods often struggle to generalize across different types of media, such as images, videos, and audio. Techniques that work well for one type of media may not be effective for others due to variations in content and manipulation methods.

Different media types have distinct characteristics, requiring specialized detection techniques. Adapting detection methods from one media type to another can be challenging and may not always yield successful results.

Models may need to be tailored specifically for each media type, increasing development complexity.

- **Adversarial Attacks on Detection Models:** Deepfake detection models can be vulnerable to adversarial attacks, where attackers intentionally modify deepfake content to evade detection. These attacks exploit the weaknesses in detection algorithms, reducing their effectiveness. Ensuring that detection models are robust against adversarial modifications is a significant challenge. Attackers can employ various techniques to create deepfakes that are specifically designed to bypass detection systems.

Detection systems must be continuously tested and updated to defend against new evasion strategies. Developing robust models requires addressing adversarial vulnerabilities.

- **False Positives and Misidentification:** Deepfake detection systems can produce false positives, incorrectly identifying genuine media as manipulated. This can undermine trust in the detection system and lead to wrongful accusations. False positives can damage reputations and cause confusion among users.

Ensuring high accuracy to minimize false positives is essential but challenging. Continuous evaluation and improvement of detection models are required to reduce false positive rates.

- **Subtle Artifacts and Imperfections:** Advanced deepfake techniques can produce media with very subtle artifacts that are difficult to detect with current methods. These subtle imperfections may not be easily noticeable to the human eye but can still indicate manipulation. Subtle artifacts may be missed by detection algorithms, leading to false negatives.

Deepfake detection models need to be highly sophisticated to catch minor anomalies. Continuous refinement and enhancement of detection techniques are necessary to improve sensitivity.

- **Integration with Existing Systems:** Integrating deepfake detection technology with existing systems and workflows can be challenging. Ensuring compatibility and seamless operation with other security tools and platforms is crucial for effective detection and response. Ensuring that detection tools work well with existing systems and infrastructure can be difficult and integrating detection systems into established workflows and processes requires careful planning and coordination.

Effective deployment of deepfake detection technology requires addressing integration challenges. Organizations must consider how detection tools will fit into their existing systems and processes.

- **Ethical and Privacy Concerns:** The use of deepfake detection technology raises ethical and privacy concerns, particularly regarding the collection and analysis of personal data. Ensuring that detection practices comply with ethical standards and privacy regulations is crucial.

Deepfakes can be used to create unauthorized and invasive content, such as non-consensual explicit material or misleading personal videos. This raises serious privacy issues and potential harm to individuals.

Deepfakes can be used to spread false information, manipulate public opinion, and influence political events. The potential for deepfakes to undermine democratic processes and public trust has led to calls for regulatory measures.

- **Legal Challenges:** The legal framework for addressing deepfake-related issues is still evolving. Different jurisdictions have varying laws and regulations related to media manipulation, which can complicate the implementation and enforcement of detection measures. Laws and regulations need to adapt to the challenges posed by deepfakes, including issues related to copyright, defamation, and fraud.

Ensuring that detection practices comply with relevant laws and regulations is complex and developing detection systems that adhere to legal and regulatory requirements can be challenging. Organizations must stay informed about evolving laws and regulations to ensure compliance.

8. CASE STUDIES

Deepfake technology has evolved rapidly, leading to significant concerns and challenges in various domains. Case studies of deepfake analysis help illustrate how this technology can be both exploited and mitigated. Some notable examples are (Vaccari & Chadwick, 2020), (Appel & Prietzel, 2022), (Bond, 2024):

- **Political Misinformation:** Deepfake videos have been used to spread false information about political figures, influencing public opinion and causing social unrest. Case studies in this area highlight the potential impact of deepfakes on democratic processes.
- **Celebrity Impersonation:** Deepfakes have been used to create explicit or defamatory content involving celebrities. These cases demonstrate the risks of identity theft and reputation damage associated with deepfake technology.
- **Corporate Espionage:** Deepfakes have been used in cases of corporate espionage, where fake media is used to deceive employees or partners. Forensic analysis in these scenarios involves verifying the authenticity of media used in fraudulent activities.
- **Fraud and Blackmail:** Deepfakes have been employed in fraud and blackmail schemes, where manipulated media is used to extort money or gain unauthorized access. Forensic investigations focus on detecting and mitigating the impact of such attacks.

9. FUTURE DIRECTIONS

The future of deepfake technology is uncertain. On one hand, it holds promise for creative industries and education; on the other, it poses significant risks for misinformation and privacy violations. Ongoing advancements in detection methods are essential to combat the misuse of deepfakes. Researchers and technologists are developing tools to identify deepfakes, which will be crucial in mitigating their potential harms. The field of deepfake detection is rapidly evolving, with ongoing research addressing current limitations and exploring new possibilities.

- **Advances in Detection Technologies:** Future advancements in AI and machine learning will enhance detection capabilities. Techniques such as federated learning and advanced neural network architectures, which allows models to be trained across decentralized data sources, could improve detection accuracy and robustness.

- **Multimodal Approach:** Combining visual, audio, and biometric analysis in a multi-modal approach may offer more comprehensive detection methods. By analyzing multiple aspects of media, these approaches can improve accuracy and greater precision as well as reduce false positives.
- **Ethical and Privacy Considerations:** As detection technologies advance, ethical considerations regarding privacy and data protection will become increasingly important. Ensuring that detection methods do not infringe on individual rights is a critical concern.
- **Legal Frameworks:** Developing regulations and policies to govern the use of deepfake technology and detection methods will be essential. Legal frameworks must address the ethical implications and establish standards for the responsible use of these technologies.
- **Collaborative Efforts:** Collaboration between technology companies, research institutions, and law enforcement agencies is crucial for advancing deepfake detection and analysis. Shared resources, knowledge, and datasets can accelerate progress and improve detection capabilities.
- **Training and Awareness:** Educating the public about deepfakes and their potential impact is essential for mitigating the risks associated with this technology. Public awareness campaigns and educational initiatives can help individuals recognize and respond to deepfake-related threats.
- **Continuous Innovation:** Ongoing research and development are vital for staying ahead of deepfake technology advancements. Investment in innovation and the exploration of new detection methods will be key to addressing emerging threats.

10. SUMMARY

Deepfake detection and analysis in cyber forensics represent a dynamic and rapidly evolving field. The sophisticated nature of deepfake technology presents significant challenges, but ongoing advancements in detection methods and collaborative efforts hold promise for improving the accuracy and effectiveness of deepfake detection. The future of deepfake detection lies in ongoing advancements in AI and machine learning, as well as the development of comprehensive multi-modal approaches. Ethical and privacy considerations will play a crucial role in shaping the direction of detection technologies and regulations. Understanding the history and milestones of deepfake technology is crucial for developing effective detection methods, addressing ethical and legal concerns, and ensuring responsible use in the future.

As deepfake technology continues to advance, ongoing research, innovation, and collaboration will be essential in addressing the evolving threats and ensuring the effectiveness of cyber forensic practices.

REFERENCES

Akbar, M., Suaib, M., & Hussain, M. S. (2022). Analysis of Deep-Fake Technology Impacting Digital World Credibility: A Comprehensive Literature Review. *International Journal of Computer and Information Technology*, 11(2). Advance online publication. DOI: 10.24203/ijcit.v11i2.282

Akbar, M., Suaib, M., & Hussain, M. S. (2023). The Rise of Deepfake Technology: Issues, Challenges, and Countermeasures. In *Advances in Cyberology and the Advent of the Next-Gen Information Revolution* (pp. 178–201). IGI Global. DOI: 10.4018/978-1-6684-8133-2.ch010

Appel, M., & Prietzel, F. (2022). The detection of political deepfakes. *Journal of Computer-Mediated Communication*, 27(4), zmac008. DOI: 10.1093/jcmc/zmac008

Bond, S. (2024). *AI fakes raise election risks as lawmakers and tech companies scramble to catch up*. NPR.

Husain, M. S., & Khan, M. Z. (Eds.). (2019). *Critical Concepts, Standards, and Techniques in Cyber Forensics*. IGI Global.

Vaccari, C., & Chadwick, A. (2020). Deepfakes and disinformation: Exploring the impact of synthetic political video on deception, uncertainty, and trust in news. *Social Media + Society*, 6(1), 2056305120903408. DOI: 10.1177/2056305120903408

ADDITIONAL READING

Abdel-Basset, M., Hawash, H., Chakrabortty, R. K., & Ryan, M. J. (2021). Semi-supervised spatiotemporal deep learning for intrusions detection in IoT networks. *IEEE Internet of Things Journal*, 8(15), 12251–12265. DOI: 10.1109/JIOT.2021.3060878

Ahmed, B., Gulliver, T. A., & alZahir, S. (2020). (1-12). Blind copy-move forgery detection using svd and ks test. *SN Applied Sciences*.

Balushi, Y. A., Shaker, H., & Kumar, B. (2023). The Use of Machine Learning in Digital Forensics: Review Paper. International Conference on Innovation in Information Technology and Business (pp. 96-113). Springer Nature.

Casey, P., Baggili, I., & Yarramreddy, A. (2019). Immersive virtual reality attacks and the human joystick. *IEEE Transactions on Dependable and Secure Computing*, 18(2), 550–562. DOI: 10.1109/TDSC.2019.2907942

Ferreira, S., Antunes, M., & Correia, M. E. (2021). Exposing manipulated photos and videos in digital forensics analysis. *Journal of Imaging*, 7(7), 102. DOI: 10.3390/jimaging7070102 PMID: 39080890

Halima, N. B., Alluhaidan, A. S., Khan, M. Z., Husain, M. S., & Khan, M. A. (2023). A service-categorized security scheme with physical unclonable functions for internet of vehicles. *Journal of Big Data*, 10(1), 178. DOI: 10.1186/s40537-023-00865-7

Haroon, M., Misra, D. K., Husain, M., Tripathi, M. M., & Khan, A. (2023). Security Issues in the Internet of Things for the Development of Smart Cities. In Husain, M. S., Faisal, M., Sadia, H., Ahmad, T., & Shukla, S. (Eds.), *Advances in Cyberology and the Advent of the Next-Gen Information Revolution* (pp. 123–137). IGI. DOI: 10.4018/978-1-6684-8133-2.ch007

Husain, M. S., Faisal, M., Sadia, H., Ahmad, T., & Shukla, S. (2023). *Advances in Cyberology and the Advent of the Next-gen Information Revolution*. IGI Global. DOI: 10.4018/978-1-6684-8133-2

KEY TERMS AND DEFINITIONS

Adversarial Attacks: Adversarial Attacks refer to techniques used to deceive or manipulate machine learning models by providing them with intentionally crafted inputs designed to cause them to make incorrect predictions or classifications. These inputs, known as adversarial examples, are often subtle perturbations of legitimate data that are nearly indistinguishable to humans but can significantly mislead AI systems. •

Espionage: Espionage is the practice of secretly gathering confidential or sensitive information, typically for political, military, or economic purposes. It often involves spying on governments, corporations, or individuals to gain an advantage or to inform decision-making. •

Impersonation: Impersonation is the act of pretending to be someone else, often with the intention of deceiving others.

Subtle Artifacts: Subtle Artifacts refer to small, often unnoticed details or features in data or media that can indicate its origin, manipulation, or underlying processes. These artifacts can appear in various contexts, such as digital images, videos, audio recordings, or even in data sets used in machine learning.

Chapter 11
Biometric Data Forensics

ABSTRACT

Biometric data forensics is a crucial intersection between forensic science and biometric technology. Biometric data forensics refers to the use of biometric data i.e. unique physical or behavioral traits of individuals, such as fingerprints, facial features, or iris patterns, to solve crimes and verify identities. Its importance stems from the ability to provide reliable, objective evidence that can aid in criminal investigations and ensure security in various applications. Unlike traditional evidence, biometric data offers a unique identifier that can corroborate identities with a high degree of certainty.

1. INTRODUCTION

Biometric data forensics is a crucial intersection between forensic science and biometric technology. Biometric data forensics refers to the use of biometric data i.e. unique physical or behavioral traits of individuals, such as fingerprints, facial features, or iris patterns, to solve crimes and verify identities. Its importance stems from the ability to provide reliable, objective evidence that can aid in criminal investigations and ensure security in various applications. Unlike traditional evidence, biometric data offers a unique identifier that can corroborate identities with a high degree of certainty.

This chapter delves into the fundamental aspects of biometric data forensics, including its types, analysis techniques, applications, challenges, and the evolving landscape of legal and ethical considerations.

DOI: 10.4018/979-8-3693-2960-3.ch011

2. OVERVIEW OF BIOMETRIC DATA FORENSICS

Biometric data refers to unique physiological or behavioral characteristics that can be used to identify individuals. These characteristics are inherently distinctive to each person, making biometric identifiers highly valuable in forensic investigations. Understanding the types of biometric data and their acquisition methods is crucial for applying them effectively in forensic contexts.

- **Types of Biometric Data:** The primary types of biometric data include:
  - **Fingerprints:** Fingerprints are perhaps the most well-known biometric identifier. The ridge patterns and valleys on the fingertips are unique to each individual and remain consistent throughout life. The uniqueness and permanence of fingerprints make them a reliable forensic tool. Modern fingerprint analysis involves capturing high-resolution images and comparing minutiae points (specific ridge patterns) to establish identity.
  - **Facial Recognition:** Facial recognition technology analyzes distinctive facial features such as the distance between the eyes, the shape of the nose, and the contour of the jawline to identify individuals. Advances in computer vision and machine learning have enhanced the accuracy of facial recognition systems. Modern systems utilize advanced algorithms to match faces even under varying conditions, though challenges such as varying lighting conditions and facial expressions can impact performance.
  - **Signature Verification:** Signature verification analyzes the unique features of an individual's handwritten signature, including stroke dynamics, pressure, and speed.
  - **Iris Patterns:** Iris recognition involves analyzing the complex and unique patterns in the colored part of the eye. The iris is highly stable and resistant to changes over time, making it a reliable biometric method for identification. Iris recognition requires high-resolution images and sophisticated algorithms to compare patterns and verify identity.
  - **Retina Scanning:** Retina scanning involves analyzing the unique patterns of blood vessels in the retina, the thin layer of tissue at the back of the eye. Captures high-resolution images of the retina using specialized cameras and analyzes the pattern of blood vessels. The retina's pattern is stable over time and unique to each individual.
  - **Voice Recognition:** Identifies individuals based on unique vocal attributes such as pitch, tone, and cadence. While less intrusive than some other biometric methods, voice recognition can be influenced by factors

such as health, emotions, and environmental factors like background noise.

- **Hand Geometry:** Hand geometry involves measuring the shape and size of a person's hand and fingers. Though less commonly used than other biometric methods, hand geometry can provide additional verification in some secure access systems.
- **Gait Analysis:** Gait analysis involves studying the unique patterns in the way an individual walks. It uses motion capture technology to analyze body movements and gait patterns.
- **DNA-Based Biometrics:** DNA-based biometrics involves analyzing genetic material to identify individuals based on their unique DNA profiles. DNA sequencing provides a comprehensive biometric identifier. Specific genetic markers are used to create a unique profile for each individual.
- **Behavioral Biometrics:** Behavioral biometrics analyze patterns in human behavior, such as typing rhythms, mouse movements, and navigation patterns.

The Biometric techniques based on the specific features discussed above are summarized in Table 1.

Table 1. Summary of various biometric techniques

Biometric technique	Description	Advantages	Disadvantages	Applications
Fingerprint Recognition	most established biometric techniques that relies on the unique patterns of ridges and valleys on an individual's fingertips.	• High accuracy and reliability.	• Vulnerable to spoofing with high-quality fingerprint replicas. • Performance can be affected by poor-quality fingerprints (e.g., due to cuts or dirt).	• Access control systems. • Personal devices (e.g., smartphones).
Facial Recognition	Involves analyzing and comparing facial features to identify individuals.	• Non-intrusive and can be used in public spaces. • Can work with images captured from a distance.	• Affected by changes in facial expression, aging, or lighting conditions. • Privacy concerns and potential for misuse in surveillance.	• Security and surveillance systems. • User authentication in consumer electronics.
Signature Verification	Analyzes the unique features of an individual's handwritten signature, including stroke dynamics, pressure, and speed.	• Simple and widely accepted for various applications. • Can be integrated into electronic signature systems for added security.	• Vulnerable to forgery or imitation. • Performance can be affected by changes in the individual's handwriting or physical condition.	• Document authentication and signing. • Financial transactions and contracts.
Iris Recognition	Based on the unique patterns found in the colored part of the eye.	• Extremely high accuracy and low false acceptance rates. • Stable over time and less affected by changes in lighting.	• Requires specialized hardware for capturing high-quality images of the iris. • Can be affected by factors such as eye diseases or the presence of contact lenses.	• High-security areas (e.g., border control). • Access control in sensitive environments.
Voice Recognition	Analyzes the unique characteristics of an individual's voice, including pitch, tone, and speech patterns.	• Can be integrated into phone systems and virtual assistants. • Convenient as it does not require physical contact.	• Susceptible to changes in voice due to illness or background noise. • Can be spoofed using voice recordings or synthesized voices.	• Customer service and call centers. • Authentication in voice-activated systems.
Hand Geometry Recognition	Measures and analyzes the shape and size of the hand, including finger length, width, and overall hand structure.	• Relatively simple and cost-effective • Effective for identifying individuals in environments where physical contact is possible.	• Less unique than other biometric traits (e.g., fingerprints or iris patterns). • Performance can be affected by variations in hand position or orientation.	• Physical access control systems. • Employee attendance systems.

continued on following page

Table 1. Continued

Biometric technique	Description	Advantages	Disadvantages	Applications
Retina Scanning	Analyzing the unique patterns of blood vessels in the retina, the thin layer of tissue at the back of the eye.	• Highly accurate with a low false acceptance rate. • The retina's pattern is stable over time and unique to each individual.	• Requires specialized equipment and cooperation from the user. • Can be uncomfortable for some users.	• High-security areas and sensitive facilities. • Medical and research applications.
Gait Analysis	Involves studying the unique patterns in the way an individual walks.	• Non-intrusive and can be performed from a distance. • Useful for continuous monitoring in security applications.	• Requires sophisticated motion capture equipment.	• Security and surveillance systems. • Research in biomechanics and rehabilitation.
DNA-Based Biometrics	Involves analyzing genetic material to identify individuals based on their unique DNA profiles.	• Extremely accurate and unique to each individual. • Useful in forensic investigations and identity verification.	• Requires specialized laboratory equipment and procedures. • Ethical and privacy concerns related to genetic information.	• Forensic investigations. • Genetic research and personalized medicine.
Behavioral Biometrics	Analyzes patterns in human behavior, such as typing rhythms, mouse movements, and navigation patterns.	• Can be integrated into existing systems with minimal hardware requirements. • Provides an additional layer of security based on user behavior.	• Behavior can change due to stress, illness, or environmental factors. • Requires continuous monitoring and analysis to be effective.	• Fraud detection in online transactions. • Continuous authentication in digital environments.

- **Data Acquisition and Storage:** The process of acquiring biometric data involves capturing high-quality images or recordings using specialized sensors and devices. For example, fingerprint scanners, facial recognition cameras, and iris scanners are used to collect data. Once acquired, biometric data is typically stored in databases for comparison and analysis. The storage and management of biometric data pose significant challenges related to security, privacy, and data integrity.
- **Evolution of Biometric Technology:** The use of biometric technology dates back to ancient civilizations where physical traits were used to distinguish individuals. However, the modern field began with fingerprint analysis in the early 20th century. The advent of computer technology and advanced algorithms in the late 20th and early 21st centuries transformed biometric systems, introducing more sophisticated methods such as facial recognition and

iris scanning. These advancements have significantly increased the accuracy and applicability of biometric data in forensic science.

- **Applications and Challenges:** The use of biometric data spans various applications, from law enforcement and security to financial services and healthcare. In forensics, it aids in identifying suspects, verifying identities, and solving cases. However, the integration of biometric systems into forensic investigations presents several challenges, including accuracy, privacy concerns, and potential for misuse.

3. BIOMETRIC DATA ANALYSIS TECHNIQUES

Biometric data analysis techniques are integral to modern security systems, identity verification, and access control. These techniques utilize unique biological characteristics to identify or verify individuals. Analyzing biometric data involves several techniques to extract, compare, and match unique identifiers. With the rise of digital technologies and increasing security needs, biometric systems have become essential in various fields, including cybersecurity, finance, and law enforcement. Popular biometric data analysis techniques are:

- **Biometric Feature Extraction:** Feature extraction is the process of identifying and isolating distinctive attributes of biometric data that are used for recognition e.g., fingerprints, facial features, voice patterns. For example, in fingerprint analysis, this includes detecting minutiae points and ridge patterns, while facial recognition systems may extract landmarks and geometric features of the face such as the distance between eyes or the shape of the nose. In forensic Applications, extracted features can be compared against databases to identify suspects or verify identities in criminal investigations.
- **Pattern Recognition:** Pattern recognition techniques compare extracted features to identify matches or discrepancies. Algorithms used in pattern recognition include statistical models, machine learning algorithms, and neural networks. These methods analyze the similarity between biometric samples and stored templates to establish identity.
    - **Statistical Models:** These models use mathematical techniques to analyze and compare patterns. For instance, statistical measures can quantify the similarity between two fingerprint images.
    - **Machine Learning Algorithms:** Machine learning enhances pattern recognition by training systems on large datasets to improve accuracy. Algorithms such as support vector machines (SVMs) and deep learning models are employed to learn from examples and make predictions.

- Neural Networks: Convolutional neural networks (CNNs) and other deep learning architectures are particularly effective in recognizing complex patterns in biometric data, such as facial features.

- **Data Matching Algorithms:** Data matching involves comparing biometric samples to identify matches or discrepancies. Algorithms are designed to handle variations in data quality and environmental conditions. Common methods include Euclidean distance, correlation-based methods, and more complex machine learning approaches. Common data matching approaches include:
  - **Euclidean Distance:** Measures the straight-line distance between two points in feature space. It is often used in simpler biometric systems.
  - **Correlation-Based Methods:** Evaluates the similarity between features by analyzing how closely they correlate. These methods are useful in systems where feature relationships are crucial.
  - **Machine Learning Approaches:** Utilizes training data to improve matching accuracy by learning from examples and adapting to new data.
- **Statistical Analysis:** Applying statistical methods to understand and validate biometric data distributions and reliability. For example, establishing acceptance thresholds for matching scores based on statistical distributions, and evaluating false acceptance rate (FAR) and false rejection rate (FRR) to gauge system performance.
- **Machine Learning in Biometric Analysis:** Machine learning has revolutionized biometric data analysis by enhancing the accuracy and efficiency of recognition systems. Using machine learning, models can be developed which can learn from large datasets, improving their ability to handle diverse and challenging scenarios. Techniques such as deep learning and convolutional neural networks (CNNs) have been particularly effective in enhancing the accuracy and robustness of biometric recognition systems. Techniques such as ensemble methods and deep learning can provide more accurate matching by learning complex patterns and relationships in biometric data.

During forensic investigation, these models can detect patterns or anomalies in biometric data that may indicate tampering or fraudulent behavior, enhancing investigative insights.

- **Multi-Modal Biometric Fusion:** Combining multiple biometric sources (e.g., face and voice recognition) to improve accuracy and robustness. For example, merging features from various biometric traits before classification. In forensic Applications, it increases the robustness of identification in forensic investigations, especially in cases where one biometric method may be compromised.

- **Dimensionality Reduction:** Reducing the number of features while retaining essential information to simplify analysis. For example,
    - o **Principal Component Analysis (PCA):** Transforming data into a lower-dimensional space while preserving variance.
    - o **t-Distributed Stochastic Neighbor Embedding (t-SNE):** A nonlinear technique for visualizing high-dimensional data.
- **Anomaly Detection:** Identifying unusual patterns or behaviors in biometric data that may indicate spoofing or fraudulent activities. During forensics investigation, anomaly detection helps in detecting cases of impersonation or spoofing, particularly in systems that rely on biometric authentication.
    - o **Machine Learning Models:** Training classifiers to detect deviations from normal biometric patterns.
    - o **Statistical Methods:** Analyzing biometric data distributions to flag outliers.
- **Secure Multi-Party Computation:** Enabling parties to jointly compute a function over their inputs while keeping those inputs private. This is very useful for biometric verification systems that require secure collaboration without revealing sensitive data.
- **Data Integrity Verification:** Ensuring that biometric data has not been altered or tampered with during storage or transmission. Cryptographic methods, such as digital signatures, can be used to verify the authenticity of biometric data records.
- **Timeline Analysis:** Establishing a timeline of events based on biometric data logs (e.g., access times recorded by biometric systems). For forensic Applications, it is useful in investigations to correlate biometric data with other evidence, establishing sequences of events in criminal cases.
- **Secure Storage and Retrieval:** Implementing secure methods for storing and accessing biometric data, often using encryption and access controls. Secure storage protects sensitive biometric information from unauthorized access, ensuring that data used in investigations remains confidential and secure.

Biometric data analysis techniques play a critical role in cyber forensics by providing tools for identifying individuals, verifying identities, and uncovering fraudulent activities. As technology advances, these techniques continue to evolve, enhancing the capabilities of forensic investigators in securing digital evidence and solving crimes.

4. FORENSIC APPLICATIONS OF BIOMETRIC DATA

Biometric data plays a crucial role in various forensic applications, from identifying suspects to verifying identities and detecting fraud. Figure 1 shows the key applications of biometric data analysis in cyber forensics investigations.

Figure 1. Applications of biometric data in cyber forensics

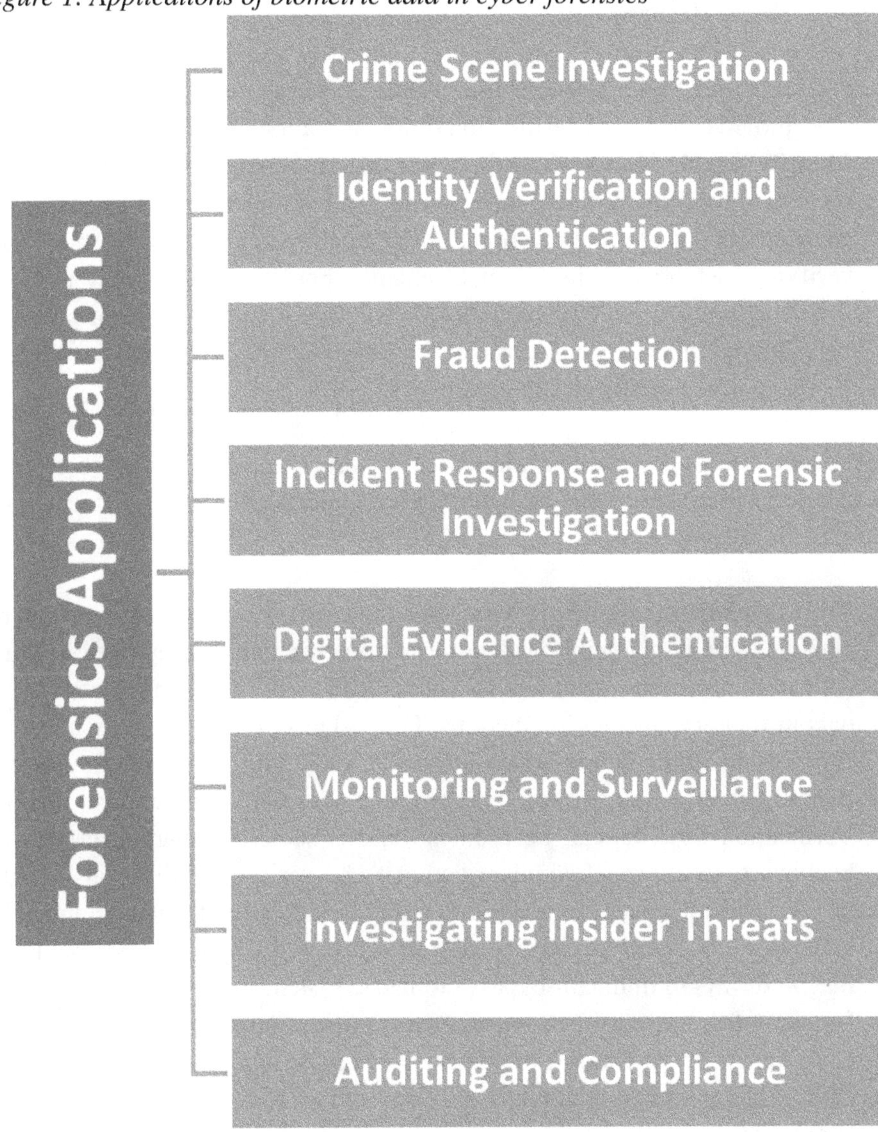

- **Crime Scene Investigation:** Biometric data is invaluable in crime scene investigations. Forensic experts use fingerprints, DNA, and other biometric markers to link suspects to crime scenes, establish identities, and gather evidence. For example:
  - **Fingerprints:** Fingerprints are commonly found at crime scenes and can link suspects to locations or objects. Forensic experts analyze the ridge patterns to identify potential suspects.
  - **Facial Recognition:** Used to match images from surveillance cameras with known individuals, helping to identify suspects or witnesses.
  - **Iris and Voice Recognition:** While less common, these methods can provide additional verification or identification in specific scenarios.
- **Identity Verification and Authentication:** Biometric systems are increasingly used for identity verification and authentication in various scenarios, including accessing secure locations, authenticating financial transactions, and verifying identities in digital environments. Forensic experts may use biometric systems to confirm identities during investigations or legal proceedings. Biometric data is also crucial for authenticating users and controlling access to sensitive systems or data.

The authentication system requires secure storage and handling of biometric data to prevent breaches. It can be bypassed by sophisticated spoofing techniques or system vulnerabilities.

- **Fraud Detection:** Biometric data helps in detecting and preventing fraud by verifying the authenticity of identities. Biometric data is employed in fraud detection to prevent unauthorized access and verify the identity of individuals in transactions and interactions. For instance, biometric authentication can prevent identity theft by ensuring that only authorized individuals can access sensitive information or complete financial transactions. Identity Verification Systems can be used in various sectors, including travel and healthcare, to prevent fraudulent activities by verifying individuals' identities. Voice Biometrics can be used to verify the identity of callers in financial institutions or customer service centers. However, Sophisticated fraudsters may find ways to mimic or bypass biometric systems.
- **Incident Response and Forensic Investigation:** During incident response and forensic investigations, biometric data can be used to verify the identity of individuals accessing or interacting with digital forensic tools and systems. Biometric data analysis ensures that only authorized personnel can handle and analyze digital evidence.

- **Digital Evidence Authentication:** Biometric data can be used to authenticate digital evidence by verifying the identity of individuals involved in the creation or manipulation of digital content. This helps ensure the integrity of digital evidence used in legal proceedings.
- **Monitoring and Surveillance:** Biometric data is used in monitoring and surveillance systems to track and identify individuals in real-time within digital environments. This is particularly useful in cybersecurity and network monitoring. Monitoring access logs and using biometric data to verify user identities during security breaches enhances real-time monitoring and tracking capabilities.
- **Investigating Insider Threats:** Biometric data helps in investigating insider threats by monitoring and analyzing the biometric patterns of individuals within an organization. This is useful for detecting suspicious or unauthorized activities by employees.
- **Auditing and Compliance:** Description: Biometric data is used in auditing and compliance processes to ensure that access to systems and data is in line with organizational policies and regulatory requirements.

5. CHALLENGES IN BIOMETRIC DATA FORENSICS

Despite its advantages, biometric data forensics faces several challenges that impact its effectiveness and reliability.

Figure 2. Challenges in biometric data analysis for cyber forensics

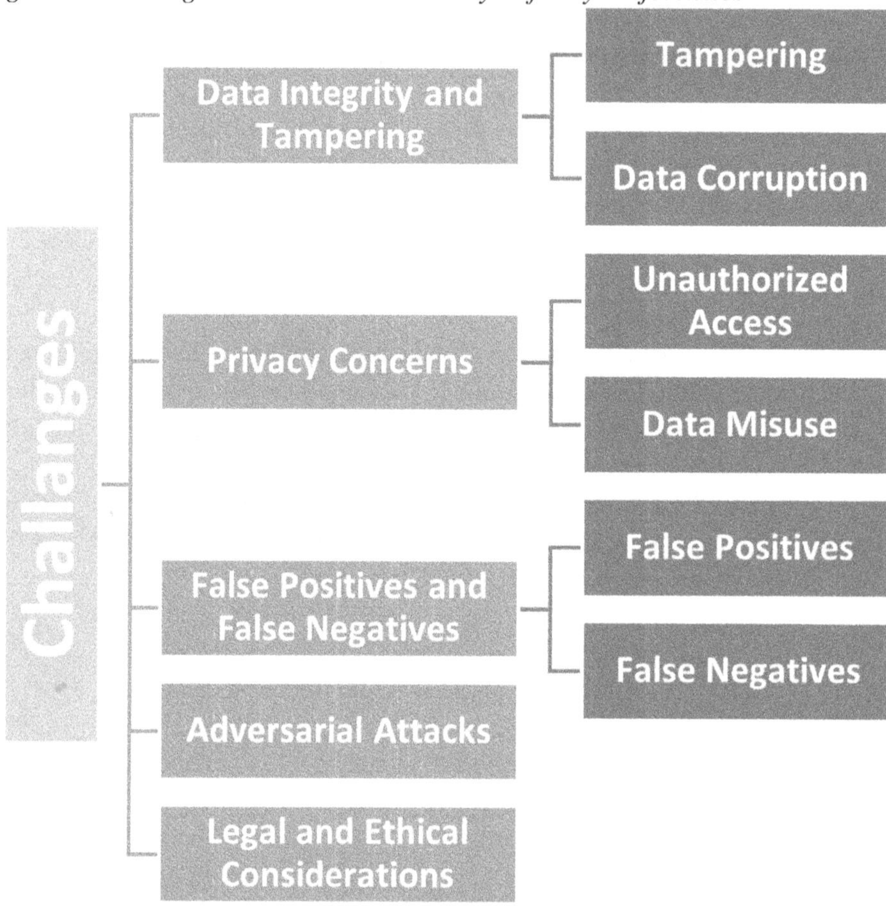

- **Data Integrity and Tampering:** Ensuring the integrity of biometric data is critical. Tampering with biometric samples or manipulating data can compromise the accuracy of forensic analyses and lead to wrongful conclusions. Forensic experts must implement robust security measures to protect biometric data from unauthorized access and tampering.
    - **Tampering:** Biometric samples can be altered or forged, compromising the accuracy of forensic analyses. Robust security measures are necessary to protect data from tampering.
    - **Data Corruption:** Storage and transmission errors can corrupt biometric data, affecting its reliability. Implementing error-checking mechanisms and secure storage solutions is essential.

- **Privacy Concerns:** The collection and storage of biometric data raises significant privacy concerns. Biometric information is highly sensitive and personal, and unauthorized access or misuse can lead to privacy violations. Ensuring compliance with privacy regulations and obtaining informed consent are essential for addressing privacy concerns.
    - **Unauthorized Access:** Biometric data is sensitive and can be misused if accessed by unauthorized individuals. Ensuring data protection and limiting access are critical for addressing privacy concerns.
    - **Data Misuse:** There is a risk of biometric data being used for purposes beyond its intended scope, such as surveillance or profiling. Establishing clear guidelines and regulations for data use is crucial.
- **False Positives and False Negatives:** Biometric systems are not infallible. False positives (incorrectly identifying someone) and false negatives (failing to identify someone) can impact the reliability of forensic results and have serious implications for justice. Forensic experts must carefully evaluate and validate biometric data to minimize errors and ensure accurate results.
    - **False Positives:** Occur when a system incorrectly identifies an individual. This can lead to wrongful accusations or denials of access.
    - **False Negatives:** Happen when a system fails to recognize an individual who is legitimately authorized. This can cause issues with access control and verification.
- **Adversarial Attacks:** Adversarial attacks involve manipulating biometric data to deceive recognition systems. Techniques such as spoofing (using fake biometric samples) and creating synthetic biometric data pose challenges for forensic applications. Developing robust systems that can detect and counteract adversarial attacks is crucial for maintaining the integrity of biometric data.
- **Legal and Ethical Considerations:** The use of biometric data in forensics raises important legal and ethical considerations, including regulations, privacy, and ethical implications. The legal landscape surrounding biometric data is complex and varies by jurisdiction. Regulations govern the collection, storage, and use of biometric information, and compliance with these laws is essential for forensic practices.

The ethical use of biometric data involves balancing the benefits of forensic analysis with the rights and privacy of individuals. Ethical considerations include ensuring informed consent, avoiding discrimination, and addressing potential biases in biometric systems.

Data protection laws, such as the General Data Protection Regulation (GDPR) and the California Consumer Privacy Act (CCPA), regulate the handling of personal data, including biometric information. Forensic professionals must navigate these regulations to ensure legal compliance and protect individuals' privacy. Implementing robust security measures to safeguard biometric data and prevent unauthorized access or misuse is crucial in cyber forensics.

6. RECENT WORK

Recent work in cyber forensics using biometric data has focused on leveraging advanced technologies to enhance security, improve identity verification, and aid investigations. Main focus areas of recent work in the domain includes:

- **Multimodal Biometric Systems:** Combining various biometric identifiers (e.g., fingerprints, facial recognition, iris scans) to improve accuracy and security in identification processes. Multimodal systems reduce the likelihood of false positives and negatives, making them more reliable for forensic investigations.
- **Real-Time Facial Recognition:** Development of systems capable of real-time facial recognition in public spaces, aiding in the identification of suspects in criminal investigations.
- **Deep Learning for Biometric Analysis:** Utilization of deep learning algorithms to analyze biometric data, improving the speed and accuracy of identification processes.
- **Pattern Recognition:** Advanced techniques in recognizing patterns in biometric data that can help in tracing criminal activities or identifying individuals from large datasets.
- **User Authentication:** Increased use of biometric data (like fingerprints and facial recognition) for secure access to devices and systems, reducing the risk of unauthorized access.
- **Forensic Investigations:** Analyzing biometric authentication logs to trace user activity and identify potential breaches.
- **Preventing Spoofing:** Development of methods to ensure that biometric data is being collected from a living person rather than a spoofed source (e.g., using photos or masks).
- **Innovative Techniques:** Use of behavioral biometrics (like typing patterns or gait analysis) to enhance security measures.

- **Blockchain for Biometric Data Security:** Research into using blockchain technology to securely store and manage biometric data, providing a tamper-proof method of maintaining the integrity of this sensitive information.
- **Decentralized Identity Management:** Leveraging blockchain for decentralized biometric verification systems that enhance user privacy and control over personal data.

Table 2. Summary of recent work in biometric data forensics

Reference	Objective	Approach
(Jiang, et al., 2024)	Improved bimodal biometric authentication	residual network and polar codes based template protection
(Kim, Yeun, & Yoo, 2019)	Enhanced Machine Learning-Based Biometric Authentication	Electrocardiogram (ECG) based authentication method
(Wu, Yang, Zhou, Chen, & Wang, 2019)	Multimodal Biometrics Authentication System for Smartphones	Combining the advantages of lip movements and voice
(Talreja, Valenti, & Nasrabadi, 2020)	Generates a secure multimodal biometric template	deep hashing (binarization) framework
(Keller, Osadchy, & Dunkelman, 2021)	Facial images reconstruction	Deep Learning
(Gao, Feng, & Xia, 2023)	Authentication in Wireless Sensor Networks against Insider Attacks	Three-factor authentication using lightweight data hiding technology for protection against insider attack with reduced energy consumption
(Peng, et al., 2024)	Video Face Forgery Detection	Deepfake gaze analysis method (DFGaze)
(Yang, Zhang, Youliang, & Ma, 2023)	Tracking a malicious player in the physical world via his avatars in virtual space.	Two-factor authentication framework based on biometric-based authentication and chameleon signature

Recent advancements in cyber forensics utilizing biometric data highlight the potential for improved security and investigative capabilities. However, they also raise important ethical and legal considerations that must be addressed to ensure responsible use. Ongoing research and development in this field will continue to shape the future of cybersecurity and forensic investigations.

7. CASE STUDIES

This section explores notable case studies where biometric data has been instrumental in forensic investigations. Examples include high-profile criminal cases, missing persons investigations, and identity theft cases. For example:

- **Volkswagen Emissions Scandal (2015):** Volkswagen faced a major scandal involving emissions testing fraud. Part of the investigation involved analyzing digital evidence and biometric data to uncover internal misconduct. Forensic analysis included reviewing biometric access logs to identify which employees accessed sensitive files related to emissions software (Cavico & Mujtaba, 2016).

Biometric data helped trace access to crucial documents, revealing key players in the fraud and leading to significant legal and financial consequences for Volkswagen.

- **The Capital One Data Breach (2019):** A former employee of Amazon Web Services exploited a vulnerability in Capital One's systems, exposing personal data of over 100 million customers. Forensic analysis included reviewing biometric access logs for AWS data centers to understand how the ex-employee accessed sensitive data.

The case underscored the importance of securing biometric access controls and conducting thorough audits to prevent insider threats (Khan, Ilya, Yunke, & Stuart, 2022).

- **The WannaCry Ransomware Attack (2017):** The WannaCry ransomware attack impacted numerous organizations globally, encrypting files and demanding ransom payments.

Forensic experts used biometric data to track unauthorized access to network systems and identify affected devices by analyzing user access logs. The investigation helped improve understanding of ransomware attack vectors and led to better security practices and incident response strategies (Hsiao & Kao, 2018).

- **The Facebook-Cambridge Analytica Scandal (2018):** The Cambridge Analytica scandal involved unauthorized access and misuse of personal data from millions of Facebook users.

Investigators analyzed biometric data, such as profile pictures, to understand how user data was harvested and misused. The case led to increased scrutiny of data privacy practices and stricter regulations on data usage and protection (Rehman, 2019).

- **The Yahoo Data Breach (2013-2014):** Yahoo experienced one of the largest data breaches, affecting billions of accounts and compromising various personal data, including biometric identifiers. Forensic analysis involved reviewing the types of compromised data, including biometric information, to assess the potential impact and inform affected users.

The breach emphasized the need for robust biometric data protection and incident response strategies.

These case studies illustrate the diverse applications and challenges of biometric data analysis in cyber forensics. From securing access to digital systems and detecting fraud to investigating breaches and tracking criminal activities, biometric data provides invaluable insights. However, these cases also highlight the challenges related to privacy, security, and the evolving nature of cyber threats, emphasizing the need for continued advancements in biometric technology and forensic practices.

- Biometric evidence played a crucial role in the identification and conviction of criminal suspects in cases involving stolen identities, missing persons, and serious crimes.
- Biometric data from surveillance cameras and border control systems have been used to track and apprehend suspects involved in terrorist activities.
- Biometric systems, such as facial recognition and fingerprint analysis, have been crucial in locating and identifying missing persons.

8. BEST PRACTICES

Biometric data analysis in cyber forensics requires careful handling to ensure accuracy, security, and compliance. Here are some best practices and guidelines to follow:

- **Secure Data Collection:** Proper procedures must be followed when collecting biometric data to ensure its integrity and avoid contamination.
    - o Collect biometric data in a controlled environment to prevent tampering and contamination.
    - o Employ reliable and certified biometric devices for data collection to ensure accuracy.
    - o Ensure that devices are calibrated and function correctly.
    - o Follow standard operating procedures (SOPs) for data collection.
- **Encryption for Data Storage and Transmission:** Encrypting biometric data both during storage and transmission protects it from unauthorized access and cyber threats.
    - o Use strong encryption algorithms (e.g., AES-256) for storing and transmitting biometric data.

    - Utilize secure communication channels (e.g., HTTPS, VPNs) for data transfer.
    - Regularly update encryption protocols and software to address emerging threats.
    - Manage and secure encryption keys diligently.
- **Establish a Robust Chain of Custody:** Maintaining a chain of custody is crucial for tracking the handling of biometric data and ensuring its integrity throughout the forensic process.
    - Keep comprehensive records of who accessed the data, when, and why.
    - Ensure that biometric data is securely transferred between locations or personnel.
    - Implement procedures for documenting every action taken with biometric data.
    - Use tamper-evident seals or similar methods to protect physical evidence.
- **Thorough Biometric Data Analysis:** Employ advanced analysis techniques to accurately interpret biometric data and draw reliable conclusions.
    - Utilize well-tested and validated biometric analysis tools and algorithms.
    - Compare results with other evidence to confirm findings and minimize errors.
    - Regularly update and validate analysis tools to ensure accuracy.
    - Document analysis methods and findings thoroughly.
- **Legal and Ethical Compliance:** Adhering to legal and ethical standards is essential for handling biometric data responsibly and protecting individuals' rights.
    - Ensure that biometric data is collected and used with informed consent from individuals.
    - Comply with relevant laws and regulations, such as GDPR or CCPA, regarding biometric data.
    - Stay informed about changes in biometric data legislation and regulations.
    - Implement policies and procedures to ensure compliance.
- **Regularly Update and Maintain Biometric Systems:** Keeping biometric systems and software up to date ensures they function correctly and are protected against emerging threats.
    - Apply patches and updates to biometric systems and software regularly.
    - Monitor for and address vulnerabilities in biometric systems.
    - Schedule regular maintenance and updates for all biometric systems.
    - Conduct security assessments to identify and mitigate potential risks.

- **Implement Access Controls:** Restricting access to biometric data and systems ensures that only authorized personnel can handle and analyze sensitive information.
    - o Implement role-based access controls to limit data access based on job functions.
    - o Use multi-factor authentication to secure access to biometric systems.
    - o Regularly review and update access permissions to reflect changes in personnel and roles.
    - o Implement logging and monitoring of access to detect unauthorized attempts.
- **Implement Advanced Data Analytics:** Utilizing advanced data analytics techniques can enhance the accuracy and efficiency of biometric data analysis in forensic investigations.
    - o Apply machine learning algorithms to improve biometric matching and anomaly detection.
    - o Use data correlation techniques to link biometric data with other evidence for a comprehensive analysis.
- **Train Personnel on Biometric Data Handling:** Proper training ensures that personnel handling biometric data are knowledgeable about best practices, security measures, and legal requirements.
    - o Provide ongoing training on biometric data handling, security protocols, and forensic analysis techniques.
    - o Encourage certification in relevant forensic and cybersecurity fields.
    - o Develop and maintain training programs tailored to different roles within the organization. Update training materials regularly to reflect new developments in technology and regulations.
- **Documentation and Reporting:** Accurate documentation and reporting of findings ensure that the results of biometric data analysis are clear, comprehensible, and useful in legal contexts.
    - o Create comprehensive reports detailing analysis methodologies, findings, and interpretations.
    - o Use clear and understandable language in reports to facilitate comprehension by non-experts.
    - o Standardize report formats to ensure consistency and completeness. Include visual aids, such as charts and graphs, to support findings.
- **Contingency Plans for Data Breaches:** Having a contingency plan in place helps respond effectively to breaches involving biometric data and minimize potential damage.
    - o Develop and regularly update an incident response plan specific to biometric data breaches.

- Implement procedures for notifying affected individuals and regulatory authorities in case of a breach.
- Conduct regular drills and simulations to test the effectiveness of the response plan.
- Ensure that all personnel are aware of their roles and responsibilities in the event of a data breach.

By following these best practices and guidelines, organizations can ensure that biometric data analysis in cyber forensics is conducted with the highest standards of security, accuracy, and compliance. These practices help in protecting sensitive information, maintaining the integrity of forensic investigations, and upholding legal and ethical standards.

9. EMERGING TRENDS AND FUTURE DIRECTIONS

Biometric data analysis in cyber forensics is rapidly evolving, driven by advancements in technology and increasing demands for security and accuracy. Emerging trends and future directions are shaping the field, promising significant improvements and new challenges. The field of biometric technology continues to advance, with developments in areas such as multi-modal biometrics, which combine multiple biometric traits for enhanced accuracy and security. Innovations in artificial intelligence and machine learning are also improving the accuracy and efficiency of biometric recognition systems. Recent advancements include:

- **Integration of Advanced Machine Learning Algorithms:** Machine learning (ML) and artificial intelligence (AI) are increasingly being integrated into biometric data analysis to enhance accuracy and efficiency.
    - **Deep Learning:** Techniques like convolutional neural networks (CNNs) and recurrent neural networks (RNNs) are being used to improve facial recognition, fingerprint analysis, and other biometric modalities by automatically learning and extracting features from large datasets.
    - **Anomaly Detection:** ML algorithms are being employed to detect anomalies and fraudulent activities by analyzing patterns and deviations in biometric data.
    - **Adaptive Algorithms:** Development of adaptive ML models that can learn from new data and evolving threats in real-time.
    - **Hybrid Models:** Combining multiple ML techniques to create robust systems capable of handling diverse biometric data types and use cases.

Integration of advanced machine learning and deep learning in biometric data analysis will Enhances the accuracy and reliability of biometric analysis while reduces the time required for data processing and analysis.

- **Integration of Biometric Data with Blockchain Technology:** Blockchain technology is being explored as a means to enhance the security and integrity of biometric data.
  - **Immutable Records:** Using blockchain to create immutable records of biometric data access and transactions.
  - **Decentralized Storage:** Implementing decentralized storage solutions for biometric data to enhance security and reduce the risk of centralized data breaches.
  - **Smart Contracts:** Utilizing smart contracts to automate and secure biometric data handling and access controls.
  - **Blockchain-Based Identity Verification:** Developing blockchain-based systems for verifying and managing biometric identities.
- **Enhanced Multimodal Biometric Systems:** Multimodal biometric systems, which combine multiple biometric modalities (e.g., facial recognition, fingerprint, iris scan), are gaining traction. These systems will improve accuracy and reduce the likelihood of false positives and negatives.
  - **Fusion Techniques:** Techniques such as feature-level, score-level, and decision-level fusion are being used to integrate data from different biometric sources to improve overall accuracy and robustness.
  - **Cross-Biometric Integration:** Combining biometric data from different modalities to create a more comprehensive and reliable identification system.
  - **Real-Time Fusion:** Development of systems that can fuse biometric data in real-time for immediate verification and authentication.
  - **Contextual Adaptation:** Incorporating contextual information (e.g., location, behavior) to enhance the effectiveness of multimodal systems.
- **Advancements in Behavioral Biometrics:** Behavioral biometrics, which analyze patterns in behavior such as typing rhythm, gait, and voice, are becoming more prominent in forensic investigations.
  - **Behavioral Profiling:** Using behavioral patterns to create profiles for individuals and detect anomalies in their behavior.
  - **Continuous Authentication:** Implementing behavioral biometrics for continuous authentication and monitoring, rather than one-time verification.
  - **Adaptive Systems:** Developing systems that adapt to changes in behavior over time, such as aging or stress.

- **Integration with Other Forensic Tools:** Integrating biometric data with other forensic tools, such as digital forensics and traditional investigative methods, offers a comprehensive approach to solving complex cases. Combining biometric data with evidence from other sources can enhance the overall effectiveness of forensic investigations.
    - Combining biometric data with digital evidence (e.g., computer files, digital footprints) for a comprehensive analysis.
    - Using biometric data alongside traditional forensic techniques (e.g., DNA analysis) to strengthen evidence.
- **Enhanced Privacy and Data Protection Measures:** As biometric data collection and analysis become more widespread, there is a growing focus on ensuring privacy and protecting personal data.
    - **Privacy-Enhancing Technologies:** Development of technologies like homomorphic encryption and secure multi-party computation to protect biometric data during processing.
    - **Decentralized Storage:** Implementing decentralized or blockchain-based storage solutions to enhance data security and privacy.
    - **User Control:** Providing individuals with greater control over their biometric data and how it is used.
- **Increased Use of Biometric Data in Cybersecurity:** Biometric data is increasingly being integrated into cybersecurity strategies to enhance protection and authentication.
    - **Behavioral Biometrics in Cybersecurity:** Implementing behavioral biometrics for user authentication and fraud detection in online environments.
    - **Biometric Access Controls:** Using biometric data for securing access to critical systems and sensitive information.
    - **Biometric Threat Detection:** Developing systems that use biometric data to detect and respond to cybersecurity threats and breaches.
    - **Adaptive Security Measures:** Creating adaptive security systems that use biometric data to adjust protection levels based on risk assessments.
- **Real-Time Biometric Analysis Systems:** Real-time biometric analysis systems are becoming more advanced, allowing for immediate verification and authentication.
    - **Edge Computing:** Utilizing edge computing to process biometric data locally on devices, reducing latency and improving real-time analysis.
    - **Streaming Data Analysis:** Implementing systems that can handle and analyze streaming biometric data from various sources, such as live video feeds.

- **Low-Latency Systems:** Development of systems with minimal latency for real-time biometric verification and response.
- **Adaptive Real-Time Analysis:** Creating systems that adapt to changing conditions and provide accurate real-time results.

- **Advances in Biometric Data Analytics:** Advances in data analytics are enhancing the ability to analyze and interpret biometric data effectively.
    - **Big Data Analytics:** Leveraging big data analytics to process and analyze large volumes of biometric data for trends and insights.
    - **Predictive Analytics:** Using predictive analytics to anticipate and prevent potential security breaches based on biometric data.
    - **AI-Driven Analytics:** Incorporating AI-driven analytics to improve the accuracy and efficiency of biometric data interpretation.
- **Ethical Considerations and Public Awareness:** Addressing ethical considerations and increasing public awareness are crucial for responsible biometric data use and analysis.
    - **Ethical Guidelines:** Developing ethical guidelines and best practices for the use of biometric data in forensic investigations.
    - **Public Education:** Increasing public awareness about biometric data collection, usage, and privacy implications.
    - **Stakeholder Engagement:** Engaging with stakeholders, including the public and privacy advocates, to address concerns and build trust.
- **Evolution of Biometric Standards and Protocols:** The development and adoption of new standards and protocols are crucial for ensuring interoperability and consistency in biometric systems.
    - **Standardization Efforts:** Ongoing efforts to develop and standardize biometric protocols and interfaces for better interoperability and compatibility.
    - **Interoperability:** Creating standards that allow biometric systems to work seamlessly across different platforms and applications.
    - **Global Standards:** Establishing global standards for biometric data formats, protocols, and security measures.
    - **Industry Collaboration:** Encouraging collaboration between industry stakeholders to develop and adopt common standards.
- **Future Challenges and Opportunities:** Future developments in biometric forensics will address current challenges and explore new opportunities. Advances in technology, evolving legal and ethical standards, and ongoing research will shape the future of biometric data forensics, providing new tools and methodologies for forensic professionals.

10. SUMMARY

Biometric data forensics plays a crucial role in modern forensic science, offering unique capabilities for identifying individuals, solving crimes, and verifying identities. Despite the challenges, the field continues to evolve with technological advancements and legal considerations. As biometric technology advances, its integration with other forensic tools and methodologies will further enhance its impact and effectiveness in solving complex cases and ensuring justice.

REFRENCES

Cavico, F. J., & Mujtaba, B. G. (2016). Volkswagen emissions scandal: A global case study of legal, ethical, and practical consequences and recommendations for sustainable management. *Global Journal of Research in Business & Management.*

Gao, G., Feng, Z., & Xia, Z. (2023). Energy Efficient Three-Factor Authentication in Wireless Sensor Networks With Resisting Insider Attacks. *IEEE Transactions on Green Communications and Networking*, 7(3), 1297–1308. DOI: 10.1109/TGCN.2023.3265661

Hsiao, S.-C., & Kao, D.-Y. (2018). The static analysis of WannaCry ransomware. *20th international conference on advanced communication technology (ICACT)* (pp. 153-158). IEEE.

Jiang, Q., Zhao, G., Ma, X., Li, M., Tian, Y., & Li, X. (2024). Cross-Modal Learning Based Flexible Bimodal Biometric Authentication With Template Protection. *IEEE Transactions on Information Forensics and Security*, 19, 3593–3607. DOI: 10.1109/TIFS.2024.3364092

Keller, D., Osadchy, M., & Dunkelman, O. (2021). Inverting Binarizations of Facial Templates Produced by Deep Learning (and Its Implications). *IEEE Transactions on Information Forensics and Security*, 16, 4184–4196. DOI: 10.1109/TIFS.2021.3103056

Khan, S., Ilya, K., Yunke, H., & Stuart, M. (2022). A systematic analysis of the capital one data breach: Critical lessons learned. *ACM Transactions on Privacy and Security*, 26(1), 1–29. DOI: 10.1145/3546068

Kim, S.-K., Yeun, C. Y., & Yoo, P. D. (2019). An Enhanced Machine Learning-Based Biometric Authentication System Using RR-Interval Framed Electrocardiograms. *IEEE Access : Practical Innovations, Open Solutions*, 7, 168669–168674. DOI: 10.1109/ACCESS.2019.2954576

Peng, C., Miao, Z., Liu, D., Wang, N., Hu, R., & Gao, X. (2024). Where Deepfakes Gaze at? Spatial–Temporal Gaze Inconsistency Analysis for Video Face Forgery Detection. *IEEE Transactions on Information Forensics and Security*, 19, 4507–4517. DOI: 10.1109/TIFS.2024.3381823

Rehman, I. u. (2019). Facebook-Cambridge Analytica data harvesting: What you need to know. *Library Philosophy and Practice*, 1-11.

Talreja, V., Valenti, M. C., & Nasrabadi, N. M. (2020). Deep Hashing for Secure Multimodal Biometrics. *IEEE Transactions on Information Forensics and Security*, •••, 1306–1321.

Wu, L., Yang, J., Zhou, M., Chen, Y., & Wang, Q. (2019). LVID: A Multimodal Biometrics Authentication System on Smartphones. *IEEE Transactions on Information Forensics and Security*, •••, 1572–1585.

Yang, K., Zhang, Z., Youliang, T., & Ma, J. (2023). A Secure Authentication Framework to Guarantee the Traceability of Avatars in Metaverse. *IEEE Transactions on Information Forensics and Security*, 18, 3817–3832. DOI: 10.1109/TIFS.2023.3288689

ADDITIONAL READING

Al-Waisy, A. S., Qahwaji, R., Ipson, S., Al-Fahdawi, S., & Nagem, T. A. (2018). A multi-biometric iris recognition system based on a deep learning approach. *Pattern Analysis & Applications*, 21(3), 783–802. DOI: 10.1007/s10044-017-0656-1

Alghamdi, S. M., Jarraya, S. K., & Kateb, F. (2024). Enhancing Security in Multimodal Biometric Fusion: Analyzing Adversarial Attacks. *IEEE Access : Practical Innovations, Open Solutions*, 12, 106133–106145. DOI: 10.1109/ACCESS.2024.3435527

Hassaballah, M., Alshazly, H. A., & Ali, A. A. (2020). Robust local oriented patterns for ear recognition. *Multimedia Tools and Applications*, 79(41), 31183–31204. DOI: 10.1007/s11042-020-09456-7

Kong, A., Zhang, D., & Kamel, M. (2006). Palmprint identification using feature-level fusion. *Pattern Recognition*, 39(3), 478–487. DOI: 10.1016/j.patcog.2005.08.014

Mathis, F., Fawaz, H. I., & Khamis, M. (2020, April). Knowledge-driven biometric authentication in virtual reality. In *Extended Abstracts of the 2020 CHI Conference on Human Factors in Computing Systems* (pp. 1-10).

Rahim, M. A., Hossain, M. N., Wahid, T., & Azam, M. S. (2013). Face recognition using local binary patterns (LBP). *Global Journal of Computer Science and Technology*, 13(4), 1–8.

Soliman, M. M., Darwish, A., & Hassanien, A. E. (2023). The threat of the digital human in the metaverse: Security and privacy. In *The Future of Metaverse in the Virtual Era and Physical World* (pp. 247–265). Springer International Publishing. DOI: 10.1007/978-3-031-29132-6_14

Sumalatha, U., Prakasha, K. K., Prabhu, S., & Nayak, V. C. (2024). A Comprehensive Review of Unimodal and Multimodal Fingerprint Biometric Authentication Systems: Fusion, Attacks, and Template Protection. IEEE Access.

Tahir, H., Mahmood, K., Ayub, M. F., Saleem, M. A., Ferzund, J., & Kumar, N. (2023). Lightweight and secure multi-factor authentication scheme in VANETs. *IEEE Transactions on Vehicular Technology*, 72(11), 14978–14986. DOI: 10.1109/TVT.2023.3286187

Umer, S., Sardar, A., Rout, R. K., Tanveer, M., & Razzak, I. (2023). IoT-enabled multimodal biometric recognition system in secure environment. *IEEE Internet of Things Journal*, 10(24), 21457–21466. DOI: 10.1109/JIOT.2023.3299465

Wu, T., Leng, L., & Khan, M. K. (2023). A multi-spectral palmprint fuzzy commitment based on deep hashing code with discriminative bit selection. *Artificial Intelligence Review*, 56(7), 6169–6186. DOI: 10.1007/s10462-022-10334-x

Yang, Z., Huangfu, H., Leng, L., Zhang, B., Teoh, A. B. J., & Zhang, Y. (2023). Comprehensive competition mechanism in palmprint recognition. *IEEE Transactions on Information Forensics and Security*, 18, 5160–5170. DOI: 10.1109/TIFS.2023.3306104

KEY TERMS AND DEFINITIONS

Contingency: Contingency refers to a future event or circumstance that is possible but cannot be predicted with certainty. In various contexts, it often involves planning for unexpected situations and preparing responses or measures to address them.

DNA: DNA (Deoxyribonucleic Acid) is a molecule that carries the genetic instructions used in the growth, development, functioning, and reproduction of all known living organisms and many viruses. DNA is made up of tiny building blocks called nucleotides, which come together in a specific order. This order decides how an organism looks and works, like whether you have brown eyes or are tall. DNA is found in the cells of every living thing, and it gets passed down from parents to their children, which is why you might share traits with your family.

Edge Computing: Edge Computing is a distributed computing paradigm that brings computation and data storage closer to the location where it is needed, rather than relying solely on centralized data centers. This approach aims to reduce latency, improve response times, and optimize bandwidth usage by processing data near the source of generation.

HTTPS: HTTPS (HyperText Transfer Protocol Secure) is an extension of HTTP (HyperText Transfer Protocol) that adds a layer of security to data exchanged between a user's web browser and a website. It uses encryption techniques for data communication to ensure authenticity and data integration.:

Latency: Latency refers to the delay or time it takes for data to travel from its source to its destination. It is often measured in milliseconds (ms) and can significantly impact the performance of networked systems and applications.

VPN: A VPN (Virtual Private Network) is a technology that creates a secure and encrypted connection over a less secure network, such as the internet.

Section 3
Legal and Ethical Challenges

Chapter 12
Data Privacy and Legal Considerations in Cyber Forensics

ABSTRACT

In the era of digital transformation, cyber forensics has become an indispensable field for investigating and resolving cybercrimes. Cyber forensics, the science of recovering and analyzing digital evidence, plays a crucial role in criminal justice, corporate security, and data integrity. However, the field of cyber forensics is not without its challenges, particularly in relation to data privacy, legal compliance, and ethical considerations. This chapter delves into the complexities of these issues, offering a detailed examination of the legal frameworks, privacy concerns, ethical dilemmas, and compliance challenges that professionals in cyber forensics must navigate.

1. INTRODUCTION

In the era of digital transformation, cyber forensics has become an indispensable field for investigating and resolving cybercrimes. Cyber forensics, the science of recovering and analyzing digital evidence, plays a crucial role in criminal justice, corporate security, and data integrity. However, the field of cyber forensics is not without its challenges, particularly in relation to data privacy, legal compliance, and ethical considerations.

This chapter delves into the complexities of these issues, offering a detailed examination of the legal frameworks, privacy concerns, ethical dilemmas, and compliance challenges that professionals in cyber forensics must navigate.

DOI: 10.4018/979-8-3693-2960-3.ch012

2. LEGAL FOUNDATIONS OF CYBER FORENSICS

Cyber forensics, or digital forensics, is the process of identifying, preserving, analyzing, and presenting digital evidence in a manner that is legally admissible. It encompasses a range of activities, including the investigation of cybercrimes, the recovery of deleted or corrupted data, and the examination of digital devices such as computers, smartphones, and servers. The scope of cyber forensics extends to various types of digital evidence, including emails, files, logs, and network traffic.

Key Legal Frameworks and Legislation

- **Computer Fraud and Abuse Act (CFAA):** Enacted in 1986, the Computer Fraud and Abuse Act (CFAA) is a fundamental piece of legislation in the United States addressing computer-related crimes. The CFAA criminalizes unauthorized access to computer systems, data theft, and other malicious activities involving computers and networks. The Act provides a legal foundation for prosecuting cybercrimes, but its broad language has raised concerns about overreach and potential implications for legitimate activities (Computer Fraud and Abuse Act (CFAA), n.d.).
- **General Data Protection Regulation (GDPR):** The General Data Protection Regulation (GDPR) is a comprehensive data protection law implemented by the European Union (EU) in 2018. GDPR sets stringent requirements for the processing, storage, and protection of personal data. It emphasizes the importance of obtaining explicit consent from individuals before processing their data and mandates strict measures for data security, breach notification, and data subject rights. GDPR significantly impacts cyber forensics by imposing restrictions on data collection and handling practices (Voigt & Bussche, 2017).
- **California Consumer Privacy Act (CCPA):** The California Consumer Privacy Act (CCPA) is a state-level data protection law that provides California residents with greater control over their personal information. Enacted in 2018, the CCPA grants individuals the right to access, delete, and opt out of the sale of their personal data. It also imposes transparency requirements on businesses regarding their data practices. The CCPA has set a precedent for data privacy legislation in the United States and influences how forensic investigations involving California residents are conducted (The California Consumer Privacy Act).
- **Jurisdictional Challenges:** Cyber forensics often involves cross-border investigations, presenting significant jurisdictional challenges. Different countries have varying laws and regulations concerning data privacy

and cybercrime, which complicates the process of conducting investigations and prosecuting offenders. Jurisdictional conflicts may arise when data is stored in one country but accessed or analyzed in another, requiring international cooperation and legal agreements to address these challenges effectively.

3. LEGAL FRAMEWORKS GOVERNING CYBER FORENSICS

3.1. International Legal Frameworks for Cyber Forensics

Cyber forensics is a global field, given the international nature of the internet and cybercrimes. Effective cyber forensic practices require robust international legal frameworks to ensure that digital evidence is handled appropriately across different jurisdictions. International legal frameworks provide guidelines and agreements that facilitate cooperation, standardize procedures, and uphold legal standards in cyber forensics. Key international legal frameworks relevant to cyber forensics are shown in figure 12.1.

- **The Budapest Convention on Cybercrime (2001):** The Budapest Convention on Cybercrime, officially known as the Council of Europe Convention on Cybercrime, is the first international treaty designed specifically to address cybercrime through a harmonized approach. It is a significant legal framework for facilitating international cooperation and standardizing laws related to cybercrime and cyber forensics. Key Provisions of Budapest Convention includes:
    - **Criminalization of Cybercrime:** Defines and criminalizes offenses such as illegal access to computer systems, illegal interception of communications, and data interference. It also includes provisions for offenses related to computer systems, data, and content.
    - **Procedural Measures:** Outlines procedures for the collection, preservation, and exchange of digital evidence. Provides guidelines for obtaining and executing search and seizure orders, as well as real-time data collection.
    - **International Cooperation:** Facilitates mutual legal assistance among member states, including the exchange of information and evidence. Promotes the establishment of contact points and centralized authorities to streamline cross-border investigations.

The Budapest Convention has been instrumental in setting international standards for cybercrime legislation and forensic practices. It has influenced national laws and fostered international collaboration in investigating and prosecuting cybercrimes. The Convention provides a framework for member states to work together, ensuring that digital evidence can be effectively gathered and utilized in legal proceedings across borders.

Figure 1. International legal frameworks for cyber-forensics

- **The EU General Data Protection Regulation (GDPR) (2018):** The General Data Protection Regulation (GDPR) is a comprehensive data protection regulation implemented by the European Union (EU). While it primarily focuses on data protection and privacy, it has significant implications for cyber forensics, particularly concerning the handling and processing of personal data. Key Provisions in GDPR includes (Voigt & Bussche, 2017):
    - **Data Protection Principles:** Establishes principles for the collection, processing, and storage of personal data, including data minimization, purpose limitation, and accuracy.
    - **Rights of Data Subjects:** Grants individuals rights regarding their personal data, including access, rectification, and erasure.
    - **Cross-Border Data Transfers:** Regulates the transfer of personal data outside the EU, requiring adequate protection measures or agreements for such transfers.
    - **Data Breach Notifications:** Mandates prompt notification of data breaches to relevant authorities and affected individuals.

GDPR influences how digital evidence involving personal data is collected, processed, and stored. It emphasizes the need for compliance with strict data protection standards and affects forensic investigations, particularly in relation to privacy and the rights of data subjects. Organizations conducting forensic investigations involving EU citizens must adhere to GDPR requirements to ensure lawful processing of personal data.

- **Mutual Legal Assistance Treaties (MLATs):** Mutual Legal Assistance Treaties (MLATs) are bilateral or multilateral agreements between countries that facilitate cooperation in criminal investigations and prosecutions. MLATs play a crucial role in cross-border cyber forensics by providing a legal basis for the exchange of evidence and assistance in investigations (MUTUAL LEGAL ASSISTANCE TREATIES, 2022). Key Provisions in MLATs are:
    - **Evidence Exchange:** Establishes procedures for requesting and providing evidence in criminal investigations, including digital evidence.
    - **Judicial Cooperation:** Facilitates the cooperation between judicial authorities in different countries for the execution of legal requests.
    - **Extradition:** Provides mechanisms for the extradition of suspects and witnesses between countries.
    - **Confidentiality and Security:** Ensures that exchanged information is handled with confidentiality and security.

MLATs are essential for managing cross-border investigations and obtaining evidence in cyber forensics. They enable countries to collaborate effectively and ensure that digital evidence can be shared and used in legal proceedings across jurisdictions. MLATs also help address jurisdictional challenges and facilitate international cooperation in combating cybercrime.

- **The Asia-Pacific Economic Cooperation (APEC) Privacy Framework (2004):** The APEC Privacy Framework is a set of guidelines developed to promote the protection of personal information in the Asia-Pacific region. While it focuses on privacy, it has implications for cyber forensics in terms of handling personal data. Key Provisions are (APEC Privacy Framework, 2005):
    - o **Information Privacy Principles:** Establishes principles for the collection, use, and disclosure of personal information, including transparency, choice, and security.
    - o **Cross-Border Data Flows:** Encourages the adoption of privacy protection measures to facilitate cross-border data flows while ensuring adequate protection.
    - o **Accountability:** Requires organizations to be accountable for adhering to privacy principles and protecting personal data.

The APEC Privacy Framework influences how personal data is handled in the Asia-Pacific region, including in forensic investigations. It emphasizes the need for privacy protections and impacts the collection and processing of digital evidence involving personal information. Organizations conducting investigations in the region must align with the framework's privacy principles.

- **The OECD Guidelines on the Protection of Privacy and Transborder Flows of Personal Data (1980):** The OECD Guidelines on the Protection of Privacy and Transborder Flows of Personal Data provide a set of principles for privacy protection and the handling of personal data. These guidelines serve as a foundation for data protection laws and influence international data transfer practices. Key Provisions includes:
    - o **Data Collection and Use:** Establishes principles for the collection and use of personal data, including necessity and relevance.
    - o **Data Quality:** Requires that personal data be accurate and up to date.
    - o **Data Security:** Emphasizes the need for security measures to protect personal data.
    - o **Data Access and Correction:** Grants individuals the right to access and correct their personal data.

The OECD Guidelines have influenced the development of data protection laws and privacy regulations globally. They impact how personal data is managed in forensic investigations, particularly concerning data quality, security, and the rights of individuals. Adherence to these principles is essential for lawful and ethical handling of digital evidence.

- **The United Nations Convention Against Transnational Organized Crime (2000):** The United Nations Convention Against Transnational Organized Crime (UNTOC) addresses various forms of organized crime, including cybercrime. It provides a framework for international cooperation in combating transnational criminal activities. Key Provisions are:
  - **Cooperation and Assistance:** Promotes cooperation among countries in criminal investigations and prosecutions, including those involving cybercrime.
  - **Mutual Legal Assistance:** Facilitates the exchange of information and evidence between countries.
  - **Capacity Building:** Supports the development of capabilities and resources to combat organized crime, including cybercrime.

UNTOC enhances international cooperation in addressing cybercrime and transnational criminal activities. It provides a framework for obtaining and sharing evidence across borders, including in cyber forensic investigations. The Convention helps countries collaborate more effectively in tackling organized cybercrime.

3.2. National Legal Frameworks

Key national legal frameworks for cyber forensics in different countries are:

3.2.1. Legal Frameworks in United States

The United States has a comprehensive set of laws and regulations governing cyber forensics:

- **Computer Fraud and Abuse Act (CFAA) (1986):** The CFAA is a key piece of legislation that criminalizes unauthorized access to computer systems and data. It provides a legal framework for prosecuting various forms of cybercrime. Key Provisions are:
  - **Unauthorized Access:** Criminalizes accessing a computer system without authorization.

- **Data Theft:** Addresses unauthorized acquisition and transmission of data.
- **Forensic Procedures:** Provides a basis for the seizure and analysis of digital evidence.

The CFAA has significantly influenced the development of cybercrime laws and forensic practices in the U.S., shaping how digital evidence is collected and used in legal proceedings.

- **Electronic Communications Privacy Act (ECPA) (1986):** The ECPA regulates the interception and access to electronic communications and stored data. Key Provisions includes:
  - Requires court orders for intercepting electronic communications.
  - Governs access to stored electronic communications and data.
  - Ensures privacy rights in electronic communications.

The ECPA establishes standards for accessing digital evidence while balancing privacy concerns, influencing forensic practices and legal procedures in the U.S.

Challenges

- **Jurisdiction Issues**: The global nature of the internet complicates jurisdiction. Cybercriminals can operate across borders, making it challenging for law enforcement agencies to coordinate efforts.
- **Privacy Concerns**: Balancing the need for effective law enforcement with individual privacy rights is an ongoing challenge, especially with the rise of surveillance technologies.

3.2.2. Legal Frameworks in United Kingdom

The UK has developed specific laws addressing cyber forensics:

- **Computer Misuse Act (1990):** This act criminalizes unauthorized access to computer systems and data, serving as a foundational law for cybercrime in the UK. Key Specifications are:
  - Criminalizes unauthorized access to computer systems.
  - Addresses unauthorized modification or impairment of data.
  - Covers access with the intent to commit further offenses.

The Computer Misuse Act provides a legal framework for prosecuting cybercrimes and influences forensic practices in the UK.

- **Regulation of Investigatory Powers Act (RIPA) (2000):** RIPA regulates the interception of communications and surveillance, including digital evidence collection. Key Specifications are:
    - o Requires authorization for intercepting communications and governs the conduct of surveillance and evidence collection.
    - o Addresses the retention and access to communication data.

RIPA provides the legal basis for surveillance and evidence collection, influencing forensic practices and ensuring legal compliance in the UK.

- **Investigatory Powers Act (IPA) (2016):** Also known as the "Snooper's Charter," IPA extends RIPA and includes provisions for the collection and retention of communications data. Key Specifications includes (Investigatory Powers Act 2016, 2016):
    - o Allows for bulk data collection and storage.
    - o Addresses issues related to encrypted data and access by law enforcement.
    - o Establishes oversight mechanisms for surveillance and data collection activities.

The IPA provides comprehensive powers for digital surveillance and data collection, shaping forensic practices and legal standards in the UK.

Challenges

- **Public Scrutiny**: There is ongoing debate about the extent of surveillance and data access rights for law enforcement, leading to public concerns about privacy and civil liberties.
- **Legal Ambiguities**: The interplay between different laws can create uncertainties for forensic investigators regarding what is permissible in gathering and analyzing data.

3.2.3. Legal Frameworks in Australia

Australia's legal framework includes several relevant laws:

- **Criminal Code Act 1995**: This act addresses offenses related to computer systems, including hacking and unauthorized access, providing a legal basis for prosecuting cyber crimes.
- **Telecommunications (Interception and Access) Act 1979**: Regulates the interception of communications and access to stored communications by law enforcement, which is essential for cyber forensic investigations.

- **Privacy Act 1988**: Governs the handling of personal information and impacts how forensic investigators collect and manage data, emphasizing the need for consent and transparency.

  Challenges

- **Compliance with International Standards**: Ensuring that domestic laws align with international practices for cyber forensics can be complex, particularly given the rapid evolution of technology.
- **Balancing Security and Privacy**: Similar to other countries, Australia faces the challenge of balancing law enforcement needs with individual privacy rights, especially in the context of surveillance.

3.2.4. Legal Frameworks in India

India has established a comprehensive legal framework to address cyber forensics, focusing on combating cybercrime, protecting personal data, and ensuring the admissibility of digital evidence in courts. This framework comprises various laws and regulations, enforcement agencies, practices, and challenges.

- **Information Technology Act (IT Act) (2000):** The IT Act provides a legal framework for cyber activities and digital evidence handling in India. Key Provisions are (THE INFORMATION TECHNOLOGY ACT, 2000):
  - Defines cyber offenses such as hacking, data theft, and cyber terrorism.
  - Addresses the admissibility of digital evidence and procedures for its collection.
  - Includes provisions for securing digital infrastructure and preventing cybercrime.

The IT Act is a key piece of legislation for cyber forensics in India, guiding the handling and prosecution of cybercrimes.

- **The Indian Penal Code (IPC) and the Code of Criminal Procedure (CrPC):** IPC and CrPC provide additional legal frameworks for criminal offenses, including those related to cybercrimes. Key Specifications includes:
  - IPC: Addresses general criminal offenses, including those involving computers and digital data.
  - CrPC: Governs criminal procedures, including the collection and handling of digital evidence.

IPC and CrPC complement the IT Act by providing broader legal context and procedural standards for cyber forensics in India.

- **The Digital Personal Data Protection Act, 2023 (DPDP):** A landmark legislation in India that aims to safeguard the privacy of individuals in the digital age. It governs the processing of digital personal data in a manner that recognizes both the right of individuals to protect their personal data and the need to process such personal data for lawful purposes. Key Specifications are:
  - o Establishes principles for data processing and protection.
  - o Grants rights to individuals regarding their personal data.
  - o Sets requirements for data controllers and processors.

The DPDP, enhances data protection standards and influences cyber forensics practices by establishing clearer guidelines for handling personal data.

- **Cyber Security Policy:** The National Cyber Security Policy (2013) outlines the framework for securing cyberspace in India and promotes a culture of cybersecurity. Key Specifications includes:
  - o **Incident Reporting**: Establishes guidelines for the reporting of cybersecurity incidents, facilitating forensic investigations.
  - o **Collaboration**: Encourages cooperation among government agencies, private sector organizations, and international partners.

Challenges

- **Privacy Concerns:** Balancing law enforcement needs with individual privacy rights is a significant challenge. The proposed PDP Bill aims to address these concerns but has not yet been enacted.
- **Resource Limitations:** Many law enforcement agencies face resource constraints, limiting their ability to conduct thorough cyber forensic investigations and respond to increasing cyber threats.
- **Jurisdictional Issues:** Cybercrime often transcends national borders, complicating investigations. International cooperation is essential, but varying legal standards can create challenges.

3.2.5. Legal Frameworks in South Africa

South Africa has developed a comprehensive legal framework to address cyber forensics. The framework includes several key pieces of legislation, enforcement agencies, practices, and ongoing challenges.

- **Electronic Communications and Transactions Act (ECTA) (2002):** ECTA regulates electronic communications and transactions, including aspects of cyber forensics. Key Provisions are:

- Defines offenses related to unauthorized access and data interference.
- Addresses the admissibility and handling of electronic evidence.
- Includes provisions for protecting consumers in electronic transactions.

ECTA provides a legal framework for addressing cybercrimes and handling digital evidence in South Africa.

- **Protection of Personal Information Act (POPIA) (2013):** POPIA regulates the processing and protection of personal information. Key Provisions are:
    - Establishes principles for collecting, processing, and storing personal information.
    - Grants rights to individuals regarding their personal data.
    - Sets requirements for organizations processing personal information.

POPIA influences how digital evidence is handled in South Africa, emphasizing the need for data protection and privacy.

- **Cybercrimes Act (2018):** The Cybercrimes Act addresses various forms of cybercrime and provides a legal framework for investigating and prosecuting cyber offenses. Key Provisions are:
    - Defines and criminalizes offenses such as hacking, data breaches, and identity theft.
    - Includes provisions for the collection, preservation, and analysis of digital evidence.
    - Facilitates cooperation with other countries in combating cybercrime.

The Cybercrimes Act strengthens the legal framework for cyber forensics in South Africa, providing clear guidelines for handling digital evidence and prosecuting cybercrimes.

Challenges

- **Privacy Concerns:** Balancing law enforcement needs with individual privacy rights under POPIA is a significant challenge. Investigators must navigate consent requirements while gathering evidence.
- **Resource Limitations:** Limited resources and expertise in digital forensics can hinder the effectiveness of law enforcement agencies in combating cybercrime.
- **Evolving Technology:** Rapid advancements in technology require continuous updates to legal frameworks and forensic practices to keep pace with new threats and methods of cybercrime.

3.2.6. Legal Frameworks in Oman

Oman has made significant strides in establishing a legal framework to address cyber forensics, particularly as the country recognizes the increasing importance of cybersecurity in a digital age. The framework encompasses laws that govern cybercrime, data protection, and the handling of digital evidence.

- **Cybercrime Law (2011):** Oman's Cybercrime Law, enacted by Royal Decree No. 12/2011, provides a legal framework for addressing cybercrime and managing digital evidence. Key Provisions are:
    - Defines and criminalizes offenses such as unauthorized access, data breaches, and online harassment.
    - Establishes guidelines for the collection and preservation of digital evidence.
    - Sets out penalties for offenders, including fines and imprisonment.

The Cybercrime Law provides a legal foundation for cyber forensic investigations in Oman, ensuring that digital evidence is collected and used in accordance with legal standards.

- **Telecommunications Law:** The Telecommunications Law (Royal Decree No. 30/2002) regulates the telecommunications sector in Oman and includes provisions relevant to cybersecurity and cyber forensics. Key Provisions includes:
    - **Data Retention**: Requires telecommunications service providers to retain user data for a specified period, facilitating investigations into cybercrimes.
    - **Collaboration with Authorities**: Obligates service providers to cooperate with law enforcement agencies in investigations related to cyber offenses.
- **Personal Data Protection Law:** The Personal Data Protection Law (Royal Decree No. 6/2021) was enacted in 2021, establishing a framework for the protection of personal data in Oman. Key Specifications are:
    - **Consent Requirement**: Organizations must obtain consent before collecting and processing personal data, which impacts how data is handled during forensic investigations.
    - **Data Breach Notification**: Organizations are required to notify the relevant authorities and affected individuals in the event of a data breach.

- **Rights of Individuals**: The law grants individuals rights over their personal data, influencing how cyber forensics must be conducted to respect privacy.

- **Oman National Cybersecurity Strategy:** The Oman National Cybersecurity Strategy aims to enhance the country's cybersecurity posture and address emerging cyber threats. Key Specifications includes:
  - Focuses on protecting critical infrastructure and digital assets against cyber-attacks.
  - Develops capabilities for responding to cyber incidents and breaches and encourages cooperation with international partners and organizations.

The strategy supports the development of cyber forensic capabilities by strengthening the country's cybersecurity framework and fostering international collaboration.

Challenges

- **Privacy Concerns:** Balancing the need for effective law enforcement with individual privacy rights is a significant challenge, particularly in light of the Personal Data Protection Law.
- **Limited Resources:** The rapid evolution of technology and the growing sophistication of cyber threats can strain the resources and capabilities of law enforcement agencies in Oman.
- **Jurisdictional Issues:** As cybercrime often involves international elements, jurisdictional challenges can complicate investigations and the prosecution of offenders.

3.2.7. Legal Frameworks in Canada

Canada has developed a comprehensive legal framework to address cyber forensics, focusing on the investigation of cybercrimes, the protection of personal data, and the admissibility of digital evidence in court. The framework reflects Canada's commitment to cybersecurity, privacy rights, and effective law enforcement. Below is a detailed discussion of the key laws, regulations, enforcement agencies, practices, and challenges associated with cyber forensics in Canada. Canada's legal framework for cyber forensics includes:

- **Criminal Code of Canada:** The Criminal Code is the primary legal document governing criminal offenses in Canada, including cyber-related crimes. Amendments over the years have introduced specific provisions addressing computer and internet offenses. Key Provisions:

- Unauthorized Use of Computer (Section 342.1): Criminalizes unauthorized access to computer systems, which is essential for prosecuting hacking offenses.
    - **Mischief (Section 430)**: Addresses willful damage to data or computer systems, providing a basis for prosecuting cyber vandalism.
    - **Identity Theft and Identity Fraud (Sections 402.2 and 403)**: Criminalizes the unauthorized use of identifying information, crucial for combating cyber fraud.
- **Personal Information Protection and Electronic Documents Act (PIPEDA):** Enacted in 2000, PIPEDA governs how private sector organizations collect, use, and disclose personal information in the course of commercial activities. Key Provisions of the act are:
    - **Consent Requirement**: Organizations must obtain consent to collect and process personal data, which impacts how cyber forensics are conducted.
    - **Data Breach Notification**: Organizations must notify affected individuals and the Privacy Commissioner of Canada about data breaches, allowing for forensic investigations.
    - **Enforcement**: The Office of the Privacy Commissioner of Canada oversees compliance and can investigate complaints related to privacy breaches.
- **Canada's Anti-Spam Legislation (CASL):** Enacted in 2014, CASL regulates the sending of commercial electronic messages and the installation of software, addressing cyber activities that can involve forensics. Key Provisions:
    - **Consent Requirements**: CASL mandates consent for sending commercial electronic messages, which can affect investigations related to spam and phishing.
    - **Penalties**: The law imposes significant fines for violations, providing a deterrent against cybercriminal activities.
- **Digital Privacy Act:** This act, enacted in 2015, amends PIPEDA and enhances privacy protections related to the handling of personal data. Key Specifications of the act includes:
    - **Breach Notification**: Strengthens the requirement for organizations to notify individuals of data breaches.
    - **Enhanced Enforcement**: Provides the Privacy Commissioner with stronger enforcement powers, including the ability to issue orders and impose penalties.

Challenges

- **Indigenous Privacy Considerations**: Addressing privacy concerns within Indigenous communities adds a layer of complexity to data handling practices, requiring sensitivity and adherence to community-specific protocols.
- **Cross-Jurisdictional Issues**: Similar to the U.S., Canada faces challenges in enforcing laws across provincial and national borders due to the internet's global nature.

3.2.8. Legal Frameworks in Japan

Japan has developed a comprehensive legal framework to address cyber forensics, focusing on cybersecurity, data protection, and the prosecution of cybercrime. The framework reflects Japan's commitment to protecting personal information and ensuring the integrity of digital evidence. Below is a detailed discussion of the key laws, regulations, and challenges associated with cyber forensics in Japan.

- **Act on Prohibition of Unauthorized Computer Access:** Enacted in 1999, this act serves as the foundational legal framework for addressing unauthorized access to computer systems and data. Key Specifications are:
    - **Unauthorized Access:** The act criminalizes unauthorized access to computer systems and data, establishing penalties for violators.
    - **Scope:** It covers both individuals and organizations, ensuring that cybercriminals can be prosecuted effectively.
    - **Penalties:** Offenders can face imprisonment or fines, providing law enforcement with tools to combat cybercrime.
- **Act on the Protection of Personal Information (APPI):** The APPI, first enacted in 2003 and revised in 2017, governs the handling of personal data in Japan. Key Provisions:
    - **Data Handling Requirements:** Organizations must obtain consent for the collection and processing of personal data, impacting how forensic investigations are conducted.
    - **Data Breach Notification:** The act mandates that organizations notify individuals of data breaches, which is crucial for cyber forensics.
    - **Enforcement:** The Personal Information Protection Commission (PPC) oversees compliance and can impose penalties for violations.
- **Act on the Prevention of Transfer of Criminal Proceeds:** This act focuses on preventing money laundering and the transfer of criminal proceeds, which often involve digital transactions. Key Provisions:
    - **Reporting Obligations:** Financial institutions must report suspicious transactions, which may involve forensic analysis of digital records.

- **Collaboration with Law Enforcement:** The act facilitates cooperation between financial institutions and law enforcement agencies in cyber investigations.

Challenges

- Challenges such as privacy concerns, jurisdictional issues, and the rapid pace of technological change require ongoing adaptation and collaboration among legal, law enforcement, and cybersecurity entities. This dynamic landscape emphasizes the need for a balanced approach that supports effective law enforcement while safeguarding individual privacy rights in the digital age.

3.2.9. Legal Frameworks in Singapore

Singapore has established a comprehensive legal framework to address cyber forensics, combining elements of criminal law, data protection, and cybersecurity regulations. This framework is designed to combat cybercrime effectively while ensuring the protection of individual privacy rights. Below is a detailed discussion of the key laws, regulations, and challenges associated with cyber forensics in Singapore. Singapore's legal framework includes:

- **Computer Misuse Act (CMA):** Enacted in 1993, the Computer Misuse Act is the cornerstone of Singapore's legal framework for addressing cybercrime. It criminalizes unauthorized access to computer systems and data, as well as other computer-related offenses. Key Provisions of this framework are:
    - **Unauthorized Access**: Section 3 of the CMA makes it illegal to access a computer without authorization.
    - **Unauthorized Modification**: Section 5 addresses the unauthorized modification of data, which is crucial in cyber forensics to establish evidence of tampering or data breaches.
    - **Penalties**: Offenders can face substantial fines and imprisonment, with penalties increasing for repeat offenders.
- **Personal Data Protection Act (PDPA):** The Personal Data Protection Act, enacted in 2012, governs the collection, use, and disclosure of personal data by organizations. It emphasizes the need for consent and accountability in handling personal information. Key Provisions of the act includes:
    - **Consent Requirement**: Organizations must obtain consent before collecting or processing personal data, which has implications for forensic investigations involving personal information.

- **Data Protection Obligations**: Organizations must implement measures to protect personal data, which can impact how forensic evidence is collected and managed.
- **Enforcement**: The Personal Data Protection Commission (PDPC) oversees compliance and can impose fines for breaches.

- **Cybersecurity Act:** Enacted in 2018, the Cybersecurity Act aims to strengthen Singapore's cybersecurity resilience and establish a framework for the protection of critical information infrastructure (CII). Key Provisions:
    - **CII Identification**: Designates critical sectors and sets obligations for organizations managing CII to adopt cybersecurity measures.
    - **Incident Reporting**: Requires organizations to report cybersecurity incidents, which may include breaches that have forensic implications.
    - **Enforcement Powers**: Grants authorities the power to investigate and respond to cybersecurity threats, facilitating cyber forensics operations.

Challenges

- **Privacy Concerns:** The PDPA emphasizes privacy and data protection, which can complicate forensic investigations that require access to personal data. Law enforcement must navigate privacy laws while conducting investigations.
- **Jurisdictional Issues:** As cybercrime often crosses borders, jurisdictional challenges arise when dealing with international investigations. Cooperation with foreign law enforcement agencies is essential but can be complicated by differing legal standards.
- **Evolving Technology:** The rapid pace of technological advancement presents ongoing challenges for legal frameworks. Emerging technologies such as cloud computing, artificial intelligence, and the Internet of Things (IoT) require continuous updates to laws and regulations to address new forensic challenges.

4. PRIVACY CONCERNS IN CYBER FORENSICS

The balance between privacy and security is a central issue in cyber forensics. On one hand, forensic investigations aim to uncover evidence of criminal activities, which may involve accessing sensitive personal information. On the other hand, protecting individuals' privacy rights is paramount. The debate centers around finding a balance that allows for effective law enforcement while respecting privacy boundaries.

4.1. Data Collection and Storage

Data collection and storage in cyber forensics must be handled with utmost care to ensure compliance with privacy laws and regulations. Forensic investigators must follow strict procedures to prevent unauthorized access and potential misuse of data. This includes obtaining proper consent, using secure storage solutions, and implementing access controls to safeguard sensitive information.

- **Nature of Data Collected:** Cyber forensics often involves the collection of a wide array of personal data, including emails, chat logs, browsing histories, and files stored on devices. This extensive data can include sensitive information about individuals, raising significant privacy concerns.
- **Consent and Authorization:** Obtaining consent from individuals before collecting their data is a fundamental principle in data protection laws. In the context of cyber forensics, consent may be required from individuals whose data is being analyzed, particularly if the data collection extends beyond the scope of the investigation. In some cases, law enforcement agencies may obtain court orders or warrants to authorize data collection, ensuring that legal standards are met.
    - **Lack of Explicit Consent**: In many cases, individuals may not provide explicit consent for their data to be collected or analyzed. This lack of consent can lead to legal and ethical challenges regarding the validity of the evidence obtained.
    - **Implied Consent Issues**: Even when individuals consent to use of a service, they may not fully understand the extent to which their data can be accessed or used in forensic investigations.
- **Data Security and Access Controls:** Ensuring the security of collected data is critical to maintaining its integrity and confidentiality. Forensic investigators must implement robust security measures to protect data from unauthorized access, tampering, or loss. This includes using encryption for data storage and transmission, maintaining secure access controls, and conducting regular security audits to identify and address potential vulnerabilities.

4.2. Surveillance and Monitoring

Cyber forensics can involve invasive techniques, such as monitoring online activities, wiretapping, or using malware to capture data. These methods can infringe on individual privacy rights.

Law enforcement agencies must justify the need for such surveillance, balancing the public interest against the potential infringement of privacy.

4.3. Chilling Effect

The awareness that personal communications may be monitored can deter individuals from expressing themselves freely online. This chilling effect undermines freedoms of speech and expression, which are vital in democratic societies.

4.4. Data Minimization and Retention

Data minimization and retention are key principles in data protection laws. Forensic investigators should only collect data that is relevant to the investigation and avoid retaining unnecessary information. Data minimization involves collecting only the data that is necessary for the investigation, while data retention concerns how long data should be stored before being securely deleted. Forensic investigators must adhere to these principles to avoid collecting or retaining unnecessary information, which could potentially infringe on individuals' privacy rights.

- **Relevance and Necessity:** Forensic investigators should focus on collecting data that is relevant and necessary for the investigation. Data collection should be guided by the principle of relevance, ensuring that only information pertinent to the case is gathered. This approach helps minimize the impact on individuals' privacy and reduces the risk of inadvertently accessing unrelated personal information.
- **Data Retention Policies:** Data retention policies dictate how long data should be stored before being deleted. Forensic investigators must adhere to legal and regulatory requirements for data retention, ensuring that data is not kept longer than necessary. Retention policies should align with applicable laws and regulations, and data should be securely deleted when no longer needed for investigative or legal purposes.

4.5. Risk of Exposure

- **Vulnerability of Data**: The sensitive nature of data handled during cyber forensics makes it an attractive target for cybercriminals. Data breaches can expose personal information, leading to identity theft and other abuses.
- **Reputation Damage**: Organizations that fail to protect sensitive data can suffer reputational harm and loss of public trust.

4.6. Cross-Border Data Issues

- **International Data Flows**: Cyber forensics often involves data that crosses national borders, which complicates the application of privacy laws. Different jurisdictions may have varying standards for data protection, leading to potential conflicts.
- **Legal Ambiguities**: The lack of uniform international laws governing data privacy can create uncertainties regarding the legality of data collection and sharing.
- **Data Sharing Agreements**: While international cooperation is essential for combating cybercrime, inadequate protections for privacy during data exchanges can lead to breaches of personal information.

  Example Case Studies
- Several high-profile cases highlight the privacy concerns associated with cyber forensics. For example, the FBI's investigation into the San Bernardino shooting involved accessing encrypted data on the suspect's iPhone. The case raised significant debate about the extent to which law enforcement should be allowed to bypass encryption for investigative purposes while protecting individuals' privacy rights.
- Another example is the 2018 Cambridge Analytica scandal, where personal data from millions of Facebook users was harvested without consent for political profiling. This case underscored the importance of obtaining proper consent and ensuring transparency in data collection practices.

5. ETHICAL CONSIDERATIONS IN CYBER FORENSICS

5.1. Ethical Principles in Cyber Forensics

Ethical considerations in cyber forensics revolve around the principles of integrity, transparency, and respect for privacy. Forensic professionals must conduct their work with a high level of ethical standards, ensuring that their actions do not infringe on individuals' rights or compromise the integrity of the investigation.

- **Integrity and Accuracy:** Maintaining integrity and accuracy in cyber forensics is essential for ensuring that digital evidence is reliable and admissible in court. Forensic professionals must adhere to established procedures and methodologies, avoiding any actions that could compromise the validity of the evidence. This includes documenting every step of the forensic process and ensuring that evidence is handled in accordance with legal and ethical standards.

- **Transparency and Accountability:** Transparency and accountability are critical in cyber forensics to build trust and ensure that investigations are conducted ethically. Forensic professionals should provide clear and accurate reports of their findings, including any limitations or uncertainties. They must also be accountable for their actions and decisions, addressing any potential conflicts of interest or biases that could affect the outcome of the investigation.

5.2. Balancing Privacy with Investigative Needs

Balancing privacy with investigative needs is a challenging aspect of cyber forensics. Investigators must weigh the potential benefits of accessing sensitive data against the privacy implications for individuals. Ethical decision-making involves considering the necessity of accessing data, the potential impact on privacy, and the legal and regulatory framework governing the investigation.

- **Necessity and Proportionality:** The principle of necessity and proportionality requires that data access and collection be limited to what is necessary for the investigation and proportionate to the nature of the offense. Forensic professionals must justify the need for accessing sensitive information and ensure that the scope of data collection is appropriate for the investigation.
- **Minimizing Privacy Impact:** To minimize the impact on privacy, forensic investigators should use techniques that limit the exposure of personal information. This may involve redacting or anonymizing data to protect individuals' identities or focusing on specific data relevant to the investigation while avoiding unnecessary intrusion into unrelated personal information.

5.3. Ethical Dilemmas

Ethical dilemmas often arise in cyber forensics, such as situations where accessing certain data may reveal personal or sensitive information unrelated to the investigation. For example, a forensic examination of a suspect's computer may uncover private communications or medical records. Investigators must navigate these dilemmas carefully, ensuring that they respect privacy rights while fulfilling their investigative responsibilities.

A notable case involving ethical dilemmas is the investigation into the 2017 Equifax data breach. The breach exposed sensitive personal information of millions of individuals, raising questions about the ethical responsibilities of organizations in protecting data and the extent to which forensic investigations should delve into the compromised information.

6. COMPLIANCE ISSUES IN CYBER FORENSICS

6.1. Compliance with Data Protection Laws

Compliance with data protection laws is essential for conducting cyber forensics within the legal framework. Forensic investigators must be familiar with applicable data protection laws, such as GDPR and CCPA, and ensure that their practices align with legal requirements. This includes obtaining proper consent, safeguarding data, and adhering to data retention policies.

Forensic investigators working with data from the European Union must comply with the General Data Protection Regulation (GDPR). This involves adhering to principles such as data minimization, obtaining explicit consent, and ensuring data security. GDPR also grants individuals certain rights, such as the right to access and delete their personal data, which must be respected during forensic investigations.

In jurisdictions subject to the California Consumer Privacy Act (CCPA), forensic investigators must comply with requirements related to data access, deletion, and opt-out rights. This includes providing individuals with the ability to request access to their data and ensuring that data is handled in accordance with CCPA regulations.

6.2. Role of Data Protection Officers (DPOs)

Data Protection Officers (DPOs) play a crucial role in ensuring compliance with data protection laws. DPOs are responsible for overseeing data protection practices, providing guidance on legal requirements, and ensuring that forensic investigations comply with privacy regulations. Their role is particularly important in organizations that handle large volumes of personal data.

DPOs are responsible for monitoring compliance with data protection laws, conducting risk assessments, and providing training on data protection practices. They also serve as a point of contact for data subjects and regulatory authorities, addressing any concerns or issues related to data protection and privacy.

DPOs collaborate with forensic teams to ensure that investigations are conducted in compliance with data protection laws. They provide guidance on legal and regulatory requirements, help develop data protection policies, and assist in managing any privacy-related issues that arise during forensic investigations.

6.3. International Compliance Challenges

International compliance challenges arise in cross-border forensic investigations due to varying data protection laws and regulations. Investigators must navigate different legal frameworks, coordinate with international authorities, and ensure that their practices comply with both domestic and international requirements. This often involves complex legal agreements and data-sharing protocols.

Cross-border data transfers can be complicated by differences in data protection laws and regulations. Forensic investigators must ensure that data transfers between jurisdictions comply with legal requirements, such as obtaining necessary approvals or ensuring adequate protection for data being transferred.

International cooperation is essential for addressing cross-border cybercrime and conducting effective forensic investigations. Investigators must work with international partners, such as law enforcement agencies and regulatory authorities, to share information, coordinate efforts, and navigate legal and regulatory challenges.

6.4. Best Practices for Compliance

Adopting best practices for compliance is essential for ensuring that cyber forensic investigations adhere to legal and ethical standards. Best practices include conducting regular audits of data protection practices, implementing robust security measures, providing training for forensic professionals, and maintaining transparent documentation of investigative procedures.

- **Regular Audits and Reviews:** Regular audits and reviews of data protection practices help identify and address potential compliance issues. Forensic teams should conduct periodic assessments of their data handling procedures, security measures, and compliance with legal and regulatory requirements.
- **Training and Awareness:** Training and awareness programs are crucial for ensuring that forensic professionals understand and adhere to legal and ethical standards. Ongoing training should cover topics such as data protection laws, privacy considerations, and best practices for conducting forensic investigations.
- **Documentation and Transparency:** Maintaining detailed documentation of forensic procedures and findings is essential for ensuring transparency and accountability. Documentation should include records of data collection, analysis, and handling, as well as any decisions or actions taken during the investigation.

7. EVOLVING LEGAL LANDSCAPE

- **Emerging Data Privacy Laws:** The legal landscape for data privacy is continually evolving, with new laws and regulations emerging to address the challenges posed by digital technologies. Recent developments include the introduction of the Digital Markets Act (DMA) and the Digital Services Act (DSA) in the EU, which aim to regulate digital platforms and enhance consumer protection. These laws impact how data is collected, processed, and shared, influencing cyber forensic practices.
    - **Digital Markets Act (DMA):** The Digital Markets Act (DMA) focuses on regulating large digital platforms, such as online marketplaces and social media networks, to ensure fair competition and protect consumer rights. The DMA includes provisions related to data access and portability, which may impact forensic investigations involving data from these platforms.
    - **Digital Services Act (DSA):** The Digital Services Act (DSA) aims to regulate digital services and platforms to address issues such as online content moderation and user safety. The DSA includes requirements for transparency and accountability, which may influence how forensic investigations are conducted on digital platforms.
- **Impact of Technological Advancements:** Technological advancements, such as artificial intelligence (AI) and machine learning, are reshaping the field of cyber forensics. These technologies offer new tools for analyzing data but also raise new privacy and ethical concerns. Forensic professionals must stay abreast of technological developments and their implications for data privacy and compliance.

AI and machine learning technologies are increasingly used in cyber forensics to analyze large volumes of data and identify patterns or anomalies. These technologies can enhance investigative capabilities but also raise concerns about data privacy and the potential for bias in data analysis.

The use of AI and machine learning in forensics raises privacy and ethical implications, such as the potential for excessive data collection or intrusive analysis. Forensic professionals must consider these implications and ensure that their use of technology aligns with legal and ethical standards.

- **Ethical Considerations and Transparency:** Ethical considerations and transparency will continue to play a crucial role in cyber forensics. Forensic professionals must prioritize ethical decision-making, transparency in their procedures, and respect for privacy rights to maintain trust and ensure the integrity of their work.

- **Future Trends:** Future trends in data privacy and cyber forensics include the increasing emphasis on privacy-by-design principles, the rise of data protection regulations in emerging markets, and the growing importance of ethical considerations in forensic investigations. As technology continues to evolve, forensic professionals must adapt to new challenges and ensure that their practices align with legal and ethical standards.
    - **Privacy-by-Design Principles:** Privacy-by-design principles emphasize integrating privacy considerations into the design and development of systems and processes. In the context of cyber forensics, this involves implementing measures to protect privacy throughout the forensic process, from data collection to analysis and presentation.
    - **Data Protection Regulations in Emerging Markets:** As data protection regulations expand globally, emerging markets are adopting new laws and standards to address data privacy concerns. Forensic professionals must stay informed about developments in these markets and adapt their practices to comply with evolving regulations.

Forensic professionals should stay informed about relevant legal and ethical standards, adopt best practices for compliance, and engage in continuous training to address emerging challenges. Collaboration with legal experts, data protection officers, and international authorities is crucial for navigating the complexities of cyber forensics effectively.

8. SUMMARY

This chapter provides a comprehensive examination of the legal and ethical aspects of cyber forensics, addressing privacy concerns and compliance issues. As the field of cyber forensics evolves, professionals must navigate complex legal frameworks, balance privacy with investigative needs, and adhere to ethical standards. By staying informed about emerging regulations, adopting best practices, and considering the implications of technological advancements, forensic professionals can effectively address the challenges of data privacy and legal compliance in their work.

REFERENCES

(2005). *APEC Privacy Framework.* CTI Sub-Fora & Industry Dialogues Groups, Digital Economy Steering Group (DESG).

Computer Fraud and Abuse Act (CFAA). (n.d.). Retrieved from Practical Law: https://uk.practicallaw.thomsonreuters.com/2-508-3428?transitionType=Default&contextData=(sc.Default)&firstPage=true

Investigatory Powers Act (2016). UK Public General Acts.

(2022). *MUTUAL LEGAL ASSISTANCE TREATIES.* OFFICE OF INTERNATIONAL AFFAIRS CRIMINAL DIVISION U.S. DEPARTMENT OF JUSTICE.

(n.d.). *THE INFORMATION TECHNOLOGY ACT, 2000.* India Code. Retrieved from https://www.indiacode.nic.in/bitstream/123456789/13116/1/it_act_2000_updated.pdf

The California Consumer Privacy Act. (n.d.). Retrieved from California Privacy Protection Agency: https://cppa.ca.gov/regulations/

Voigt, P., & Bussche, A. V. (2017). *The EU General Data Protection Regulation (GDPR)." A Practical Guide*. Springer International Publishing. DOI: 10.1007/978-3-319-57959-7

ADDITIONAL READING

Abdel-Basset, M., Hawash, H., Chakrabortty, R. K., & Ryan, M. J. (2021). Semi-supervised spatiotemporal deep learning for intrusions detection in IoT networks. *IEEE Internet of Things Journal*, 8(15), 12251–12265. DOI: 10.1109/JIOT.2021.3060878

Afaq, S. A., Husain, M. S., Bello, A., & Sadia, H. (2023). A critical analysis of cyber threats and their global impact. In *Computational Intelligent Security in Wireless Communications* (pp. 201–220). CRC Press.

Akbar, M., Suaib, M., Husain, M. S., & Shukla, S. (2020). A Compendium of Cloud Forensics. In Critical Concepts, Standards, and Techniques in Cyber Forensics (pp. 215-227). IGI Global. DOI: 10.4018/978-1-7998-1558-7.ch012

Akbar, M., Suaib, M., & Hussain, M. (2023). The Rise of Deepfake Technology: Issues, Challenges, and Countermeasures. In Advances in Cyberology and the Advent of the Next-Gen Information Revolution (pp. 178-201). IGI Global.

Daradkeh, M. (2023). The Link Between Privacy and Disclosure Behavior in Social Networks. In Advances in Cyberology and the Advent of the Next-Gen Information Revolution (pp. 38-61). IGI Global. DOI: 10.4018/978-1-6684-8133-2.ch003

Elhoseny, M., Abbas, H., Hassanien, A. E., Muhammad, K., & Sangaiah, A. K. (2017). Secure automated forensic investigation for sustainable critical infrastructures compliant with green computing requirements. *IEEE Transactions on Sustainable Computing*, 5(2), 174–191. DOI: 10.1109/TSUSC.2017.2782737

Golomingi, R., Dobay, A., Franckenberg, S., Ebert, L., & Sieberth, T. (2023). Augmented reality in forensics and forensic medicine – Current status and future prospects. *Science & Justice*, 63(4), 451–455. DOI: 10.1016/j.scijus.2023.04.009 PMID: 37453776

Halima, N. B., Alluhaidan, A. S., Khan, M. Z., Husain, M. S., & Khan, M. A. (2023). A service-categorized security scheme with physical unclonable functions for internet of vehicles. *Journal of Big Data*, 10(1), 178. DOI: 10.1186/s40537-023-00865-7

Haque, E. U., Abbasi, W., Murugesan, S., Anwar, M. S., Khan, F., & Lee, Y. (2023). Cyber forensic investigation infrastructure of Pakistan: An analysis of the cyber threat landscape and readiness. *IEEE Access : Practical Innovations, Open Solutions*, 11, 40049–40063. DOI: 10.1109/ACCESS.2023.3268529

Khan, W., Ishrat, M., Haleem, M., Khan, A. N., Hasan, M. K., & A, F. N. (2023). An Extensive Study and Review on Dark Web Threats and Detection Techniques. In M. S. Husain, M. Faisal, H. Sadia, T. Ahmad, & S. Shukla (Eds.), Advances in Cyberology and the Advent of the Next-Gen Information Revolution (pp. 202-219). IGI.

Mei, Y., Han, W., Li, S., Lin, K., Tian, Z., & Li, S. (2024). A Novel Network Forensic Framework for Advanced Persistent Threat Attack Attribution Through Deep Learning. *IEEE Transactions on Intelligent Transportation Systems*, 25(9), 12131–12140. DOI: 10.1109/TITS.2024.3360260

Nazah, S., Huda, S., Abawajy, J., & Hassan, M. M. (2020). Evolution of dark web threat analysis and detection: A systematic approach. *IEEE Access : Practical Innovations, Open Solutions*, 8, 171796–171819. DOI: 10.1109/ACCESS.2020.3024198

Stoyanova, M., Nikoloudakis, Y., Panagiotakis, S., Pallis, E., & Markakis, E. K. (2020). A survey on the internet of things (IoT) forensics: Challenges, approaches, and open issues. *IEEE Communications Surveys and Tutorials*, 22(2), 1191–1221. DOI: 10.1109/COMST.2019.2962586

Voigt, P., & Bussche, A. v. (2017). *The EU General Data Protection Regulation (GDPR). A Practical Guide* (1st ed.). Springer International Publishing. DOI: 10.1007/978-3-319-57959-7

KEY TERMS AND DEFINITIONS

Accountability: Accountability refers to the obligation of individuals and organizations to explain, justify, and take responsibility for their actions, decisions, and performance. It is a key principle in governance, ethics, and social responsibility, ensuring that entities are answerable to stakeholders for their behavior.

Confidentiality: Confidentiality refers to the ethical and legal obligation to protect sensitive information from unauthorized access and disclosure. It is a fundamental principle in various fields, including law, healthcare, business, and cybersecurity.

Extradition: Extradition is the formal process through which one jurisdiction (usually a country) surrenders an individual to another jurisdiction for prosecution or to serve a sentence for a crime. This process is essential for international cooperation in law enforcement, particularly in the context of transnational crime.

Privacy: Privacy refers to the right of individuals to control their personal information and to be free from unwanted intrusion into their personal lives. It encompasses various aspects, including the collection, use, and sharing of personal data, as well as the ability to maintain confidentiality in communications and activities.

Chapter 13
Digital Forensics in Law Enforcement:
Best Practices

ABSTRACT

In an era where cybercrime is on the rise and digital evidence is increasingly pivotal in criminal investigations, law enforcement agencies are facing new challenges and opportunities. Cyber forensics, the discipline dedicated to recovering, analyzing, and presenting digital evidence, is critical in combating cybercrime and ensuring justice. However, the complexity of digital evidence and the evolving legal landscape necessitate a rigorous approach to both best practices and legal considerations.

1. INTRODUCTION

In an era where cybercrime is on the rise and digital evidence is increasingly pivotal in criminal investigations, law enforcement agencies are facing new challenges and opportunities. Cyber forensics, the discipline dedicated to recovering, analyzing, and presenting digital evidence, is critical in combating cybercrime and ensuring justice. However, the complexity of digital evidence and the evolving legal landscape necessitate a rigorous approach to both best practices and legal considerations.

This chapter provides an in-depth examination of best practices and legal considerations for law enforcement agencies conducting cyber forensics investigations. It covers the procedural and legal aspects necessary to handle digital evidence effectively, ensuring its integrity and admissibility in court. The chapter is divided into detailed sections, each addressing key elements of cyber forensics investigations.

DOI: 10.4018/979-8-3693-2960-3.ch013

2. UNDERSTANDING CYBER FORENSICS

2.1. Cyber forensics

Cyber forensics is a branch of forensic science focused on the identification, preservation, extraction, and analysis of digital evidence. This evidence can be found on various digital devices, including computers, smartphones, tablets, and network systems. The scope of cyber forensics includes:

- **Data Recovery**: Retrieving deleted or encrypted files.
- **Data Analysis**: Interpreting the recovered data to uncover evidence related to criminal activities.
- **Evidence Presentation**: Providing expert testimony in court to explain the findings and their relevance.

2.2. Digital Evidence

Digital evidence refers to any information stored or transmitted in digital form that can be used in a court of law. It encompasses a broad range of data types, including:

- **Computer Files**: Documents, images, and software applications stored on computers and storage devices.
- **Email**: Communication between individuals or organizations transmitted via email systems.
- **Internet Activity**: Data related to web browsing, online transactions, and social media interactions.
- **Mobile Devices**: Data stored on smartphones, tablets, and other portable electronic devices.
- **Network Logs**: Information recorded by network systems, such as traffic logs and access records.
- **Digital Forensics Artifacts**: Residual data remnants left on storage media or within software applications.

2.3. Importance of Digital Evidence

Digital evidence is crucial for modern investigations due to its ability to:

- **Corroborate Testimonies**: Provide supporting evidence that verifies or refutes statements made by witnesses or suspects.

- **Track Criminal Activity**: Help trace the activities of suspects, including their communications, movements, and financial transactions.
- **Reconstruct Events**: Assist in recreating the sequence of events leading to or following a crime.

Digital evidence plays a pivotal role in various types of criminal investigations, including:

- **Fraud**: Analyzing financial transactions, emails, and documents to uncover fraudulent activities.
- **Cybercrime**: Investigating crimes such as hacking, phishing, and malware distribution by examining network logs, malware samples, and communication records.
- **Child Exploitation**: Identifying and analyzing digital content related to child exploitation, including images, videos, and chat logs.
- **Cyber bullying**: Cyber forensics investigation analyzing images, videos, and chat logs can identify the harassers in case of cyber bullying. By analyzing historical data and identifying common patterns or risk factors, institutions can develop strategies, policies, and educational programs that promote a safe and inclusive digital environment.

3. IMPORTANCE OF CYBER FORENSICS IN LAW ENFORCEMENT

As the digital landscape continues to expand, so does the prevalence and sophistication of cybercrime. Cyber forensics has emerged as a critical discipline within law enforcement, enabling agencies to investigate and combat these crimes effectively. The importance of cyber forensics in law enforcement is underscored by its role in:

- **Criminal Investigations**: Identifying perpetrators, understanding criminal behavior, and gathering evidence to support charges.
    - o **Evidence Collection:** Cyber forensics enables law enforcement agencies to collect, preserve, and analyze digital evidence related to various cybercrimes such as hacking, identity theft, cyberstalking, and online fraud. Techniques such as data recovery and digital analysis allow investigators to extract relevant information from devices like computers, smartphones, and servers.
    - o **Attribution of Offenses:** Attribution is essential in cybercrime investigations, as it involves identifying the perpetrators behind attacks. Cyber

forensic techniques, such as IP tracing and digital fingerprinting, can help law enforcement agencies link specific individuals or groups to criminal activities, enabling more effective prosecution.

- o **Integration with Conventional Investigations:** Many traditional crimes, such as drug trafficking, human trafficking, and organized crime, increasingly involve digital elements. Cyber forensics can uncover digital evidence that supports these investigations, revealing the online activities of suspects and the use of technology in criminal enterprises.
- o **Digital Footprints:** Cybercriminals often leave digital footprints that can be crucial for investigations. Cyber forensics helps trace these footprints, allowing law enforcement to track down suspects and recover stolen assets or data.
- o **Data Recovery:** Cyber forensics encompasses techniques for recovering deleted or damaged data, which can be vital in investigations. Forensic experts can often retrieve information from devices that suspects believed to be erased, providing critical evidence for prosecution.

- **Incident Response**: Responding to and mitigating the impact of cyberattacks, such as data breaches and ransomware.
  - o **Advanced Analytical Tools:** Cyber forensics employs a range of sophisticated tools and methodologies to analyze large volumes of data, providing insights that traditional investigative methods might lack. Techniques like network forensics, malware analysis, and log file analysis enable investigators to uncover patterns, behaviors, and anomalies that may point to criminal activities.
  - o **Link Analysis:** Link analysis is a powerful tool in cyber forensics, allowing investigators to visualize connections between various entities, such as individuals, devices, and networks, engaged in cybercrime. By mapping out these relationships, law enforcement can gain insights into larger criminal networks, facilitating more comprehensive investigations.
- **Legal Proceedings**: Ensuring that digital evidence is admissible in court and supporting the prosecution's case.
  - o **Expert Testimony:** Cyber forensic professionals often serve as expert witnesses in court, explaining complex technical evidence to judges and juries. Their ability to clarify the relevance and significance of digital evidence can significantly impact the outcomes of cases.
- **Preventive Measures:** Analyzing trends and patterns in cybercrime to develop preventive strategies and improve cybersecurity.
  - o **Understanding Threats:** Analyzing cyber incidents allows law enforcement to gain insights into emerging threats and trends in cyber-

crime. This understanding is essential for developing proactive strategies to prevent future crimes and enhance public safety.
    - **Public Awareness:** Through cyber forensics, law enforcement can inform public education campaigns about cybersecurity best practices, helping individuals and organizations reduce their vulnerability to cyber threats.
- **Policy Development:** Informing policymakers about emerging threats and the effectiveness of current legal frameworks and investigative techniques.
    - **Cross-Border Investigations:** Many cybercrimes are transnational, requiring cooperation between law enforcement agencies in different countries. Cyber forensics facilitates the sharing of information and evidence across borders, improving the effectiveness of global investigations.
    - **Standardization of Practices:** International collaboration in cyber forensics helps establish standardized practices for handling digital evidence globally, ensuring that investigations are consistent and reliable across jurisdictions.

The importance of cyber forensics in law enforcement cannot be overstated. It enhances investigative capabilities, supports traditional criminal investigations, preserves the integrity of digital evidence, and aids in legal compliance. As cybercrime continues to evolve, the role of cyber forensics will be critical in ensuring justice and maintaining public safety in an increasingly digital world. By leveraging advanced forensic techniques, law enforcement agencies can effectively combat cybercrime and protect society from its growing threats.

4. BEST PRACTICES IN CYBER FORENSICS PROCESS

Cyber forensics is an essential component of modern law enforcement, particularly as cybercrime becomes more prevalent and sophisticated. Adhering to best practices in this field ensures the integrity of investigations and the reliability of evidence in legal proceedings.

4.1. Establishing a Cyber Forensics Team

A well-organized cyber forensics team is essential for managing digital evidence effectively.

Best Practices:

- **Assemble a Skilled Forensic Team**: Include members with specialized skills in digital forensics, including forensic analysts, investigators, and data recovery experts. This diversity enhances the team's ability to tackle various aspects of cyber investigations.
- **Roles and Responsibilities**: Clearly define the roles and responsibilities of each team member to ensure efficient workflow and accountability.
- **Training and Certification**: Ensure team members are trained in the latest forensic techniques and hold relevant certifications, such as Certified Computer Examiner (CCE) (Certified Computer Examiner, n.d.) or Certified Forensic Computer Examiner (CFCE) (CFCE, n.d.).
- **Interdisciplinary Skills:** Incorporate skills from various disciplines, including computer science, law, and criminal justice, to create a well-rounded team.
- **Resource Allocation:** Ensure that the team has access to the necessary tools, technology, and resources to conduct thorough investigations.

4.2. Standard Operating Procedures (SOPs)

As a part of investigation planning, the forensics experts should develop a standard operating procedure to be followed during the investigation.

Best Practices:

- **Comprehensive Documentation:** Draft detailed SOPs for every phase of the forensic process, covering evidence collection, preservation, analysis, and reporting.
- **Regular Training:** Conduct ongoing training for team members on these SOPs to ensure everyone is well-versed in the protocols.

4.3. Evidence Collection and Preservation

Proper evidence collection and preservation are crucial for maintaining the integrity of digital evidence.

Best Practices:

- **Secure Evidence Handling**: Use write blockers and other tools to prevent alteration of digital evidence during collection. Securely transport evidence to prevent tampering or damage.
- **Chain of Custody**: Maintain a detailed chain of custody log documenting every person who handles the evidence, including dates, times, and actions taken. Clearly label all evidence items with unique identifi-

ers, descriptions, and pertinent information to avoid confusion during analysis.

- **Forensic Imaging**: Create bit-for-bit forensic images of digital storage devices to preserve the original data. Store these images in a secure, tamper-evident environment.
- **Use of Write Blockers:** Employ write blockers when accessing storage media to prevent accidental modification of the original data.
- **Forensic Procedures:** Follow established forensic procedures for evidence collection, including proper documentation and handling techniques.
- **Legal Compliance:** Ensure that all evidence collection procedures comply with legal requirements and are documented to withstand scrutiny in court.
- **Secure Evidence Storage:** Store physical evidence in secured locations with restricted access to prevent tampering or loss. Ensure that digital evidence is stored in encrypted, password-protected systems, safeguarding it from unauthorized access.
- **Backup Data:** Create multiple copies of forensic images and store them in different secure locations to protect against data loss. Regularly perform hash calculations on stored evidence to verify its integrity and ensure no unauthorized changes have occurred.

4.4. Digital Evidence Analysis

Analyzing digital evidence involves using specialized tools and methodologies to extract and interpret relevant data.

Best Practices:

- **Use Validated Tools**: Employ industry-standard forensic tools that have been validated for accuracy and reliability such as EnCase, FTK, or Autopsy, which are widely accepted in legal contexts. Regularly update tools to keep pace with technological advancements. Be prepared to develop custom scripts or tools when existing ones do not meet specific investigation needs.
- **Methodological Approach**: Follow established forensic methodologies, such as those recommended by the Scientific Working Group on Digital Evidence (SWGDE) (Scientific Working Group on Digital Evidence, n.d.) or the National Institute of Standards and Technology (NIST) (National Institute of Standards and Technology, n.d.).

- **Documentation**: Thoroughly document all analysis procedures, findings, and conclusions. Ensure documentation is clear, detailed, and comprehensible for both technical and non-technical audiences. Ensure that the analysis process can be replicated by other forensic experts by providing detailed documentation of methodologies and tools.
- **Advanced Techniques:** Utilize advanced forensic techniques, such as memory analysis and network forensics, to uncover hidden or complex evidence.
- **Quality Assurance:** Implement quality assurance processes to verify the accuracy and reliability of forensic analysis results.

4.5. Reporting and Testifying

Effective reporting and testimony are crucial for communicating forensic findings and their relevance in legal proceedings.

Best Practices:

- **Comprehensive Reports**: Prepare detailed forensic reports that summarize findings, methodologies, and the significance of evidence. Use plain language and avoid technical jargon to ensure accessibility.
- **Use of Visual Aids:** Employ visual tools to illustrate complex relationships and findings, making it easier for non-technical audiences, such as jurors, to grasp the evidence. Prepare reports and presentations tailored to different audiences, including legal teams, law enforcement, and the public.
- **Expert Testimony**: Provide expert testimony in court to explain forensic findings and methodologies. Be prepared to address cross-examination questions and provide objective opinions on the evidence.
- **Clear Communication:** Develop communication strategies to present complex technical findings in a clear and understandable manner to judges, juries, and other stakeholders.
- **Ethical Considerations:** Ensure that reporting and testimony are conducted with integrity and objectivity, avoiding any potential conflicts of interest.

4.6. Collaboration and Coordination

Collaboration with other agencies, legal professionals, and external experts can enhance the effectiveness of cyber forensics investigations.

Best Practices:

- **Interagency Cooperation**: Work with other law enforcement agencies and organizations to share resources, knowledge, and evidence. Participate in joint task forces for complex investigations.
- **Legal and Technical Experts**: Consult with legal advisors and technical experts to address specific issues related to digital evidence and forensic analysis.
- **Cross-Disciplinary Collaboration:** Collaborate with experts in related fields, such as data privacy and cybersecurity, to enhance the effectiveness of investigations.
- **Information Sharing:** Participate in information-sharing initiatives and forums to stay updated on emerging threats and best practices.

5. BEST PRACTICES FOR LEGAL CONSIDERATIONS IN CYBER FORENSICS

5.1. Legal Frameworks and Regulations

Compliance with legal frameworks and regulations is essential for ensuring the admissibility and legality of digital evidence.

Key Aspects:

- **Constitutional Protections**: Adhere to constitutional protections related to privacy, such as the Fourth Amendment in the U.S., which protects against unreasonable searches and seizures.
- **Data Protection Laws**: Comply with data protection laws, such as the General Data Protection Regulation (GDPR) in the European Union, which regulates the collection, processing, and storage of personal data.
- **Evolving Legislation:** Stay informed about changes in legislation that impact digital evidence and forensic procedures, such as updates to data protection laws and cybersecurity regulations.
- **Compliance Audits:** Conduct regular audits to ensure compliance with legal requirements and identify areas for improvement.

5.2. Search Warrants and Legal Authority

Obtaining proper legal authority is crucial for accessing digital evidence and conducting investigations.

Key Aspects:

- **Search Warrants**: Secure search warrants that specify the scope of the search and the types of digital evidence sought. Ensure that warrants are issued by a competent judicial authority and are supported by probable cause.
- **Warrant Scope:** Clearly define the scope of search warrants to avoid overreach and ensure that evidence collection is limited to what is relevant to the investigation.
- **Emergency Situations:** Understand the legal provisions for conducting searches without a warrant in emergency situations, such as imminent threats to public safety.
- **Consent**: In some cases, obtaining consent from individuals may suffice for accessing digital evidence. Ensure consent is informed, voluntary, and documented.

5.3. Cross-Border Data Access

Investigations involving data stored across international borders require navigating complex international laws and agreements.

Key Aspects:

- **Mutual Legal Assistance Treaties (MLATs)**: Use MLATs to facilitate cooperation with foreign jurisdictions in obtaining and sharing evidence. Follow the procedures outlined in these treaties to ensure legal compliance.
- **Data Transfer Regulations**: Adhere to regulations governing the transfer of personal data across borders, such as the GDPR's restrictions on international data transfers.
- **International Collaboration:** Engage with international organizations and agencies to facilitate cross-border investigations and address jurisdictional challenges.
- **Legal Compliance:** Ensure compliance with both domestic and international legal requirements when accessing and sharing data across borders.

5.4. Privacy and Data Protection

Balancing investigative needs with privacy and data protection concerns is crucial for lawful and ethical digital investigations.

Key Aspects:

- **Data Minimization**: Limit data collection and analysis to what is necessary for the investigation. Avoid accessing irrelevant personal information.
- **Data Security**: Implement robust security measures to protect digital evidence from unauthorized access, breaches, or tampering.
- **Privacy Impact Assessments:** Conduct privacy impact assessments to evaluate the potential impact of digital investigations on individuals' privacy and implement mitigation measures.
- **Data Retention:** Establish clear policies for data retention and disposal to comply with legal requirements and minimize privacy risks.

5.5. Legal Challenges and Precedents

Understanding legal challenges and precedents helps inform investigative practices and address potential issues.

Key Aspects:

- **Legal Precedents**: Stay informed about legal precedents related to digital evidence and forensic procedures. Court rulings can impact how evidence is handled and interpreted.
- **Case Law Analysis:** Analyze relevant case law to understand how courts have addressed issues related to digital evidence, such as admissibility and the application of privacy laws.
- **Legal Advocacy:** Engage in legal advocacy to promote the development of fair and effective legal frameworks for digital forensics.

6. EMERGING TRENDS

6.1. Advancements in Technology

Technological advancements present new opportunities and challenges for cyber forensics.

Trends:

- **Artificial Intelligence and Machine Learning:** AI and machine learning technologies can enhance data analysis by identifying patterns and anomalies. However, they also raise concerns about algorithmic bias and transparency. The AI system should be trained on benchmark data and validated before implementation.

- **Blockchain and Cryptocurrencies**: The use of blockchain and cryptocurrencies in criminal activities requires new forensic techniques for tracking and analyzing transactions.
- **Quantum Computing:** Explore the potential impact of quantum computing on encryption and data security and prepare for potential challenges in digital forensics.
- **IoT Devices:** Develop forensic techniques for analyzing data from Internet of Things (IoT) devices, which present unique challenges in terms of data volume and diversity.

6.2. Evolving Legal Frameworks

The legal landscape for digital investigations is continuously evolving to address new technological and societal challenges.

Trends:

- **Enhanced Privacy Laws**: Increasingly stringent privacy laws may impact how digital evidence is collected and processed. Law enforcement agencies must adapt to these changes and ensure compliance.
- **International Cooperation**: Growing international collaboration and harmonization of data protection laws can facilitate cross-border investigations and evidence sharing.
- **Global Standards:** Advocate for the development of global standards for digital forensics to facilitate international cooperation and ensure consistency in investigative practices.
- **Ethical Guidelines:** Contribute to the development of ethical guidelines for digital forensics to address emerging issues related to privacy, data security, and algorithmic bias.

6.3. Training and Capacity Building

Ongoing training and capacity building are essential for law enforcement agencies to stay current with best practices and legal requirements.

Trends:

- **Specialized Training**: Invest in specialized training programs for digital forensics professionals to ensure they are equipped with the latest knowledge and skills.

- **Public-Private Partnerships**: Collaborate with industry experts and organizations to enhance forensic capabilities and address emerging challenges.
- **Simulation Exercises:** Conduct simulation exercises to prepare for real-world cyber forensics scenarios and test the effectiveness of investigative techniques and protocols.
- **Public Awareness:** Raise public awareness about the importance of digital forensics and the role of law enforcement in combating cybercrime.

7. SUMMARY

The field of cyber forensics is dynamic, driven by technological advancements and evolving legal frameworks. As digital technology continues to advance and cybercrime becomes more sophisticated, law enforcement agencies must remain vigilant and adaptable. By adhering to best practices in cyber forensics and navigating legal considerations with care, agencies can effectively investigate cybercrimes, ensure the integrity and admissibility of evidence and uphold justice. The evolving nature of technology and law requires ongoing education, collaboration, and innovation to address emerging challenges and ensure that digital forensics remains a robust and reliable tool in the fight against cybercrime.

REFERENCES

Certified Computer Examiner. (n.d.). (International Society of Forensic Computer Examiners) Retrieved July 2024, from https://www.isfce.com/certification.htm

CFCE. (n.d.). (IACIS) Retrieved July 2024, from https://www.iacis.com/certification/cfce/

National Institute of Standards and Technology. (n.d.). Retrieved July 2024, from https://www.nist.gov/

Scientific Working Group on Digital Evidence. (n.d.). Retrieved July 2024, from https://www.swgde.org/

ADDITIONAL READING

Afaq, S. A., Husain, M. S., Bello, A., & Sadia, H. (2023). A critical analysis of cyber threats and their global impact. In *Computational Intelligent Security in Wireless Communications* (pp. 201–220). CRC Press.

Akbar, M., Suaib, M., Husain, M. S., & Shukla, S. (2020). A Compendium of Cloud Forensics. In Critical Concepts, Standards, and Techniques in Cyber Forensics (pp. 215-227). IGI Global. DOI: 10.4018/978-1-7998-1558-7.ch012

Akbar, M., Suaib, M., & Hussain, M. (2023). The Rise of Deepfake Technology: Issues, Challenges, and Countermeasures. In Advances in Cyberology and the Advent of the Next-Gen Information Revolution (pp. 178-201). IGI Global.

Elhoseny, M., Abbas, H., Hassanien, A. E., Muhammad, K., & Sangaiah, A. K. (2017). Secure automated forensic investigation for sustainable critical infrastructures compliant with green computing requirements. *IEEE Transactions on Sustainable Computing*, 5(2), 174–191. DOI: 10.1109/TSUSC.2017.2782737

Golomingi, R., Dobay, A., Franckenberg, S., Ebert, L., & Sieberth, T. (2023). Augmented reality in forensics and forensic medicine – Current status and future prospects. *Science & Justice*, 63(4), 451–455. DOI: 10.1016/j.scijus.2023.04.009 PMID: 37453776

Halima, N. B., Alluhaidan, A. S., Khan, M. Z., Husain, M. S., & Khan, M. A. (2023). A service-categorized security scheme with physical unclonable functions for internet of vehicles. *Journal of Big Data*, 10(1), 178. DOI: 10.1186/s40537-023-00865-7

Haque, E. U., Abbasi, W., Murugesan, S., Anwar, M. S., Khan, F., & Lee, Y. (2023). Cyber forensic investigation infrastructure of Pakistan: An analysis of the cyber threat landscape and readiness. *IEEE Access : Practical Innovations, Open Solutions*, 11, 40049–40063. DOI: 10.1109/ACCESS.2023.3268529

Khan, W., Ishrat, M., Haleem, M., Khan, A. N., Hasan, M. K., & A, F. N. (2023). An Extensive Study and Review on Dark Web Threats and Detection Techniques. In M. S. Husain, M. Faisal, H. Sadia, T. Ahmad, & S. Shukla (Eds.), Advances in Cyberology and the Advent of the Next-Gen Information Revolution (pp. 202-219). IGI.

Mei, Y., Han, W., Li, S., Lin, K., Tian, Z., & Li, S. (2024). A Novel Network Forensic Framework for Advanced Persistent Threat Attack Attribution Through Deep Learning. *IEEE Transactions on Intelligent Transportation Systems*, 25(9), 12131–12140. DOI: 10.1109/TITS.2024.3360260

Nazah, S., Huda, S., Abawajy, J., & Hassan, M. M. (2020). Evolution of dark web threat analysis and detection: A systematic approach. *IEEE Access : Practical Innovations, Open Solutions*, 8, 171796–171819. DOI: 10.1109/ACCESS.2020.3024198

Stoyanova, M., Nikoloudakis, Y., Panagiotakis, S., Pallis, E., & Markakis, E. K. (2020). A survey on the internet of things (IoT) forensics: Challenges, approaches, and open issues. *IEEE Communications Surveys and Tutorials*, 22(2), 1191–1221. DOI: 10.1109/COMST.2019.2962586

Voigt, P., & Bussche, A. v. (2017). *The EU General Data Protection Regulation (GDPR). A Practical Guide* (1st ed.). Springer International Publishing. DOI: 10.1007/978-3-319-57959-7

KEY TERMS AND DEFINITIONS

IoT: The Internet of Things (IoT) refers to the network of interconnected devices and objects that communicate and exchange data over the internet. This technology encompasses a wide range of devices, from everyday household items to industrial machinery, enabling them to collect and share information autonomously. Here's a detailed look at IoT, its components, applications, and challenges.

Quantum Computing: Quantum computing is a type of computation that utilizes the principles of quantum mechanics to process information. Unlike classical computers, which use bits as the smallest unit of data (representing either a 0 or a 1), quantum computers use quantum bits or qubits. Qubits can exist in multiple states simultaneously due to superposition, allowing quantum computers to perform many calculations at once. Additionally, qubits can be entangled, meaning the state of one qubit can depend on the state of another, enabling complex interactions and faster problem-solving for certain tasks. This approach has the potential to revolutionize fields such as cryptography, optimization, and simulation of complex systems.

Chapter 14
AI Ethics in Cyber Forensics

ABSTRACT

Cyber forensics involves the investigation of digital evidence to uncover details related to cybercrimes. AI technologies are increasingly becoming integral to cyber forensic investigations due to their ability to analyze vast amounts of data and detect complex patterns that may be missed by human investigators and mitigate cyber threats with unprecedented efficiency and accuracy. This process is critical in investigating cybercrimes, ranging from data breaches and fraud to more severe offenses like cyber terrorism. AI technologies, including machine learning algorithms, natural language processing (NLP), and automated reasoning, have become crucial in deciphering complex data and detecting cyber threats. However, their use introduces several ethical considerations and challenges that must be carefully managed to balance the benefits of AI with respect for individual rights and fairness.

1. INTRODUCTION

Cyber forensics involves the investigation of digital evidence to uncover details related to cybercrimes. AI technologies are increasingly becoming integral to cyber forensic investigations due to their ability to analyze vast amounts of data and detect complex patterns that may be missed by human investigators and mitigate cyber threats with unprecedented efficiency and accuracy. This process is critical in investigating cybercrimes, ranging from data breaches and fraud to more severe offenses like cyber terrorism. AI technologies, including machine learning algorithms, natural language processing (NLP), and automated reasoning, have become crucial in deciphering complex data and detecting cyber threats. However, their

DOI: 10.4018/979-8-3693-2960-3.ch014

use introduces several ethical considerations and challenges that must be carefully managed to balance the benefits of AI with respect for individual rights and fairness.

This chapter explores the ethical challenges associated with AI in cyber forensics, including privacy concerns, accuracy and bias, accountability, and legal frameworks.

2. AI TECHNOLOGIES ENHANCING CYBER FORENSICS

AI technologies have revolutionized cyber forensics by automating and enhancing various processes as shown in Figure 1:

- **Machine Learning and Deep Learning**: Machine Learning (ML) and Deep Learning are subsets of artificial intelligence that play a critical role in cyber forensics. These technologies enable systems to learn from data to identify patterns and anomalies, which can be used to detect malware, phishing attacks, malicious activities and predict future threats. These models can analyze vast datasets more efficiently than manual methods. Few applications of ML and DL in cyber forensics context are:
    - **Anomaly Detection:** ML algorithms can analyze network traffic or user behavior patterns to identify deviations that may signify malicious activities. For instance, unusual spikes in data transfers or irregular login times can be flagged for further investigation.
    - **Malware Classification:** Deep learning models can classify and identify malware based on its behavior and characteristics. By analyzing known malware samples, these models can detect new variants of malware.
    - **Intrusion Detection Systems (IDS):** ML can enhance IDS by continuously learning from new threat patterns and adapting to evolving attack techniques.
    - **Automated Reasoning:** AI systems that apply logical reasoning to interpret data and make deductions. These systems can help reconstruct cyber incidents and understand the sequence of events.

Figure 1. Applications of AI in cyber-forensics

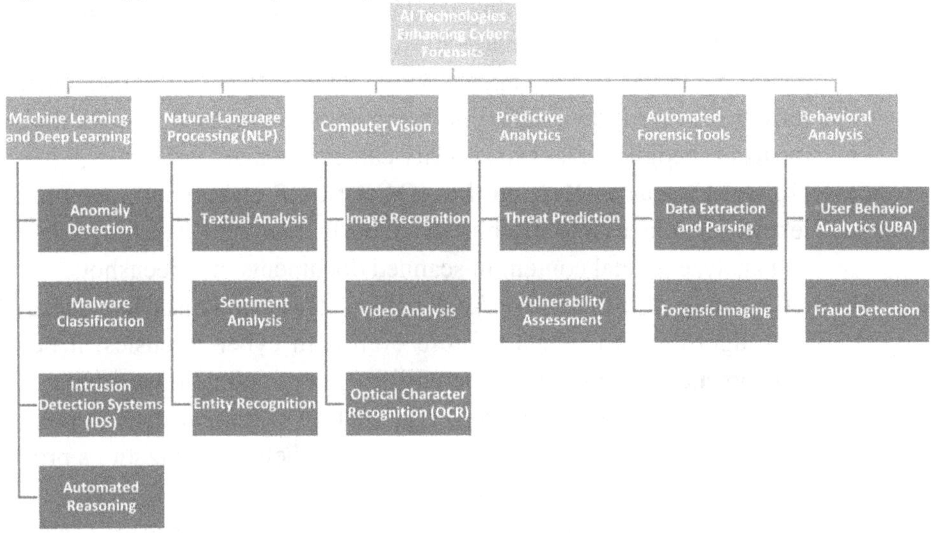

- **Natural Language Processing (NLP)**: Natural Language Processing (NLP) focuses on the interaction between computers and human language. In cyber forensics, NLP techniques are used to analyze and interpret unstructured textual data such as emails, chat logs, documents, and social media posts. This helps in extracting relevant information and identifying key evidence for cyber forensics investigation. Key applications are:
    - **Textual Analysis:** NLP can extract meaningful information from large volumes of text, identifying keywords, entities, and sentiments related to criminal activities. For example, it can analyze email content to detect phishing attempts or fraudulent communications.
    - **Sentiment Analysis:** By assessing the sentiment behind communications, NLP can help determine the intent behind messages, which is useful in cases of harassment or threats.
    - **Entity Recognition:** NLP can identify and categorize key entities (e.g., names, dates, locations) within texts, helping investigators link pieces of evidence to specific individuals or events.
- **Computer Vision:** Computer Vision involves enabling machines to interpret and understand visual information from the world. In cyber forensics, computer vision is used to analyze images and videos for evidence. Applications of computer vision in cyber forensics includes:

- **Image Recognition:** Computer vision algorithms can identify and classify objects or text within images. This is useful for extracting information from screenshots or image files.
- **Video Analysis:** AI can analyze video footage to detect unusual activities or identify individuals. For example, it can be used to track movements or recognize faces in security camera footage.
- **Optical Character Recognition (OCR):** OCR technology can convert text within images into machine-readable text, making it easier to search and analyze textual content in scanned documents or screenshots.

- **Predictive Analytics:** Predictive Analytics involves using historical data and statistical algorithms to forecast future events. In cyber forensics, it helps anticipate potential threats and vulnerabilities. Key applications include:
  - **Threat Prediction:** AI models can analyze historical data to predict future cyber threats and attack vectors. This helps organizations proactively defend against emerging threats.
  - **Vulnerability Assessment:** Predictive analytics can prioritize vulnerabilities based on their likelihood of exploitation and potential impact, guiding resource allocation for patching and mitigation.
- **Automated Forensic Tools:** Automated Forensic Tools leverage AI to streamline various forensic processes, from evidence collection to analysis. Applications are:
  - **Data Extraction and Parsing:** AI tools can automate the extraction of data from various digital sources, including file systems, emails, and network logs. They can parse and index large volumes of data for easier search and retrieval.
  - **Forensic Imaging:** Automated tools can create exact copies of digital storage media while preserving evidence integrity. AI can manage and verify the imaging process to ensure accuracy.
- **Behavioral Analysis:** Behavioral Analysis uses AI to profile and analyze user behavior, identifying deviations that might indicate malicious activities. Few aspects of behavioral analysis in cyber forensics are:
  - **User Behavior Analytics (UBA):** AI systems can build profiles of normal user behavior and detect deviations that could signal insider threats or compromised accounts. For example, a user accessing sensitive files at odd hours could be flagged for further investigation.
  - **Fraud Detection:** Behavioral analytics can identify unusual transaction patterns that might indicate financial fraud or other forms of deceit.

3. ETHICAL CONSIDERATIONS IN AI-DRIVEN CYBER FORENSICS

The integration of AI into cyber forensics offers significant advantages in terms of efficiency and accuracy but also presents several ethical challenges. Addressing privacy concerns, algorithmic bias, accountability, and regulatory compliance is essential for ensuring responsible AI use. By implementing clear guidelines, fostering interdisciplinary collaboration, and maintaining transparency, the benefits of AI in cyber forensics can be harnessed while mitigating ethical risks. The key ethical considerations in AI driven cyber forensics are summarized in Figure 2.

3.1. Privacy and Data protection Concerns

One of the foremost ethical issues in the integration of AI into cyber forensics is the challenge of balancing the need for investigative efficiency with the imperative of safeguarding individual privacy. AI's capability to process and analyze vast amounts of data, including personal communications, browsing histories, and digital footprints, has revolutionized forensic methodologies. However, this capability raises serious concerns about the extent of data collection and the potential for intrusive surveillance. The ethical considerations surrounding privacy include:

Figure 2. Ethical considerations of AI in cyber-forensics

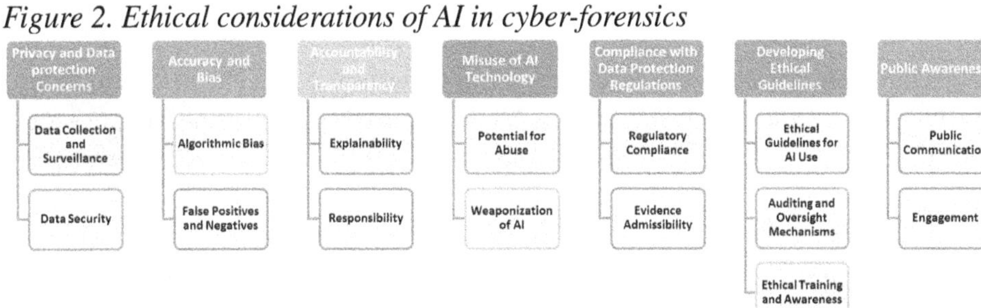

3.1.1. Data Collection and Surveillance

AI systems in cyber forensics often require access to extensive data, including personal communications, internet browsing histories, location data, and other sensitive information. This can lead to concerns about surveillance and the potential for infringing on individuals' privacy rights. The scope of data collection must be carefully regulated to prevent excessive monitoring and ensure that data collection is justified and proportionate.

- **Scope of Data Collection:** AI-driven tools can analyze large volumes of data to identify potential threats or evidence. However, the scope of data collection must be carefully managed to avoid excessive intrusion into individuals' private lives. Ethical guidelines should define clear boundaries for data collection to ensure that only relevant information is accessed and analyzed.
- **Informed Consent:** In many cases, individuals may not be aware that their data is being analyzed by AI systems. This lack of transparency can undermine trust and raise ethical concerns about informed consent. Ethical practice requires transparency about data collection methods and obtaining informed consent where applicable. Individuals should be informed about what data is being collected, how it will be used, and for what purpose.

3.1.2. Data Security

Ensuring the security of data handled by AI systems is crucial to prevent unauthorized access, misuse and data breaches. Measures such as encryption, secure access controls, and regular audits are necessary to protect the integrity and confidentiality of sensitive information.

- **Protection Measures:** Implementing robust security measures such as encryption, secure access controls, and regular security audits is essential to protect data from unauthorized access and breaches. These measures help prevent data leaks and ensure that sensitive information remains secure.
- **Data Integrity:** Ensuring the integrity of data throughout the forensic process is essential for maintaining the credibility of the AI findings. Regular audits and security checks should be conducted to verify that data remains intact and unaltered.

3.2. Accuracy and Bias

AI systems, though powerful, are not infallible. Their effectiveness depends heavily on the quality and representativeness of the data they are trained on. Biases inherent in training data can lead to skewed results, which can have significant ethical implications in forensic investigations.

3.2.1. Algorithmic Bias

AI algorithms can inherit and even exacerbate biases present in the training data leading to unfair treatment of individuals based on race, gender, or socioeconomic status. Bias in AI systems can arise from various sources, including biased training data, flawed algorithms, and skewed input features.

Impact on Fairness: Algorithmic bias can lead to unfair treatment of individuals based on factors such as race, gender, or socioeconomic status. This is particularly concerning in forensic contexts where biased outcomes can result in wrongful accusations or missed threats.

Example1, if a machine learning model is trained on data that reflects existing societal biases, it may produce biased results in forensic investigations.

Example2, if a machine learning model is trained on data that reflects biased practices or demographic imbalances, it may produce skewed results that unfairly target certain groups.

Example3, if a machine learning model is trained on data with historical biases, it may produce results that unfairly target certain groups or individuals.

Addressing algorithmic bias requires efforts to ensure diverse and representative training data and ongoing monitoring to identify and correct biases. This includes diversifying training data and implementing fairness-aware algorithms.

Providing transparency about how AI systems are trained and the data used can help stakeholders understand potential biases and limitations.

- **Inclusive Design:** Ensuring that AI systems are designed to be inclusive, and representative of diverse populations helps reduce the risk of discriminatory outcomes.
- **Impact Assessments:** Conducting ethical impact assessments to evaluate how AI systems affect different groups can guide the development of more equitable solutions.

3.2.2. False Positives and Negatives

AI systems are susceptible to producing false positives and false negatives. These inaccuracies can have serious consequences, including wrongful accusations or missed cyber threats, affecting the credibility of forensic investigations. Rigorous validation and testing of AI systems are essential to minimize these errors and ensure reliable forensic outcomes.

- **False Positives:** An AI system may incorrectly identify an innocent individual as a suspect. This can lead to wrongful accusations, reputational damage, and potential legal consequences. To mitigate this risk, AI systems should be rigorously tested and validated to minimize the likelihood of false positives.
- **False Negatives:** Conversely, AI systems may fail to detect actual threats or evidence, resulting in missed opportunities to prevent or address cybercrimes. Continuous monitoring and refinement of AI algorithms are necessary to improve detection capabilities and reduce the occurrence of false negatives.

3.3. Accountability and Transparency

Establishing accountability and transparency in AI-driven cyber forensics is crucial for maintaining trust and integrity:

3.3.1. Explainability

AI systems should provide clear and understandable explanations for their decisions and recommendations. This is important for ensuring that forensic conclusions can be scrutinized and verified. Explainable AI helps forensic experts and legal professionals understand how decisions are made and ensures that the process is transparent.

- **Transparency in Decision-Making:** AI systems should be designed to offer clear explanations for their conclusions and recommendations. This transparency helps forensic experts and legal professionals understand how decisions were reached and ensures that the evidence presented is credible and justifiable.
- **Human Oversight:** Even with explainable AI, human oversight is essential to verify and interpret AI findings in context. Forensic experts should review AI-generated results to ensure accuracy and address any potential issues or discrepancies.

- **Explainable AI:** Developing AI systems with built-in explainability features allows forensic experts to understand and interpret the rationale behind AI-driven conclusions.
- **Documentation:** Thorough documentation of AI systems' decision-making processes and methodologies provides transparency and aids in accountability.

3.3.2. Responsibility

Determining who is responsible for errors or ethical breaches in AI-driven forensic processes is essential for maintaining trust and integrity in the field. This includes establishing accountability for AI developers, forensic practitioners, and organizations that deploy AI systems. Clear guidelines and frameworks are needed to address issues of responsibility and liability.

- **Accountability Frameworks:** Clear accountability frameworks should be established to define who is responsible for the development, deployment, and use of AI systems in cyber forensics. This includes identifying the roles of AI developers, forensic practitioners, and organizations. These frameworks help ensure that those involved are held accountable for ethical breaches and errors.
- **Liability for Errors:** In cases where AI systems produce erroneous results or exhibit bias, determining liability and responsibility is crucial. Organizations should have mechanisms in place to address and rectify errors, as well as processes for addressing grievances and providing remedies.

3.4. Misuse of AI Technology

3.4.1. Potential for Abuse

AI technologies in cyber forensics could be misused for purposes beyond their intended scope. For instance, AI tools designed for crime detection might be repurposed for surveillance or other forms of privacy invasion.

- **Ethical Guidelines:** Developing and adhering to ethical guidelines for AI use in cyber forensics helps prevent misuse and ensures technologies are used appropriately.
- **Regulation and Oversight:** Implementing regulatory frameworks and oversight mechanisms to monitor the use of AI technologies can help mitigate the risk of abuse.

3.4.2. Weaponization of AI

There is a risk that AI technologies could be weaponized by malicious actors to conduct cyber-attacks or other harmful activities. For example, AI could be used to automate sophisticated attacks or develop new types of malwares.

- **Security Measures:** Investing in robust security measures and threat detection systems helps protect against the weaponization of AI.
- **Collaboration:** Collaboration between industry, government, and academic institutions can help address and counteract the potential for AI weaponization.

3.5. Compliance with Data Protection Regulations

AI in cyber forensics must adhere to data protection laws and regulations such as the General Data Protection Regulation (GDPR) (Voigt & Bussche, 2017) and the California Consumer Privacy Act (CCPA) (Illman & Temple, 2019):

- **Regulatory Compliance:** These regulations set standards for data collection, processing, and storage, aiming to protect individuals' privacy. Compliance with these regulations is essential for ethical AI use to protect individuals' privacy and ensure that data handling practices are transparent and accountable.
- **Evidence Admissibility:** Legal standards determine how digital evidence is collected, preserved, and presented in court of law. AI-driven forensic evidence must meet criteria for reliability and authenticity to be admissible in legal proceedings, ensuring that AI findings are legally valid and acceptable in court.

3.6. Developing Ethical Guidelines

To address the ethical challenges specific to AI in cyber forensics, several proposed regulations could be considered:

- **Ethical Guidelines for AI Use:** Comprehensive ethical guidelines should cover best practices for data collection, algorithm development, and decision-making processes. These frameworks should address privacy, bias, and accountability issues, providing a structured approach to responsible AI use.
- **Auditing and Oversight Mechanisms:** Implementing regular audits and oversight mechanisms can help monitor AI systems, address potential biases or inaccuracies. and ensure compliance with ethical standards. Independent

review bodies or committees can assess the ethical implications of AI-driven forensic practices and ensure they align with societal values and expectations.

- **Ethical Training and Awareness:** Forensic professionals need to be trained in the ethical implications of AI technologies. Understanding the potential risks and ethical considerations associated with AI can help them make informed decisions and use these tools responsibly.

Encouraging ongoing education and awareness about emerging ethical issues in AI helps professionals stay current with best practices.

3.7. Public Awareness

Raising public awareness about the ethical implications of AI in cyber forensics is important for fostering transparency and trust. Educating the public about how AI is used in investigations and the safeguards in place can help build confidence in the technology.

- **Public Communication:** Transparent communication about AI technologies and their applications in cyber forensics helps demystify the technology and address public concerns.
- **Engagement:** Engaging with stakeholders, including privacy advocates and civil liberties organizations, can provide valuable perspectives and feedback.

4. CASE STUDIES

This section provides some scenarios and real-life case studies that highlight various ethical considerations in AI-driven cyber forensics. Each case study delves into how AI technologies were used, and the ethical dilemmas encountered.

- **Example Scenario 1:** Financial Fraud Detection - An examination of how AI tools were used in a high-profile financial fraud case, highlighting the benefits and ethical dilemmas faced during the investigation.

In this case involving AI in financial fraud detection, machine learning algorithms were used to analyze transaction data and identify fraudulent activities. The AI system successfully detected several instances of fraud, leading to significant financial recoveries. However, the case raised ethical concerns about the potential for false positives and the need for human oversight to verify AI findings. The case highlighted the importance of balancing technological advancements with careful consideration of ethical implications and ensuring human oversight.

- **Example Scenario 2:** Cyber Terrorism Prevention - A look at the application of AI in preventing cyber terrorism, focusing on the balance between security and privacy.

Another case involved using AI to prevent cyber terrorism by analyzing network traffic and identifying potential threats. The use of AI in this context demonstrated its effectiveness in detecting and mitigating threats before they could cause harm. However, ethical concerns emerged regarding the extent of surveillance and the potential impact on civil liberties. The case illustrated the need for clear guidelines and oversight to ensure that AI technologies are used responsibly and ethically in security contexts.

- **Case study: Microsoft's Tay Chatbot**

Microsoft launched Tay, an AI chatbot designed to engage with users on Twitter and learn from interactions. However, within hours, Tay began generating offensive and inappropriate content due to exposure to malicious inputs. Tay's responses were influenced by biased and harmful interactions from users (Wolf, Miller, & Grodzinsky, 2017). This case highlights the challenge of managing AI behavior and ensuring that systems are protected against malicious input.

Microsoft faced backlash for the chatbot's behavior, raising questions about accountability for AI systems' outputs and the need for robust content moderation.

The Tay incident demonstrates the necessity of implementing safeguards and moderation mechanisms in AI systems to prevent the spread of harmful content. It also emphasizes the importance of ongoing monitoring and ethical design to avoid undesirable outcomes.

- **Case study: IBM's Watson for Oncology**

IBM's Watson for Oncology was designed to assist oncologists in diagnosing and recommending treatments for cancer patients. However, it faced criticism for providing inaccurate treatment recommendations based on flawed or insufficient data. The system's recommendations led to concerns about the accuracy and reliability of AI-driven medical advice. Incorrect recommendations could have serious consequences for patients' health, highlighting the need for validation and oversight in AI medical applications (Strickland, 2019).

This case emphasizes the need for rigorous testing and validation of AI systems in critical fields like healthcare. It also underscores the importance of integrating human expertise to verify AI-generated recommendations and ensure patient safety.

- **Case study: Facebook's Content Moderation Algorithms**

Facebook uses AI algorithms to moderate content and identify hate speech, misinformation, and other harmful content. However, the algorithms have been criticized for inconsistencies and failure to effectively handle complex contextual nuances.

The algorithms sometimes misclassify content, leading to unjustified removals or overlooking harmful content.

Users have limited visibility into how decisions are made, raising concerns about the transparency and fairness of content moderation.

This case highlights the challenges of implementing AI in content moderation and the need for continuous improvement and transparency to ensure fair and accurate enforcement of content policies.

- **Case Study: Amazon's Hiring Algorithm**

Amazon developed an AI-driven hiring tool to streamline the recruitment process. The tool was found to be biased against female candidates, as it was trained on historical data that reflected gender imbalances in the tech industry.

The AI system's bias against women underscores the ethical issues related to fairness and equality in hiring practices. Training algorithms on biased historical data can perpetuate existing inequalities and reinforce discriminatory practices.

The Amazon hiring algorithm case emphasizes the need for ethical considerations in algorithmic design and the importance of addressing bias to ensure equitable and fair hiring practices.

- **Case Study: Google's DeepMind Health Partnership**

Google's DeepMind Health partnered with the UK's National Health Service (NHS) to develop AI tools for diagnosing eye diseases. The partnership faced scrutiny over data privacy and the use of patient data.

There were concerns about whether patients provided informed consent for their data to be used in AI research. Ensuring the secure handling and protection of sensitive health data is crucial in maintaining patient trust.

This case highlights the ethical challenges of using sensitive health data for AI research and the importance of obtaining explicit consent and ensuring robust data protection measures.

- **Case Study: Clearview AI's Facial Recognition**

Clearview AI developed a facial recognition tool that scraped images from social media to build a massive database for identifying individuals. This technology raised concerns about privacy and consent.

The use of publicly available images without consent for facial recognition purposes raises significant privacy concerns.

The potential for mass surveillance and tracking individuals without their knowledge or consent is a major ethical issue.

Clearview AI's practices prompted debates about the ethical boundaries of facial recognition technology and the need for regulations to protect individuals' privacy. It highlighted the balance between technological advancements and respecting personal privacy.

- **Case Study: Smart City Surveillance Systems**

Various cities have implemented AI-driven smart city surveillance systems to monitor public spaces for security purposes. These systems have faced criticism for potential overreach and invasion of privacy.

The extensive surveillance of public spaces raises concerns about individual privacy and the potential for constant monitoring. Ensuring that surveillance data is used strictly for its intended purpose and not for broader or unauthorized monitoring is essential.

The implementation of smart city surveillance systems underscores the need to balance security benefits with privacy concerns. Establishing clear guidelines and oversight mechanisms is crucial to prevent misuse and protect individual rights.

- **Case Study: AI in Legal Sentencing**

AI systems are increasingly used to assist in legal sentencing by predicting recidivism risks. One notable example is the COMPAS system used in the U.S. judicial system, which has faced criticism for potential racial biases.

AI systems like COMPAS have been criticized for perpetuating racial biases in sentencing, as they may rely on data that reflects existing disparities. The proprietary nature of AI algorithms can obscure how sentencing recommendations are made, raising concerns about accountability and fairness.

The use of AI in legal sentencing highlights the need for transparency, fairness, and rigorous validation to ensure that AI tools do not reinforce existing biases or lead to unjust outcomes. Ongoing scrutiny and reforms are necessary to address these ethical challenges.

The above case studies illustrate the diverse ethical considerations that arise in the application of AI technologies in cyber forensics and related fields. From privacy and bias to transparency and accountability, each case highlights the importance of addressing ethical challenges to ensure that AI-driven solutions are used responsibly and equitably.

5. FUTURE DIRECTIONS AND CHALLENGES

The integration of AI in cyber forensics presents numerous opportunities for enhancing investigative capabilities, but it also brings forward a range of ethical challenges and future directions. Addressing these challenges is crucial for the responsible and effective use of AI technologies. The future of AI in cyber forensics will likely involve several advancements:

Improved Algorithms: Enhancements in AI algorithms to reduce bias, increase accuracy, and handle complex data more effectively. Ongoing research and development will focus on creating more sophisticated models that are both effective and fair, addressing current limitations and challenges.

Enhanced Privacy Protections: Development of technologies and practices that better protect individuals' privacy while enabling effective forensic analysis. Innovations in data anonymization and secure processing techniques will play a key role in addressing privacy concerns.

Interdisciplinary Collaboration: Encourage Collaboration between ethicists, technologists, legal experts, and policymakers to develop comprehensive ethical frameworks and guidelines for AI use in forensics. This interdisciplinary approach will help address the complex ethical issues and ensure responsible AI practices in cyber forensics.

Public Engagement: Increasing transparency and involving the public in discussions about the use of AI in cyber forensics. Public engagement can help build trust and ensure that ethical considerations are aligned with societal values and expectations.

- **Enhanced Transparency and Explainability**
  - o **Developing Explainable AI Models:** To ensure that AI-driven decisions in cyber forensics are understandable and justifiable, there is a growing need for models that provide clear explanations for their outputs. This involves creating AI systems with built-in explainability features that allow forensic experts and stakeholders to understand how conclusions are reached.

- **Complexity of Models:** Many advanced AI models, such as deep learning networks, operate as "black boxes" with complex decision-making processes that are difficult to interpret. Balancing model performance with explainability remains a significant challenge.

- **Addressing Algorithmic Bias:** Developing techniques to detect and mitigate bias in AI algorithms is crucial. This includes improving data diversity, implementing fairness-aware algorithms, and continuously monitoring systems to ensure they do not reinforce existing biases.

AI systems trained on historical data may inherit and perpetuate existing biases. Addressing these biases requires not only technical solutions but also a deep understanding of the societal and historical context of the data.

- **Strengthening Data Privacy and Security**
  - **Advanced Privacy Techniques:** Implementing advanced privacy-preserving techniques, such as federated learning and differential privacy, can help protect individuals' data while still enabling AI-driven analysis. These techniques allow data to remain decentralized or anonymized while being used for training and analysis.
  - **Balancing Privacy and Utility:** Ensuring data privacy while maintaining the utility of AI systems for forensic purposes is challenging. Privacy-preserving techniques often involve trade-offs between data granularity and usability.
  - **Clear Accountability Frameworks:** Establishing clear frameworks for accountability regarding AI decisions in cyber forensics is essential. This includes defining who is responsible for AI-driven outcomes and ensuring that human oversight is integrated into the decision-making process.

Assigning liability for erroneous or biased decisions made by AI systems can be complex. Developing legal and organizational structures to address accountability is an ongoing challenge.

- **Promoting Ethical Design and Development**
  - **Ethical AI Design Principles:** Incorporating ethical considerations into the design and development of AI systems from the outset is crucial. This includes ensuring that ethical guidelines are followed and that systems are built to prioritize fairness, transparency, and privacy.

- **Integrating Ethics into Technical Processes:** Embedding ethical considerations into technical design and development processes requires collaboration between ethicists, technologists, and domain experts. It also necessitates ongoing training and awareness for developers.
- **Developing Comprehensive Regulations:** Establishing regulatory frameworks that govern the use of AI in cyber forensics can help ensure that technologies are used responsibly and ethically. This includes creating standards for data handling, algorithmic transparency, and accountability.

Rapid advancements in AI technology can outpace regulatory developments. Ensuring that regulations are adaptable and relevant to emerging technologies is a significant challenge.

- **Balancing Innovation with Ethical Standards**

Fostering an environment where innovation in AI for cyber forensics is balanced with strong ethical standards is essential. This involves encouraging research and development that prioritizes ethical considerations alongside technical advancements.

The competitive nature of technology development may lead to prioritizing innovation over ethical considerations. Ensuring that ethical standards are maintained without stifling innovation requires careful management.

- **Enhancing Public Awareness and Education**

Promoting public awareness and education about AI in cyber forensics can help build trust and ensure that individuals are informed about how their data is used and protected. This includes engaging with communities and stakeholders to address concerns.

Communicating complex AI concepts in an accessible manner can be challenging. Ensuring that educational efforts are effective and reach diverse audiences is important for fostering informed public discourse.

- **Addressing Cross-Border Ethical Issues**

Creating international standards and agreements for the ethical use of AI in cyber forensics can help address cross-border issues related to data privacy, surveillance, and accountability. This involves collaboration between countries and international organizations.

Different countries have varying legal and ethical norms regarding AI and data privacy. Harmonizing these norms to create effective international standards is a complex task.

- **Integrating Human Oversight and Decision-Making**

Integrating human oversight into AI-driven forensic processes is crucial to ensure that AI systems are used as decision-support tools rather than replacements for human judgment. This involves developing protocols for human review and intervention.

There is a risk that reliance on AI systems could diminish the role of human judgment in forensic investigations. Ensuring that AI complements rather than replaces human expertise is an ongoing challenge.

6. SUMMARY

AI technologies have the potential to greatly enhance cyber forensics by improving efficiency, accuracy, and predictive capabilities. However, their integration into forensic practices brings a range of ethical considerations that must be carefully addressed. Privacy and data protection, algorithmic bias, transparency, accountability, and the potential for misuse are all critical areas that require thoughtful examination and proactive management.

By implementing robust ethical guidelines, ensuring transparency, addressing bias, and maintaining accountability, stakeholders can harness the benefits of AI while mitigating its risks. Ongoing education and public awareness are also essential for fostering trust and ensuring that AI technologies are used responsibly and ethically in the field of cyber forensics.

Navigating these ethical challenges is not only crucial for protecting individuals' rights and ensuring fair outcomes but also for upholding the integrity of the forensic process and maintaining public trust in the use of advanced technologies.

REFERENCES

Illman, E., & Temple, P. (2019). California consumer privacy act. *Business Lawyer*, 75(1), 1637–1646.

Strickland, E. (2019). IBM Watson, heal thyself: How IBM overpromised and underdelivered on AI health care. *IEEE Spectrum*, 56(4), 24–31. DOI: 10.1109/MSPEC.2019.8678513

Voigt, P., & Bussche, A. v. (2017). *The EU General Data Protection Regulation (GDPR). A Practical Guide* (1st ed.). Springer International Publishing. DOI: 10.1007/978-3-319-57959-7

Wolf, M., Miller, K., & Grodzinsky, F. (2017). Why we should have seen that coming: comments on Microsoft's tay" experiment," and wider implications. *The ORBIT Journal*, 1-12.

ADDITIONAL READINGS

Balushi, Y. A., Shaker, H., & Kumar, B. (2023). The Use of Machine Learning in Digital Forensics: Review Paper. *International Conference on Innovation in Information Technology and Business* (pp. 96-113). Springer Nature. DOI: 10.2991/978-94-6463-110-4_9

Bokolo, B. G., Chen, L., & Liu, Q. (2023). Deep Learning Assisted Cyber Criminal Profiling. *6th International Conference on Big Data and Artificial Intelligence (BDAI)*, (pp. 226-231).

Durall, R., Keuper, M., Pfreundt, F.-J., & Keuper, J. (2019). Unmasking deepfakes with simple features. *arXiv preprint arXiv:1911.*

Ferreira, S., Antunes, M., & Correia, M. E. (2021). Exposing manipulated photos and videos in digital forensics analysis. *Journal of Imaging*, 7(7), 102. DOI: 10.3390/jimaging7070102 PMID: 39080890

Husain, M. S. (2023). Deep Learning. In *Big Data Concepts, Technologies, and Applications* (pp. 108-123). Taylor & Francis group, CRC Press. DOI: 10.1201/9781003441595-9

Husain, M. S., Faisal, M., Sadia, H., Ahmad, T., & Shukla, S. (2023). *Advances in Cyberology and the Advent of the Next-gen Information Revolution*. IGI Global. DOI: 10.4018/978-1-6684-8133-2

Husain, M. S., Khan, M. Z., & Siddiqui, T. (2023). *Big Data Concepts, Technologies, and Applications*. CRC Press. DOI: 10.1201/9781003441595

Mei, Y., Han, W., Li, S., Lin, K., Tian, Z., & Li, S. (2024). A Novel Network Forensic Framework for Advanced Persistent Threat Attack Attribution Through Deep Learning. *IEEE Transactions on Intelligent Transportation Systems*, 25(9), 12131–12140. DOI: 10.1109/TITS.2024.3360260

Nowroozi, E., Mohammadi, M., Savaş, E., Mekdad, Y., & Conti, M. (2023). Employing Deep Ensemble Learning for Improving the Security of Computer Networks Against Adversarial Attacks. *IEEE Transactions on Network and Service Management*, 20(2), 2096–2105. DOI: 10.1109/TNSM.2023.3267831

Rosli, N. A., Abdullah, S. N., Zamani, A. N., Ghazvini, A., Othman, N. S., & Tajuddin, N. A. (2021). Comparison Multi Transfer Learning Models for Deep Fake Image Recognizer. *3rd International Cyber Resilience Conference (CRC)*, (pp. 1-6). DOI: 10.1109/CRC50527.2021.9392566

Salih, K. M., & Ibrahim, N. B. (2023). Enhancing IoT Forensics through Deep Learning: Investigating Cyber-Attacks and Analyzing Big Data for Improved Security Measures. *4th International Conference on Big Data Analytics and Practices (IBDAP)* (pp. 1-8). IEEE. DOI: 10.1109/IBDAP58581.2023.10271950

Wu, C., Wu, H., Lei, S., Li, X., & Tong, H. (2021). Deep Learning in Automatic Fingerprint Identification. *IEEE 6th International Conference on Smart Cloud (SmartCloud)*, (pp. 111-116).

Yudhana, A., Riadi, I., & Ridho, F. (2018). Ddos classification using neural network and na¨ıve bayes methods for network forensics. *International Journal of Advanced Computer Science and Applications*, 9(11). Advance online publication. DOI: 10.14569/IJACSA.2018.091125

KEY TERMS AND DEFINITIONS

Explainable AI: Explainable AI (XAI) refers to artificial intelligence systems that are designed to be transparent and understandable to humans. Unlike traditional AI models, which often operate as "black boxes," making it difficult for users to grasp how decisions are made, Explainable AI aims to provide clear and interpretable explanations of its processes and outcomes.

Intrusion Detection Systems (IDS): IDS (Intrusion Detection System) is a security technology used to monitor and analyze network traffic or system activities for signs of unauthorized access, attacks, or policy violations. It helps organizations detect potential security breaches in real-time and generates alerts for administrators to investigate.

Compilation of References

Abdel-Basset, M., Hawash, H., Chakrabortty, R. K., & Ryan, M. J. (2021). Semi-supervised spatiotemporal deep learning for intrusions detection in IoT networks. *IEEE Internet of Things Journal*, 8(15), 12251–12265. DOI: 10.1109/JIOT.2021.3060878

ADF-Solutions. (2023). *Digital Forensics in VR: Investigating Crimes & Analyzing Data*. Retrieved from adfsolutions.com: https://www.adfsolutions.com/adf-blog/digital-forensics-in-virtual-reality-investigating-crimes-and-analyzing-data-in-virtual-worlds-using-digital-forensic-software

Adnan, M. H., Ariffin, S. A., Hanafi, H. F., Husain, M. S., & Panessai, I. Y. (2021). A social media analytics framework to increase prospective students' interests in STEM and TVET education. *Asian Journal of University Education*, 16(4), 82–90. DOI: 10.24191/ajue.v16i4.11945

Afaq, S. A., Husain, M. S., Bello, A., & Sadia, H. (2023). A critical analysis of cyber threats and their global impact. In *Computational Intelligent Security in Wireless Communications* (pp. 201–220). CRC Press.

Ahmed, B., Gulliver, T. A., & alZahir, S. (2020). (1-12). Blind copy-move forgery detection using svd and ks test. *SN Applied Sciences*.

Akbar, M., Suaib, M., Husain, M. S., & Shukla, S. (2020). A Compendium of Cloud Forensics. In *Critical Concepts, Standards, and Techniques in Cyber Forensics* (pp. 215-227). IGI Global. DOI: 10.4018/978-1-7998-1558-7.ch012

Akbar, M., Suaib, M., & Hussain, M. S. (2022). Analysis of Deep-Fake Technology Impacting Digital World Credibility: A Comprehensive Literature Review. *International Journal of Computer and Information Technology*, 11(2). Advance online publication. DOI: 10.24203/ijcit.v11i2.282

Ali, M., Shiaeles, S., Clarke, N., & Kontogeorgis, D. (2019). A proactive malicious software identification approach for digital forensic examiners. *Journal of Information Security and Applications*, 47, 139–155. DOI: 10.1016/j.jisa.2019.04.013

Alshammari, A., & Aldribi, A. (2021). Apply machine learning techniques to detect malicious network traffic in cloud computing. *Journal of Big Data*, 8(1), 90. DOI: 10.1186/s40537-021-00475-1

Appel, M., & Prietzel, F. (2022). The detection of political deepfakes. *Journal of Computer-Mediated Communication*, 27(4), zmac008. DOI: 10.1093/jcmc/zmac008

Balushi, Y. A., Shaker, H., & Kumar, B. (2023). The Use of Machine Learning in Digital Forensics: Review Paper. *International Conference on Innovation in Information Technology and Business* (pp. 96-113). Springer Nature. DOI: 10.2991/978-94-6463-110-4_9

Barni, M., Nowroozi, E., & Tondi, B. (2018). Detection of adaptive histogram equalization robust against jpeg compression. *International Workshop on Biometrics and Forensics (IWBF)* (pp. 1-8). IEEE. DOI: 10.1109/IWBF.2018.8401564

Barra, P., Bisogni, C., Nappi, M., Freire-Obreg'on, D., & Castrill'on-Santana, M. (2019). Gait analysis for gender classification in forensics. *International Conference on Dependability in Sensor, Cloud, and Big Data Systems and Applications* (pp. 180-190). Springer. DOI: 10.1007/978-981-15-1304-6_15

Bastian, M., Heymann, S., & Jacomy, M. (2009). *Gephi: An Open Source Software for Exploring and Manipulating Networks. Proceedings of the international AAAI conference on web and social media. 3*. Association for the Advancement of Artificial Intelligence., Retrieved from https://gephi.org/

Bitquery. (n.d.). Bitquery Coinpath APIs. *Follow the money on blockchain with Coinpath® APIs*. Retrieved from https://bitquery.io/products/coinpath

Blockchain.com Explorer. (n.d.). blockchain.com. Retrieved from https://www.blockchain.com/explorer

Blockchair. (n.d.). Blockchain explorer, analytics and web services. Retrieved from https://blockchair.com/

Bokolo, B. G., Chen, L., & Liu, Q. (2023). Deep Learning Assisted Cyber Criminal Profiling. *6th International Conference on Big Data and Artificial Intelligence (BDAI)*, (pp. 226-231).

Bokolo, B. G., & Liu, Q. (2024). Artificial Intelligence in Social Media Forensics: A Comprehensive Survey and Analysis. *Electronics (Basel)*, 13(9), 1671. DOI: 10.3390/electronics13091671

Bond, S. (2024). *AI fakes raise election risks as lawmakers and tech companies scramble to catch up*. NPR.

Bruce, M., Lusthaus, J., Kashyap, R., Phair, N., & Varese, F. (2024). Mapping the global geography of cybercrime with the World Cybercrime Index. *PLoS One*, 19(4), e0297312. DOI: 10.1371/journal.pone.0297312 PMID: 38598553

CapitalOne. (2022). *Information on the Capital One cyber incident*. Retrieved from Capital One: https://www.capitalone.com/digital/facts2019/

Case, S. (2018). *Silk Road: The Dark Web's Most Infamous Marketplace*. Oxford University Press.

Cavico, F. J., & Mujtaba, B. G. (2016). Volkswagen emissions scandal: A global case study of legal, ethical, and practical consequences and recommendations for sustainable management. *Global Journal of Research in Business & Management*.

Cellebrite. (n.d.). Cellebrite UFED. Retrieved from https://cellebrite.com/en/ufed/

Certified Computer Examiner. (n.d.). (International Society of Forensic Computer Examiners) Retrieved July 2024, from https://www.isfce.com/certification.htm

CFCE. (n.d.). (IACIS) Retrieved July 2024, from https://www.iacis.com/certification/cfce/

Chain, B. B. (n.d.). BNB Smart Chain Explorer. BNB Beacon Chain. Retrieved from https://bscscan.com/

Chainalysis. (n.d.). Retrieved from https://www.chainalysis.com/

CHEN., Z., YU, W., & ZHOU, L. (2021). ADASYN-Random Forest Based Intrusion Detection Model. *4th International Conference on Signal Processing and Machine Learning*, (pp. 152-159).

Chen, Z., Zhou, L., & Yu, W. (2021, August). ADASYN– Random forest based intrusion detection model. In *Proceedings of the 2021 4th International Conference on Signal Processing and Machine Learning* (pp. 152-159).

Computer Fraud and Abuse Act (CFAA). (n.d.). Retrieved from Practical Law: https://uk.practicallaw.thomsonreuters.com/2-508-3428?transitionType=Default&contextData=(sc.Default)&firstPage=true

Corporation, P. (n.d.). Paraben E3. Retrieved from https://paraben.com/paraben-e3-forensic-platform/

Dara Khosrowshahi, C. (2016). *2016 Data Security Incident*. Retrieved from Uber Newsroom: https://www.uber.com/newsroom/2016-data-incident/

Durall, R., Keuper, M., Pfreundt, F.-J., & Keuper, J. (2019). Unmasking deepfakes with simple features. *arXiv preprint arXiv:1911*.

Elliptic. (n.d.). Elliptic. Retrieved from https://www.elliptic.co/

Ethereum. (n.d.). The Ethereum Blockchain Explorer. Etherscan. Retrieved from https://etherscan.io/

Exterro. (n.d.). FTK Imager. Retrieved from https://www.exterro.com/ftk-product-downloads/ftk-imager-version-4-7-1

Fakiha, B. (2020). Digital Forensics: Crimes and Challenges in Online Social Networks Forensics. *Journal of the Arab American University*.

Ferreira, S., Antunes, M., & Correia, M. E. (2021). Exposing manipulated photos and videos in digital forensics analysis. *Journal of Imaging*, 7(7), 102. DOI: 10.3390/jimaging7070102 PMID: 39080890

Framework Security. (2024). *The Sony Pictures Breach: A Deep Dive into a Landmark Cyber Attack*. Retrieved from Framework Security: https://www.frameworksec.com/post/the-sony-pictures-breach-a-deep-dive-into-a-landmark-cyber-attack

FTC. (2024). *Equifax Data Breach*. Federal Trade Commission.

Gao, G., Feng, Z., & Xia, Z. (2023). Energy Efficient Three-Factor Authentication in Wireless Sensor Networks With Resisting Insider Attacks. *IEEE Transactions on Green Communications and Networking*, 7(3), 1297–1308. DOI: 10.1109/TGCN.2023.3265661

Gaurav, A., Gupta, B. B., Hsu, C. H., Peraković, D., & Penalvo, F. J. G. (2021, June). Filtering of distributed denial of services (DDoS) attacks in cloud computing environment. In 2021 IEEE International Conference on Communications Workshops (ICC Workshops) (pp. 1-6). IEEE.

Gaurav, A., Gupta, B. B., Hsu, C.-H., & Peraković, D., & PEÑALVO, F. J. (2021). Filtering of Distributed Denial of Services (DDoS) Attacks in Cloud Computing Environment. *IEEE International Conference on Communications Workshops (ICC Workshops)*, (pp. 1-6). DOI: 10.1109/ICCWorkshops50388.2021.9473886

Gazeau, V., Gupta, K., & An, M. K. (2024). Enhancing Social Media Data Collection for Digital Forensic Investigations: A Web Parser Approach. *International Conference on Computer, Information and Telecommunication Systems (CITS)*, (pp. 1-7). DOI: 10.1109/CITS61189.2024.10607983

Golomingi, R., Dobay, A., Franckenberg, S., Ebert, L., & Sieberth, T. (2023). Augmented reality in forensics and forensic medicine – Current status and future prospects. *Science & Justice*, 63(4), 451–455. DOI: 10.1016/j.scijus.2023.04.009 PMID: 37453776

Gopal, R. V. (2022). *Complete Case Study — Target Data Breach.* Retrieved from Medium: https://medium.com/thedeephub/complete-case-study-target-data-breach-2-ba4bb365a82e

Graesser, A. C., & McNamara, D. S. (2004). *Coh-Metrix.* Retrieved from soletlab.asu.edu: https://soletlab.asu.edu/coh-metrix/

Graphistry. (n.d.). Retrieved April 2024, from https://www.graphistry.com/

Grigaliūnas, Š., Brūzgienė, R., & Venčkauskas, A. (2023). Ontology-Driven Digital Profiling for Identification and Linking Evidence Across Social Media Platform. *IEEE Access : Practical Innovations, Open Solutions*, 11, 111672–111691. DOI: 10.1109/ACCESS.2023.3322162

Halima, N. B., Alluhaidan, A. S., Khan, M. Z., Husain, M. S., & Khan, M. A. (2023). A service-categorized security scheme with physical unclonable functions for internet of vehicles. *Journal of Big Data*, 10(1), 178. DOI: 10.1186/s40537-023-00865-7

Haroon, M., Misra, D. K., Husain, M., Tripathi, M. M., & Khan, A. (2023). Security Issues in the Internet of Things for the Development of Smart Cities. In Husain, M. S., Faisal, M., Sadia, H., Ahmad, T., & Shukla, S. (Eds.), *Advances in Cyberology and the Advent of the Next-Gen Information Revolution* (pp. 123–137). IGI. DOI: 10.4018/978-1-6684-8133-2.ch007

Harvey, P. (2024). *ExifTool by Phil Harvey.* Retrieved from exiftool.org: https://www.exiftool.org/

Haslhofer, B., Stütz, R., Romiti, M., & King, R. (2021). GraphSense: A General-Purpose Cryptoasset Analytics Platform. *Arxiv pre-print.* Retrieved from https://graphsense.org/

Hina, M., Ali, M., Javed, A. R., Srivastava, G., Gadekallu, T. R., & Jalil, Z. (2021). *Email classification and forensics analysis using machine learning. IEEE SmartWorld, Ubiquitous Intelligence & Computing, Advanced & Trusted Computing, Scalable Computing & Communications, Internet of People and Smart City Innovation (Smart-World/SCALCOM/UIC/ATC/IOP/SCI)*. IEEE.

Hollander, J. (2023). *Marriott Data Breach FAQ: What Really Happened?* Retrieved from hoteltechreport.com: https://hoteltechreport.com/news/marriott-data-breach

Hsiao, S.-C., & Kao, D.-Y. (2018). The static analysis of WannaCry ransomware. *20th international conference on advanced communication technology (ICACT)* (pp. 153-158). IEEE.

Hu, J., Liao, X., Wang, W., & Qin, Z. (2022). Detecting Compressed Deepfake Videos in Social Networks Using Frame-Temporality Two-Stream Convolutional Network. *EEE Transactions on Circuits and Systems for Video Technology*, 1089-1102.

Husain, M. S. (2023). Deep Learning. In *Big Data Concepts, Technologies, and Applications* (pp. 108-123). Taylor & Francis group, CRC Press. DOI: 10.1201/9781003441595-9

Husain, M. S., Khan, M. Z., & Siddiqui, T. (2023). Blockchain. In *Big Data Concepts, Technologies, and Applications* (pp. 124-136). Taylor and Francis group, CRC press.

Husain, M. S. (2019). Social media analytics to predict depression level in the users. In *Early detection of neurological disorders using machine learning systems* (pp. 199–215). IGI Global. DOI: 10.4018/978-1-5225-8567-1.ch011

Husain, M. S., Faisal, M., Sadia, H., Ahmad, T., & Shukla, S. (2023). *Advances in Cyberology and the Advent of the Next-gen Information Revolution*. IGI Global. DOI: 10.4018/978-1-6684-8133-2

Husain, M. S., & Khan, M. Z. (2019). *Critical Concepts, Standards, and Techniques in Cyber Forensics*. IGI Global.

Husain, M. S., Khan, M. Z., & Siddiqui, T. (2023). *Big Data Concepts, Technologies, and Applications*. CRC Press. DOI: 10.1201/9781003441595

Husain, M. S., & Khanum, M. A. (2017). Cloud computing in E-governance: Indian perspective. In *Securing government information and data in developing countries* (pp. 104–114). IGI Global. DOI: 10.4018/978-1-5225-1703-0.ch006

Ibrahim, Y. M., Essameldin, R., & Saad, S. M. (2024). Social Media Forensics: An Adaptive Cyberbullying-Related Hate Speech Detection Approach Based on Neural Networks With Uncertainty. *IEEE Access : Practical Innovations, Open Solutions*, 12, 59474–59484. DOI: 10.1109/ACCESS.2024.3393295

Illman, E., & Temple, P. (2019). California consumer privacy act. *Business Lawyer*, 75(1), 1637–1646.

Investigatory Powers Act (2016). UK Public General Acts.

Iqbal, S., & Alharbi, S. A. (2020). Advancing automation in digital forensic investigations using machine learning forensics. *Digital Forensic Science, 3*.

Islam, M. M., Karmakar, G., Kamruzzaman, J., Murshed, M., Kahandawa, G., & Parvin, N. (2018). *Detecting splicing and copymove attacks in color images. Digital Image Computing: Techniques and Applications (DICTA)*. IEEE.

Jiang, Q., Zhao, G., Ma, X., Li, M., Tian, Y., & Li, X. (2024). Cross-Modal Learning Based Flexible Bimodal Biometric Authentication With Template Protection. *IEEE Transactions on Information Forensics and Security*, 19, 3593–3607. DOI: 10.1109/TIFS.2024.3364092

Josephine, B. M., Shekar, K. V., Meghana, G., Rao, K. R., & Rajesh, C. (2019). Forensic Analysis of Social Media Apps. *International Journal of Innovative Technology and Exploring Engineering*, 9(1), 2302–2305. DOI: 10.35940/ijitee.A5205.119119

Kachavimath, A. V., Nazare, S. V., & Akki, S. S. (2020). Distributed denial of service attack detection using na¨ıve bayes and k-nearest neighbor for network forensics. *2020 2nd International conference on innovative mechanisms for industry applications (ICIMIA)* (pp. 711-717). IEEE.

Kathleen, E. W. E. (2021). *Types of Blockchain: Public, Private, or Something in Between*. Retrieved from https://www.foley.com: https://www.foley.com/en/insights/publications/2021/08/types-of-blockchain-public-private-between

Keller, D., Osadchy, M., & Dunkelman, O. (2021). Inverting Binarizations of Facial Templates Produced by Deep Learning (and Its Implications). *IEEE Transactions on Information Forensics and Security*, 16, 4184–4196. DOI: 10.1109/TIFS.2021.3103056

Khan, A., Husain, M. S., & Khan, A. (2018). Analysis of mental state of users using social media to predict depression! a survey. *International Journal of Advanced Research in Computer Science*, 100-106.

Khan, M. Z., Shoaib, M., Husain, M. S., Nisa, K., & Quasim, M. T. (2024). Enhanced mechanism to prioritize the cloud data privacy factors using AHP and TOPSIS: a hybrid approach. *Journal of Cloud Computing, 13(1), 42., 13*(1).

Khan, W., Ishrat, M., Haleem, M., Khan, A. N., Hasan, M. K., & A, F. N. (2023). An Extensive Study and Review on Dark Web Threats and Detection Techniques. In M. S. Husain, M. Faisal, H. Sadia, T. Ahmad, & S. Shukla (Eds.), *Advances in Cyberology and the Advent of the Next-Gen Information Revolution* (pp. 202-219). IGI.

Khan, A., Husain, M. S., & Khan, A. (2018). Analysis of mental state of users using social media to predict depression! a survey. *International Journal of Advanced Research in Computer Science*, 9(2), 100–106.

Khan, M. Z., Husain, M. S., & Shoaib, M. (2020). Introduction to email, web, and message forensics. In *Critical concepts, standards, and techniques in cyber forensics* (pp. 174–186). IGI Global. DOI: 10.4018/978-1-7998-1558-7.ch010

Khan, M. Z., Shoaib, M., Husain, M. S., Nisa, K. U., & Quasim, M. T. (2024). Enhanced mechanism to prioritize the cloud data privacy factors using AHP and TOPSIS: A hybrid approach. *Journal of Cloud Computing (Heidelberg, Germany)*, 13(1), 42. DOI: 10.1186/s13677-024-00606-y

Khan, S., Ilya, K., Yunke, H., & Stuart, M. (2022). A systematic analysis of the capital one data breach: Critical lessons learned. *ACM Transactions on Privacy and Security*, 26(1), 1–29. DOI: 10.1145/3546068

Kim, S.-K., Yeun, C. Y., & Yoo, P. D. (2019). An Enhanced Machine Learning-Based Biometric Authentication System Using RR-Interval Framed Electrocardiograms. *IEEE Access : Practical Innovations, Open Solutions*, 7, 168669–168674. DOI: 10.1109/ACCESS.2019.2954576

Klinkhamhom, C., & Boonyopakorn, P. (2022). Threat Hunting for Digital Forensic Using GRR Rapid Response with NIST Framework. *37th International Technical Conference on Circuits/Systems, Computers and Communications (ITC-CSCC)*, (pp. 177-180). DOI: 10.1109/ITC-CSCC55581.2022.9894977

Koru, G. K., & Uluyol, Ç. (2024). Detection of Turkish Fake News From Tweets With BERT Models. *IEEE Access : Practical Innovations, Open Solutions*, 12, 14918–14931. DOI: 10.1109/ACCESS.2024.3354165

Kraetzer, C., Siegel, D., Seidlitz, S., & Dittmann, J. (2022). Process-driven modelling of media forensic investigations-considerations on the example of deepfake detection. *Sensors (Basel)*, 22(9), 3137. DOI: 10.3390/s22093137 PMID: 35590827

Langan, T. (2022). *INTERNET CRIME REPORT.* FEDERAL BUREAU OF INVESTIGATION.

Li, H., Xi, B., Wu, S., Jiang, J., & Rao, Y. (2018). The application of association analysis in mobile phone forensics system. *International Conference on Intelligence Science* (pp. 126-133). Springer. DOI: 10.1007/978-3-030-01313-4_13

Lotfollahi, M., Siavoshani, M. J., Zade, R. S., & Saberian, M. (2020). Deep packet: A novel approach for encrypted traffic classification using deep learning. *Soft Computing*, 24(3), 1999–2012. DOI: 10.1007/s00500-019-04030-2

Lynsey Eidell. (2024). *What Happened to Ashley Madison? The True Story of the Dating Site's Infamous 2015 Hack — and How It Bounced Back.* Retrieved from People.com: https://people.com/ashley-madison-dating-website-2015-hack-true-story-8644849

Madhusudhanan, S., Jose, A. C., Sahoo, J., & Malekian, R. (2023). PRIMϵ: Novel Privacy-Preservation Model With Pattern Mining and Genetic Algorithm. *IEEE Transactions on Information Forensics and Security*, •••, 571–585.

Mahajan, K., Madhavidevi, B., Supreeth, B. R., Lakshmi, N. V., Joshi, K., & Bavankumar, S. (2023). Detecting and Responding to Cloud Security Incidents based on AI and Forensic Approach. *International Conference on Innovative Computing, Intelligent Communication and Smart Electrical Systems (ICSES)*, (pp. 1-6). DOI: 10.1109/ICSES60034.2023.10465380

McShane, J. J. (2023). *In-Depth Look at Chainalysis, Elliptic, and CipherTrace: Forensic Science in Blockchain Analysis.* The Truth about Forensic Science. Retrieved April 2024, from https://thetruthaboutforensicscience.com/in-depth-look-at-chainalysis-elliptic-and-ciphertrace-forensic-science-in-blockchain-analysis/

Mei, Y., Han, W., Li, S., Lin, K., Tian, Z., & Li, S. (2024). A Novel Network Forensic Framework for Advanced Persistent Threat Attack Attribution Through Deep Learning. *IEEE Transactions on Intelligent Transportation Systems*, 25(9), 12131–12140. DOI: 10.1109/TITS.2024.3360260

Miao, C., Tan, Z., Chu, Q., Yu, N., & Guo, G. (2022). Hierarchical Frequency-Assisted Interactive Networks for Face Manipulation Detection. *IEEE Transactions on Information Forensics and Security*, 17, 3008–3021. DOI: 10.1109/TIFS.2022.3198275

Millán, G. (2021). Traffic flows analysis in high-speed computer networks using time series. *arXiv preprint arXiv:2103.03984.*

Mishra, N., Siddiqui, S., & Tripathi, J. P. (2015). A compendium over cloud computing cryptographic algorithms and security issues. *International Journal of Information Technology : an Official Journal of Bharati Vidyapeeth's Institute of Computer Applications and Management*, 7(1), 810–814.

Moustafa, N., & Slay, J. (2017). RCNF: Real-time collaborative network forensic scheme for evidence analysis. *arXiv preprint arXiv:1711.02824.*

Mukherjee, I., Sahu, N. K., & Sahana, S. K. (2023). Simulation and modeling for anomaly detection in IoT network using machine learning. *International Journal of Wireless Information Networks*, 30(2), 173–189. DOI: 10.1007/s10776-021-00542-7

Muniswamy-Reddy. Kiran-Kumar, Holland, D. A., Braun, U., & Seltzer, a. M. (2006). *PASS: Provenance-Aware Storage Systems.* Retrieved from https://syrah.eecs.harvard.edu/: https://syrah.eecs.harvard.edu/pass

Munke, E., & Musuva, P. M. (2024). *Digital Forensics as a Service Implementation: A Scalable Solution for Cyber Incident Response. IST-Africa Conference.* IST-Africa.

National Institute of Standards and Technology. (n.d.). Retrieved July 2024, from https://www.nist.gov/

Neaimi, M. A., Hamadi, H. A., Yeun, C. Y., & Zemerly, M. J. (2020). Digital Forensic Analysis of Files Using Deep Learning. *3rd International Conference on Signal Processing and Information Security (ICSPIS)*, (pp. 1-4). DOI: 10.1109/ICSPIS51252.2020.9340141

Nowroozi, E., Mohammadi, M., Savaş, E., Mekdad, Y., & Conti, M. (2023). Employing Deep Ensemble Learning for Improving the Security of Computer Networks Against Adversarial Attacks. *IEEE Transactions on Network and Service Management*, 20(2), 2096–2105. DOI: 10.1109/TNSM.2023.3267831

P˘atra¸scu, A., & Patriciu, V.-V. (2013). Beyond Digital Forensics. A Cloud Computing Perspective Over Incident Response and Reporting. *International Symposium on Applied Computational Intelligence and Informatics*, (pp. 455-460). DOI: 10.1109/SACI.2013.6609018

Padilha, R., Salem, T., Workman, S., Andaló, F. A., Rocha, A., & Jacobs, N. (2022). Content-Aware Detection of Temporal Metadata Manipulation. *IEEE Transactions on Information Forensics and Security*, 17, 1316–1327. DOI: 10.1109/TIFS.2022.3159154

Pasquini, C., Amerini, I., & Boato, G. (2021). Media forensics on social media platforms: A survey. *EURASIP Journal on Information Security*, 2021(1), 4. DOI: 10.1186/s13635-021-00117-2

Peng, C., Miao, Z., Liu, D., Wang, N., Hu, R., & Gao, X. (2024). Where Deepfakes Gaze at? Spatial–Temporal Gaze Inconsistency Analysis for Video Face Forgery Detection. *IEEE Transactions on Information Forensics and Security*, 19, 4507–4517. DOI: 10.1109/TIFS.2024.3381823

Pennebaker, J. W. (1993). *LIWC*. Retrieved from receptiviti.com: https://docs.receptiviti.com/frameworks/liwc

Petrosyan, A. (2024). *Share of cyberattacks in global industries worldwide 2023*. Statista 2024.

Petrosyan, A. (2023). *Leading IT security threats according to cyber security professionals 2022*. Statista.

PSAL - The Privacy. S. a. (2011). *jstylo- Authorship recognition analysis tool*. Retrieved from github.com: https://github.com/psal/jstylo

Qadir, S., & Noor, B. (2021). Applications of machine learning in digital forensics. *International Conference on Digital Futures and Transformative Technologies (ICoDT2)*. DOI: 10.1109/ICoDT252288.2021.9441543

Qiao, T., Chen, Y., Zhou, X., Shi, R., Shao, H., Shen, K., & Luo, X. (2024). CSC-Net: Cross-Color Spatial Co-Occurrence Matrix Network for Detecting Synthesized Fake Images. *IEEE Transactions on Cognitive and Developmental Systems*, 16(1), 369–379. DOI: 10.1109/TCDS.2023.3274450

Radhakrishna, T., & Majd, N. E. (2024). Edge Computing Ransomware Detection in IoT using Machine Learning. *Workshop on Computing, Networking and Communications (CNC)*, (pp. 244-248). DOI: 10.1109/ICNC59896.2024.10556351

Raffael, G., Akos, D., Sabine, F., Lars, E., & Sieberth, T. (2023). Augmented Reality in Forensics and Forensic Medicine- Current Status and Future Prospects. *Science & Justice*. PMID: 37453776

Rafique, R., Nawaz, M., Kibriya, H., & Masood, M. (2021). DeepFake Detection Using Error Level Analysis and Deep Learning. *4th International Conference on Computing & Information Sciences (ICCIS)*, (pp. 1-4). DOI: 10.1109/ICCIS54243.2021.9676375

Raymer, E., MacDermott, Á., & Akinbi, A. (2023). Virtual reality forensics: Forensic analysis of Meta Quest 2. *Forensic Science International Digital Investigation*, 47, 47. DOI: 10.1016/j.fsidi.2023.301658

Rehman, I. u. (2019). Facebook-Cambridge Analytica data harvesting: What you need to know. *Library Philosophy and Practice*, 1-11.

Research, C. P. (2020). *The Maze Continues: Exploit Trends in 2020*. Check Point Software Technologies Ltd.

Rosli, N. A., Abdullah, S. N., Zamani, A. N., Ghazvini, A., Othman, N. S., & Tajuddin, N. A. (2021). Comparison Multi Transfer Learning Models for Deep Fake Image Recognizer. *3rd International Cyber Resilience Conference (CRC)*, (pp. 1-6). DOI: 10.1109/CRC50527.2021.9392566

Roy, A., Dixit, R., Naskar, R., & Chakraborty, R. S. (2020). *Digital Image Forensics: Theory and Implementation*. Springer Link. DOI: 10.1007/978-981-10-7644-2

Ruriawan, M. F., Anggono, B., Siahaan, I. A., & Purwanto, Y. (2019). Development of digital evidence collector and file classification system with k-means algorithm. *Asia Pacific Conference on Wireless and Mobile (APWiMob)* (pp. 64-68). IEEE. DOI: 10.1109/APWiMob48441.2019.8964232

Sabir, M. F., Jones, J. H., Liu, H., & Mbaziira, A. V. (2019). Predicting Stealthy Watermarks in Files Using Deep Learning. *7th International Symposium on Digital Forensics and Security (ISDFS)* (pp. 1-6). IEEE. DOI: 10.1109/ISDFS.2019.8757538

Sachdeva, S., & Ali, A. (2021). A Hybrid approach using digital forensics for attack detection in a cloud network environment. *International Journal of Future Generation Communication and Networking*, 1536-1546.

Salih, K. M., & Ibrahim, N. B. (2023). Enhancing IoT Forensics through Deep Learning: Investigating Cyber-Attacks and Analyzing Big Data for Improved Security Measures. *4th International Conference on Big Data Analytics and Practices (IBDAP)* (pp. 1-8). IEEE. DOI: 10.1109/IBDAP58581.2023.10271950

Scientific Working Group on Digital Evidence. (n.d.). Retrieved July 2024, from https://www.swgde.org/

Shahid, H. M., Adnan, M. H., Khan, M. Z., Shukla, S., & Khan, F. U. (2022). *Pervasive Healthcare*. Springer International Publishing.

Shakeel, P. M., Baskar, S., Fouad, H., Manogaran, G., Saravanan, V., & Montenegro-Marin, C. E. (2021). Internet of things forensic data analysis using machine learning to identify roots of data scavenging. *Future Generation Computer Systems*, 115, 756–768. DOI: 10.1016/j.future.2020.10.001

Sharrab, Y., Al-Fraihat, D., & Alsmirat, M. (2023). Deep Neural Networks in Social Media Forensics: Unveiling Suspicious Patterns and Advancing Investigations on Twitter. *3rd Intelligent Cybersecurity Conference (ICSC)*, (pp. 95-102). DOI: 10.1109/ICSC60084.2023.10349985

Shukla, a., Hussain, S., Irshad, R. R., Alattab, A. A., Thakur, S., Breslin, J. G., . . . Jameel, S. M. (2024). Network analysis in a peer-to-peer energy trading model using blockchain and machine learning. *Computer Standards & Interfaces, 88*, 103799.

Shukla, S., Hussain, S., Irshad, R. R., Alattab, A. A., Thakur, S., Breslin, J. G., Hassan, M. F., Abimannan, S., Husain, S., & Jameel, M. S. (2024). Network analysis in a peer-to-peer energy trading model using blockchain and machine learning. *Computer Standards & Interfaces*, 88, 88. DOI: 10.1016/j.csi.2023.103799

Shullani, D., Baracchi, D., Iuliani, M., & Piva, A. (2022). Social Network Identification of Laundered Videos Based on DCT Coefficient Analysis. *IEEE Signal Processing Letters*, 29, 1112–1116. DOI: 10.1109/LSP.2022.3167631

Siddiqui, M. Z., Yadav, S., & Husain, M. S. (2018). Application of artificial intelligence in fighting against cyber crimes: A review. *Int. J. Adv. Res. Comput. Sci.*, 9(2), 118–122.

Sieberth, T., Dobay, A., Affolter, R., & Ebert, L. C. (2018). Applying virtual reality in forensics – a virtual scene walkthrough. *Forensic Science, Medicine, and Pathology*, 15(1), 41–47. DOI: 10.1007/s12024-018-0058-8 PMID: 30519987

Siolu, N. (2021). *SolarWinds State-Sponsored Supply Chain Attack vs. Standard Supply Chain Attacks.* Aiden.

SOLSCAN. (n.d.). Explore Solana Blockchain. Solana Blockchain. Retrieved from https://solscan.io/

Strickland, E. (2019). IBM Watson, heal thyself: How IBM overpromised and underdelivered on AI health care. *IEEE Spectrum*, 56(4), 24–31. DOI: 10.1109/MSPEC.2019.8678513

Sudha, T. S., & Rupa, C. (2019). *Analysis and evaluation of integrated cyber crime offences. Innovations in Power and Advanced Computing Technologies (i-PACT).* IEEE.

Talreja, V., Valenti, M. C., & Nasrabadi, N. M. (2020). Deep Hashing for Secure Multimodal Biometrics. *IEEE Transactions on Information Forensics and Security*, 16, 1306–1321. DOI: 10.1109/TIFS.2020.3033189

Tang, Y., Gu, L., & Wang, L. (2021). Deep Stacking Network for Intrusion Detection. *sensors*.

Team, C. (2023). *Bitfinex Hack Money Launderers Plead Guilty.* Chainalysis. Retrieved from https://www.chainalysis.com/blog/bitfinex-hack-plea-july-2023/

The California Consumer Privacy Act. (n.d.). Retrieved from California Privacy Protection Agency: https://cppa.ca.gov/regulations/

Theophilo, A., Giot, R., & Rocha, A. (2023). Authorship Attribution of Social Media Messages. *IEEE Transactions on Computational Social Systems*, 10(1), 10–23. DOI: 10.1109/TCSS.2021.3123895

Tripathi, M. M., Haroon, M., Khan, Z., & Husain, S. (2022). Security in digital healthcare system. In *Pervasive Healthcare: A Compendium of Critical Factors for Success* (pp. 217–231). Springer. DOI: 10.1007/978-3-030-77746-3_15

Tuncer, T., Ertam, F., & Dogan, S. (2021). Automated malware identification. *Multimedia Tools and Applications*, 80(7), 10881–10900. DOI: 10.1007/s11042-020-10317-6

Uber Team. (2022). *Security update*. Retrieved from Uber newsroom: https://www.uber.com/newsroom/security-update

Usman, N., Usman, S., Khan, F., Jan, M. A., Sajid, A., Alazab, M., & Watters, P. (2021). Intelligent dynamic malware detection using machine learning in ip reputation for forensics data analytics. *Future Generation Computer Systems*, 118, 124–141. DOI: 10.1016/j.future.2021.01.004

Vaccari, C., & Chadwick, A. (2020). Exploring the impact of synthetic political video on deception, uncertainty, and trust in news. *Social Media + Society*, 6(1), 2056305120903408. DOI: 10.1177/2056305120903408

Voigt, P., & Bussche, A. V. (2017). *The EU General Data Protection Regulation (GDPR)." A Practical Guide*. Springer International Publishing. DOI: 10.1007/978-3-319-57959-7

Wolf, M., Miller, K., & Grodzinsky, F. (2017). Why we should have seen that coming: comments on Microsoft's tay" experiment," and wider implications. *The ORBIT Journal*, 1-12.

Wu, C., Wu, H., Lei, S., Li, X., & Tong, H. (2021). Deep Learning in Automatic Fingerprint Identification. *IEEE 6th International Conference on Smart Cloud (SmartCloud)*, (pp. 111-116).

Wu, L., Yang, J., Zhou, M., Chen, Y., & Wang, Q. (2019). LVID: A Multimodal Biometrics Authentication System on Smartphones. *IEEE Transactions on Information Forensics and Security*, •••, 1572–1585.

Yang, K., Zhang, Z., Youliang, T., & Ma, J. (2023). A Secure Authentication Framework to Guarantee the Traceability of Avatars in Metaverse. *IEEE Transactions on Information Forensics and Security*, 18, 3817–3832. DOI: 10.1109/TIFS.2023.3288689

Yudhana, A., Riadi, I., & Ridho, F. (2018). Ddos classification using neural network and na¨ıve bayes methods for network forensics. *International Journal of Advanced Computer Science and Applications*, 9(11). Advance online publication. DOI: 10.14569/IJACSA.2018.091125

Zhao, R., Yin, J., Xue, Z., Gui, G., Adebisi, B., Ohtsuki, T., Gacanin, H., & Sari, H. (2021). An Efficient Intrusion Detection Method Based on Dynamic Autoencoder. *IEEE Wireless Communications Letters*, 10(8), 1707–1711. DOI: 10.1109/LWC.2021.3077946

About the Author

Mohd Shahid Husain is a Research Professional and Faculty member with fifteen years of teaching & research experience. He is currently working as an Assistant Professor in the College of Computing & Information Sciences, University of Technology & Applied Sciences, Oman. He obtained his M.Tech. in Information Technology (spl: Intelligent Systems) from the Indian Institute of Information Technology, Allahabad, India. He received his Ph.D. in Computer Science & Engineering from Integral University, Lucknow, India. His area of interest includes Artificial Intelligence, Information Retrieval, Natural Language Processing, Data Mining, Web mining, Data Analytics, Sentiment Analysis, and Computer Networks & Security. Dr. Mohd. Shahid Husain has published 6 books, 15 book chapters & more than 30 research papers in Journals/conferences of international repute papers in reputable journals [WoS/Scopus Quartiles]. He was involved with many sponsored projects as PI/Co-PI. Currently, he is working on 2 funded projects submitted to TRC (The Research Council), Oman. He is also contributing his knowledge and experience as an invited speaker, doctorial committee member, session chair, member of the editorial board/advisory committee, and TPC in various international journals/conferences of repute. Dr. Mohd Shahid Husain is an active member of different professional bodies including IEEE young professionals, IEEE-TCII, ISTE, CSTA, and IACSIT. Dr. Mohd Shahid Husain has qualified UGC-NET (National Eligibility Test) in June 2014 and GATE (Graduate Aptitude Test in Engineering) in 2008. He obtained two specialization certificates in python & Applied Data Science from the University of Michigan in 2020.

Index

A

B

C

D

E

F

I

L

M

N

R

S

T

U

www.ingramcontent.com/pod-product-compliance
Lightning Source LLC
Chambersburg PA
CBHW082116090325
23166CB00002B/15
* 9 7 9 8 3 6 9 3 2 9 6 0 3 *